MW01074447

RUSSIAN NUCLEAR ORTHODOXY

DMITRY (DIMA) ADAMSKY

RUSSIAN NUCLEAR ORTHODOXY

Religion, Politics, and Strategy

STANFORD UNIVERSITY PRESS

STANFORD, CALIFORNIA

Stanford University Press
Stanford, California

©2019 by the Board of Trustees of the Leland Stanford Junior University. All rights reserved.

No part of this book may be reproduced or transmitted in any form or by any means, electronic or mechanical, including photocopying and recording, or in any information storage or retrieval system without the prior written permission of Stanford University Press.

Printed in the United States of America on acid-free, archival-quality paper

Library of Congress Cataloging-in-Publication Data
Names: Adamsky, Dmitry, author.
Title: Russian nuclear orthodoxy : religion, politics, and strategy / Dmitry (Dima) Adamsky.
Description: Stanford, California : Stanford University Press, [2019] | Includes bibliographical references and index.
Identifiers: LCCN 2018041926 (print) | LCCN 2018043465 (ebook) | ISBN 9781503608658 (e-book) | ISBN 9781503608054 (cloth : alk. paper) | ISBN 9781503608641 (pbk. : alk. paper)
Subjects: LCSH: Nuclear weapons—Russia (Federation) | Nuclear weapons—Government policy—Russia (Federation) | Nuclear warfare—Religious aspects—Russkaia pravoslavnaia tserkov. | Church and state—Russia (Federation) | Church and state—Russkaia pravoslavnaia tserkov. | Russkaia pravoslavnaia tserkov—Political activity. | Russia (Federation)—Military policy.
Classification: LCC UA770 (ebook) | LCC UA770 .A573 2019 (print) | DDC 355.02/170947—dc23
LC record available at https://lccn.loc.gov/2018041926

Typeset by Westchester Publishing Services in 10.75/15 Adobe Caslon

For my grandmother, who took me as a child to walk and draw in the yard of the Novodevichy Monastery.

CONTENTS

ACKNOWLEDGMENTS

This book was the longest, and one of the most difficult and amazing, projects I have ever done. I had been thinking about it and collecting materials since 2010, but things did not progress. There were various reasons for that, plus writer's block. Then, everything changed. The muse, who brought unmatched inspiration, came to me in May 2015. This encounter has enormously empowered me in certain ways and immensely complicated my life in others. That said, I guess I was more fortunate than not and was grateful to the muse.

Uri Bar-Joseph provided me with ideas for all my previous books. This is the first book that I conceived myself. Still, I was fortunate to have him as my teacher and mentor during this project. Coffee sessions on the bench in the yard of the old Jaffa church enabled me to better imagine the book, not to lose faith, and to complete the project.

The book's theme was prompted by conversations with Jacqueline Newmyer Deal, Andrew W. Marshall, and Stephen P. Rosen. Their questions made me pay greater attention to what until then looked like just a footnote in my larger work on Russian nuclear strategy. Their interest, encouragement, and advice in the following years enabled me to structure the book.

I am grateful to several Russian, American, European, and Israeli scholars, officials, and clerics who provided counsel and assistance, on the condition of anonymity. My conversations with one of them in particular have been indispensable over the years. He has been very generous with his time, attention, and wisdom. I benefited enormously from his phenomenal knowledge of religious affairs and history. His genuine faith and devoted service has given me a better sense of the Russian Orthodoxy coming from the heart and mind of a true believer.

Nehemia Burgin encouraged me nonstop to move forward, asked difficult questions, and assisted with advice and unique sources. He invested more time in this manuscript than anyone else and provided the most valuable insights. I am very thankful to him.

Numerous conversations and professional fun with Yaacov (Kobi) Falkov, an authority on Russian history and politics, enabled me to better refine my arguments. Daniel Rakov, a wise and modest scholar, was supportive in his unique way with critique and opinion.

MS was indispensable. As with my previous projects, he was puzzled by what I am doing and why anyone would care; he assisted in getting to the most important sources and places and shared his wisdom, kindness, and humor. On our unforgettable trips I learned a great deal, about the subject, life, and myself.

MZ was always there for me. In addition to endless personal and professional support, he has taught me, by example, how to strive against the odds, to remain unbreakable, and to succeed time and again.

I was lucky to have an unparalleled and dedicated research assistant, who asked for anonymity. Her initiative, creativity, and professionalism, with which she met my endless requests, were superb. Most importantly, a great scholar, she was passionate about the subject, asked intriguing questions, and provided outstanding comments.

Through these years, I have been fortunate to count on Morielle Lotan and Leehe Friedman, directors of the Honors Track in Strategy and Decision Making, which I am heading at the Interdisciplinary Center (IDC) Herzliya. They brilliantly carried out their academic-administrative responsibilities, which saved me time and energy for the work on the book.

I have benefited much from the advice, remarks, and questions of Uzi Arad, Yossi Baidatz, Eliot Cohen, Thomas Erhard, Gideon Frank, Amos Gilad, Ori Goldberg, Gershon Hacohen, Ben Lamont, Ariel (Eli) Levite, Keir Lieber, Andrew May, Dan Meridor, Phillip Pournelle, Daryl Press, Yoav Rosenberg, and Keren Yarhi-Milo. Itai Brun generously shared with me the contours of the analytical framework for faith-military relations. I am indebted to Yaacov (Yasha) Kedmi for unique reflections on Vladimir Putin and other senior Russian officials, as well as his ideas and advice on the themes central to the book. I am thankful to Morielle

Lotan for her insights on the strategic role of nuclear operators. Felix Motzkin shared his unique experiences with the Soviet political officers and with their Russian reincarnations, for which I am indebted to him.

The School of Government at the IDC Herzliya has been an exceptional professional home. My thanks go to Uriel Reichman, the president; Alex Mintz, the provost; and Boaz Ganor, the dean, who have enabled me to benefit from the IDC's success story and to be part of this remarkable academic institution, the genuine academia of the twenty-first century. I have also been exceptionally fortunate to have kind colleagues at the school. I would like to thank especially Assaf Moghadam and Asif Efrat, who always found time for me and were generous with their wisdom and advice. Also, I have benefited enormously from the questions and observations of the IDC students, particularly those of the Honors Track and of my seminar on Russian foreign and security policy.

Ron Hassner provided priceless theoretical and methodological advice, which significantly improved the final product. David Holloway, on a walk in the woods during the Nuclear Boot Camp in Italy, provided sharp and prudent counsel about what to do and what not to do in the book, and how to proceed. I am very grateful to both. I would also like to extend my thanks to three anonymous reviewers for their insightful comments. Ruvik Danieli did a superb editing job of unparalleled professionalism. It has been a privilege and pleasure to work with Alan Harvey and Leah Pennywark of the Stanford University Press.

I was very close to my grandmother and was lucky to share the book's idea with her. I told her that my passion for the subject probably has something to do with early childhood experiences, when as a good Jewish grandmother she took me to walk and draw in one of the most picturesque places of Moscow—the Novodevichy Monastery. She was thrilled to hear it. She passed away halfway through my work. This book is a tribute to everything she did for me and is dedicated to her memory.

LIST OF TERMS AND ABBREVIATIONS

AF—Russian Air Force

Akafist—an Orthodox hymn dedicated to a saint

Archangel—a chief angel

Arkhiepiskop—honorary title granted by the patriarch to the *episcop* (bishop)

Arkhierei—a general term for the senior-level monastic clergy

Arkhimandrit—rank of a monastic priest who heads the monastery

Blagochinie—the ROC's administrative division, merging several parishes of one eparchy, equivalent to a deanery in the Roman Catholic Church; its head, *blagochinii*, is subordinate to the *arkhierei*

Confessor (*dukhovnik*)—a priest who accepts confessions and gives pardon and spiritual counsel

Cosmodrome—Russian term for the space launch site

Cross procession / procession of the cross (*krestnyi khod*)—carrying of the cross in outdoor processions, usually during the major holidays, festal occasions, or the veneration of relics

CTBT—Comprehensive Test Ban Treaty

C2—command and control

Dedovschina—Russian colloquial expression for physical and psychological brutalization of junior conscripts by senior servicemen

Diakon—deacon, the lowest rank of the priesthood

DM—defense minister

DOSAAF—the Soviet paramilitary sport organization

Enthronization—the religious ceremony of installing a new patriarch in the ROC

Eparkhiia—eparchy, an administrative division of the ROC headed by an *episcop* and consisting of several *blagochinie*

Episcop—bishop, senior cleric heading an *eparkhiia*

EW—early warning

FOC—Faculty of Orthodox Culture

FSB—Russian Federal (Internal) Security Service

GPW—Great Patriotic War (1941–45)

GRU—Russian military intelligence

GS—General Staff

GUMO—the 12th Main Directorate of the Ministry of Defense, responsible for storage, maintenance, safety, transportation, and delivery of the arsenals to all legs of the nuclear triad

House church (*Domovaia tserkov' / domovoi khram*)—a church building or part of the dwelling designated for performing religious services and ceremonies by members of a household or an institution

ICBM—intercontinental ballistic missile

Ierei—the second rank of the Orthodox priesthood

Ieromonk—a monk combining his duties with serving as a priest

Igumen—a monk, head of the monastery, with duties equivalent to an *arkhimandrit*, but considered to be the lower rank of the two

Khorugv'—an Orthodox heraldic banner used for liturgies

Kupel' (baptismal font)—a water basin used during the baptismal ceremony

Lavra—a monastery consisting of a cluster of hermit monks' cells

Legenda—Soviet and Russian intelligence jargon for an operative's cover story

LRA—Long Range Aviation

Maskirovka—Russian military term for the range of deception, camouflage, and denial methods

Metropolitan—the highest administrative clerical rank beneath patriarch, heading several eparchies and ruling a certain territory

MIFI—Moscow Engineering and Physics Institute

MINATOM—Russian Ministry of Nuclear Affairs, predecessor of *ROSATOM*

MoD—Ministry of Defense

Moleben—supplication service

Moschevik—icon embedded with pieces of saints' remains

NF—Northern Fleet

ORBAT—order of battle

PF—Pacific Fleet

Podvizhnichestvo—philanthropic labor for the sake of a higher goal and for the good of mankind; a *podvizhnik* is someone who conducts this labor

Pokazukha—Russian colloquial expression for staging an event for show

Polygon—Russian term for testing range

Prikhod—parish; a *blagochinie* consists of several parishes

PRO (Protivoraketnaia oborona)—Anti-Missile Defense corps (troops)

Protoierei—a priest of a rank higher than *ierei*

Pustynnik (desert person)—an Orthodox ascetic tradition emanating from the early Christian practice of monks and nuns in the desert of Egypt, also known as Desert Fathers and Mothers

RISI—Russian Institute of Strategic Research

ROSATOM—Russian State Atomic Energy Corporation, successor of MINATOM

ROSCOSMOS—Russian State Space Corporation

RPTs/ROC—*Russkaia Pravoslavnaia Tserkov'* / Russian Orthodox Church

RVSN (Raketnye voiska strategicheskogo naznacheniia)—Strategic Mission Missile Forces

SF—Space Forces

Siloviki—Russian colloquial expression for politicians from the security and military services, usually of the Soviet era

Skete (skit)—an isolated community of hermit monks

Sobor—cathedral; the main temple of the eparchy

SPRN (Sistema preduprezhdeniia o raketnom napadenii)—System of Missile Attack Warning

SSB—submarine capable of launching ballistic missiles

SSBN—nuclear-powered submarine

Starets—an elder monk who functions as spiritual leader, with wisdom and powers acquired directly from God; ascetic experiences of prayer and fasting enable him to heal, provide spiritual guidance, and prophesy

START—Strategic Arms Reduction Treaty

SVR—Russian Foreign Intelligence Service

Synod—the supreme administrative governing organ of the ROC

Temple (*khram*)—synonymous with *church* in Russian, but used in reference to the physical building and not the institution

TsNII / CSRI—Tsentral'nyi Nauchno-Issledovatel'skii Institut / Central Scientific-Research Institute

V-Day—Victory Day in the Great Patriotic War (9 May 1945), the Soviet and Russian national holiday

VDV—Russian Airborne Troops

VNIIEF—All-Russian Research Institute of Experimental Physics, in Sarov (former Arzamas-16)

VRNS (*Vsemirnyi russkii narodnyi sobor*)—World Russian People's Council

RUSSIAN NUCLEAR ORTHODOXY

CHAPTER 1

INTRODUCTION

SINCE THE COLLAPSE of the Soviet Union, religion and nuclear weapons have grown immensely in significance, reaching a peak in Russian ideology and strategy. Faith has a high profile in the president's public and private conduct and in domestic and foreign policy, and it is a measure of national identity. It has also saturated Russian nuclear military-industrial complex. Each leg of the nuclear triad has its patron saint, and their icons hang on the walls of the consecrated headquarters and command posts. Icons appear on the nuclear platforms; aerial, naval, and ground processions of the cross are a routine; the military clergy provide regular pastoral care to the nuclear corps' servicemen and function as official assistants of the commanders for the work with personnel. Within each big base there is a garrison church, chapel, or prayer room. The nuclear priesthood and commanders jointly celebrate religious and professional holidays, and catechization is an integral part of the military and civilian higher nuclear education. A similar situation prevails within the nuclear weapons industry.

Supplication services and the sprinkling of holy water occur during parades, the oath of allegiance, exercises, maneuvers, space and nuclear launches, and combat duties. Nuclear priests are integrated in professional activities through the whole chain of command and join their flock during operational missions on the ground and underwater. Pilots of strategic bombers consecrate their jets before combat sorties, and icons are attached to the maps they take to the cockpit. Mobile temples accompany intercontinental ballistic missiles, and nuclear-armed submarines have their portable churches. Within the Russian military, in particular within the nuclear forces, the scope and frequency of clerical activities fostering patriotism, morale, and human reliability have made the priests almost equivalent to Soviet-era political officers. History had come full circle. In the Soviet era "red corners" were located in public places to present an iconostasis of the "new saints" of Marxism-Leninism, replacing the Orthodox icons.[1] Now, the new mythology and iconography have replaced the Soviet iconostasis with a new-old one, in which traditional Russian and newly canonized saints and warriors from Russian and Soviet history harmoniously coexist. Incrementally, the Russian Orthodox Church (ROC) crafted a new pantheon of military heroes and a new professional ethos emerged.

In parallel, during the past decade the West has perceived Russia's nuclear theory and practice as the most assertive ever. Indeed, Russian strategists more readily than in the past have incorporated nuclear tools in their military planning and employed coercive nuclear signaling during a crisis. Exercises with nonstrategic nuclear weapons and the deployment of nuclear-capable, dual-use platforms in Ukraine and in Syria demonstrate this trend, and nuclear intimidations have been evident in Russia's conduct in its European periphery. The ROC's role is not the only, and not even the main, factor behind the Kremlin's nuclear credo and foreign policy, but the moral-ideational climate fostered by the ROC provided Moscow with the needed legitimacy. The ROC has systematically and openly supported the Kremlin's foreign policy gambits involving nuclear weapons. For these moves by the Kremlin, the ROC has steadily generated social backing through its indoctrination and educational activities, among both the general public and the military. In contrast to other antinuclear Christian denominations, the ROC has promoted a "pronuclear" worldview within Russian society. At a time of economic austerity, it supports the Kremlin's national security course and legitimizes budget allocations to the defense sector. The ROC's position provided nuclear weapon designers with some sort of moral legitimacy for research and development (R&D) programs on the nuclear weapons' modernization, as it also indirectly legitimized the Russian strategic community's reluctance to consider further arms control agreements.

The ROC has positioned itself as one of the main guardians of the state's nuclear potential and, as such, claims the role of one of the main guarantors of Russian national security. Many in the broader strategic community have come to share this self-assessment of the church. The ROC capitalized on this reputation and became one of the designers of the new professional identity of the Russian military in general, and of the nuclear corps in particular, and has utilized the nuclear community as a tool to enhance its social and political influence. In short, the practices and rituals within the Russian military, especially within the nuclear community, are in line with Ron Hassner's definition of a religious military organization.[2]

RESEARCH OBJECTIVES

The case at hand is the most significant and the least likely at the same time. The book provides an account of how a grassroots phenomenon of a formerly outcast religion became supported by a state and wormed its way into the most significant wing of one of the most powerful military organizations in the world no less. It is not only the story of the crucial role that religion plays today in the Russian military and in a state from which it was banned until the early 1990s, but also the dramatic tale of how it came to play that assertive role within a very short span of time. The story is so much more impressive given how very dire the status of the ROC was in the eyes of the military elite before the events described in the book. Antichurch propaganda had been especially strong within the ranks of the Soviet military, which was one of the main pillars of the most anticlerical regime in history. How did all of that come to happen?

Exploring the impact of religion on strategy in Russia is the main theme of this book. It describes the unprecedented role that the Orthodox faith has played in Russian identity, politics, and national security and focuses on the bond that has emerged between the Kremlin, the ROC, and the nuclear weapons community. The book dubs this unique three-decade-long nexus "Russian Nuclear Orthodoxy." Outlining the social and cultural causes of this overlooked phenomenon, describing its impact on Moscow's foreign and security policy and on Russian military-nuclear affairs, and discussing the consequences of this neglected singularity for international security theory are this book's primary aims. How has this church-nuclear nexus evolved? What have been its effects on Russian national security policy? What are the implications for Moscow's future political trajectory? What insights does this phenomenon suggest regarding other members of the nuclear club where religion is interwoven with strategy? What are the broader ramifications for international relations (IR) theory and practice? These are the main questions with which this book grapples.

The following three corps of literature are most relevant for explaining this intriguing phenomenon: works on religion and IR, since this book is essentially about the role of faith in international security; scholarship on state-church relations in Russia, since the phenomenon is a unique part of Russian political history; and works on the role of religion on the battlefield, since the book explores how faith conditions military strategy and operations. This book makes use of this important scholarship, though it suffers from certain lacunae. First, despite a consensus that religion matters, the causal mechanism that links faith to strategy is, for the most part, unclear.[3] The growing literature on religion and IR has examined how faith influences international cooperation and conflict;[4] how religious identities drive peace and war;[5] and how religion shapes warriors' self-perception, wars' duration, and the appropriateness of weapons,[6] and it has analyzed the concept of just war.[7] Notwithstanding these important contributions, international security literature is still closer to the first than to the last word on the issue of faith's influence on states' militaries.[8] The scholarship suffers from a case-selection bias. With few exceptions,[9] the majority of the literature has focused on Islamic radicalism and non-state actors,[10] but paid little attention to the nexus between nuclear weapons and religion in the militaries of the Christian world.

Second, the book corresponds with works on the role of religion in Russian politics. The history of Russian church-military relations remains entirely unwritten. Although the literature has scrutinized Russian church-state relations,[11] the ROC's role within the strategic community has received little notice.[12] The burgeoning scholarship on Russian security has completely passed over the theocratization of the nuclear complex, although its significance is hard to underestimate. No existing work identifies the Russian church-nuclear nexus or explains its sources and effects. The book shares an analytical focus with John Garrard and Carol Garrard's work, which sets the stage for exploring the resurgence of the ROC in Russian national security, and also with Irina Papkova's and John Burgess's works, which provide a broad discussion on state-church relations.[13] However, Burgess and Papkova leave the national security dimension outside their main focus, while Garrard and Garrard make passing and chronologically limited reference to this topic. This book offers the first comprehensive analysis of the church-nuclear nexus in Russia from its inception to the present day and examines its impact on national security policy.

Third, the book is part of the evolving wave of scholarship on religion in militaries and on battlefields worldwide. Ron Hassner's works are setting the theoretical tone in the field.[14] The book strongly resonates with this scholarship analytically and methodologically. However, Hassner's works do not cover Orthodox Christianity and the Russian military, and are confined to conventional affairs, leaving the nuclear realm beyond their scope. In this book, in contrast, these subjects are at the center of scrutiny.

The book seeks to extend our knowledge beyond these shortcomings. By shifting the research emphasis to exploring the nexus of Orthodox Christianity and the Russian nuclear complex, it expands the database empirically and functionally. The book portrays the symbiotic relationship between religious beliefs, nuclear policy, and military organizations. Building on standing theoretical insights and generalizing from the findings, it advances a debate about religion and international security toward a more coherent theory of the field. The book situates the findings in the comparative context and uses a nuanced understanding of the Russian case to hypothesize about the role of religion in modern militaries and draw conclusions that are applicable to other members of the nuclear club. The book takes the first steps in the direction of a parsimonious model of faith-driven modern militaries. Its generalization about the mechanism that transforms religious content into policy outcomes advances theory building on the subject of religion and strategy. Methodologically, the book offers a multifaceted analytical perspective, emanating from religious studies, political science, and Russian area studies. As such, it further refines the techniques applicable in other cases looking at religion and military affairs. Finally, the empirical findings on the role of ecclesiastical ideas in Russian national security highlight the implications for practitioners.

STRUCTURE

The book traces the evolution of Russian nuclear orthodoxy since the Soviet collapse. Each part covers roughly one decade, examining its overriding trend, and scrutinizes the coming together of strategy and religion within the political leadership, the national security elite, and the nuclear complex—the Strategic Mission Missile Forces, Long Range Aviation, the Space Forces, the Early Warning Corps, the Nuclear Submarine Fleet, the nuclear custodians of the Ministry of Defense (MoD), and the nuclear weapons industry. Consequently, each part first describes the state-church relations, then narrows the focus to state-military relations, and finally concentrates on the main topic of inquiry—Russian Nuclear Orthodoxy. In addition, each part covers the evolution of strategic mythmaking during the discussed decade and its impact on the national security discourse. Since the book is focused on the nuclear dimension, it does not discuss in detail the religious renaissance in the other military services. It only describes the general trend of the decade under scrutiny to contextualize the state of nuclear-faith affairs. Detailed analysis of the overall religious penetration inside the Russian strategic community and military establishment is a topic for a separate work and is beyond the scope of this book.

The first part of the book describes the inception of the church-nuclear nexus in the early 1990s. During this period the quest for religiosity emerged as a grassroots phenomenon within the nuclear complex, and the latter entered into a covenant with the ROC. The book defines it as the "genesis decade." The second part of the book covers the period from the early 2000s to 2010, during which the churching of the nuclear complex coincided with the increasing role of religion in Russian politics.

Russian Nuclear Orthodoxy initially emerged as a bottom-up phenomenon. However, when the leadership began flirting with faith, a top-down trend supplemented the initial grassroots impulse. The book defines it as the "conversion decade." The third part of the book, covering the period from 2010 onward, describes how these bottom-up and top-down tendencies have merged, reaching a peak of clericalization in state-church relations. The book defines this period as the "operationalization decade." During this period the nuclear arsenal has become one of the major instruments of national security, while religion has gained extraordinary prominence in national ideology.

Aiming to demonstrate how and to what extent religion has conditioned Russian nuclear affairs, the book's chapters examine the following questions: What set of values does the ROC's pastoral care cultivate within the nuclear forces? What theological motifs feature in the nuclear forces' professional activities and rituals? How do nuclear commanders use religious norms and myths to express their professional credo and to envision the appropriate behavior of the nuclear officer? How do such outlooks affect the routine of the nuclear corps? To what extent has the encounter with the ROC shaped nuclear modernization, arms control initiatives, doctrine, and strategy, and do any or all of these deviate from earlier practices?

The conclusion and epilogue situate the main empirical findings in a comparative context, generalize them into generic theoretical insights, and hypothesize about the emerging role of religion in modern militaries worldwide, to facilitate broader generalizations about faith and strategy. The insights they offer are applicable to other members of the nuclear club and make it possible to generate hypotheses for further theory development and to pose several policy-relevant questions. Also, to provide a solid basis for practitioners seeking to engage Moscow on a host of geopolitical issues, both concluding chapters speculate how the Kremlin's emphasis on religious ideology and nuclear weapons may manifest itself in prospective diplomatic and military initiatives.

ARGUMENTS AND FINDINGS

This book tells the story of how the ROC came to permeate the Russian nuclear military-industrial complex. This story reflects the general tendency of the time—religious saturation began simultaneously from the 1990s across the entire strategic establishment. However, within this large-scale penetration by the ROC the nuclear community has been special. The scale of the church-nuclear bond dwarfs any comparable developments, in terms of scope and longevity, and hence the main focus of the book. The book demonstrates how this development occurred and grounds it within the broader contexts of state-church affairs and church-military (non-nuclear) relations. This unique story of the nuclear community partially demonstrated the ROC's prioritization dictum—first and foremost, to concentrate on the services that are most important for national security and that operate under the most difficult, risky, and stressful conditions. Also, it seems, the ROC considered the centrality of the complex to public perception and at the same time its relative compactness, which made penetration optimal.

Although some of the clergy and some senior nuclear officials have credited the ROC with "delivering" the Kremlin's backing for nuclear issues, the book does not argue that greater penetration into the nuclear community resulted in greater resourcing. The services that the ROC penetrated most deeply indeed received the majority of allocated resources, but this was a matter more of correlation than of causality. Evidence, presented in competition with other explanations, is needed to make the case that the ROC made the difference. However, the clergy, and in some cases the services, have attributed this impact to the ROC and have tried to position the church as a provider of political support, to increase its legitimacy and political-organizational influence. The book describes this narrative, which the ROC has promoted.

The analysis offered in the book concludes with the following findings. First, the penetration of faith into politics has been so wide, deep, and continuous, with so many vested interests across the political landscape and strategic community, that it is likely to outlive President Vladimir Putin. Nuclear orthodoxy manifests more continuity than change within the Russian political-military tradition and, as such, is likely to remain a durable phenomenon. Second, since the ROC's role continues to expand, it may become a tool of influence in bureaucratic rivalries among organizations competing for resources within and outside the Russian strategic community, especially in the era of austerity. Third, the ROC is likely to continue serving as a mobilization tool ensuring the quality and quantity of the draft, as well as a tool of social mobilization for national security enterprises. This relates to attracting qualified youth for the elite units of the nuclear forces and the elite technological detachments. Commanders of the nuclear corps may increasingly seek Orthodox draftees, viewing them as more reliable and motivated. Fourth, in the current political-ideational reality in Russia where faith has become mixed with national identity and patriotism, being Orthodox may become a promotion multiplier within the institutions of the strategic community. Similarly, association with influential senior clerics within the Kremlin's court may positively affect career paths. Fifth, the theocratization of the Russian strategic community may project on the conflict duration and escalation dynamics. Presumably, the Russian nuclear clergy is less likely to constrain conflict. It might even ensure a relatively easier path to escalation, by legitimizing a belligerent political course and ensuring public support for it. Moreover, the Kremlin may promote its image of a faithful strategic actor in the eyes of its counterparts and utilize it for more effective coercion across various domains while managing its national security policy.

The penetration of organized religion into the professional life of state militaries is not a phenomenon peculiar to Russia and is increasingly observable worldwide. The resurgence of religiosity in state militaries is not a binary situation, and each case can be placed on a continuum spanning three ideal types. The first type—"enabling faith"—refers to cases in which a state military enables servicemen to practice their personal religious obligations while conducting military duty. The second type—"faith as enabler"—refers to state military organizations where religion has penetrated the national ideology and is equated with patriotism. The third type—"military theocratization"—is a situation where religion shapes the strategic thinking and operational behavior of a military organization. Presumably, the closer a military organization is to the third type, the greater the probability that religious jurisprudence related to military affairs will emerge and, with it, operators' demand for the counsel of theological experts.

Russia today, the empirical evidence suggests, seems to be within the "faith as enabler" category and possibly in the initial stages of the path toward the "theocratization" type. This juxtaposition makes it possible to offer a set of hypotheses pertaining to nuclear religious jurisprudence and to the conduct and reliability of nuclear operators. On the first matter, Orthodox nuclear jurisprudence dealing with the main questions of nuclear strategy and operations seems to be, as of now, nonexistent. However, the organizational-conceptual conditions and settings for joint explorations of these issues do exist both within the Russian nuclear community and within the ROC. One could argue that given the current level of theocratization of the nuclear establishment and operationalization of the nuclear clergy, the latter will be interested and compelled by the potential demand from the former to explore these questions in depth and in a more elaborate manner than has been done until recently. The more the priesthood is involved in operational issues and the keener its professional contacts with the operators, the greater the likelihood that a demand for nuclear Orthodox jurisprudence will emerge.

On the second matter, it is unclear how the Orthodox faith and priests project on the human reliability of the nuclear chain of command. On the one hand, religiosity may enhance obedience and commitment to turning the key when the order arrives, and not turning it when there is no order. Discipline, motivation, the fulfillment of patriotic duty, and service to a higher cause are the dominant values that the Russian nuclear clergy has promoted. Thus, the nuclear priesthood is likely to serve to enhance the legitimation and execution of orders. One could argue that when it comes to ordering nuclear battlefield use, under the influence of the ROC, strategists and operators will more easily overcome moral and ethical self-restraints and execute missions exactly as ordered. On the other hand, it is not inconceivable that nuclear operators, driven by faith and encouraged by the clergy, may, under certain circumstances, establish pockets of disobedience. Although one might have difficulty imagining the patriarch opposing the nuclear initiatives of the political leadership for theological reasons, disagreements and tensions in state-church relations have been on display in modern Russia and historically. The current cooperative and close nature of the state-church relationship is not predetermined. Theoretically, voices from within the church may question certain aspects of nuclear policy. This counterintuitive scenario is now more likely than before, given the political power and social influence that the ROC has accumulated. If an order from the political leadership runs against both the operators' professional intuition and nuclear jurisprudence, the nuclear clergy multiplies the probability of disobedience.

The findings of the book suggest that the closer the situation approaches a protracted geopolitical crisis, the more prominent the role and involvement of the nuclear priests in the decision-making might become. If nuclear commanders and operators seek a priest's guidance to deal with the moral and ethical questions raised by an order from the political leadership, this could mean that, de facto, there might be two parallel lines of command authority. It is thus conceivable that in a crisis situation accompanied by civil-church and civil-military tensions, the nuclear priesthood might become part of the decision-making on matters of national security. Hence, the most basic takeaway from the book is a need to incorporate religion into any future analysis of strategic affairs in general, in the Russian case in particular.[15] The book argues that it is essential to follow the metamorphosis of the state-church contract in Russia and to explore how it projects on national security policy, in particular in the nuclear realm. This is a major discontinuity from the past.

METHOD AND AUDIENCES

The book employs several academic disciplines to investigate a topic at the intersection of military affairs, religion, and international politics. It uses primary sources that are for the most part unknown to Western audiences—government and ecclesiastical documents and materials, military and religious professional periodicals, movies and TV programs, interviews with clergy and military brass, and a content analysis of iconography and heraldic symbols. These primary sources have their strengths and weaknesses. They afford a unique glimpse, but often present a tendentious narrative. Also, reliable, nonofficial sociological-statistical data on the most important issues is unavailable. The book highlights these biases, critically discusses them, and conditions its conclusions.

Where possible the book uses the English equivalents of Orthodox religious and Russian military terms. In the places where the book keeps the Russian term, military or religious, it offers an explanation on its first appearance and then refers to the glossary of terms and abbreviations. The term *consecration* is preferred over the term *sanctification* to translate the Russian word *osviatschenie*, which stands for the religious ritual of the sacralization of material objects. Also, the book translates the Russian term *votserkvlenie* as "churching," which stands for the active, and not merely nominal and declarative, practice of faith. Unless otherwise stated all English translations are by the author. The book adopts an interdisciplinary research methodology, used by scholars of culture, strategy, and religion, and international politics. To trace the causal link, it investigates the religious foundations of a phenomenon and then moves on to the political outcome, constructing successive layers of explanation. Insights yielded by this method are generalized into broader conclusions about faith-based behavior on the international level of analysis. The purpose is to delineate the role of religion in strategy and to determine whether a connection is correlative, causal, or constitutive.[16]

Essentially an international security studies endeavor, this book does not limit itself to a single field, but engages with a topic situated at the intersection of religion, Russian politics, and IR scholarship, in particular dealing with nuclear affairs. Its appeal is therefore broad and diverse. The first audience is the readership on international security and nuclear strategy. For students, scholars, and practitioners who are interested in contemporary military affairs, specifically in the role of nuclear weapons in IR, and in Russian nuclear modernization, the book is a case study in itself and an empirical building-block for general theorization. The second audience is the readership on Russian affairs. No less than to the international security generalists, the book will also appeal to academics and wide public audiences interested in contemporary Russian politics, national security, anthropology, and contemporary history. The book's audience also includes practitioners who have to contend with a host of challenges thrown up by Russia's current geopolitical assertiveness. The third audience the book will draw is both academics and general readers interested in the impact of religion on IR and military affairs. It provides a timely addition to the growing wave of theoretical scholarship on the subject and, as such, speaks directly to the theoreticians of this field of political science. Also, practitioners interested in engaging with religion-driven and nuclear-capable actors should find the book of immediate relevance.

It is both remarkable and worrisome how little practitioners and scholars of IR on both sides of the Atlantic understand a subject of such unquestionable importance. If anything, the resurgence of religiosity in several state militaries worldwide has driven home the urgency of a book-length study on this issue and the pressing need to educate on the phenomenon of Russian Nuclear Orthodoxy.

Part I
THE GENESIS DECADE: 1991–2000

CHAPTER 2

STATE-CHURCH RELATIONS

ON 25 DECEMBER 1991, the Russian tricolor replaced the red flag over the Kremlin. The president of the Soviet Union, Mikhail Gorbachev, resigned and handed over power to Boris Yeltsin, the president of Russia. The next day the Supreme Soviet declared the dissolution of the Union, acknowledged the independence of the former Soviet republics, and established the Commonwealth of Independent States (CIS). Although it was a natural progression from the previous events, the collapse was a colossal surprise to the millions of Soviet citizens across the eleven time zones of the biggest country in the world. The move was rapid, difficult to grasp, and extremely disorienting. The social-professional group that experienced the deepest shock and the most profound systemic crisis was what had been until the previous day the bulk of the Soviet military and had just become the Armed Forces of the Russian Federation. When the collapse overturned the political, economic, and social order, the world fell apart for the military. It was the final blow after perestroika, when the military had been harshly criticized as a source of the state's many troubles and torn apart by moral dilemmas, ideological contradictions, and financial difficulties.

In parallel, the Soviet regime's last years created the optimal conditions for religion's entry into Russian social and political life. Economic decline went hand in hand with ideological exhaustion and cultural-spiritual impoverishment, making the society, at the dusk of the Soviet era, unprecedentedly receptive to faith. The predisposition toward religiosity in the hearts and minds of the masses was genuine, if not always deep.[1] The Russian clergy saw this popular spiritual hunger and the overall religious renaissance as "the second baptism of Russia" of sorts. Sensing the winds of change still under the Soviet regime, the ROC's hierarchs called on the clergy to exploit the unprecedented political freedoms brought by perestroika, urged the most active stand on the pressing national issues, and encouraged them to use every opportunity to engage with society and state.[2] The clergy rushed toward political influence "in a fit of revenge for decades of persecution, oppression, and restrictions."[3] Within this engagement, the then patriarch, Alexey, and the then head of the ROC's External Relations Department, Metropolitan Kirill, the future patriarch, envisioned the work with the military as one of the most important courses of action.[4]

The initial mastermind behind church-military relations was Alexey. As the metropolitan of Leningrad, he was among the first senior clerics to sense that the military could become the ROC's major social ally.[5] Under him, the first significant encounter between the two occurred. Returning the bones of saints to their reliquaries became one of the main state-church enterprises during the perestroika era. One year before his enthronization, in 1989, Alexey regained St. Alexander Nevsky's relics. These bones were special. When Peter the Great built and declared St. Petersburg the capital in the eighteenth century, he had installed Nevsky's relics in the main cathedral. The bones were there until 1922, when the Bolsheviks confiscated them. Now the Soviet authorities handed them back. The ceremony took place in the Kazan Cathedral, which also hosts the tomb of Mikhail Kutuzov, a major Russian military hero and the victor over Napoleon. Alexey skillfully exploited this coincidence. He put the Nevsky relics near Kutuzov's tomb and called on the crowd to join him in a prayer of "eternal memory," which he publicly dedicated to all Russian soldiers who had ever fallen in the Motherland's defense. Several uniformed officers participated and Soviet television broadcast it live.[6]

It is difficult to overestimate the magnitude of this event, as Alexander Nevsky resonates so powerfully within the Russian psyche. A thirteenth-century prince who was called Nevsky after defeating the Teutonic Knights on the banks of the Neva, he is one of the most venerated in the Russian pantheon of heroes. Canonized in the sixteenth century, he became so popular in national folklore that every Soviet atheist knew him. During the famous Red Square address on 7 November 1941, aimed at suppressing panic when the Wehrmacht tanks were less than fifty kilometers from the Kremlin, Joseph Stalin mentioned Nevsky first among the Russian heroes, and Kutuzov last.[7] In 1989 the Soviet military, probably at its lowest point since 1941, needed a moral boost as never before. Troops had departed from Afghanistan that year after a humiliating decade of futile war, with thousands killed or wounded. The Warsaw Pact had collapsed and troops were withdrawing from Europe. Thus, "saluting the memory of the country's greatest military hero" and dedicating a prayer to all fallen soldiers served as a powerful tribute to the Soviet military's recent sacrifices and humiliations.[8]

This skillful move, a prelude to the reinvigoration of church-military relations, went largely unnoticed in the turmoil of the disintegrating regime. The big leap forward occurred right after the Soviet collapse. When the Union vanished, the ROC was fully alerted to engage with its main target of opportunity—the Russian military. In January 1992, about two weeks following Gorbachev's dissolution of the Soviet Union, to meet the situation of collapse, about five thousand senior commanders from all the corps, services, and military districts gathered in the Kremlin. The first head of the just-established CIS Armed Forces led the meeting. The presidents of Russia and Kazakhstan were present. The atmosphere was charged and gloomy.

There was a puzzling twist to the agenda: among the keynote speakers was Metropolitan Kirill, the head of the ROC's External Relations Department. An address by a high-ranking cleric to such a senior military audience was unheard of. Kirill's speech, however, was perfectly tailored to resonate with the burning problems in the military's hearts and minds. Kirill positioned himself as someone deeply concerned with the implications of the collapse for the military and the ROC as its reliable political-social ally. His address was historical; it gave the initial impulse to a monumental restoration of military-church relations.[9] His first message related to the moral-ethical grounds of the military and to the responsibility of the church to pastor it. To the astonishment of the secular audience of senior commanders, he said that during each of the ROC's services the priests pray to strengthen the moral-spiritual powers of the military. He asserted that it is the only professional category that the ROC prays for, because more than anyone else it is responsible for the destiny of the nation, the state, and the people's lives, since the price of a mistake is devastating and since military duty demands the most terrible thing—life's sacrifice for the higher cause.

Kirill argued that the warriors, like no one else, needed to preserve their ideals and maintain ethical coherence. Without that, moral motivation is lacking, warriors turn into mercenaries, and the military loses its ability to defend the Motherland and endangers its people.[10] As Kirill's words make plain, the ROC was staking a claim also as the military's advocate vis-à-vis society. He remarked on the military's recent social-economic sacrifices and argued that the demonizing public attitude of recent years toward the military, which was operating on the highest moral grounds, had to stop.[11] The second message envisioned the ideological foundations of the new state and its relations with the Near Abroad. Despite the tendency at the time toward national self-determination, Kirill emphasized the importance of the faith-based geopolitical solidarity of the thousand-year-old communality of nations baptized in the same Kiev baptismal font (*kupel'*) and inhabiting the Motherland. The policy of radical sovereignty, according to him, risked inflicting huge moral-ethical damage on what he would later call the "Russian World."

Finally, Kirill touched on the then most sensitive issue among the officers—the new oaths of allegiance emanating from the division of the Soviet military among newly established states, which risked dividing the Russia nation. "What will happen if father and son swear an oath of allegiance to different states? What will happen if these states [that is, Russia and Ukraine], God forbid, decide to resolve their issues with arms? Today, on all of us, and on the politicians, there lies an epochal responsibility": to ensure harmony between the development of the independent states and preserving the historical communalism of the nations inhabiting Russia.[12]

Kirill communicated more than empathy. He argued that the ROC could assist the new military with its three burning professional issues: motivating the soldiers, providing new meanings under new geopolitical circumstances, and preventing civil war. To the secular senior officers, still the products of the Soviet mentality, Kirill's address was unusual. Nevertheless, after years of humiliation, social ostracism, and balancing on the brink of civil war, his words were music to their ears. Summarizing the event, the commander of the CIS forces said: "With regard to the relationship with the ROC on the matter of bringing up the military youth, we are ready for cooperation to strengthen the patriotic spirit, the high moral grounds, and to overcome national conflicts in the military."[13]

Tremendous problems were indeed tearing the military apart. The conscripts felt miserable. Their morale was low; they lacked a sense of purpose, often starved, suffered from *dedovschina* (physical and psychological brutalization by senior conscripts), and if unlucky enough not to dodge the draft by bribes, medical fraud, or pretense, often deserted or even committed suicide. The officers' corps felt equally dejected. Defeat in Afghanistan, public critique, the collapse of the Warsaw Pact, and withdrawal from Europe had brought them to the lowest point of their careers. The military shrank, lost large arsenals and personnel to the former republics, and was plundered by corruption, drinking, and disciplinary problems. The ROC could not have wished for a better constellation for engagement.[14]

Kirill, who was experienced in collaboration with the state organs, realized that only a formal agreement would afford military-church relations practical space for maneuvering. In June 1993, President Yeltsin, Defense Minister (DM) Pavel Grachev, and Metropolitan Kirill greeted the graduates of the military academies at the Kremlin. Following the official ceremony, Kirill secured a personal meeting with Grachev, and their first official get-together occurred in July. Among others, the head of the Ministry of Defense (MoD) Main Educational Work Directorate participated. This organ—like its predecessor, the Main Political Directorate that once oversaw the work of the political officers—was responsible for the discipline, ideology, and moral-psychological aptitude of the military. The meeting explored church-military cooperation in the field of spiritual-ethical education and gave the impulse to the staff work out-lining its ends and means.[15] The leadership's assertion that "orientation on a religious worldview should ensure better management of social and state institutions, including the military," provided the necessary legitimacy for cooperation.[16]

The MoD's and the ROC's interests converged. The latter could deliver remedies for the former's professional problems: motivation and discipline, social critique, and an ideological vacuum. In turn, the church saw the military as a vehicle that could allow it to play an important role in society by outreaching to all possible groups and to expand its influence in the government. Both shared a desire to construct a new identity—national in the case of the church and professional in the case of the military. Less than a year later, in March 1994, the patriarch and the DM signed the Joint Declaration on Cooperation.[17] By the time of the signing, the ROC and the military, according to the DM, already shared a common language, and clerics were permitted into the units. The declaration, however, legalized the cooperation in educating recruits, fostering a patriotic spirit in them, and strengthening the spiritual-moral aspects of the service.[18] In April, the Holy Synod of the ROC, the supreme clerical organ, designated cooperation with the military as one of the ROC's main aims.[19] By summer 1994, the MoD ordered the intensification of "military-patriotic education of the soldiers and youth," and the General Staff (GS) introduced, within the organs of the Main Educational Work Directorate in all the corps, services, and districts, the position of an officer charged with cooperating with religious organizations.[20]

The military internalized the subtle message: only the representatives of the ROC would get access to the soldiers. "Orthodox meant our own, a patriot; someone of a different faith meant the stranger, an agent of enemy influence." The perception of the ROC as one of the state pillars, in the spirit of the tsarist slogan "Orthodoxy, Autocracy, Peoplehood," began to revive.[21] Though the military's faith was not necessarily deeply rooted, affection for the church was authentic. When the military realized the ROC's social-political potential, it changed its attitude toward religion as something backward and obsolete and was inclined to cooperate. People wearing insignia on their shoulders traditionally have been more conservative, perceiving themselves as keepers of the national values, and have therefore sympathized with other groups of similar psychology. Commanders sought ideological symbols in support of discipline. They attributed the acute problems to the moral crisis corrupting the military and nostalgically recalled the Soviet past, when soldiers were properly motivated, ready to execute orders, and sacrifice lives. Finally, the military's renunciation of the Communist ideology stimulated professional soul-searching, and many commanders saw in a return to Orthodoxy something genuinely Russian that could recapture the lost meanings and values.[22]

To engage the hearts and minds of the senior but still secular commanders, the Moscow Patriarchate and the MoD organized two conferences in 1994: "Spiritual-Ethical and Orthodox Traditions of the Military" and "Orthodoxy and the Russian Army." Both conventions hosted hundreds of senior commanders and were held in no less than the General Staff (GS) Academy—the most prestigious and high-ranking Russian military education institution. Patriarch Alexey and the first deputy DM headed the venue, but it was Metropolitan Kirill who played the central role. His speech analyzed the pre-Soviet history of the church-military relations, presented the current nexus as an extension of the then-extant reality, and outlined goals for the future.[23] He aimed to convince the audience that cooperation with the ROC was the most natural and timely enterprise. The address was of historical importance, since Kirill outlined the ROC's strategic goal with regard to the military (that is, the introduction of the military clergy and maximum churching of the armed forces) and the operational principles of its realization.

First, Kirill positioned the church and the military as "brothers in arms." He presented both as central institutions excluded from political life; both perceiving themselves, due to their similar spiritual-ethical values, as the main defenders of the Motherland; and their professions not as "jobs" but as "services" of total commitment and self-sacrifice. Thus, the ROC, according to Kirill, had been and would continue to be the strongest ally of the military when it came to justifying its mission in the eyes of Russian society, sustaining the necessary levels of public and political support, and ensuring the draft.[24] Second, Kirill presented the

ROC's relevancy to the servicemen, especially when conducting combat duties under difficult circumstances. The ROC, promised Kirill, would provide the meaning for the service, motivation for sacrifice, and moral-psychological support to overcome combat difficulties.[25] Third, Kirill stated his strategic goal: reviving the institution of the military clergy. Being realistic about his limitations, Kirill argued that this mission was still just a dream, beyond realization.

Nonetheless he outlined activities aimed at laying the foundations for its fulfillment. Kirill suggested involving priests in military ceremonies, including the oath of allegiance, and in predraft educational activities, to cultivate motivation. To him, the voice of a priest addressing draftees concerned with dedovschina could be more convincing than that of an officer holding a negative image of the military. Kirill urged the clergy to regularly visit the bases and conduct pastoral conversations with the soldiers, especially where there were risks of stress, psychological breakdowns, and suicidal inclinations. He urged local clergy to take responsibility over bases and units deployed within their eparchies and to establish close working and personal contacts with the officers responsible for educational activities there.[26]

For the military, this encounter with religion was as natural as it was controversial. On the one hand, it looked like just another metamorphosis in a longtime trend. The tsars had established the military clergy in 1800 and fully integrated this corps into the armed forces. By 1917 the institution numbered about six hundred military priests, the majority of whom the Soviet authorities physically liquidated. To replace the dismantled corps, the Red Army introduced political officers, or commissars, charged with ensuring each unit's ideological discipline, morale, and combat spirit.[27] Essentially the new organ strongly resonated with its predecessor, but the size, authority, responsibility, and influence of the GS Main Political Directorate dwarfed those of the tsarist Chaplain Corps. Another metamorphosis, then, came with the Soviet collapse. The Main Educational Work Directorate inherited essential functions from its predecessor, plus the new-old mission—cooperation with the church. Thus, within the broader context, it all looked natural. The adoption of faith as a substitute for the civil religion and the reinstitution of the military clergy would be just another reincarnation of a centuries-old practice.

On the other hand, even putting aside commanders' still very superficial religiosity and Russia's multi-confessionalism, there were two big issues. First, a majority of the Soviet commanders detested political officers, whom they saw as good-for-nothing loafers, dangerous troublemakers, and professional careerists. Rebranding the Political Directorate did not change this attitude much in the beginning, as in many cases these were still the same political officers who until recently had lectured on atheism and forced commanders and soldiers to join Komsomol and the Communist Party. Now, the new agreement required the same people to interact with the priests. This seemed hypocritical. The second major concern related to tsarist times. Russian senior commanders, then still predominantly secular, suspected that the restoration of the church-military relations might resurrect "faith-based strategy, tactics and logistics." According to the Garrards, in the post-Communist military there was a widespread notion, probably cultivated during Soviet times, that Nikolai II, one of the most pious tsars, had been a disastrous commander in chief due to his faith-based approach in assuming that icons and prayers could substitute for sound strategic planning and ammunition.[28]

Wise strategists and effective managers, the patriarch and the metropolitan realized that the ROC, which had just started to revive, was not yet ready to take on the reinstitution of the military clergy in the absence of a qualified cadre.[29] They also realized that the catechization of the senior military, which had just recently rediscovered faith, would be a long process and that confining activities only to the senior members could turn into *pokazukha* (Russian colloquial expression for staging an event for show), compromising the whole enterprise.[30] Aware of these challenges, they adopted a sophisticated approach: without institutionalizing the military priesthood, the ROC would offer its services voluntarily and would provide pastoral care to the best of its ability, incrementally churching the whole chain of command. In 1994 the patriarch instructed all the senior clerics at the eparchies to designate local priests responsible for cooperation with the military.[31] These low-ranking priests were advised to establish relations with the commanders of military districts, corps, and units deployed in their parishes, and they delegated authority to coordinate all church-military activities and serve as contacts for all local military commanders seeking cooperation.[32] Metropolitan Kirill, commenting on the patriarch's directive, emphasized the importance of conceptual sync at all levels of operation—the patriarchate, eparchies, and parishes.[33]

Experienced in organizational politics, Kirill realized that a formal organ was needed to coordinate these activities and translate the patriarch's vision into actions on the ground.[34] In July 1995, the Holy Synod, the supreme administrative governing body of the ROC, established the Synodal Department of the Moscow Patriarchate for Cooperation with the Armed Forces and Law Enforcement Organs (Synodal Department)[35]—an organizational vehicle that was charged with this mission. Eparchies established desks with the same title and charged specific priests to pastor military units. In the space of ten years there would be four hundred priests subordinate to the Synodic Department in parishes across Russia.[36] To prioritize the numerous efforts in this realm, Kirill introduced the main guiding principle: first and foremost, concentration on the corps and services that have the most strategically important national security tasks (the nuclear triad) and that operate under the most difficult, risky, and stressful conditions (Airborne Troops and the Navy).[37]

The ROC grasped that to outreach to members of the military and their families across Russia, massive preparations were required. In addition to securing the political will of the state leadership, it started to formulate a positive social attitude. It engaged with the bureaucracy and social audiences to demonstrate its bond with the strategic community and defended the military from demonizing social critique—a minority position in those days.[38] In parallel, the ROC established publishing and informational enterprises tailored to the needs and mentality of the military flock, which differed from the civilian congregations. For this effort, Kirill urged the use of printed and mass media and the introduction of religious components into the state TV programs addressing the military.[39] Around 1996 the ROC issued its first catechism adapted for the military and short prayers for the warrior.[40]

The ROC sensed that in order to establish itself as a permanent social force it had to link faith, patriotism, and the military. Rebuilding the Cathedral of Christ the Savior, the biggest Russian temple, and turning it into one of the central brands of the new state enabled that.[41] In 1812 Tsar Alexander I had ordered the construction of the cathedral to commemorate the victory over Napoleon in the Russian "Patriotic War." Although Stalin had ordered the temple destroyed, Soviet ideology co-opted the war's title and linked that former victory with the Soviet triumph in the "Great Patriotic War." Both events resonated in public memory, and in the post-Soviet rebranding the cathedral started to symbolize willingness to sacrifice for the Motherland.[42] Faith and patriotism began merging in the collective psyche, further underscored by the new cathedral's architectural layout.[43] To co-opt this military-national narrative, the patriarch blessed the cathedral's cornerstone, as had been done in 1812, on Christmas Day of 1995, in the presence of Russia's president and prime minister and Moscow's mayor. Around the same time the construction of churches and chapels within the military units began to gather momentum.[44] The trend started when the head of the GS approved construction of the house church[45] in the GS Academy—the highest educational institution of the military.[46] "At the heart of the military science and at the heart of the spiritual life of the military," the new church sent down a clear signal regarding the preference of the GS and the new professional identity.[47] The patriarch consecrated the temple in December 1995 and called it after the main guardian angel of Orthodox Christianity— Archistrategos Archangel Michael, the Supreme Commander of the Heavenly Forces.[48] A former Soviet major became the temple's priest.[49]

In sum, mutual learning, efforts to overcome previous stereotypes, and objective difficulties characterized the decade. The ROC's initial encounters with the corps, services, and military districts were rather sporadic. The ROC forced itself to reconcile with the Soviet past and positioned itself toward the military as a provider of ideological meanings, as pastor, and as a shield from public critique.[50] However, it lacked experience, and its ability to catechize the armed forces was limited. Pastoring the military in addition to the routine responsibilities in the parishes, which provided the priests with daily bread, was often beyond their capacity. Neither on the ROC's nor the MoD's payrolls, they usually confined their activities to involving the servicemen in the life of local congregations, conversations and blessings during holidays, episodic baptism of the draftees, and the dissemination of icons and literature.[51] Around that time some priests introduced a religious element into the oath of allegiance and the ceremonial for the burial of the fallen.[52] The clergy tried, but was still less instrumental in addressing the main burning issues—dedovschina, suicides following depression, alcohol consumption leading to crimes, and the use of weapons against fellow servicemen.[53]

Within the military, up to the 2000s, the dynamic of the church-military relations was bottom-up rather than top-down. Despite acknowledgment of the need to utilize the ROC for professional purposes, caution was exercised. Many senior officers, still the old Soviet guard, had no idea what to expect from the priests and how to interact with them.[54] At the lower levels of command, in the places of permanent deployment of specific units, a deeper connection began to evolve. This grassroots nexus, also varying across the military, emerged less by order from the top than as a natural bonding between commanders and the local priests, whose churches were located next to the bases. The commanders' quest for personal ties with local clergy reflected the then overall restoration of religiosity in Russian society, both as a genuine return to faith and as a ritualistic facade.[55] Thus, cooperation much depended on the personal connection of the local priests to the local commanders.[56] The interests, worldviews, and intentions of the mid- and low-level officials, military and civilian, and the personal religiosity of specific corps' and units' commanders determined the level of cooperation.[57] Across the Russian strategic community, cooperation and clerical penetration was deepest and most significant in the nuclear corps and in the nuclear industry.

CHAPTER 3

FAITH-NUCLEAR NEXUS

NUCLEAR INDUSTRY

The Brief Encounter

The deterioration in the country's international prestige, the worst economic situation since the Great Patriotic War, a disastrous fall in the standard of leaving, loss of communal feeling, and disillusionment with Communism—this was the zeitgeist at the dusk of the Soviet era. According to the Garrards, the gloomy mood prompted increasing numbers of Soviet citizens "[to seek] another set of prophecies, ones that held out hope [. . .] of better things to come" and which promised that all the suffering had not been in vain.[1] The ROC exploited this spiritual hunger to expand its influence.[2] Among its efforts in this regard, the utilization of St. Seraphim Sarovsky, one of the most renowned Russian saints, stands out. The saint became the key figure in forging the nexus between the ROC and the Russian nuclear weapons community.

The most celebrated member of the Russian ascetic movement, St. Seraphim, born Prokhor Moshnin (1754–1833), was the most popular elder monk (*starets*) of the nineteenth century. Russian startsy, like biblical prophets, function as spiritual leaders, with wisdom and powers given them directly from God. Ascetic experiences of prayer and fasting enable them to heal, provide spiritual guidance, and prophesy. After fifteen years in solitude as a *pustynnik*[3] in the forest near the city of

Sarov, the hermit Seraphim became an elder in the Diveevo Monastery. He received an endless stream of pilgrims from all over Russia, mostly peasants, seeking spiritual and physical healing. Popular belief attributed to his blessings the power of enabling women to conceive sons. More than half a century after Seraphim's death, this caught the attention of Tsar Nikolai II and his wife, who desperately hoped for a successor. The tsar ordered that Seraphim be exhumed and canonized and then reburied. During the canonization service, in July 1903, the tsar carried a reliquary containing Seraphim's bones, while the tsarina stood and prayed. When a year later she gave birth to the tsarevich, Seraphim's tomb became an even more sought-after pilgrimage destination.[4]

Seraphim's disciples compiled every testimony related to his prophesies into the *Diveevo Chronicle*. Among other things, it included his "Letter to the Future," in which Seraphim promised: "The Lord will have mercy on Russia and will lead it along the path of suffering to great glory." First published in 1898, it was reprinted several times.[5] The Soviet regime, aware of Seraphim's centrality to the masses as a Russian-born saint and due to his link to the tsar, made a monumental effort to erase him from public memory. In 1920 a special commission arrived in Diveevo to demonstrate to the "ignorant masses" that what the church called his "incorruptible remains" was a lie. The commission "removed the skeleton from the reliquary and uncovered it for the populace." In 1927 the authorities seized the Diveevo and Sarov Monasteries, confiscated their riches, including Seraphim's bones, drove out the nuns, and executed many of the monks.[6]

The Sarov Monastery, built over Seraphim's hermit cell, became a prison of the People's Commissariat for Internal Affairs (NKVD). During the war, it hosted a factory that produced Katyusha missiles. In 1946, with the beginning of the nuclear project, the Kremlin designated the monastery as the site where the first Soviet bomb would be produced.[7] Renamed first Arzamas-16 and then Kremlev, this top-secret town became the heart of the Soviet system of closed nuclear cities. The brain of the nuclear project—design bureau KB-11, which produced the first atomic and hydrogen bombs and the subsequent generations of weapons— was located in the buildings of the Sarov Monastery. In the 1950s, it split into what are today the two main nuclear weapons design centers—the VNIIEF in Sarov (the former Arzamas-16)[8] and the VNIITF in Snezhinsk (the former Chelyabinsk-70).[9] The ROC, in the meantime, lost track of the saint's relics and considered them to have vanished.

In December 1990, the Leningrad authorities returned to the ROC the Kazan Cathedral, which had functioned as the Museum of Atheism. As part of the inventory activities, the metropolitan Alexey "miraculously" discovered in the museum's warehouse the relics of St. Seraphim wrapped in fabric.[10] The recovery of the bones opened huge opportunities. With the relics in his hands, the next year, by then as patriarch, Alexey started to satisfy the spiritual hunger of the desperate masses. He cultivated the image of Seraphim as a Russian Nostradamus of sorts and popularized his predictions, situating them within the context of the then socialpolitical reality. "The hermit had predicted that the country would pass through a time of great torment, but would find once again the path of 'great glory.'" These allusions strongly resonated with many who aspired to a better life and believed that Seraphim "could 'explain' all the heartbreak of the twentieth century and point the way to a glorious future." For people disillusioned with the politicians, to hear from the patriarch this encouraging prophecy attributed to the saint was a powerful experience. According to the Garrards, Alexey directly linked the country's recovery with the resurgence of faith and made the Seraphim relics "a magnet for the sense that the Russian nation itself was reviving."[11]

The public resonance was astonishing. First, the patriarch moved the relics among the Leningrad cathedrals, enabling the public to venerate them. Daily, Soviet TV covered the endless flow of worshippers. Then, escorted by the mass media, the relics were moved to Moscow and stayed there for several months, attracting thousands. The Garrards describe the highly publicized pilgrimage as a series of "ecstatic ceremonies" blending nationalism and religiosity.[12] As the climax of the entire enterprise, Alexey intended to return the relics to where they belonged—the Diveevo Monastery. This final accolade, which the patriarch orchestrated for the month of July to synchronize with Seraphim's original 1903 canonization, was not trivial. Some of the Diveevo temples had been returned to the ROC earlier that year and the services renewed in the monasteries.

However, access to this location, especially in numbers, was not obvious at all in 1991. The whole area around Diveevo was still a restricted zone, let alone the most secret town of the Soviet Union—the closed nuclear city Arzamas-16. Most Soviet citizens had never heard of it. The city appeared neither on the maps nor on bus, rail, or air transportation schedules. Its name was never mentioned in public and was known only to a very narrow circle. The first Soviet article about the "city that is not on the map," published in December 1990, became a sensation.[13]

For four days the patriarch led a procession of about twenty thousand pilgrims from Moscow to Diveevo, visiting several places to pray and rest. Eventually, on 31 July 1991, unstopped, the procession entered the forbidden zone, and St. Seraphim returned to his grave in the most joyful religious celebration.[14] The next day, 1 August, the patriarch passed through the three circles of electric barbed wire guarded by the State Security Committee (KGB), and arrived at the heart of the Soviet nuclear empire, Arzamas-16, the former Sarov, the original locus of St. Seraphim, after which he had been called Sarovsky. To the pilgrims and to the people following the procession en masse, this entrance to the most secret Soviet city, where the party and the KGB were still alive and kicking, was more than surprising; it was a miracle. This was exactly what the patriarch wanted to communicate, that Seraphim's prophecy was coming true: "Time was turning around, and a new age was beginning."[15] The patriarch's smooth passage to Arzamas-16, however, was neither a miracle nor an accident. The entrance to the closed city and the events there had been approved in advance and carefully preplanned. The nuclear hosts were ready for the visit and had big expectations of it.

Spiritually, as elsewhere in Russia, the publicized celebrations of the baptism of Rus in 1988 revived the interest in Orthodoxy among the residents of Arzamas-16, several years before the visit. Paying tribute to the celebrations, in April 1988, the VNIIEF newspaper interviewed the metropolitan of Gorky and Arzamas about potential church-state cooperation in spiritual education within the closed city.[16] Joint activities became possible when in 1989 a former VNIIEF senior official, Valerii Takoev, was elected to head the city in the first-ever democratic procedure. The local party nomenclature cast him as a semi-dissident for his support of religious life revival in the city.[17] Back then, however, the municipal authorities rejected the request to register the Orthodox congregation, in order not to compromise the secrecy regime through confessions,[18] but approved the metropolitan's stopover in the city in September 1990. The first cleric to visit the sacred places since the 1930s, Metropolitan Nikolai consecrated the spring near the stone on which Seraphim had prayed, prayed with all the willing, and then met the VNIIEF's scientific intelligentsia.[19]

When in January 1991 the patriarch announced his intention to return the relics to Diveevo, Takoev, in coordination with the VNIIEF leadership, secured the approval of the minister of atomic energy and of the secretary of the Central Committee to personally invite the patriarch.[20] Approval was psychologically uneasy to everyone, but the pressing needs of Arzamas-16 overrode the Soviet mentality.[21] Metropolitan Nikolai mediated, and the city head met the patriarch to discuss the pilgrimage arrangements several months prior to the visit.[22] Immediately afterward, the VNIIEF and city authorities launched a crash program of preparations to impress the patriarch during the forthcoming visit. A special nuclear industry construction unit renovated the Diveevo Monastery, and in very little time, to enable consecration during the patriarch's visit, it planned and built the chapel in the city cemetery.[23] A local sculptor designed and produced a monument of St. Seraphim praying on the stone, which, like the chapel, was constructed within Arzamas-16. Due to the rush, one day before the patriarch's visit, while being unloaded from a truck, the statue fell and was damaged. It was decided that the patriarch would consecrate only the chapel and the cornerstone of the monument. Boris Nemtsov, then representing the district in the Supreme Soviet, provided the patriarch with his personal car to take him to Arzamas-16.[24]

Why were the nuclear hosts so proactive? Beyond the above-mentioned emerging religiosity, the city authorities and the VNIIEF had huge practical expectations of the visit, which came upon them, indeed upon the whole Soviet nuclear industry, at a moment of enormous frustration. The systemic crisis brought on by perestroika had hit all sectors, but especially the nuclear weapons industry—once the crème de la crème of the Soviet elite. Political support, ideological meanings, social status, and public re-spect, even basic food supplies—all of it had vanished at once. The in-dustrial functioning of the atomic project and social-economic mainte-nance of its closed cities was falling apart.[25] The miserable reality depicted in the first article about Arzamas-16 reflected the gloomy situation in other closed cities:

> Life is not easy here. All the food and goods, even matches, are sold only with special tokens. Each person has about forty of those of different kinds. Scientists and engineers creating the state's nuclear shield receive four hun-dred grams of meat a month and one liter of milk a week. They don't com-plain, keep on working, and try to manage: [they] plant potatoes at their dachas and pickle cabbages for winter. Concerned with life's difficulties, they are, however, anxious about the principal issues: the professional cadre is get-ting older, but nothing lures the youth into the closed zone. Back in the day there were salary advantages and better food supplies, but not anymore. [. . .] Worst of all, the strong media press makes young physicists, mathematicians, and engineers doubt the necessity of the VNIIEF's work.[26]

The industry seniors believed that social disagreement over the role of nu-clear weapons had been one of the main reasons for the devastation. During the perestroika era many within the Soviet scientific community, for ethical reasons, started to treat "nuclear scientists" as not a part of it, arguing that their research does not advance pure science but serves the needs of the military-industrial complex. Operating under a regime of se-crecy, nuclear scientists could not counterattack either in public debates or in personal conversations. To the industry's frustration, "the public was aware neither of the motives of the renowned Soviet nuclear scientists nor of the magnitude of the difficult tasks of the nuclear project." The nu-clear community basically lost the state's patronage and was left de-fenseless in the face of public critique. International disarmament, Cher-nobyl, and the removal of censorship resulted in the strongest wave of condemnation. The media called the nuclear weapons industry a "plane-tary catastrophe," a "source of deadly evil," and a "meaningless consumer of resources," its scientists "hawks and war inflamers" who should "be sunk," and criticized its production as purposeless and "generating constant safety maintenance expenses." Although this reference to the then demonization of nuclear science may seem today a bit overstated, according to an industry senior at that time, "It was an atmosphere of full-blown catastrophe."[27] That's how they felt, whether or not it was actually the case.

In 1990, Yulii Khariton, one of the fathers of the first Soviet bomb and director of the VNIIEF, sent a personal letter to Gorbachev, requesting a meeting to communicate the humiliating state of affairs. A response never arrived.[28] Feeling on "the brink of collapse because of the leadership's total indifference and naive nuclear-free world dreaming,"[29] the industry's seniors sought to exploit the moment of unprecedented public exposure brought by the patriarch's visit, to correct the demonized image of the nuclear complex, its capital, and its specialists.[30] Expecting that improved publicity would bring "more food supplies and resources," they sought to convince the patriarch that the industry consisted of professionals operating on high moral grounds and respectful of religious heritage and to persuade him that the nuclear complex had made a significant contribution to the state in the past and that it would be important for its future.[31]

On 30 July 1991, one day before the patriarch's visit, with the encouragement of the nuclear industry, Soviet TV aired the first-ever report on Arzamas-16. One of the then most renowned journalists, Alexander Nevzorov, submitted the report in his political-social investigative program *600 Seconds*, watched by millions all over the Union. The report depicted the terrible state of affairs in Arzamas-16 and conveyed the breadth and depth of the nuclear industry's anguish. Dozens of its demoralized most senior officials, seated around Khariton in Arzamas-16, voiced their helplessness. "We have no hope; we turned to the president with no luck. To whom else can we turn?" When Nevzorov asked the circle to define the state of the industry in one word, they replied "collapse," "degradation," "lack of perspective," "no need for our work," and "betrayal." "Confidentially, I have a feeling," said Khariton, who in the 1940s stood upright in front of Stalin, but now looked like a broken old man with tears in his eyes, "that someone is purposely disarming the country."[32] Aired on the eve of Seraphim's reburial celebration, the report linked the two events—in the intercut between the report's two parts, a monk wearing an Orthodox hermit's black robe appeared to underscore the drama of the moment and to allude to the image of St. Seraphim.

Upon arrival, Alexey visited the *dal'niaia pustyn'ka* (far desert)—a location in the outskirts of the city where Seraphim had built his anchoretic cell and spent years as a hermit.[33] The patriarch consecrated the cornerstone of the monument commemorating the stone on which Seraphim allegedly prayed and the newly built cemetery chapel nearby and continued to the city's House of the Scientists to meet the public.[34] The hall was fully packed. The audience—nuclear scientists and their families—roughly comprised two groups: the small core of true believers and the majority of the entirely secular Soviet "scientific intelligentsia," who saw in the patriarch their hope of salvation from socioeconomic woes. The patriarch told the story of Seraphim, his connection to the city, and his prophecy about the fall and subsequent restoration of Russia's greatness and alluded to the return of the relics as being a sign of the prophecy's coming true. He thanked the authorities for allowing him to enter the city and expressed hope for further cooperation. Nevzorov's movie screening was followed by a long question-and-answer session.[35]

Then the VNIIEF leadership met the clergy. The organizers were concerned—this would be an encounter of people who had never met before and who had hardly heard of each other: Yulii Khariton, the Soviet "nuclear patriarch," and Patriarch Alexey, the metropolitan of Moscow and all Rus.[36] The head of the VNIIEF and his seniors greeted the ROC hierarchs at the entrance to the City Theater, the building that was originally the church where Seraphim prayed. As an act of respect, in the group photo taken against the background of this church-theater, Khariton and Alexey sat next to each other.[37] Originally dubbed "Two Patriarchs," today this picture is called "Three Patriarchs"—in ten years Kirill, then the metropolitan of Kaliningrad, sitting at Alexey's left hand, would become patriarch himself. The seating arrangement in the assembly hall was also an innovation. According to Soviet bureaucratic etiquette, the guests and the hosts were to have sat across from each other. "This time we decided to do it differently and mixed the participants—Patriarch Alexey II next to the patriarch of nuclear affairs Yulii Khariton, then a metropolitan next to another director, then another metropolitan next to a senior scientific officer, and so on." This proved to be conducive to conviviality: "Our concerns evaporated quickly as the table grew loud with everyone actively talking." In the official summary, the hosts concluded: "The hierarchs of the church and the creators of nuclear weapons are people of the same circle who perceive state interests in the same way. Both defend the people: one physically and the other morally."[38] Following the meeting, the hosts presented to the patriarch a picture taken a few hours earlier at the entrance to the church-theater and a scale model of the Sarov Monastery produced especially for him.[39]

Acceleration of Relations

This brief encounter incepted a long-lasting affection and liaison between the ROC and the nuclear complex and gave a strong impulse to the acceleration of their relations. While the increase in religiosity among the nuclear complex's workers was still gradual, its leadership began steadily to perceive the ROC as the main vehicle for promoting the nuclear industry's agenda vis-à-vis the state and society, especially after the August 1991 coup d'état, which gave the ROC even greater political-social power. In September 1991, the city council deputies approved the establishment of the local Orthodox congregation, headed by the director of the VNIIEF laboratories and a permanent priest. It also filed a request with the Supreme Soviet to return the historical name of Sarov to the city. A year later, the city would return to the congregation the first church, which had been a store until then. In November 1992, the cross would be erected, and the church itself was consecrated in 1993.[40]

The Soviet collapse worsened the situation and brought the industry to its nadir. In January 1992, President Yeltsin established the Russian Ministry of Nuclear Affairs (MINATOM) and appointed as its head Viktor Mikhailov, previously director of the VNIIEF. Yeltsin personally hosted Mikhailov and the industry seniors, for the first time since perestroika had begun, to discuss the state of the nuclear complex, and in March 1992 he visited Arzamas-16, already renamed Kremlev (until 1995) back to the original Soviet name. Despite these meetings, according to Mikhailov, the future of the nuclear industry was still doubtful. On top of the earlier troubles, like other state industries, the nuclear complex was severely crippled by the Union's collapse, and there were political forces seeking to further curtail it.[41] Not unusual in Russia's economic climate of that time, during 1992–96 even very limited budget allocations to the complex were never transferred in full. The average salary was USD 50, and the routine three-month delay in its payment resulted in an exodus of qualified workers.[42]

The biggest frustration was the inability to get information from the politicians and to shape the course of events. Upset by the government irresponsiveness, in June 1993 the VNIIEF and the city council conducted a roundtable for the industry seniors to seek solutions. Inspired by the per-estroika experience, when social activists influenced the political course, participants decided to use public opinion as leverage. However, they saw no actor that could introduce the problem to the public discourse and to the Kremlin's agenda, given the image of the nuclear complex at the time.[43] The ROC, which was then intensifying its contacts with the state across the board, grasped this opportunity and eagerly took patronage over the complex's troubles. From this moment on it became the nuclear weapons complex's main vehicle for communicating with the Russian state and society.

In July and August 1993, the ROC together with the VNIIEF orga-nized in Diveevo and Sarov celebrations to commemorate the ninetieth anniversary of Seraphim's canonization. As part of the event, the patri-arch came to Sarov to meet the VNIIEF leadership. Accompanied by the ROC hierarchs and Diveevo nuns, he visited the secret VNIIEF Museum of Nuclear Weapons, left an encouraging note in the guestbook, and then, sitting in an informal circle of clergy mixed with the industry seniors, dis-cussed the problems of the nuclear complex.[44] It had been exactly two years since their first encounter; both parties knew each other better, so the atmosphere was intimate, the discussion lengthier and practical.[45] After the meeting, joint activities began that were aimed at ensuring gov-ernment and public support and appealing to politicians, the business elite, and the intelligentsia. The VNIIEF and the ROC began sending delegates to different social, political, and entrepreneurial forums to ex-plain the importance of the closed cities and the nuclear industry. The biggest of these gatherings, "Nuclear Shield and Russia: Morality, Ideology, and Politics," took place in Moscow in 1994. The first issue of the VNIIEF's new journal *Atom*, in reviewing the event, opened with a blessing from the Sarov priest.[46]

In parallel, the nuclear industry began participating in the ROC's activities, including the annual 1995 World Russian People's Council (VRNS).[47] Its head, Metropolitan Kirill, encouraged participants to establish VRNS regional units, and in January 1996 the Sarov branch opened, headed by the local metropolitan and the VNIIEF's deputy director.[48] The first meeting of the branch aimed at articulating the social-professional problems of the nuclear cities and the industry, linking them to the all-Russian agenda and seeking ways to survive.[49] Turning the ROC into the main vehicle for the articulation of problems was somewhat bizarre to many within the industry. However, in the absence of any alternative social-political power to lean upon, similar church-nuclear forums started to emerge in other closed cities, and growing numbers within the industry started perceiving the church-nuclear nexus as natural and useful.[50]

The biggest boost that the ROC provided the nuclear weapons complex, and which, according to its seniors, enabled the industry to survive the time of troubles, occurred in November 1996. Patriarch Alexey and the VNIIEF organized in the Danilov Monastery, the patriarch's residency, a conference titled "Nuclear Weapons and Russian National Security." Government officials, Parliament members, military seniors, including from the nuclear triad, prominent public figures, and clergy participated. Although it does not seem from today's perspective that the Russian nuclear weapons were in any danger of totally going away, participants back then saw those days as the moment of destiny for the Russian nuclear arsenal, a Shakespearean juncture of "to be or not to be,"[51] as the National Security Council had conducting during that time staff work on the future of the nuclear complex. The nuclear seniors took part in this endeavor, but were unsure of the outcome.[52]

The nuclear community had three expectations from the event: to present the indispensable role it plays in the framework of national security, to outline the problems that had almost devastated the nuclear triad and the industry supporting it, and to publicly legitimize its requests and communicate them to the Kremlin. The conference was a microcosm of the emerging nuclear-church bond. For the nuclear industrial complex and the military, the gathering became an opportunity to exploit the ROC, with its political and public popularity, as a vehicle for exerting influence on the Kremlin. For the ROC, it became an occasion to forge influence within two major professional sectors and potential congregations and to adopt a visible national-level public and political role.

Patriarch Alexey and Metropolitan Kirill orchestrated the event. Their opening statements, which dubbed the nuclear weapons specialists "the eremites" (*podvizhniki*), proclaimed its credo: to assist the nuclear complex in overcoming the most pressing problems, to ensure its influence in national security policy, and to cultivate a respectful image of it among the Russian public.[53] For the nuclear industry officials, this was the highest-profile forum they had ever joined in post-Soviet Russia. They arrived armed with a survival strategy formulated at the Sarov branch of the VRNS: to abandon partial solutions, to convince the government of their importance, and to translate this understanding into a steady budget allocation and state orders.[54]

First, participants outlined national security concerns justifying the need for the nuclear arsenal. In a nutshell, according to the threat perception of more than a dozen speakers, the Soviet collapse, the change in the geopolitical situation, and unilateral disarmament had produced no genuine partnership with the West. Moscow had decreased its conventional and nuclear arsenals and dissolved the Warsaw Pact, but the North Atlantic Treaty Organization (NATO), exploiting the unipolar moment, had expanded eastward. The emerging U.S. position on missile defense, poor Russian performance in Chechnya, and evolving hostile actors on all fronts raised concerns. In such a reality, participants suggested, further nuclear reductions, in keeping with the pledges of the Soviet leadership, should be seen as a genuine security threat. Such a course, according to them, would erode the country's deterrence credibility and might result in exclusion from the United Nations Security Council and the imposition of sanctions supported by military threats to influence Moscow's course. In their view, the nuclear arsenal and the industrial-scientific complex supporting it were the only reason why Russia still preserved its sovereignty and some influence in the world.[55]

Second, they outlined the main problems plaguing the nuclear military-industrial complex. The biggest issue was the lack of a respectful social attitude toward the people developing and operating nuclear weapons. Participants felt that if they could not sway public consciousness and activism in the informational sphere, they were doomed.[56] This deficit of "social-psychological support" emanated, according to them, from public naïveté and Western subversion. In their view, "nuclear altruism" had deeply penetrated public consciousness in the time of Gorbachev. The thesis that disarmament would increase national security was widespread among the general public, which had been "infected by pacifism" and believed that Russia had no enemies after the Cold War and therefore did not need nukes.[57] Participants agreed that "disarmament brainwash promoted by democrats and pacifists for more than a decade" had been so effective "that the majority of the population believed in this propagandistic fairy tale."[58]

Participants perceived this to be more than just innocent naïveté on the part of the populace, but rather a disarmament stratagem on the part of the West, and saw the Western discrediting of the Russian arsenal's safety as a tactic to take control over it.[59] In a similar vein, they perceived ecological activism and the exploitation of the Chernobyl tragedy as skillful foreign subversion. In their view, the United States had co-opted and cultivated "green movements" that demonized the Russian nuclear industry and then exploited this public image and internal tensions to elect Parliament members promoting antinuclear policies. Ecological activism, according to them, was part of the Western disarmament strategy, which included arms control, the financing of the nuclear weapons' decommissioning, and the purchase of Russian uranium.[60]

The next big issue was technological, as the industry lacked normal work conditions. Maintaining safety, preserving a qualified scientific cadre, and conducting fundamental research had become tremendously difficult due to political neglect. The Comprehensive Test Ban Treaty (CTBT), signed several months before the conference, magnified the problem.[61] Under this new treaty, fundamental R&D became totally dependent on modernization of the calculation-computation base and experimental modeling laboratories, both of which demanded huge investments. Although presidential decrees and parliamentary decisions nominally allocated funds for the nuclear industry, actually it was not getting enough funding for salaries and food supplies.[62] The patriotic connotation of "serving" in the nuclear weapons complex had evaporated, and the media image depicting nuclear specialists as mass murderers scared young scientists away. The brain drain turned fifty-plus into the average age in the industry.[63]

Finally, the psychological climate within the industry projected on nuclear technological safety. As one speaker put it: "If the wife, bluntly speaking, meets her husband, a nuclear operator working on the reactor's control system, with a rolling pin and asks—'Why haven't you brought home any salary for five months?'—tomorrow he may push the wrong button."[64] This was no exaggeration. Gorbachev's *conversion* policy—the transformation of military manufacturing into civilian production—affected about 25 percent of the population.[65] The social implications of conversion were enormous, especially for its main victim—the nuclear industry. According to the director of Sarov's city hospital, the post-Soviet political-social reforms drove the closed cities to the brink of a demographic-psychological catastrophe.[66]

The suicide of Vladimir Nechai, the head of the VNIITF (Chelyabinsk-70), was symptomatic of the prevailing fatalism. One of the inventors of the thermonuclear weapons, Nechai had participated in all the nuclear tests since 1958, directed the VNIITF since 1988, and shot himself a day before the conference. His necrology reads:

> In the last years Nechai did everything he could to preserve the scientific cadre and continue research on the newest weapons. He constantly tried to make subordinates internalize that they do not work for themselves but are improving Russia's capabilities. However, workers who did not get their salaries for six months were skeptical of his appeals to patriotism. Some families of the nuclear center literally eat only bread bought on credit. Physicists demanded money, but Nechai could do nothing—this once elite scientific center has lost its state funding. Constant stress drove him to suicide.[67]

The ROC met the participants' expectations in full. The church eagerly took upon itself responsibility for the spiritual-moral legitimization of the nuclear weapons, for the pastoral care of the nuclear community, and for the articulation and delivery of the message.[68] In the final proclamation delivered to the president, the government, and the Parliament, which Metropolitan Kirill outlined, the ROC emerged as the main patron of the nuclear enterprise.[69] "We, scientists, experts, military, diplomats, clergy, politicians, NGO leaders, and cultural and educational activists have gathered here with the blessing of the patriarch of Moscow and all Rus, Alexey, the head of the World Russian People's Council, in order to speak in full voice to our people and our government about the critical state of the Russian nuclear weapons complex."

Kirill skillfully interwove the socioeconomic, spiritual, and national security agendas to justify the nuclear shield. He argued that the nation's gross domestic product had decreased in half, that science, high-tech industry, and education were in deep decline, and that the destruction of the traditional values had led to a spiritual disaster and decline of morale. All of these, coupled with external dangers, threatened, according to him, the state's very existence. In the face of this multidimensional crisis "when the economy and armed forces are so weak, nuclear weapons, which have been produced by the great labor and sacrifice of the whole nation, are the sole Russian effective means of defense." Enjoying the ROC's then-growing status and influence, he adopted a harsh tone: "The constant underfunding of the nuclear weapons complex and of the related military services, and the penetration into public consciousness of the negative attitude to nuclear weapons, will unavoidably" weaken Russia. "We turn to the president, the government, and the Federal Assembly and demand that they consider carefully every step related to the destiny of our country's nuclear shield in conjunction with the long-term national interests." The proclamation demanded the full and quickest execution of the government's scientific-technological programs aimed at preserving the nuclear weapons technologies, their safety and security.

In the last paragraph, the ROC, speaking from the position of a unifying national force, gave pastoral guidance:

It's a duty of the responsible state to prevent the collapse of Russia's nuclear weapons complex. We turn to the scientists, engineers, experts, and military that work with the nuclear weapons. During the past years you have demonstrated extraordinary stamina, responsibility, and power of spirit, and you have preserved these national assets in the most difficult economic conditions, and in the midst of political and spiritual chaos. Taking into consideration all the current difficulties, we call on you to maintain calm, stamina, professional responsibility, and civil and personal solidarity. We appeal to the conscience of those who are involved in formulating public opinion. Russia needs social concord on the nuclear weapons. Problems should not conceal the main issue—the vitally important role of the nuclear weapons in preserving an independent and united Russia.[70]

The declaration reached the president, the Parliament, and government officials.[71] The event had the broadest media coverage in the major newspapers associated with different social, political, and professional groups.[72]

The organizers sought to make a genuine impact,[73] and the outcome was satisfying. The above-mentioned National Security Council staff work during the years 1996–97 resulted in a series of decisions that shaped the fate of the nuclear complex for the next decades. In December 1997, Yeltsin approved the National Security Concept, which preserved the central role of the nuclear weapons in national security.[74] He also approved the preservation of all the nuclear triad's legs, specified what each of them had to do, and outlined the nuclear force buildup for the intermediate and distant future.[75] The nuclear weapons complex sensed a huge relief. The memoirs of Viktor Mikhailov, the then minister of nuclear energy, indicate the change in the state of the nuclear industry in 1997–98 and the emergence of gradual and solid political support. Until then, the titles, content, and tone of his statements had been defensive, apologetic, and pleading for public, political, and financial support.[76]

Forging the Bond
In March 1999, Yeltsin approved the "Main Fundaments of the Russian Policy in the Field of Nuclear Deterrence." In addition to establishing an overall state commitment to nuclear orientation in strategic affairs and to

the shape of the nuclear forces, the document charged the National Security Council with specifically addressing the state of the nuclear weapons industry. In April 1999, the council held a meeting dedicated to the hardships of the nuclear industry: insufficient funding, social problems resulting in the brain drain, and an overall negative atmosphere within the complex. The meeting approved a strategic course for the industry's development to address these hardships and allocated funds in the framework of an exclusive federal program, Nuclear Weapons Complex Development Until 2005.[77] Also, in spring 1999, after almost two decades, Moscow flexed its nuclear muscles during the events associated with the start of the NATO bombing of Yugoslavia.[78]

It would be an exaggeration to attribute the Kremlin's pronuclear stand entirely to the ROC's lobbying, although the positive social-political zeitgeist that the ROC had helped to establish as the backdrop to the Kremlin's decisions was probably a necessary albeit insufficient condition. The impact of the church, however, should not be understated. The nuclear industry seniors to this day are convinced that the ROC had the most prominent influence on their destiny and have praised its unique ability to affect the course of events. Radii Il'kaev, then deputy and later head of the VNIIEF, reflecting on the impact of the conference, has praised the unparalleled role of the ROC in the survival of the nuclear weapons community:

> The harsh crisis that affected all of Russia extremely damaged the nuclear weapons complex; its very existence was under threat. In those years of trouble many influential public forces did not have confidence in the nuclear weapons industry and directed the most monstrous accusations at us. At this very time the ROC, with all of its social authority, supported the nuclear industry people, clearly outlined the all-Russian importance of our business, and thanked us, in the name of all the Russian people, for our stamina in the face of the unheard difficulties. These timely words of the ROC not only became the weightiest and most acutely needed moral support for us, but also had the strongest practical influence on the position of the then state leaders on the matter. We are thankful for this help and will remember it forever.[79]

In the following years Il'kaev, on several occasions, acknowledged the ROC's ability to outreach to the leading politicians, to convey messages important to the nuclear industry, and to shape the Kremlin's decision-making and national security discourse.[80]

> The ROC told us [in 1996] loudly and clearly: what you do is the necessary and the most important state business. Through its authoritativeness it supported our work, although there was a lot of shouting back in the day that our work is useless. After three years, what we said in the Danilov Monastery became the official policy. The public attitude to nuclear weapons and to defense fundamentally changed. I think all this is due to the huge practical help of the ROC leaders.[81]

Il'kaev expressed his confidence that this liaison was not a passing episode but a lasting resource that should be exploited for the needs of the nuclear complex. "I admit with great satisfaction that what we say in the relatively narrow circle, in two, three years, appears in the fundamental white papers and documents of the Russian state. That means that they [the Kremlin] are following our activities, exploiting them, and very seriously using them."[82] Since then, the ROC has adopted the role of proactive protagonist and propagandist for Russian nuclear affairs. Metropolitan Kirill clearly outlined this credo:

> There are several directions of the scientific research that demand public support, nuclear weapons research in particular. Many misunderstand the importance of nuclear weapons for national security. The ROC deliberately intervened in this discussion in order to emphasize the importance of the scientific research and the importance of the activity of scientific centers such as Arzamas-16. This was done in order to draw the attention of the state's leaders to support these activities.[83]

Inspired by their perceived success, in the following years the ROC and the nuclear industry focused on expanding the cooperation between faith and science beyond the nuclear realm. This nexus, in which the nuclear segment of the Russian scientific community would take the lead, gathered significant momentum in the following decade. In a nutshell, it was about several joint activities bringing together the ROC and the most prominent scientific-industrial actors of Russia. In March 1998, Sarov's VRNS branch initiated the first conference, titled "Faith and Knowledge: Science and Technology on the Eve of the Twenty-First Century." Patriarch Alexey opened the event; keynote speakers included the president of the Academy of Sciences, the minister of science and technology, and Metropolitan Kirill.[84] The final document emphasized the revival of Russian science against the backdrop of the post-Soviet spiritual-cultural disorientation and the importance of pastoral accompaniment in the potentially dangerous fields—genetic engineering, informational technologies, and nuclear research—to minimize the risk of morally wrong decisions. The scientists expressed their readiness to deepen cooperation and encouraged the ROC to ensure that its pastors were familiar with the morale problems pertaining to their professional activity and knew how to address them. Participants agreed to expand activities into higher scientific education[85]—indeed a trend that would characterize the nuclear field (on which more in the following chapters).

The nuclear weapons industry became the ROC's portal to the Russian scientific community. In March 2000, the VRNS, the VNIIEF, and Moscow State University cosponsored a conference, "The Problems of Interaction of the ROC and the Leading Scientific Centers of Russia." It brought together seniors from the ROC, the nuclear industry, MINATOM cities and scientific centers, and the Russian scientific-technological elite and lasted for three days in Moscow and in Sarov. Scientists from various industries were present, but the nuclear weapons experts organized and hosted the event. The patriarch and the president of the Academy of Sciences made opening speeches, after which Metropolitan Kirill and the head of the VNIIEF orchestrated the conference, which began with a prayer near the relics of St. Seraphim.[86] Sessions discussed key issues pertaining to faith and science: the position of the ROC on the development of science and technology; the ROC's pastoral care and the clergy's preparation for working with scientists; religious life in the main scientific cities; activities with scientific youth and students; and the ethical problems of weapons developers.[87]

The final document reaffirmed the ROC's pronuclear position and emphasized that the revival of religious life was possible without damaging the secrecy regime of the closed cities. Consequently, participants expressed their desire to sign an official cooperation agreement between the ROC and MINATOM that would expand the educational and pastoral activities in the secret institutes and design bureaus of the nuclear weapons industry. This would include access of the clergy directly to the working places of the specialists, the possible grant of security clearances to selected priests, introduction of the religious literature into the secret scientific-technological libraries, and expansion of the social-educational activities in the field of Orthodox culture in the schools of the closed cities for the scientists' children and families.[88]

During the event Il'kaev, then the director of the VNIIEF, apologized, on behalf of the nuclear scientists, for the destruction of Sarov's religious heritage, and announced the intention to restore Seraphim's church in Sarov.[89] Built over the original cell of the hermit and opened during the canonization ceremonies in 1903, from the 1950s it had hosted the city theater, with its stage located exactly where the altar used to be. During the conference, the patriarch unambiguously expressed his disappointment and expectation of change.[90] In the following year, the city authorities made the decision to remove the theater toward the hundredth-anniversary commemoration of St. Seraphim's canonization, planned for 2003.[91] In the meantime, the VNIIEF completed construction of the chapel-altar in the dal'niaia pustyn'ka. During the conference, Patriarch Alexey consecrated it as well as a cornerstone of the new church named after St. Panteleimon, the patron of the sick, on the site of the secret nuclear industry's hospital.[92]

In addition to providing practical benefits, the ROC enabled the nuclear complex to overcome the ideological disorientation. According to Il'kaev, the contacts with the ROC from 1991 onward made him and the nuclear industry seniors different people. "We became spiritually wealthier, started to look more broadly upon our work, our life goals and missions."[93] During the 2000 conference, the nuclear seniors expressed to the clergy a frank need for spiritual pastoral care. A separate session of the conference focused on the work on the nuclear weapons in an atmosphere of Orthodox culture and values,[94] especially when it came to "the ethical problems of development of the new types of weaponry."[95] Participants from other scientific fields, such as medicine, supported the religious quest of their nuclear colleagues.[96] Eventually, this led to St. Seraphim's being officially designated the patron saint of the Russian nuclear industry.[97]

Not all residents of the closed nuclear cities were devoted believers. For example, the Sarov religious lobby, which benefited from a strong administrative resource in the face of the VNIIEF leadership, still needed to overcome significant resistance from the local anticlerical forces when seeking to restitute the ROC property. It took the ROC more than ten years to acquire everything it wanted in the city.[98] Catechization, the inculcation of religiosity, and the churching of the scientists in general, in the communities of the closed cities in particular, went more slowly than the ROC and the industry leaders would have liked. According to the head of the VNIIEF laboratory, although the nuclear scientific community was aware that the head of the VNIIEF and several other seniors were practicing Orthodox, not many were quick to follow. In 2000, in ten MINATOM cities, there were only two churches. The majority of the nuclear scientific-technological intelligentsia still was oriented to the secular, Soviet values. The complex and the ROC's seniors acknowledged this and agreed to further church the nuclear community.[99] During the next decade, religious life in Sarov and the churching of its residents would take a big leap forward.

STRATEGIC MISSION MISSILE FORCES (RVSN)

The Russian Strategic Mission Missile Forces—RVSN—consist of three missile armies (twenty divisions in total) with staffs in Vladimir, Orenburg, and Omsk. The RVSN Main Staff and the Central Command and Control Post are located in the closed city of Vlasikha, near Moscow. The corps has two testing ranges (polygons): the Central Polygon in Kapustin Iar in Astrakhan and the intercontinental ballistic missile (ICBM) test impact range in Kura, in the Far East. The Peter the Great Academy (Dzerzhinsky Academy of Missile Forces until 1997), with branches in Serpukhov and Rostov-on-Don, has been the corps' main higher education institution. The MoD 4th Central Scientific-Research Institute is the corps' main R&D body. The RVSN operates training centers, arsenals, and manufacturing and repair plants all over Russia.

According to the official history of the RVSN and ROC's cooperation, Igor Sergeev, then commander of the RVSN and later DM, played a pivotal role in the inception of the nexus between the church and the most important leg of the Russian nuclear triad. Following the Soviet collapse, when Marxist materialism evaporated, Sergeev was concerned that ideologically disorientated RVSN troops were becoming receptive to spiritual alternatives promoted by what he saw as sects trying to engage the hearts and minds of the population at large. Various non-Orthodox denominations had become active all over Russia, also within the garrisons of the RVSN, including in Vlasikha, where the RVSN Main Staff is located. Sergeev decided to address the phenomenon in autumn 1995, against the backdrop of the then-emerging cooperation between the ROC and the MoD.[100] He invited the patriarch to participate in the celebrations commemorating the 175th anniversary of the Dzerzhinsky Academy—the higher education institution of the RVSN where the officers' cadre is trained.[101]

On 7 December 1995, the patriarch paid his first visit to the RVSN. The celebrations began outside the academy with a joint liturgy at the Kremlin's Uspensky Cathedral, led by the patriarch. All the RVSN senior commanders were present. The supplication service, the first joint liturgy ever for the ROC and the RVSN, asked for "peaceful rest for the souls of the academy and of the corps' founders and commemorated all the missileers and testers of the missile-nuclear weapons who had sacrificed their lives for the Fatherland."[102] The celebrations then moved to the academy. Before the official part, Sergeev and members of the RVSN High Command personally escorted the patriarch to the academy's museum to demonstrate the evolution of the Soviet nuclear-missile power.[103] This initial encounter put in motion a chain reaction. After the meeting, several commanders submitted to the RVSN Main Staff their suggestions for cooperation with the ROC. The academy seniors suggested establishing faculties of Orthodox culture within the corps' education institutes. The commanders of the then-three main testing ranges, and of two divisions, suggested establishing garrison churches and Sunday schools in the closed cities where their formations were deployed.[104]

Encouraged by the positive reaction among the corps' seniors, Sergeev invited the patriarch to visit the Vlasikha garrison and the RVSN Main

Staff and to address the Military Council—the corps' highest command forum.[105] The patriarch accepted the invitation and on 30 January 1996 arrived at the heart of the Russian nuclear missile forces. Several significant events occurred during this visit. First, the patriarch officially designated St. Varvara as the patroness of the RVSN, making it the first service to acquire a patron saint in the Russian military. The choice was driven by double logic: there was a military tradition of St. Varvara being a patroness of the artillery, to which the nuclear-missile corps was a successor; also, the feast day of this saint in the Orthodox calendar falls on 17 December—the official professional holiday of the RVSN establishment, which the corps had celebrated with great fanfare since 1959. The patriarch brought a huge icon of St. Varvara created especially for the RVSN.[106] The hosts decided to place it in the Central Command Post,[107] which maintains missiles and nuclear armaments in a state of readiness, commands the forces on combat duty, communicates orders to the command and control (C2) centers of the units, and ensures launches under any operational conditions. Daily, about six thousand people serve in the three-day-long duty shifts in the RVSN units subordinate to the Central Command Post.[108]

The head of the Synodal Department hung the icon and its sanctuary lamp above the display indicating the state of the mobile missile units and silo launchers, right next to the clocks showing the time in Moscow and Washington, D.C., and in the three missile armies, and the patriarch consecrated the post.[109] (Several years later he was nominated "Honorary Commander of the Duty Forces of the RVSN Central Command Post."[110]) By 2000, there was an icon of St. Varvara in each of the subordinate centers within the missile armies.[111] Finally, the patriarch discussed possible paths of cooperation with the high command.[112] There was no need to preach to the converted, and the Military Council approved the construction of a garrison church in Vlasikha, as a temple-memorial to all the victims who had sacrificed their lives for the corps;[113] the establishment of a faculty of Orthodox culture in the RVSN Academy; and the signing of a cooperation agreement between the ROC and the RVSN.[114]

Construction of the main RVSN garrison church in Vlasikha began immediately afterward. Donations for the temple, which the RVSN officers dubbed the "missile forces' cathedral [*sobor*]," came from the nuclear-missile and space weapons manufacturers, the corps' retired and active-duty servicemen, RVSN higher education and research institute officials, and residents of the closed city.[115] The church was built exactly on the site of the removed monument commemorating "seventy years to the October Revolution."[116] Sergeev, upon his promotion to DM in 1997, and his successor, General Vladimir Yakovlev, until then the commander of the Main Staff, personally oversaw the construction.[117] On 27 April 1998, the eve of Easter, the patriarch consecrated the church and conducted the first service in the presence of the entire RVSN High Command.[118] The RVSN garrison church, which was also the first in the Russian military,[119] was called after St. Varvara and St. Iliia—one the patroness of the corps, the other the saint whom the ROC proclaimed as patron of the RVSN High Command[120] and who features prominently in the current Russian nuclear folklore (on which more below).

The interior design of the church laid the foundations for the iconography within other temples of the Russian strategic community in the following years.[121] In addition to the canonic Orthodox iconostasis, it featured episodes from Russian military history exemplifying divine assistance to warriors, including St. Boris and St. Gleb assisting Alexander Nevsky during the battle against the Swedish; the Mother of God showing the way to the officers extricating their regiment from encirclement in the nineteenth century; and also examples from recent military history, such as Zhenia Radionov, who was decapitated for his faith during the Chechen War.[122] Another mural featured Admiral Feodor Ushakov, the most famous eighteenth-century Russian naval commander, having a nimbus, or saint's aureole, wearing the naval uniform, and holding a battleship in his palm. The walls featured battle scenes from various periods, and above the balcony, surrounded by other Russian saints, Seraphim Sarovsky occupied the center.[123]

During the first liturgy, the patriarch ordained Mikhail Vasiliev as the priest of the RVSN cathedral.[124] Since then, rising to the rank of *protoierei*, Father Mikhail also functions as the main RVSN priest responsible within the Synodal Department for the pastoral care of the corps.[125] Retrospectively reflecting on the reasons why the RVSN was the first corps to closely interact with the ROC on all levels, Father Mikhail has mentioned its being "the most intellectual of all the corps" and operating in the most dangerous context[126]—a point that echoes Kirill's above-mentioned dictum. Reflecting back on a decade of pastoral care, the protoierei argued: "There is no other service in the military as easy to work with as the RVSN. The most deadly weapon, which can destroy the planet in minutes, is in the hands of the people who pay major attention to spiritual-moral education."[127]

By order of the RVSN commander, the Faculty of Orthodox Culture (FOC) at the RVSN's Peter the Great Academy, then still under its Soviet name of Dzerzhinsky, opened on 3 October 1996. The faculty became the first extension education institution in the military under the auspices of the ROC.[128] The opening ceremonies began with a service at the Kremlin's Patriarch Compound, with the entire MoD and RVSN leadership attending, and then moved to the academy for the inauguration.[129] Protoierei Dmitry Smirnov, head of the Synodal Department (since 2001), became a dean of the faculty; the secretary of the RVSN committee for cooperation with the ROC at the rank of colonel became his deputy;[130] the patriarch, the mayor of Moscow, and the RVSN commander became the heads of the board of trustees.[131] Soon afterward, other RVSN institutes, and in the following years the higher education institutions of other corps, established similar FOCs.[132]

In the words of the then academy head, General Iurii Plotnikov, the driving force behind the project, the FOC aimed "to satisfy the missileers' demand for spiritual-moral development, for the acquisition of Orthodox foundations to underlie their personal worldviews, and for revival of the spiritual educational traditions within the officers' corps."[133] According to the deputy dean, the decision to establish the FOC reflected RVSN commanders' understanding that at a time when a majority of the Russian people had lost the "faith of the fathers," the "deep meaning of serving the Motherland," and "immunity to spiritual and psychological violence," there was a need to ensure that RVSN soldiers understood that every military conflict has ideological-spiritual drivers and that Western powers "spend huge budgets on informational-psychological" subversion aimed at Russia.[134]

Initially, the FOC's curriculum consisted of four modules.[135] Cadets and undergraduate lieutenants and also captains, majors, lieutenant colonels, and colonels, who attended the FOC as part of their postgraduate education, spent about eleven hundred hours at the services and seminars within the churches.[136] External donations laid the foundations for the FOC's pedagogical-material basis.[137] During the decade, the faculty issued several brochures and manuals for pastoral care in the RVSN, including the textbook *Military Didactics*, as supplementary material for the educational officers and clergy working in the field.[138] According to the deputy dean, many graduates were able "to organize effective countermeasures to internal and external forces of spiritual aggression aiming to demoralize and degrade their military units."[139] Annually, about a hundred cadets, both male and female, graduate from the FOC.[140] Since 1997 the graduation ceremonies of the cum laude cadets take place on Easter Monday, at the Kremlin's Uspensky Cathedral.[141] According to Patriarch Kirill, "It was the RVSN Academy where the fundament of the spiritual life of the Russian Armed Forces was incepted."[142]

During 1996–97, following the cooperation agreements signed by the patriarch and the RVSN commander, the majority of the RVSN C2 posts in the missile armies and divisions all over Russia were consecrated, often during combat duty, and many of them by the patriarch himself.[143] The RVSN Educational Work Department became the ROC's main point of contact. Its commander actively encouraged the RVSN higher education institutes and units to establish garrison churches and faculties of Orthodox culture.[144] In 1999 the RVSN designated 24 October as the corps' official commemoration day for all who fell in action during the testing of the missile weapons. Since then, all the RVSN garrison churches conduct commemorative liturgies mentioning the names of all the corps' fallen specialists and the corps commanders who have passed away.[145]

Establishment of the corps' main temple in the garrison church in Vlasikha gave an impetus to similar activities in other units. However, the majority of the garrison churches that appeared at that time in the missile armies were not constructed especially for the units. Often these were old and neglected small churches located next to, not within, the bases, without permanent clergy, and which the commanders started to restore.

Most of these were the so-called affiliated temples (*pripisnye khramy*) of the bigger churches functioning in the congregations near the units' bases, with their priests providing pastoral care.[146]

The religiosity gathering momentum in Russian society, and the RVSN commander's openly pro-Orthodox position, gradually projected down the chain of command, legitimizing even nonofficial contacts with the ROC. It is hard to establish when exactly Sergeev, the RVSN commander, turned to faith, but by the time of his promotion to DM in 1997 he was actively promoting clericalization within the RVSN.[147] According to Father Mikhail, the main nuclear priest, all five subsequent RVSN commanders also provided him with uninterrupted support and assistance and were personally involved in solving problems pertaining to pastoral care and spiritual activities within the corps.[148] However, during the first post-Soviet decade, with no strict and clear orders from the RVSN Main Staff and with no material support and guidance from the patriarchate, as a rule, cooperation depended on the personal contacts of specific division commanders with the archbishops (archiepiscops) in the local parishes.[149] It was up to the latter to establish contacts with the former and to prove their usefulness to them. Priests' pastoral and catechization work within the missile units totally depended at that time on the commanders' personal religiosity. The Orthodox mind-set of the commanders opened up space for pastoral maneuvering of the clergy in the missile armies or divisions.[150]

LONG RANGE AVIATION (LRA)

Long Range Aviation (LRA), the aerial leg of the Russian nuclear triad, went through several organizational transformations after the Soviet collapse. Called interchangeably the 37th Air Army or LRA command, it comprises two divisions. One, also known as Engels Air Base, with headquarters in the Saratov region, is located in the European part of Russia. It includes four air regiments operating Tu-160, Tu-95MS, and Tu-22M3 strategic bombers and is deployed in three bases (Engels, Shaikovka, and Soltsy). Another division, also known as Ukrainka Air Base, with headquarters in the Amur region, is located in the Far East. It includes four air regiments operating Tu-95MS and Tu-22M3 strategic bombers and is deployed in three bases (Ukrainka, Belaia, and Vozdvizhenka). Air tankers and training bases are located in central Russia. The LRA operates more than a dozen bases, airfields, and services dispersed all over the country. Its Main Staff is in Moscow.

An inclination toward, and contacts with, religion emerged in the LRA in a bottom-up manner. The fairly small size of the service and the religiosity of its commander and of the commanders of selected bases made the LRA relatively easy to church. The main constraint was budgetary, as until the mid-2000s the LRA was probably the most underfunded leg of the triad. The first encounter with faith occurred still under Soviet rule in the Soltsy base. According to the secretary of the LRA Military Council, in the final stages of the war in Afghanistan, pilots of the base requested that their strategic bombers be consecrated.[151] Then, in 1995, against the backdrop of the first Chechen war, the LRA commander approved the request of the Soltsy base commander General Major Igor' Khvorov (the LRA commander 2002–7) that all the Tu-22M3 bombers of the regiment, which at that time was conducting sorties in the Caucasus, be consecrated.[152] The pilots who initiated the request sought support in the face of a demoralizing public attitude toward the war and negative media coverage of their bombing missions. "With heavy hearts, seeking to minimize possible civilian casualties and to ensure precise completion of the combat missions, the pilots decided to consecrate the airplanes." The archiepiscop of Novgorod formulated a special sanctification rite for the combat airplanes, which the patriarch approved.[153] It was the first time in the Russian Air Force (AF) that an entire regiment was consecrated.[154] Soltsy was also the first air base of the LRA in which a garrison chapel appeared at around the same time.[155]

In parallel, during the early to mid-1990s, contacts started between the LRA commander and senior officers of the Main Staff and the priests of the Moscow Transfiguration Church in Tushino—Fathers Fedor Sokolov and Konstantin Tatarintsev.[156] Both priests became the driving force behind the LRA's conversion over the next decades.[157] The then patriarch handpicked Father Konstantin and blessed him to interact with the military, realizing the potential of his biography.[158] In the late 1980s, before becoming a priest, Konstantin Tatarintsev graduated as a physics engineer from the Moscow Technical University. In line with the then Soviet practice, he was drafted, assigned to the LRA due to his academic background, and awarded officer rank (captain) and spent his mandatory service in the above-mentioned Soltsy base.[159] He became a practicing Orthodox while still in the university, receiving as his spiritual father one of the central religious figures of modern Russia, Archimandrite Ioann Krestiankin, who enjoined him not to drop his studies and to go on to the military.[160] Upon his demobilization and the completion of his religious education, Konstantin became a priest. When in the early 1990s the ROC started to cultivate the nuclear weapons complex, his military-nuclear background made him a unique asset in the emerging web of church-military relations. Proximity to the leading Russian elder probably also contributed to his position within the ROC.

Father Konstantin participated in the majority of the ROC's most important meetings with the seniors of the nuclear industry and was active during the legendary 1996 conference. When in 1995 the ROC established the Synodal Department for cooperation with the military, he became the head of the AF section. In his own words, his scientific-technological and military backgrounds made him unafraid of scientific and military audiences, who were seeking to overcome a spiritual crisis and fill a moral-ideological vacuum after decades of Communist ideology.[161] His unique background as a physics engineer and retired LRA officer, coupled with his understanding of the LRA's organizational DNA, enabled him to forge strong personal ties and constructive cooperation with the corps commander and the officers of the Main Staff, by coincidence located next to his congregation. Thus, in parallel to being the priest of the Tushino church and the head of the AF section in the Synodal Department, since the mid-1990s he has been the main priest of the LRA.[162]

According to General Mikhail Oparin, the then LRA commander, to the corps' seniors Father Konstantin became a congenial pastor and useful gateway to the ROC, making connections within the Moscow clergy. As personal relations and spiritual bonds with the clerics progressed, recalls Oparin, his personal faith and participation in the life of the Tushino congregation intensified.[163] By 1997, the contacts between the clerics and the LRA seniors and their visits to the church to attend the services became regular.[164] When aviators started to promote an initiative to build the corps' temple, the Tushino priests became natural partners to discussing the construction of garrison churches at the LRA bases, with the corps' temple in the LRA Main Staff at the top of the agenda. Oparin's officers were so determined to have it that, according to him, they were "eager to build it with their own hands." Initially, however, due to the fact that the Main Staff was located in Moscow's center, without funds and with no clear administrative regulations this was not possible. Then the idea of designating the Tushino church as the main temple of the LRA arose. When permission was granted, the priests of the Tushino church became the LRA's first pastors.[165]

From the mid-1990s, churches started to appear in other LRA garrisons.[166] Initially, these were temples reviving the services in the vicinity of the military bases to which the servicemen and their families went. The AF periodical attributed this splash of churching to the changing attitude of the military and of society to religion.[167] As relations became stronger, in coordination with the LRA commander, Fathers Feodor and Konstantin started to visit the LRA garrisons to meet with the officers and soldiers serving in the corps.[168] On 23 December 1999, to commemorate the eighty-fifth anniversary of the LRA, the priests consecrated the LRA Main Staff and hung an icon of the Mother of God on the wall of the LRA's main C2 post.[169] Construction of the chapel within the Main Staff would follow soon and would be completed in the next decade.

Around 1999 the ROC designated St. Iliia as the patron saint of the LRA. As in the case of St. Varvara, the patroness of the RVSN, the choice had several layers of meaning. First, the fact that the biblical prophet Elijah (Iliia in Russian) had ascended to the skies in a chariot of fire carried symbolic meaning for Russian aviators, as it provided a divine allegory for their profession.[170] Second, the biblical story is interwoven with Orthodox folklore, which reads a local, Russian meaning into the choice of the saint. Iliia is also the name of the ancient Russian *bogatyr* from the town of Murom, the hero-warrior of the Slavic epic poems. Although the adventures of Iliia Muromets alongside his fellow bogatyri are mostly a matter of folklore, the ROC believed that this epic hero actually had a historical prototype—the medieval warrior-monk Iliia Pechersky, who was canonized in 1643 and whose relics have been preserved until today in Kiev's main monastery. For the above reasons, in 1914, the name "Iliia Muromets" was given to the first tsarist squadron of heavy bombers.[171]

Cooperation between the ROC and the LRA, as with the other legs of the nuclear triad, has been the longest and deepest as compared to other parts of the Russian military. Father Konstantin explains this in similar fashion to his RVSN colleague, in line with Metropolitan Kirill's prioritization dictum:

> People who go high in the sky [. . .] put their lives at risk even beyond the combat action. This pushes them to contemplate eternity, the brevity of life, and the great responsibility. Pilots of the LRA, which is a component of the nuclear triad, can reach any spot in the world [. . .] conducting the missions for the sake of our country. Professionals who raise to the skies such powerful weapons need spiritual care, so that not only their combat mastership but also their spirit will be strong.[172]

NUCLEAR NAVY

Grassroots religiosity began gathering momentum in the Navy immediately after the Soviet collapse. The Northern and Pacific Fleets, the Navy's most powerful, are the backbone of the naval leg of the nuclear triad. The latter leans on two detachments of nuclear-capable submarines: nuclear-powered general-purpose attack submarines (SSBNs) and submarines capable of launching nuclear-armed ballistic missiles (SSBs). The closed city of Vidiaevo, located in the Kola Peninsula beside Ara and Ura Bays, is the main base of the Northern Fleet's strategic submarines. The closed city of Viliuchinsk, located in the Kamchatka Peninsula beside Avachinsk Bay, is the main base of the Pacific Fleet's strategic submarines. As in other parts of the post-Soviet military, the state of the submarine fleet during the 1990s was steadily deteriorating, further demoralizing the officer corps. Gradual improvement would begin in the early 2000s.

Northern Fleet (NF)

A revival of religious consciousness among the crews of the atomic submarines, and within the NF in general, has been evident since the early

1990s. In 1992 officers of the K-51 nuclear submarine, which had been recommissioned after repair, requested that it be consecrated. Fleet commanders, who were still not ready for such a radical move, rejected the request, but approved changing its name from *the 25th Congress of the Communist Party* to *Verkhotur'e*, after the spiritual center of the Sverdlovsk region hosting one of the biggest Russian monasteries.[173] Progress began to be made in 1995, when the NF and the local Orthodox eparchy started cooperation. Initially, this included the restoration of several churches located near or inside the bases, clergy meetings with the servicemen, the erection of crosses commemorating fallen sailors, and giving Orthodox names to and the consecration of the Soviet vessels.[174] In the same year, the NF command for the first time approved the crew's request for sanctification of the strategic nuclear missile submarine K-117 *Briansk*.[175] Consecration and Orthodox renaming of nuclear submarines soon became a common practice, indicative of the search for new spiritual orienteers among the officers' corps.[176] At around the same time, clerics started to join vessels' sorties. During 1996–97 the episcop of Murmansk and Patriarch Alexey several times went to sea exercises on board a heavy nuclear missile cruiser. In 1998 the episcop of Petropavlovsk joined the first-ever operational voyage aboard a nuclear submarine (on which more below).[177]

In 1998 officers of the closed city of Vidiaevo officially established an Orthodox congregation. The initiators were Captain 1st Rank Vladimir Bagriantsev, chief of staff of the 7th Division of Atomic Submarines, and his wife. Both had become religious during Bagriantsev's studies at St. Petersburg's Naval Academy. The couple began to attend services and had a confessor, a well-known priest, who stayed on as their spiritual mentor when Bagriantsev became chief of staff of the nuclear submarine base. In 1996, upon graduation and arrival in Vidiaevo, the couple established a congregation. To conduct services in the garrison, the chief of staff arranged for the arrival of the priest from the nearby city, and his spouse together with other officers' wives assisted in arranging the services in the officers' club, where baptism, confession, and Communion would take place once in a while. The couple was determined to construct a garrison church with a permanent priest who would provide pastoral care within the base, but could not do so without a permit from the commanders.[178]

In April 2000, President Putin commanded the NF exercise from aboard the SSBN *Karelia*. He oversaw ballistic launches, stayed on board overnight, and was made an honorary submariner by undergoing the traditional ritual of drinking seawater. After the exercise, in June, the episcop of Murmansk consecrated the submarine.[179] In August 2000, the NF's annual maneuvers began in the Barents Sea. Captain Bagriantsev commanded the fleet's biggest undersea vessel—the nuclear-powered submarine *Kursk*. On 12 August, the *Kursk* sank with its commander, the chief of staff of the division, and 118 officers and sailors aboard. Following several days spent in Vidiaevo in failed attempts to save the submarine, Putin returned to Moscow. Upon landing, he called Patriarch Alexey and asked him to build a church in Vidiaevo, at the request of the families of the dead sailors. The patriarch immediately instructed the metropolitan of Murmansk to act, and the next day the cornerstone of the St. Nikolai church-memorial was laid at the base, not far from the pier from which the *Kursk* had departed. By the time the relatives went to the cemetery on the fortieth day, in accordance with the Orthodox tradition, construction was completed. The metropolitan consecrated the church, conducted a memorial service, and assigned a permanent priest to the Vidiaevo congregation. Since then, Father Sergei has been pastor and confessor of the nuclear submarines' crews and has conducted regular services in the base.[180]

This tragic episode gave a boost to the churching of other NF bases. Conversion went smoothly, as historically the level of religious consciousness has been very high in that region. This was probably due in part to the high concentration of churches and monasteries in the Russian north and in part to the proximity of St. Petersburg—the cradle of religious life revival. The religiosity of the Sevmash factory, based in the port city of Severodvinsk on the White Sea, attests to this. The largest Russian shipbuilding facility, it produces surface and underwater vessels for the Navy and is the only shipyard that constructs nuclear submarines for all the fleets. The shipyard and the city were built in the 1930s on the foundation of the fifteenth-century Nikolo-Korelsky Monastery. Historically, this famous monastery has been the maritime gate to Russia, and it flourished due to its location on the northern sea trade route. The Bolsheviks closed this huge complex, but when in the 1930s construction of the Sevmash started, the monastery buildings, the only suitable infrastructure in the region, became the basis of the military shipyard and of the city of Severodvinsk. Eventually, as Sevmash and the city grew, the monastery's entire area and all of its buildings became fully integrated into the gigantic shipyard.[181]

In the 1990s, the ROC reacquired some of the buildings; however, there was no way to utilize them for religious purposes, since they were located inside the top-secret facility of the closed city and served its needs.[182] In 1998 Severodvinsk celebrated its sixtieth anniversary. The local press began popularizing the city's history and the story of St. Euphemius, St. Antonii, and St. Feliks of Karelia, who founded the monastery and have been the patron saints of the region. At the request of the metropolitan of Arkhangelsk, the Sevmash administration approved the conduct of a supplication service near the walls of the monastery's main church, Nikolsky Sobor, located in the territory of the shipyard, to commemorate these patron saints. Since then, the memorial service has become an annual practice that gathers several dozens of shipyard workers. The temple and other monastery facilities continued to serve the needs of the factory; however, the process of the workers' conversion had started.[183]

Pacific Fleet (PF)

Viliuchinsk is the closed city that hosts the base of the PF nuclear submarines—the 16th Red Banner Submarine Squadron. It was established in 1968 by merging the fishing villages of Rybachii (the nuclear submarine base), Primorsky (the onshore maintenance base), and Seldevaia (the repair shipyard). Back then it was code-named, according to the Soviet practice, after the nearest major city, Petropavlovsk-Kamchatsky-50, and renamed Viliuchinsk after the nearby volcano in 1994. Dubbed "a nest of wasps" by NATO, due to the huge concentration of submarines,[184] Viliuchinsk is populated by the crews of the nuclear submarines and their families.[185]

In 1994 twenty-two families established an Orthodox congregation in the city and named it after the patron saint of the Russian Navy, St. Andrei the Apostle (Andrei the First Called). Lacking a church, they used various buildings as temporary sites for congregation and services. Once in a while, Ignatii, the archiepiscop of Petropavlovsk-Kamchatsky, would arrive to conduct services, or the congregation members drove to the church outside the base. In 1997 the authorities approved the conversion of the garrison's shop into a church. On Easter 1998, the archiepiscop consecrated the garrison church of St. Andrei and nominated a permanent priest, who since then has provided pastoral care to the squadron's servicemen and their families. As in the other legs of the nuclear triad, the temple's iconostasis featured the patron saints of the military, including the central icon of Admiral Ushakov. The banner of St. Andrei, an official flag of the Russian Navy, covered the iconostasis's "royal doors." Plaques with the names of the fallen submariners adorned both sides of the altar.[186]

In the same spring of 1998, Captain Alexander Ponamarev received an unusual order from the squadron commander. His mission was to prepare Protoierei Ignatii, the local archiepiscop, to participate in the trans-Arctic voyage aboard the nuclear-powered attack submarine *Tomsk*, which was relocating from the Sevmash shipyard to the PF. After three months of training, Archiepiscop Ignatii (today the metropolitan of South America) was ready. Upon completion of the training, he gave his instructor his blessing and enjoined him to become, upon his demobilization, the priest of the garrison church instead of the then cleric.[187] The crew arrived from the Far East to the High North to bring the submarine to the PF and the archiepiscop joined them. Admiral Vladimir Kuroedov, commander in chief of the Russian Navy, personally inspected the submarine and approved the priest's joining the cruise. During the monthlong voyage, Ignatii functioned as confessor and priest of the crew. This was the first but not the last time that clerics joined operational missions of the nuclear submarines.[188]

While the *Tomsk* was in the midst of its cruise, the patriarch satisfied the request of another PF SSB's crew to rename their vessel after a saint.

On 15 September 1998, the commander of the Russian Navy officially renamed K-433 as the *St. Georgii the Victor*. The submarine was then undergoing repair work at the Zvezda shipyard of the PF.[189] In 1999 the Petropavlovsk and Kamchatka eparchy, in line with the patriarch's guidance, signed an agreement with the Command of Forces of the Russian Northeast on "the joint strengthening of the morale-psychological state of the personnel."[190] In the same year, the St. Andrei church was awarded the status of a garrison temple. In 2000, after completing the required theological training, Captain Alexander Ponamarev, who had just retired from service, was ordained a priest, at the rank of *ierei*, and made Father Alexander—the pastor of the nuclear missile submarine squadron and confessor of its servicemen.[191]

SPACE COMPLEX

The Russian space program comprises civilian and military segments and is closely interrelated with the nuclear triad. Among its servicemen and specialists, as in the other services and the broader population, the first impulse to religiosity came still under the Soviet Union. On 28 April 1988, during a regular session with the Flight Management Center, Vladimir Titov, commander of the Soviet cosmonaut crew in orbit, who (Titov) was then still unbaptized, all of a sudden congratulated everyone on the one thousandth anniversary of the baptism of Rus. The KGB department of the cosmodrome, according to one of the witnesses, "went completely nuts."[192] The episode was symptomatic of the general trend that was gathering momentum in the civilian and military space industries.

Civilian Space

The first story about cosmonauts' worship in space relates to Valerii Poliakov. According to his account, in 1994 a fire broke out inside the Mir Space Station. As he was putting it out, he prayed in front of his small Kazan Mother of God icon, which he regularly took with him into space. In 1995 cosmonauts installed Orthodox and Catholic icons of St. Anastasia, blessed by Patriarch Alexey and Pope John Paul II, in the space station. Since this saint had been canonized before the division between Eastern and Western Christianity, both denominations revere her. The icons remained aboard for a year. Since then, taking personal icons on board has become the cosmonauts' regular practice.[193] Other religious practices became evident. Traditionally, cosmonauts have celebrated 23 February, Soviet Army Day, the main military holiday, but which also happened to be the patriarch Alexey's birthday. In February 1997, the cosmonauts, during a radio session with the Flight Management Center, congratulated the patriarch in real time.[194] In April, Alexey returned the call to the space station and wished the crew "a blessed Easter, a safe journey, and good luck on their upcoming spacewalk."[195] In 1997 the first baptism of a cosmonaut and the first consecration of a space launch took place, both in the Baikonur cosmodrome.[196] The day before the launch, the cosmonauts asked to be baptized.[197] Since then, a tradition has been established and the blessing rite has become institutionalized. It starts one day before the launch. In any weather, Father Sergei, former RVSN officer and the priest of the Baikonur congregation since 1996, approaches the rocket. Holding up the chalice of holy water, with several cosmodrome workers praying behind him, he sprinkles holy water on the rocket. He conducts the same ceremony with the crew, a few hours before the launch in the cosmonauts' hotel, and blesses the bus that drives them to the launching site. The families of the cosmonauts and the substitute crew visit his church for the blessing.[198]

Military Space

The Space Forces (SF) has always been in a symbiosis with the RVSN. From its establishment in the late 1950s, it was part of the RVSN, until the mid-1980s, when it became a separate branch. In 1997 it was resubordinated to the RVSN, then again made a separate service between 2001 and 2011. In 2015 it became a branch within the newly established Aerospace Forces. The SF's main bases are the cosmodromes in Baikonur, Plesetsk, and Svobodnyi and the Main Center for Testing and Control of the Space Systems (Civilian and Military) in Krasnoznamensk.[199] The Main Center for Missile Attack Early Warning and the Anti-Missile Defense corps (PRO) is also part of the SF. When Kazakhstan-based Baikonur became foreign territory, Plesetsk turned into the main site for military launches. Senior commanders of the SF historically have been part of the RVSN. Even when they turned into a separate corps for a while, their professional mentality and connections continued to emanate from the missile troops. As part of the RVSN in the second half of the 1990s, the SF totally internalized the zeitgeist and churched its forces accordingly. In March 1998, the episcop of Arkhangelsk consecrated the Church of St. Archestrategos Mikhail in Mirnyi, the main city of the Plesetsk cosmodrome, which was then part of the RVSN.[200] The cosmodrome's commander was among the signatories of the 1996 letter to the RVSN Military Council, asking for expanded cooperation with the ROC.[201] The establishment of the church was part of the general trend within the RVSN, and everything described in the RVSN section of this chapter relates equally to the SF.

THE 12TH MAIN DIRECTORATE OF THE MINISTRY OF DEFENSE (12TH GUMO)

The 12th GUMO is the Russian nuclear custodian, responsible for storage, maintenance, safety, transportation, and delivery of the arsenals to all legs of the nuclear triad. It comprises five components: storage bases of the nuclear arsenals, the Main Scientific-Research Institute, the Main Interservice Training Center, the Special Control Service, and the Central Nuclear Testing Range (Polygon) at Novaia Zemlia. The storage bases contain the entire nuclear arsenal that the industry commissions to the military. Upon order, assembly teams and officers of the 12th GUMO provide nuclear armaments to the platforms and means of delivery for combat use, both within the nuclear triad and in the general-purpose forces. The Main Interservice Training Center prepares personnel for conducting these missions. The Main Scientific-Research Institute conducts research and experiments together with the nuclear weapons industry. The polygon conducts experiments modeling various factors of nuclear explosions and their impact on the armaments and military technique. The Special Control Service monitors the geophysical and radiological situation worldwide and foreign nuclear tests.[202]

For the 12th GUMO, as for other parts of the Russian military, the 1990s were the most terrible period. Commanders made colossal efforts to maintain the professionalism of the service, until the situation began to improve incrementally in 2000, when funding started to flow in.[203] Until then, terrible social-economic conditions—low wages arrears, shortages of food and housing allowances—resulted in a massive brain drain, endangering the competence of the service and the safety of the arsenal.[204] A U.S. Congress report provides a vivid illustration:

> In 1997, [the service] closed a nuclear weapons storage site due to hunger strikes by the workers; in 1998, families of several nuclear units protested over wage[s] and benefit[s]. [. . .] The MoD addressed most of the arrears by early 1999, and wages are now paid regularly. Even when paid, however, officers' wages rarely exceed $70 a month and wives cannot earn a second income because the storage sites are usually located far from cities [. . .]. Housing for 12th GUMO personnel is of poor quality or nonexistent. According to the Chief of Staff of the 12th GUMO, there are 9,500 homeless active duty and retired officers. The poor living conditions of the officers—who contend with lack of heating, leaky plumbing, and deteriorating buildings—have been reported by [the] Russian press. [. . .] In October 1998, General [Igor] Valynkin [commander of the 12th GUMO] referenced serious incidents that had occurred at some of his subordinate facilities and stated that more stringent selection criteria for nuclear warhead personnel would be used.[205]

Grassroots religious activities took place within the service during the 1990s, but due to its highest secrecy, the available information is relatively limited. For the same reason, more time was probably required to become psychologically adjusted to the penetration of unsanctioned individuals into the immediate proximity of the nuclear assets. Also, from the mid-1990s the nuclear armaments complex underwent a decadelong organizational reform, bringing units of various services under the unified command. Centralization aimed at improving nuclear safety, technical reliability, and optimization of expenses without compromising combat readiness. Thus, the churching of the service has gathered momentum mainly since the 2000s, when the material and organizational factors stabilized.[206] The only available accounts from that period that illustrate the quest for religiosity among the service members relate to the revival of religious life in Belushia Guba, a settlement on Novaia Zemlia where the Central Nuclear Testing Range is located and where the 12th GUMO unit has been deployed. The functioning of the nuclear polygon at Novaia Zemlia, in the words of the commanders, has been one of the key elements of the Russian nuclear weapons complex. According to them, Russia was in compliance with the CTBT when it conducted tests aimed at verifying the storage safety of the nuclear armaments; the tests have allegedly been limited to subcritical explosions only, with no radiation output or destructive blast wave. The polygon maintains a state of readiness, in case the political leadership decides to conduct full-scale tests.[207]

In 1998 Episcop Tikhon of Arkhangelsk accepted an invitation from the polygon commander to visit the base, which, like many other places in Russia, has a religious prehistory. Since the seventeenth century, there had been a small compound of the above-mentioned Nikolo-Korelsky Monastery in Belushia Guba. Dozens of monks had run it for almost three centuries, until the Soviet authorities terminated its religious life. When the testing range was built in 1954, there were no signs of the small temple that once stood there. Commanders and officers of the base requested the episcop to restore the Nikolsky compound, rebuild the church, and send a priest to revive the congregation. The episcop consecrated the first stone in the foundation of the future temple and assigned a monk, Innokentii (Russkikh), to permanent service in Novaia Zemlia. The monk arrived at Belushia Guba in February 1999. Base commanders turned a former café into a church, and Father Innokentii started providing pastoral care to the garrison of the 12th GUMO Central Nuclear Testing Range—the most northerly Russian nuclear and military congregation.[208]

CHAPTER 4

STRATEGIC MYTHMAKING

THE QUEST OF THE RUSSIAN PEOPLE and of the Russian strategic community to reinvent themselves ideologically following the Soviet collapse resulted in, among other things, the phenomenon of national and professional mythmaking. This unique singularity, which began to emerge from the early 1990s, embodied interpretations and the rewriting and often abuse of history for the purpose of crafting a new identity. Jardar Østbø, whose work has "demythologized" current Russian ideological-philosophical scholarship, demonstrates that this distortion of history corresponds with academic definitions of political myth. The later serves state purposes by being a "carrier of ideology," "a story about a political society," and a tool for "society construction." Political myths facilitate social mobilization and advocate it. As Østbø demonstrated in his work on contemporary Russian geopolitical myths, "In many general accounts of Russian history, and, to an even greater extent, in pseudo-scholarly literature, it is difficult to discern myth from 'non-myth.'"[1]

Myths, as Østbø puts it, "make sense of human experience—and it is for this reason they are believed to be true."[2] This chapter highlights the myths that enabled the military and nuclear communities to reinvent themselves in terms of their ideological orientation, world of values, reality perception, and professional credo. Russian mythmaking in strategic affairs has involved a combination of historical facts, their interpretations, and grotesque abuses of history. The myths have often been contradictory, incoherent, and saturated with logical fallacies. But, as Østbø puts it, makers of national mythology don't seek to be scholars; they are not in the business of studying history, but in the business of making it.[3] One should therefore avoid using an academic yardstick to judge the popularizers of myths, but see them as producers of meanings that to a certain extent shape the perceptions of the national security professionals.

Two mythological narratives have been dominant within the Russian strategic community during the past three decades. The first has provided religious connotations to the history of the Great Patriotic War (GPW). The second has read divine interpretations into the Soviet nuclear history. Both myths are interrelated. The general mythmaking narrative dealing with the GPW created a fertile atmosphere for the emergence of the nuclear mythology. Although both narratives evolved almost in parallel, chronologically the general preceded the nuclear. Neither myth was invented by the leadership and then passed down to the ignorant masses; rather, both emerged as a grassroots discourse and a function of the soul-searching atmosphere. Only in the following decade would some elements of the state and of the church co-opt them for their purposes, when both myths had already been articulated and gained unprecedented popularity. The following sections trace the intellectual-social history of this phenomenon.

GENERAL MYTHMAKING

Reading divine interpretations into the history of the GPW—the most important event in Russian public memory and the main frame of reference in the contemporary Russian strategic psyche—started in the early 1990s. Independently of each other, three arguments began featuring in the public discourse. According to the first one, only when Stalin reopened the churches, returned priests from the prisons, and restored the patriarchate was the tipping point in the war reached. According to the second, several miracles and portents (*znameniia*) preceded the big Soviet victories, and there was a causal link between faith, the ROC's spiritual-material contributions, and battlefield outcomes. According to the third argument, faith and religiosity resided within the whole chain of command of the Soviet military, from Stalin at the top, through its marshals and generals, down to the rank-and-file soldiers.[4]

Different authors discussed different aspects of this myth, until 1993 when it coalesced into a coherent narrative.[5] An edited volume named *Russia before the Second Coming* offered the most articulated version of the myth and gave the strongest impulse to this mythologizing trend. One of the book's chapters, written by Protoierei Vasilii Shvets, explored the miraculous role of the Kazanskaia Mother of God icon during the GPW. In a nutshell, the narrative goes as follows: In 1941, at the most daunting juncture of the war, the patriarch of Antioch asked Orthodox believers to pray for Russia's victory. One of the first to respond was his subordinate, the metropolitan of the Lebanese mountains, Iliia. While he prayed and fasted in solitude, the Mother of God revealed to him how he could assist Russia. He was instructed to send a note to Moscow that all the churches, monasteries, and seminaries should be reopened and the priests returned from the prisons to renew the services. Most importantly, cross processions (*krestnye khodi*) should be arranged with the Kazanskaia Mother of God icon around every besieged city, to ensure salvation and battlefield success. The icon should then accompany the troops to the Soviet borders.[6]

According to the book, the metropolitan conveyed this information to the ROC representatives, and they passed it on to Stalin, who, feeling desperate in the face of the advancing Wehrmacht, implemented the guidance given as the last resort. The cross procession with the icon that was arranged in Moscow defeated the German offensive against the Soviet capital in 1941. The icon moved to Stalingrad in 1942, where it was positioned on the tiny bridgehead of the Soviet forces on the Volga's right bank, and by virtue of being there prevented its fall to the Germans. A supplication service with the icon preceded the counteroffensive in the battle of Stalingrad. In 1943 the icon moved to Leningrad and saved the besieged city. Kiev was liberated on 22 October, the icon's day in the Orthodox calendar. In 1944 a supplication service with the icon ensured the success of the offensive in Königsberg.[7]

According to the book, Stalin, driven by the dictum of the Mother of God, opened the churches and monasteries, resumed the services, and restored the patriarchate. The book claimed that Stalin prayed at the most daunting moments and accepted advice from the head of the GS, Marshal Boris Shaposhnikov, "who did not conceal his religious beliefs" and reintroduced the tsarist uniform insignia with religious connotations. The book also argued that Marshal Aleksandr Vasilevsky, who stepped in to head the GS after Shaposhnikov, was a faithful believer, as his father was a priest who spiritually guided his son. According to the same account, before battle Marshal Georgy Zhukov would always say "God be with us" and that this was not a figure of speech. The book also argued that there were reliable accounts of dying Soviet pilots who, before death, shouted "God! Accept my soul in peace!" The chapter ended with a description of how Stalin received Metropolitan Iliia in 1947 and thanked him for passing on the divine guidance.[8]

Gradually, the narrative advanced by this obscure publication began making a bigger splash, and by early 2000 it became a widespread belief. It would take more than a decade until serious research, by clerical and secular historians, would deal with this public conviction systematically and establish the groundlessness of these phantasmagoric claims. However, back in the 1990s, the publication gave a strong impulse to the wave of similar accounts describing wartime miracles and portents, while several prominent public figures became producers, consumers, and promoters of the genre. One of the reasons why the public became receptive to these interpretations was their natural resonance with the traditional folklore about divine assistance to warriors throughout Russian history, from the battle of Kulikovo to Borodino,[9] and with the traditional narrative of political-military leaders seeking the blessing of the religious authority before battle, as in the cases of Donskoy and Nevsky.

Also in 1993, another book, describing the life of St. Matrona, the blessed eldress of Moscow, popularized what would become an additional strategic myth. Together with Seraphim Sarovsky, Matrona became one of the most popular recently canonized Russian saints. Blind from birth, she was believed to have the gift of prophecy, spiritual vision, and healing, which she actively practiced in Moscow during the 1930s–50s, advising visitors and preaching for the Orthodox faith. The book, written by a woman who as a teenager allegedly shared a room with Matrona for about a decade, offered an account—among other miracles of the eldress—of Matrona's meeting with Stalin. According to the book, at the most daunting moment of the battle for Moscow, in autumn 1941, Stalin, uncertain whether to evacuate the city in the face of the approaching Wehrmacht or stay and defend it, clandestinely visited Matrona to benefit from her prophetic gift. She told Stalin that "the Russian people will win, and you will be victorious." The subtext intimated that Stalin's decision not to vacate the capital, and his subsequent success in the battle of Moscow, was the direct result of Matrona's blessing.[10]

By the mid-1990s, there was a public debate whether Zhukov, the most popular war marshal, had been a true believer. In 1996, on what would have been his one hundredth birthday, his daughter Maria, by then an actively practicing Orthodox, initiated a religious memorial service at her father's tomb near the Kremlin wall. The head of the Sretensky Monastery, Father Tikhon, who was then a young archimandrite and would later allegedly become Putin's confessor, led the ceremony. General Lieutentat Nikolai Leonov, who had just retired as the head of the KGB's Information-Analytical Directorate and also became a practicing Orthodox, was present.[11] Two years later, the Sretensky Monastery published Maria's memoirs. The book emphasized Zhukov's spirituality and the religious underpinnings of his life. It argued that Zhukov had been Orthodox by upbringing and worldview and provided examples of his practicing the faith, carrying an icon, mentioning God before major operations, and praising other believers, especially among the rank-and-file soldiers. Maria also mentioned a conversation they once had about faith. The book emphasized the symbolism of the war's end, which coincided with Easter of 1945 and the day of St. Georgii the Victor, the saint after whom Zhukov was named. Book reviews promoted by the ROC equated Zhukov with other faithful Russian military figures—Suvorov, Kutuzov, and Ushakov.[12]

NUCLEAR MYTHMAKING

At the heart of contemporary Russian nuclear mythmaking resides a notion of the divine predestination of the Soviet nuclear project, epitomized by the role of St. Seraphim and the geographic location of the first Soviet nuclear weapons design bureau. The first documented evidence of any official reference to St. Seraphim is by Viktor Mikhailov, then minister of nuclear industry, from March 1992, during President Yeltsin's visit to the VNIIEF.[13] Speaking about the national importance of Arzamas-16, to give weight to his arguments, Mikhailov mentioned the historical coincidence between the birthplace of the first Soviet nuclear bomb and the spiritual-religious center of pre-Soviet Russia.[14]

While Mikhailov's statement at the time was mainly a figure of speech, the divine role of the Russian nuclear weapons complex and the view of its creation in Sarov as an act of providence were elaborated for the first time in 1994, when the Russian nuclear industry launched a new scientific periodical—*Atom*. The first issue of the journal opened with a blessing from the priest of Sarov. The cleric argued that the Sarov land, including the closed city of Arzamas-16, has always been under Seraphim's "heavenly patronage" and therefore seen as holy by all the Orthodox. Consequently,

> there is a providential meaning in the fact that the scientific center, which works on creating Russia's nuclear shield, emerged precisely here. [. . .] The establishment of the nuclear center on the holy Sarov land did not erase the holiness of this place. [. . .] The act of bravery of the scientists who have been working here on creating the powerful shield of our Motherland multiplies the greatness of the Sarov land for Russia. Today, both of these parts of Sarov's history are indisputably valuable, interwoven, and unbreakable, respected by and meaningful to the residents of the city, who, as such, bear special civilian and religious responsibility.[15]

The divine connotation that was applied to the nuclear complex projected also on its experts. The religious lexicon began to be used to describe the labor of the nuclear scientists and thereby herald their role. In 1996 Metropolitan Kirill straightforwardly referred to the nuclear weapons specialists as "the twentieth-century devoted eremites" (*podvizhniki*):

> I must admit that visiting the nuclear centers greatly impressed me, and enabled me to understand the greatness of the act of bravery[16] performed by these outstanding people, also in the spiritual sense; I saw in front of me the eremites—persons who make sacrifices. These people who possess colossal

intellectual potential, mastering the highest technologies, who could have easily enriched themselves, have totally devoted themselves—their power, time, and lives—to preserving the security of our Fatherland and the security of the whole planet.[17]

Willingness on the part of the nuclear scientists to accept this divine interpretation was first documented during the conference "The Culture and Future of Russia," which was co-organized for the scientific intelligentsia by the ROC and the VNIIEF. The final statement of the event said: "Sarov's Pustyn [Monastery] used to be the point of spiritual gravity for Russian Orthodox people. The center for the development of the nuclear weapons that emerged here in 1946 maintained the ability of the Russian state to defend itself. Maybe such a coincidence is not accidental and demands internalization."[18] By 1996 such views had spread within the VNIIEF and were often expressed at pubic and professional events.[19] The conference "Nuclear Weapons and Russian National Security" (discussed in Chapter 3) provided ample illustrations of a merging of the metaphysical and strategic interpretations of nuclear capability.

One speaker poetically defined nuclear specialists as the guardians of Russia. According to him, the nuclear shield was protecting post-Soviet Russia not only in the geopolitical sense but also spiritually from the imposition of the Western way of life. "The genuine mission of the nuclear weapons is to deter the [Western] satanic effort to civilize Russia" and to be an "obstacle to the [Western] forces of darkness." For this reason, "every scientist, technician, and worker participating in development, production, and safeguarding of our nuclear weapons, every officer and soldier who operates our nuclear shield, is a *vitiaz'* [an epic military hero in Slavic folklore] defending the borders of Orthodox power." In his view, due to this divine mission of the Russian nuclear weapons, "the overseas civilizers" had sought to disarm Russia by means of the Strategic Arms Reduction Treaty (START) and the Comprehensive Test Ban Treaty (CTBT) and to change the balance of power in their favor.[20]

Some senior military commanders used religious figures of speech to refer to operational situations involving nuclear weapons,[21] while others straightforwardly talked about nuclear weapons in religious terms. "The most sophisticated nuclear missiles that the Americans call 'Satan' are for us the 'guardian-angels' of Russia. Nuclear weapons are our material support. Orthodoxy is our spiritual foundation."[22] The mayor of Sarov emphasized the symbolism in the creation of the nuclear bomb in the city, concluding that, as such, it "has the imprint of holiness."[23] Pavel Florensky, a professor in the Academy of Oil and Gas and the grandson of the famous religious philosopher whose writings would land on Putin's desk in the next decade, demanded an ethical differentiation between the Russian "defender-bomb" and the American "killer-bomb." According to him, the "moral nature" of the Soviet bomb was predetermined by St. Seraphim's spiritual control. He dubbed Russia's nuclear weapons developers as the successors of Seraphim's blessing "to struggle with the forces of evil by means of this terrible weapon." "There can be nothing accidental next to Father Seraphim. [. . .] If he had not preferred that in his house the nuclear shield of the Motherland be made, the bomb makers would have failed. This approval empowered them to put in the Motherland's arms terrible weapons of deterrence. [. . .] Maybe the fact that our bomb [in contrast to the American one] is not a killer bears witness to St. Seraphim's control."[24]

Similarly, Father Konstantin, the LRA pastor, distinguished between satanic and godly nuclear weapons. To him, nuclear capability, due its destructive capacity, has a demonic imprint. If the weapons are produced without a prayer, then "the original sin of the creators" projects on them:

> The solution lies in spiritualizing [*odukhotvoriat'*] those who work and construct this [nuclear] technique. [. . .] I have been to Arzamas-16 and was shocked by what I saw: many specialists have not gone on vacation for decades, and lead an ascetic way of life, conducting the important task of defending our country, working not for the money but for the idea. [. . .] This is why the pastoral care of the nuclear specialists is so important. These people sitting in front of their computers for days, solving the most difficult tasks, will find spiritualization only in the church, [where they will] satisfy the needs of their hearts. [. . .] My contacts with specialists from Arzamas-16 showed that they are thirsty for the prayer, spiritual socializing, and, finally, moral justification of their activity.[25]

Partly to pay tribute to the ROC, partly to legitimize their agenda in the eyes of the public, and partly due to a genuine return to faith, the industry seniors started mentioning religious issues with greater frequency by the late 1990s. In 1997 Mikhailov, talking about the future plans of the nuclear industry at the general assembly of the Russian Academy of Science, emphasized to the audience not only the scientific-strategic but also the religious-spiritual significance of Sarov. Holding up a nineteenth-century gravure of the Sarov Monastery, he shared with the assembly the story of St. Seraphim, the episode with the tsar's family, and the overall spiritual-religious prominence of the place in Russian history.[26] In 2000 the final statement of the joint ROC and nuclear industry conference dealing with cooperation of the two in the closed cities said: "Miraculous occurrences have always been and currently are one of the prominent aspects of church life. Often these events are not documented and lack proper assessment from the spiritual, religious, and scientific sides. It is therefore necessary to support church efforts to collect and explore data about miracles, [. . .] and to involve in this work not only the clergy but also the scientists."[27]

By 2000 the clergy formulated a theological argument about the faith-nuclear nexus, building on the most-cited verse in Seraphim's *akafist*—an Orthodox hymn dedicated to a saint—which calls him "the shield and protection of our Fatherland." Using this verse, the dean of the St. Tikhon Orthodox University read spiritual meaning into the work of the nuclear weapons specialists. According to his interpretation, it indicated the saint had foreseen that the Soviet scientists would forge—in Arzamas-16, at the site of his monastic cell—a nuclear shield for Russia.[28] Such a reading also suggested that the saint not only foresaw the Soviet nuclear project, but also approved it. Since then, this interpretation of the verse has been widely shared in the clerical and professional circles, preparing a favorable climate for the popularization of the "Nuclear Orthodoxy" concept. Nuclear Orthodoxy is an unofficial doctrine, or public belief, that has circulated in the Russian strategic community and broader public since the 2000s. In a nutshell, it argues that in order to preserve its Orthodox character, Russia needs to ensure its being a strong nuclear power, and in order to guarantee its nuclear status, Russia has to be genuinely Orthodox.

The earliest reference to *nuclear orthodoxy* dates to the late 1990s. Inception of the concept occurred in two separate, but possibly interrelated, places. The first source was popular history. In 1998 Vladimir Kucherenko, a journalist, publicist, and popular Russian military historian-futurologist, published, under the pen name Maksim Kalashnikov, a book called *The Broken Sword of the Empire*. It was one in a series of his books praising Soviet history and calling for the restoration of Russian superpower status. Far from being a work of academic research, the book offered tendentious historical interpretations leading to the revanchist demand for imperial restoration. The book went through four editions in the following years and, like many of his previous and subsequent works, became very popular, especially among the patriotic, nationalist, conservative, and radical public. In particular, a passage on the desired Russian strategic future called for revival of the Orthodox faith as the ideology of the new militaristic empire.

> The Orthodox nucleus of our empire needs to be strengthened. [. . .] We
> should revive it [the Orthodoxy] not as a circus show, as is happening now,
> with the well-fed priests consecrating almost everything, including the ca-
> sinos and nightclubs. But, [we should] revive it as the military, imperial
> Orthodoxy, blazing in super-voltage, Nuclear Orthodoxy, if you wish. [We
> should] connect the faith with cruise missiles and phase radars and [con-
> nect] the nuclear center in Arzamas-16 with the relics of Seraphim Sarovsky.
> The [public] quest for this militant Orthodoxy is evident.[29]

The second source was contemporary art. At about the same time that Kalashnikov's book made the first reference to the *Nuclear Orthodoxy* concept, Aleksei Beliaev-Gintovt and Andrei Molodkin, then relatively young Russian artists inspired by the emerging ideas of Euroasianism, were completing a big art project titled *Novosibirsk*. The exhibition opened in 2000 and moved between prestigious galleries and museums of Moscow and St. Petersburg, including the Russian Museum, Manezh, and the Schusev Museum of Architecture. In 2001 it was even presented in the Russian Duma. The centerpiece of the project consisted of large canvases dedicated to the futuristic city of Novosibirsk—the capital of the imagined Russian Eurasian Empire.[30] Seven canvases featured sites-monuments of the new capital: the gigantic neoclassical sculpture of the city's patron Apollo, standing next to the hydroelectric power station, with nuclear missiles instead of arrows in his quiver; the city's fountain, the Golden Colossus, stylized as a gigantic launching pad; and the city's cosmodrome, named after Nikolai Berdiaev, a Russian religious-political philosopher. The canvas that would become the hallmark associated with the project featured a nuclear-armed submarine, most of it covered with ice and only its tower and wings appearing above the surface, in the shape of the cross. The title of the canvas was *Nuclear Orthodoxy*.[31] The curatorial interpretation revealed artist Beliaev-Gintovt's fascination with Eurasian philosophy, particularly the ideas of Alexander Dugin, one of its leading ideologists. In the artist's words, the canvases called for the creation of the new empire and restoration of Russia's lost imperial greatness.[32]

Beliaev-Gintovt's ideational outline somewhat resonated with the political course of Putin, which started to emerge at around the same time. According to the artist,

> Imperial hierarchy should be strictly vertically oriented. As in traditional societies—at the top of the caste pyramid there are priests and warriors, and an emperor above them. [. . .] The obvious restoration of Russian statehood is the direct consequence of the positive and centrifugal process, the victory of harmony over the chaos. [. . .] Recreation of the sovereign state on the basis of the Russian Federation and strategic integration of the CIS states immediately raises the question about the location of the main city of the new entity—the center of gravity of the "Middle Empire." [. . .] Novosibirsk—the city located at the border of western and eastern Siberia, relatively close to China and India, in the geometric center of Eurasia, presumably could become the point where all the orbits of the Eurasian project merge, as Dugin described it. [. . .] Euroasianism is our chance to return to history! [. . .] Looking back, we see the main characteristics of the Big Project in the Russian and Soviet Powers [. . .] hierarchy, canon, and order.[33]

The splash of the exhibition went beyond the Russian art scene, as the artists planned *Novosibirsk* as a performance with a political statement.[34] During the exhibition's stay at the Moscow architecture museum, the artists released homing pigeons carrying a message concerning the "Great

Canon"—an appeal to the president to return art to "the bosom of the tradition." The artists saw the clamping of the notes to the birds' feet as a symbolic move, but were confident that the message reached the Kremlin. "We managed to invite the president to the exhibition through his administration," argued Beliaev-Gintovt. Putin never visited, but one of the supporters of the exhibition was the Russian Duma Committee on State Building.[35] The leading Russian art journal, which published Beliaev-Gintovt's curatorial piece, placed it right after an article by Dugin, who at that time was popularizing Eurasian ideas as the main ideology for the ruling elite and was advising the head of the Duma. Following the exhibition, Beliaev-Gintovt became a stylist of the Eurasia party and the international Euroasianist movement. By the end of the 2000s, when he received the annual Kandinsky Prize in Russian contemporary art, he acknowledged Dugin as his ideational inspiration.[36]

Cultural opposition to the West, Russian patriotism, and the theme of nuclear orthodoxy continue to feature in Beliaev-Gintovt's other projects:

> The more we presented in the West, the more obvious became the difference between the world perception of the Russians and of the so-called civilized world. [. . .] Once the annual festival in the French city of Toulouse was dedicated to the history of Russia. Everyone was there—Komar, Melamid, and Kabakov, and we, the young generation. They liked our project, and decided to put one statue from it in their city, but the mayor suddenly objected. The allegoric statue was a nuclear manhole cover with a she-wolf standing on it. It was called Nuclear Orthodoxy. The mayor became opposed since it was something beyond their understanding of Russia.[37]

The next chapter elaborates how, upon emerging out of these two rather marginal episodes, the notion of Nuclear Orthodoxy would turn during the following decade into a rather coherent and widespread doctrine.

SUMMARY REMARKS ON THE GENESIS DECADE

The church-nuclear nexus was incepted in the early 1990s. During this "genesis decade" the quest for religiosity emerged as a grassroots phenomenon within the nuclear complex, and the latter entered into a covenant with the ROC. A search for a new national and professional identity marked the exodus of the Russian strategic community, and Russia as a whole, out of the Soviet era. Within the military-industrial complex, the Union's collapse most threatened the nuclear community. For the ROC, seeking to expand its base of influence, the disoriented military-nuclear complex became a target of opportunity. The former shielded the latter from political-social ostracism, lobbied for funding, supported it in overcoming value disorientation and a miserable social attitude, helped it to reinvent its self-identity, and injected new meaning into its professional life. The decade bore witness to the introduction of religious ceremonies into the everyday functioning of the nuclear community, the designation of patron saints for nuclear institutions, and the construction of churches in the nuclear weapons industry and in the garrisons of the triad's corps. Initially, the faith-atoms nexus enjoyed only marginal state financial-administrative support. In contrast, from the beginning, the ROC's proselytism was evident from the patriarch down to the priests interacting with the nuclear forces' commanders and the industry's officials within the local parishes. Also during the decade, the phenomenon of religious-political mythmaking—the reading of divine meaning into Russian-Soviet military and nuclear history—emerged.

Part II

THE CONVERSION DECADE: 2000–2010

CHAPTER 5

STATE-CHURCH RELATIONS

THE ROC IN RUSSIAN POLITICS

During the 1990s the ROC improved its public position, acquired political influence, and made certain progress in terms of converts. However, despite its visible role in society and politics, within the framework of state-church relations, it "did not, on balance, manage to convince the state to accede to its main demands." The situation began to change during the first decade of the twenty-first century. Despite relatively low numbers of actively practicing Orthodox, as a majority of self-reported believers were still nominal, the ROC became unprecedentedly influential in promoting its agendas. Sustained lobbying by Patriarch Alexey on key issues important to the ROC prepared favorable conditions for the breakthrough, and the remarkable personal skills and political dynamism of Metropolitan Kirill, the head of the ROC's External Relations Department and patriarch from 2009, turned the ROC into one of the key players in Russian politics.[1]

Different from his predecessor in management style, the new patriarch "moved the church-state relations in directions that were only imagined under Aleksii." As Irina Papkova and Dmitry Gorenburg demonstrate, toward the end of the decade the ROC achieved its four fundamental goals: the introduction of religious instruction in public schools (the classes on "fundamentals of Orthodox culture"); revival of the institution of the military chaplaincy; federal restitution of the pre-Soviet ecclesiastical property; and marginalization of all nontraditional denominations.[2] The ROC's growing influence also sparked a reaction, as the ROC's privileges seemed to many to be contrary to the constitution.[3] Toward the end of the decade, critique of the ROC and friction between it and secular forces became widespread.[4] This anticlerical splash changed nothing and, as such, was indicative of the state-church bond.

Since the early 2000s, the ROC began saturating its religious messages with nationalistic-ideological content, ensuring greater unison between its "Holy Rus" and "Russian civilization's values" rhetoric and the Kremlin's emerging ideology.[5] Simultaneously, it adopted an active position in the sphere of national security, identity, and ideology. Metropolitan Kirill insisted that ideological subversion should be perceived as a weapon of mass destruction (WMD), as dangerous as nuclear coercion. To illustrate his point, he often referred to the Union's collapse, which happened without a major war, but through the replacement of traditional Russian spiritual values with foreign materialistic ones and the cult of profit. "We should not be ashamed to go to churches and teach our children Orthodoxy. [. . .] In that case we will have what to protect with our nuclear-armed submarines."[6] In parallel, the ROC was steadily becoming a foreign policy force. Its geopolitical vision of the "Russian World," which preached unity among the nations that share Orthodox values and a Russian cultural heritage, was in accord with official policy.[7] The ROC extended the Kremlin's concept of "spiritual security" to the Russian diasporas, further expanding Moscow's influence worldwide.[8] With an efficiency surpassing that of the Ministry of Foreign Affairs, the ROC turned into one of the major tools of Russia's soft influence—an instrument "that Moscow has long been criticized for lacking."[9]

During the decade under discussion, Putin, a pragmatist inclined to avoid ideological extremes, sought to revive Russian greatness. He "incorporated the Soviet period into the historical continuum of Russian statehood," not because he cherished the Communist ideology, but because of the Soviet superpower status.[10] Putin had no intention of restoring the Union, but sought to preserve nuclei of greatness from the then empire and to take it further. He needed a national idea that provides the ideological-spiritual staples to hold the country and the society together. A mix of Orthodoxy, nationalism, and autocracy became such a unifying narrative.[11] By the end of the decade, the contours of Putin's geopolitical worldview were largely finalized. As national ideology took shape, religious ideas and the ROC began playing an unparalleled role in it.

As the Russian ruling elite began seeing in Orthodoxy a "critical ingredient in the formation of a cohesive national identity," the adoption of Orthodox symbols and narratives gradually began on the national level.[12] This was a natural development—the leadership saw the new state as being not sui generis, but a continuity from the tsarist era through the Soviet past, from which as much was preserved as had been thrown away. After all, the people running the country and constructing the new identity were largely Soviet products. The new anthem, for example, was a restoration of the abolished Soviet one, with the same music but modified lyrics. By the mid-2000s, the ROC was allowed to encroach deeper into the authorship of the national narrative and to further shape the national symbols along Orthodox lines. In 2005 the president accepted the recommendation of the Holy Synod to abolish the holiday of 7 November, the former Soviet "Revolution Day," which had been called "Day of Concord and Reconciliation" between 1996 and 2004, in favor of 4 November.[13]

Under Putin, nuclear weapons and Orthodoxy became major aspects of Russia's greatness, both internally and externally. "Control over nuclear weapons has become the ultimate symbol of authority, an equivalent of the old-time scepter and orb." More often than his predecessor, Putin has been referred to as the commander in chief, and he has more frequently visited the nuclear forces to address the domestic and international audiences.[14] In February 2007, during an annual presidential press conference, a Sarov journalist asked about the role of Orthodoxy and nuclear weapons in Russia's future. Putin's first sentence—noting that "both themes are closely interlinked"—drew a laugh from the audience. However, those who thought it was a joke missed the point. Putin communicated his credo: "Traditional confessions and the nuclear shield are those components that strengthen Russian statehood and create the necessary preconditions for providing the state's internal and external security. Therefore, a clear conclusion can be drawn, about how the state should relate, today and in the future, to the one and to the other."[15]

Several indications from just one year at the end of Putin's second term suggest that his geopolitical and religious worldviews had become concrete and interwoven. In 2007, in addition to Putin's speech at the Munich security conference and the statement in response to the Sarov journalist, Putin for the first time officially congratulated "all the Orthodox Christians and all Russian citizens celebrating the Resurrection Sunday," and he did the same on Christmas.[16] Since then, both Dmitry Medvedev and he, as presidents, have annually repeated these blessings. In the same year, Putin encouraged Russian oligarchs to purchase parts of the Russian compound in Jerusalem and hand them over to the ROC.[17] Also in 2007, after an almost ninety-year split, the two Russian Orthodox Churches—the Moscow Patriarchate and the ROC abroad—united. Putin was personally involved in the lengthy diplomatic efforts leading to unification, which was of major religious and political significance. Following his nomination by *Time* magazine as person of the year, Putin, responding to a question about the rising role of faith in Russia, said that "first and foremost we should be governed by common sense. But common sense should be based on moral principles first. And it is not possible today to have morality separated from religious values."[18] The Moscow Patriarchate, reporting on the statement, argued that the president "repeated his conviction that moral values [. . .] can't be anything but religious ones."[19]

The state's greatness, which had coincided with Putin's personal formative experiences, loomed large for him against the backdrop of the post-Soviet times of trouble. One of his lessons from the Soviet collapse, which he saw as the biggest geopolitical catastrophe of the twentieth century, was that simply "transplanting Western institutions and ideas would create chaos." This was not mindless hostility, but a conviction that in order to become a strong state Russia must take "its own path and not slavishly follow others." Democracy, for Putin, was good as long as it didn't obstruct efficient functioning.[20] Drawing largely, just as the Soviet and pre-Soviet leaders before him did, on the Asiatic political-managerial tradition inherited from the Tatar-Mongol yoke, Putin believed that a country of Russia's dimensions, ethno-social tensions, internal contradictions, myriad natural catastrophes, and geopolitical challenges could be kept together and run effectively only through centralized vertical or authoritarian power emanating from one place—the tsar.[21]

The notion of an autocratic president demanded public legitimacy, and the ROC was eager to cultivate the support. Toward the 2007 election, hosting Orthodox hierarchs in the Kremlin, Putin hinted at the support he desired for the stability and conservatism course. The patriarch assured him that the ROC and its followers would deliver this backing on the part of the Russian citizens.[22] The ROC continued to actively instill in public consciousness the role of the Orthodox traditions in the emerging state course.[23] As part of this trend, in 2008 Archimandrite Tikhon directed and served as the main narrator of the historical documentary *The Fall of an Empire*. The movie, which was "shown three times during prime time on national TV," analyzed the collapse of Byzantium and used the story as a lesson regarding how to avoid a similar geopolitical fate.[24] Papkova has skillfully outlined the movie's main historical contention—that the Eastern Christian Empire collapsed due less to the Turkish conquest than to internal causes: the weakening of vertical power, foreign (that is, Western) political-financial machinations, the selfishness of the oligarchs, and the replacement of the traditional Orthodox values with corrupting Western (Catholic) ones, leading to spiritual degradation. The main message was straightforward: "the tragedy could have been avoided had Byzantium pursued autarchic, nationalist development." Offered by the Orthodox cleric, the analogy resonated with the collapse of the Soviet empire and subsequent times of trouble and provided legitimacy for Putin's political course.[25]

The movie popularized presenting Russia as the Third Rome. This implied that Byzantium bequeathed to Russia its civilizational burden of being the spiritual-political center of Orthodoxy. Thus, the eternal status of Holy Rus remained constant and transcendent through the centuries, from the tsarist past to the post-Soviet present, regardless of the secularity or religiosity of the regime. The timing of the movie, the identity of its narrator-director, and its analogy all suggested a connection to the administration.[26] Indeed, the Kremlin co-opted public intellectuals and nationalist ideologists who were popularizing the Third Rome notion. This political myth made it possible to determine important categories such as the definition of Russians, the centrality of political Orthodoxy, the foundation of the state and its desired boundaries, and Russian uniqueness and moral prerogative. It also situated geostrategic aspirations in the broader historical context and generated support among radically different currents of nationalism.[27] As Charles Clover put it, the movie was slightly ahead of its time.[28]

The church-state symphony continued under Medvedev. At the supplication service after the inauguration ceremony, Patriarch Alexey and the new president praised each other for the close church-state cooperation and pledged to extend it.[29] In June 2010, Medvedev, who for Christmas usually goes to the Sretensky Monastery,[30] signed the law establishing 28 July as the official commemoration day of the baptism of Russia.[31] This was the first step in the popularization of the image of the Great Prince Vladimir, which would culminate in 2016 with the erection of his statue at the entrance to the Kremlin and the release of *Viking*—one of the three most expensive Russian movies ever made, telling the story of Prince Vladimir's baptism of the Kievan Rus, an act that turned Russia into the Third Rome.

PUTIN: BETWEEN PUBLIC AND PRIVATE RELIGIOUS PERSONA

Much as Patriarch Kirill's personality is important for understanding the leap forward in the ROC's influence, it is equally essential to grasp the role that faith has played in Putin's worldview. Vladimir Vladimirovich from the start appeared to be close to the ROC and has steadily popularized the public image of himself as a true believer. The majority of experts have questioned the authenticity of the public religious persona that he has projected, seeing it as Putin's practicality at the time when the ROC and the Kremlin became allies. Indeed, both shared skepticism of Western liberalism that could corrupt the Russian way of life and a discomfort about the Western interpretation of democracy and human rights. Both converged on the notion of "managed democracy" ensuring stability through centralization—an antidote to the chaos brought on by the "unmanaged democracy." Both embraced conservative-patriotic education promoting religious values, viewing Orthodox culture as *primus inter pares*.[32] Thus, most observers saw Putin's religiosity as a manipulation by a professional Chekist (in the narrow meaning the member of Cheka, the first Soviet secret police, and in the collocual Russian, meaning the intelligence officer) to maintain a desired public image and qualified his attitude to faith as fake.[33]

Qualifying Putin's Orthodox appearance as a *legenda*—Soviet intelligence jargon for an operative's cover story—is an oversimplification. The evidence below suggests that his religiosity has gone beyond instrumental considerations.[34] Moreover, manipulating a narrative does not necessarily contradict one's being a believer. Both phenomena might coexist and be mutually reinforcing. Thus, the story that Putin wants told about his religiosity is interesting in itself, as it reveals both his genuine devotion to faith and his utilization of it for political purposes. The detailed history of Putin's conversion is yet to be written. What follows is a brief reconstruction of how religious philosophy and beliefs have become interwoven with ideology and strategy in both his public and private persona.

"Vladimir Vladimirovich Putin is probably the most pious leader since 1917," argues Nikolai Leonov, the deputy head of the KGB from 1984 to 1991 and since then an Orthodox publicist, Parliament member, and a member of the Sretensky Monastery congregation.[35] Putin's conduct indeed contrasted with that of the post-Soviet new elite—until then staunch atheists—who after 1991 transformed into zealous faithful. Standing in front of cameras in churches and kissing icons became a bon ton for these new converts. Few of them, however, were able to read the creed and "rarely knew how to hold a candle or cross themselves, but they laboriously played the role of the faithful Orthodox."[36] The trend extended also to former KGB officers, retired and serving.[37] However, upon arrival at the top of the hierarchy, Putin signaled that his faith was not for the protocol. According to John Anderson, "His participation in services clearly went beyond the lip service paid by the first generation of post- and ex-communist politicians."[38]

After Yeltsin's resignation, during his first week as acting president, in January 2000 Putin delivered the first-ever president's Christmas greetings.

He stressed the special role of Orthodoxy in Russian history, arguing that it had "determined the character of Russian civilization," and designated its values as the source of "spiritual and moral rebirth."[39] In May 2000, Putin conducted a thanksgiving service following his inauguration. The patriarch, who led the ceremony, asked him to help in "disclosing the soul of the nation."[40] Father Tikhon, already then Putin's alleged confessor, advised him to send a congratulatory note to Archimandrite Ioann Krestiankin, the most venerated among the Soviet and Russian elders.[41] The note led to a meeting, at which Putin talked to the elder for more than an hour. Many interpreted it as a blessing on the reign—an extension of the tsarist tradition and of the biblical practice of prophets anointing the kings.[42] Since then, Putin hasn't concealed his affection for the faith.[43] For Christmas he always joins the service in one of the tiny provincial Russian churches, mixing with the locals in casual dress.[44] For Easter, in official business attire, accompanied by Medvedev and his wife, and at times by the mayor of Moscow, he always joins the service at the Christ the Savior Cathedral that the patriarch leads.[45]

Putin's earliest conscious religious experience, which he publicly designates as his spiritual point of departure, dates to 1993. According to his official biography, when he went to Israel as part of the official delegation of the Leningrad city council, his mother asked him to consecrate his baptism cross in the Church of the Holy Sepulchre in Jerusalem. Putin did not wear any cross before this visit, and it is unclear when he learned about his baptism, which had been conducted clandestinely at a young age.[46] In the next decade, Putin acknowledged that the cleric who had baptized him was none other than the father of Patriarch Kirill.[47] In any case, Putin fulfilled his mother's request in 1993 and since then has not taken off the cross.[48] In September 2000, talking to television host Larry King, he added a new angle. According to the story, unmentioned in his biography, he decided always to carry the cross on his body following an episode that occurred in 1996. While spending time with friends inside a sauna at his dacha, a fire broke out. Before entering the sauna, Putin had hung the cross in the changing room, so when the fire broke out unexpectedly, he rushed to safety, leaving the cross behind. Since he cherished this cross, he asked workers at the scene to find what was left of it. "I was surprised completely when one of the workers, just muddling through those ashes of the remnants, found the cross intact. That was a surprise, a revelation, and therefore I always now keep it with me."[49] The president's press service popularized this story on the pages of a trendy Russian magazine.[50] Leonov concurs that, within narrow circles, an opinion was extant then that Putin saw this episode as a divine sign that stimulated a deeper faith.[51]

Indications of personal religiosity, beyond the public persona that he projected, were increasing steadily. To pray away from the public eye, Putin ordered a house chapel to be constructed in his official residence in the Kremlin.[52] In 2003, at the celebrations of St. Seraphim's canonization, Putin's facial expression, body language, intimacy with the patriarch, and strict observance of the Orthodox traditions were sincere or expressed a genuine desire to communicate the meaning of the moment, or both.[53] At his vacation residency near Lake Valdai, Putin constructed a house church decorated in the style of Viktor Vasnetsov, a cofounder of Russian national-romantic art, specializing in mythological subjects of folklore and history. The compound has served Putin's spiritual needs only, as this residency has been kept strictly personal and has never been shown for PR purposes. Several kilometers away from it are the Iverskaia Mother of God and the Valaam Monasteries, where Putin often spends days off and which could offer pastoral care.[54] Putin allocated funds for the monasteries' restoration, but preferred to have his own temple. "If he constructs for himself a tiny house church away from people's eyes, then he really feels from time to time a need to pray, repent, and confess."[55]

Asked in 2007 about the role of faith in his management style, Putin responded that when formulating tasks and making decisions, he was driven by common sense, based on moral principles, which in turn rest on religious values. He declined to respond whether or not he believes in God, but revealed that aboard his plane there were an icon and a Bible, which he often reads.[56] Anderson qualified Putin's commitment to faith as "personal, if theologically vague."[57] In 2008 Leonov saw Putin's religious worldview as a genuine desire to find in Orthodoxy "the source of power, which he can't find in himself,"[58] but he thought that Putin was not self-confident enough, ideologically and spiritually, to publicly position himself as "Orthodox Russian" and explain to the people "why an Orthodox president should head the state."[59] Leonov also argued that although Putin was genuinely religious, not all of his deeds were in accord with the Christian commandments.[60]

Some sources have claimed that Leonov, a frequent visitor to the Sretensky Monastery, introduced Putin to his alleged confessor, Archimandrite Tikhon—then the head of the monastery,[61] and today also a metropolite. Sources have also suggested that Tikhon served as the confessor (*dukhovnik*) of Liudmila Putina, the First Lady until 2013.[62] Having a confessor was part of the zeitgeist. Against the backdrop of the general fashion for religiosity, central figures from the business, cultural, and political elites, and even from the criminal world, developed a penchant for having a confessor. A form of psychotherapy, personal confessors were affordable only for the rich, while the mass of believers offered their quick confessions standing in the long lines in the crowded churches.[63]

According to Leonov, who has never confirmed making the connection,[64] "in the circles of the Orthodox patriotic intelligentsia, Tikhon was known for his piety, high culture, and rare personal qualities. This alone justifies taking the information seriously."[65] The two may have met when Tikhon led the construction work at the Sretensky Monastery, located down the street from the Russian Federal Security Service (FSB) headquarters in Lubianka. Putin, then head of the FSB, needed to approve the work on the site, which was surrounded by the FSB underground communications.[66] At about the same time, the FSB initiated the restoration of the Sophia Wisdom of God church within its headquarters, turning it into the house church. In August 2001, construction, which was supervised personally by Nikolai Patrushev, Putin's successor at the FSB, was completed and the church was consecrated by the patriarch.[67]

The Sretensky Monastery, which reopened in the 1990s, "has become the centre of a spiritual revival among Russia's ruling circles, who are disproportionately drawn from among the former KGB."[68] Tikhon, leading a "vibrant religious community often seen as the headquarters of the conservative nationalist wing of the church,"[69] was "eager to hammer the Soviet period into a single arc of historical Russian statehood." From his point of view, KGB officers devotedly served the then reincarnation of the Russian state, and thus he saw no contradiction in churching them.[70] Like Putin, Tikhon was a statist driven by the conservative-patriotic motto of "Orthodoxy, Autocracy, Peoplehood"[71]—a slogan encapsulating three pillars of ideology: faith, the monarch, and a pious nation loyal to him.[72] Putin, according to Fiona Hill and Clifford Gaddy, embraced this doctrine in slightly modified form, substituting "sovereign democracy" for "autocracy," implying that "Russia is accountable to no one (certainly no outside power) apart from the majority of its population," led by its national leader.[73]

Archimandrite Tikhon acquired the title of "Gray Cardinal." In 2000 he took Putin, before his inauguration, to receive a blessing from Archimandrite Ioann Krestiankin. In 2001 he guided Putin's pilgrimage to the holy places of Greece and also his excursions to Russian monasteries and to the New York meeting with the ROC abroad to discuss unification with the Moscow Patriarchate.[74] In the same year, Tikhon stated that Putin is indeed a genuine, not a nominal, Orthodox, "a person who confesses, takes Communion, and realizes his responsibility in the face of God for the high service entrusted to him and for his immortal soul."[75] Tikhon has never confirmed or denied being Putin's confessor, laughing it off by saying that he is not Cardinal Richelieu,[76] but he certainly leaves the audience with exactly that impression. The Kremlin seems to find this useful.[77] Apparently, Putin has allowed this information about his affection for the faith and his personal connections with Tikhon to circulate in public.[78]

Tikhon's proximity to Putin seems often to have been overblown for personal needs and intra-church struggles.[79] But even putting aside the possible self-promotion, Tikhon indeed has been an ecclesiastic mentor, providing pastoral guidance to political elites and to Putin's immediate entourage.[80] Whether or not Tikhon has been Putin's confessor, he is definitely his confidant and close adviser on the issues pertaining to state-church relations and matters of ritual. Clover, who has profiled Tikhon in depth, qualified him as "perhaps the most important of the new generation of ideological influencers in the orbit of the Kremlin."[81] Reportedly, Putin admires Tsar Alexander III, who suppressed liberal tendencies; cultivated the ideological hybrid of autocracy, nationalism, and Orthodoxy; and claimed that Russia has only two allies—its Army and

Navy. In the monastery's tearoom, where Tikhon accepts distinguished guests, a huge painting of this tsar hangs on the wall.[82]

Pilgrimages to sacred places in Russia and abroad, often beneath the radar, have been an important part of Putin's religious practice. A majority of these trips were not events staged for show. Leonov, commenting on Putin's trips to the small and remote northern monasteries, argued that "in these regions, located far away from the main administrative-industrial centers, there is basically nothing to do but to immerse oneself in the baptistery of spiritual cleansing, to shake off oneself the dust and web of worldly problems."[83] The fact that Putin has repeatedly allocated funds from the presidential reserve for the monasteries has hardly been publicized.[84] He has also visited several times Pereslavl-Zalesky, one of the favorite prayer sites of Ivan the Formidable and the place where the young Peter the Great conducted shipbuilding experiments.[85]

In April 2005, on the eve of the Orthodox Easter, Putin visited Jerusalem. It was the first-ever official visit of a Russian leader to Israel, and Putin's third visit to the Holy Land.[86] According to Leonov, the real goal of the trip was a pilgrimage to the Church of the Holy Sepulchre, while visits to Egypt and the Palestinian Authority and official meetings in Israel were *maskirovka*, "giving the trip a secular-political character." Putin paid lip service to the discussions on the Arab-Israeli conflict, but behaved like a true pilgrim.[87] Immediately upon landing, guided by Archimandrite Elisey, the head of the Russian Mission to Jerusalem, Putin went straight to the Holy Sepulchre.[88] After entering the church, he stopped in front of the Stone of Anointing, where allegedly Jesus was laid before burial, and stood alone and silent for a long while. Then he moved to Kuvuklia, the tiny shrine where allegedly the body of Jesus was buried, and entered it alone, spending a long while there.[89]

When he finished praying, Putin climbed up a stairway to the Rock of Golgotha (Calvary), the most decorated part of the temple, where allegedly Jesus was crucified. Putin kneeled before the altar, where the cross stood on the rock, and prayed. "Then he stood up, lit a thick candle, and was going to leave, but all of a sudden turned back, approached the cross again, and fell to his knees, to the astonishment of those around him. In front of them was not a political leader, but a faithful person, a pilgrim, seeking spiritual assistance and cleansing."[90] Following his visit to the church, the first meeting took place within the Russian Orthodox Mission in Jerusalem. Archimandrite Elisey presented Putin with an icon of the crucifixion, with a piece of Golgotha rock implanted in it. In return, the archimandrite received a huge icon of St. Seraphim decorated with gold.[91]

Putin has exploited every opportunity to undergo pilgrim experiences, some of them hardly publicized. For example, in February 2007, during an official visit to Jordan, he visited Jesus's baptismal site at the Jordan River. He first went to the spring of John the Baptist and then walked up the entire pilgrimage route to the baptismal site, where he washed, in keeping with the tradition, his face and hands in the waters of the Jordan. Among other questions discussed with the Jordanian authorities was the construction of a hostel for pilgrims from Russia, on ten hectares of land presented by Amman to Moscow.[92] Construction of the Russian compound, including the hotel and a huge chapel, under Putin's personal patronage, was completed within several years at the site. Putin opened it in 2012 and Jerusalem's patriarch consecrated it, while the choir of Moscow's Sretensky Monastery sang.[93] That visit, on which the Palestinian Authority was the first stop, as in the case of Israel, began with a visit to the Church of the Nativity in Bethlehem, only then followed by a meeting with the Palestinian leader.[94]

Putin's stance as a pious pilgrim was also evidenced in his determination to visit the holy mountain of Athos in Greece. He tried three times. In 2003 during his visit in Greece, his helicopter trip there was canceled due to the stormy weather. He rescheduled the visit for 2004, but postponed it again, due to the terrorist attack in Beslan. It was only in September 2005, after his return from Jerusalem, that he finally made it.[95] The pilgrimage included visits to all the central monasteries of the holy mountain, participation in the services, and an excursion to see all the main relics kept by the Mount Athos monks.[96] By then, pilgrimage of Russian Orthodox to the mountain had incrementally revived, reaching eleven thousand annually by 2016, including seniors from the political elite.[97]

Vladimir Yakunin, the minister of railways, who established the pilgrimage tradition among the elite, also heads the Fund of Andrei the Apostle. The latter has brought from Mount Athos for veneration in Russia the foot of St. Andrei (2003), the head of Luke the Evangelist (2007), the Belt of the Mother of God (2011), and the right hand of St. Georgii the Victor (2015). Putin personally approved bringing these relics to Moscow.[98] Also, since 2003, every year, the fund brings to Russia from Israel the Holy Fire on the Great Saturday, the day preceding the Orthodox Easter.[99] Fund representatives participate in the ceremony of the emergence of the Holy Fire at Jerusalem's Church of the Holy Sepulchre. Right after, a special plane of the Ministry of Emergency Situations, then headed by the current DM Shoigu, brings it to Moscow, directly to the patriarch's Easter service at the Christ the Savior Cathedral, which Putin attends.[100] The fire is then disseminated to congregations across Russia.

CHURCH-MILITARY RELATIONS

During the first decade of the twenty-first century, the churching and catechization of the armed forces reached a new level, with the Kremlin eventually reviving the institution of the military clergy (*voennoe dukhovenstvo*). The mastermind behind this monumental effort, which finally succeeded in 2009, was Metropolitan Kirill. To promote his agenda, he has systematically engaged with the general public and the entire chain of command—from the DM to the rank-and-file soldiers. His meetings took him to the small bases, the military education institutions, the GS Academy, and sessions with the GS and the MoD Board.[101] The favorable attitude of the MoD, whose seniors, including the minister, began adopting a genuine or nominal religiosity, helped,[102] but success stemmed mainly from the acceleration of the three ongoing efforts: churching of the military, its catechization, and a massive PR campaign. During the decade, the ROC de facto established a functioning but unofficial clerical infrastructure within the military and created a favorable public-political-professional climate. Thus, the decision to reestablish the military clergy just legitimized the existing reality.

First, the ROC increased the numbers of garrison churches and military priests. Metropolitan Kirill constantly encouraged turning the temples into the center of the pastoral work with the military and paid significant attention to the construction projects.[103] The data on the clergy's interaction with the military and on the garrison churches that were constructed during this decade is often contradictory. Still, the numbers relating to just the first half of the decade illustrate the leap forward. In October 2004, the head of the Synodal Department reported that 2,000 priests (about 8 percent of the ROC clergy) had been interacting with the military, 950 of them permanently. There were 156 churches and chapels (excluding those under construction) inside the military bases and about 400 churches located near the units and pastoring them.[104] With no budget from the ROC or the MoD, construction was usually funded by the donations of soldiers and officers and conducted using the materials and capacities of military units.[105]

New churches assisted in cultivating a new professional consciousness. For example, using donations from big state corporations, in 2002 the commander of the GS Academy initiated the renovation of its house church—the Temple of Archistrategos Mikhail.[106] The decor of the renovated temple illustrated the professional ethos of the converting military.[107] It featured guardian angels hovering overhead during the battles,[108] icons of Russian folklore heroes, and canonized warriors—Admiral Ushakov, Princes Donskoy and Nevsky—and battle scenes from the GPW. Murals on the temple's columns merged several epochs into one ideological continuum. Orthodox crosses were positioned above the two most prestigious Soviet military decorations: the Order of Victory and the Golden Star of the Hero.[109] The red flag on the ribbon of the Soviet the Golen Star medal, however, was modified to the Russian tricolor.[110]

Metropolitan Kirill, in his capacity as the head of the ROC's External Relations Department, was active across all the military, but paid special attention to naval issues, often making them the basis for interaction with other corps. Partially, this was an issue of geography—a majority of the military congregations in his eparchy were naval: the Northern and the Baltic Fleets and the Naval Staff in St. Petersburg. Also, this was an extension of the previous decade's focus on the naval component of the nuclear triad. Mainly, however, Kirill corresponded with the political constellation—the Kremlin began to pay growing attention to the renewal of naval power, and Putin demonstrated his affection for the Navy.

Katarzyna Zysk demonstrates that the spike in naval activity, including the reentry to blue water, started in 2005.[111] Discussions and fund allocations indicative of this change began earlier. Kirill seems to have pinpointed the trend and ensured ecclesiastical escort. In August 2001, in the Sanaksarsk Monastery, Patriarch Alexey canonized the most famous Russian admiral, Feodor Ushakov. The ceremony, the first of its kind, was unusual for both the ROC and the military. Commanders of the Navy Main Staff, of the Baltic, Northern, and Black Sea Fleets, and even the commander of the Ukrainian Navy were present.[112] Following the event, Kirill promoted the idea of enabling Orthodox naval servicemen to worship the saint and during 2001–2 arranged delivery of pieces of the relic to the Baltic and Black Sea Fleets.[113]

In 2002 Kirill requested to deliver to Russia a relic from the Athos Monastery—a foot of St. Andrei the Apostle.[114] Known in Russia as Andrei the First Called, this saint has special significance. According to Orthodox tradition, Andrei came to bring Christianity to Russia and his foot stepped on its soil (then the territory of the Eastern Slavs).[115] The Andreevsky flag, with a blue X-shaped cross on a white background, commemorating the martyrdom of the saint, had been the Russian Navy flag before the revolution. It was reintroduced in 2001 to substitute for its Soviet predecessor. In 2003 Putin approved the delivery by naval aviation of the foot to the Baltic, Northern, and Pacific Fleets for veneration.[116] The Fund of Andrei the Apostle, which since the same year has delivered the Holy Fire from Jerusalem, facilitated these activities.[117]

Second, the ROC co-opted the state policy for patriotic upbringing to expand catechization of the military. The ROC sought to ensure that military education includes the formulation of a religious worldview among the servicemen,[118] so when in 2001 the government approved a five-year program for citizens' patriotic upbringing it came in handy. The program obliged the MoD and the ROC to conduct conferences on church-military cooperation and to publish educational manuals for the spiritual-moral upbringing of the servicemen and predraft youth. The titles of the conferences and of the manuals speak for themselves.[119] The central event providing the impetus for catechization activities during the year became the annual Christmas educational readings, conducted since 2000 at the GS Academy. It brings together the clergy and the military, and the ROC hierarchy presents its position on internal and foreign policy, ideology, upbringing, and education.[120]

As the military's catechization progressed, a need emerged to share and develop knowledge. Since 2003, the ROC and the military have conducted educational-methodological seminars-gatherings of the clergy that, on a voluntary basis (*na vneshtatnoi osnove*), have provided pastoral care to the military and their families all over Russia. The patriarch and Metropolitan Kirill, curator of this enterprise, viewed these gatherings (*sbory voennogo dukhovenstva*) as preparation of the prospective military clergy cadre.[121] The most intensely churched corps and military educational institutions hosted the first three gatherings in 2005: the Ryazan Institute of the Airborne Troops, the GS Academy and the RVSN, and the LRA.[122] In 2006 the fourth gathering was held at the Baltic Fleet, within the eparchy headed by Kirill. Following the event, Kirill and the commander of the Baltic Fleet signed a bilateral cooperation agreement.[123] Similar agreements between local metropolitans and commanders of military districts, fleets, corps, and units became a common practice.

To educate the clerics working with the military and provide them with literature tailor-made for their flock, the ROC published several edited volumes: *Faith and Fidelity* (2005), *The Christ-Loving Warriors: Orthodox Tradition in the Russian Military* (2006), and *Science of Victory: For Faith and Fatherland* (2008).[124] The books promoted a set of interrelated arguments: the cooperation between the church and the military has been a centuries-long tradition; the Orthodox faith has been a force multiplier, an equalizer as regards material inferiority, and an assurance of victory in the Slavic, Russian, and Soviet military traditions; and in the information technology (IT) era, pastoral care to uphold the patriotic-moral stamina of the military is indispensable.[125] In 2006 professors of the RVSN Academy's FOC together with RVSN priests compiled a manual for the military pedagogues titled *Military*

Didactics.[126] Published by the MoD official press, the book instructed on how to formulate the moral, spiritual, and religious values of the students and provided methodological insights for catechization within the military institutions.[127]

Although catechization took a relative leap forward, the situation in the military still did not meet the ROC's expectations; genuine religiosity among the servicemen was low. According to a 2010 MoD study, 84 percent of the servicemen qualified themselves as Orthodox, and 80 percent of them were baptized, but only half were practicing Christians. The highest rate of those who considered themselves religious was among the junior officers (69 percent) and the lowest among the senior officers (56 percent). Based on this data, the MoD instructed educational work organs and the commanders' assistants for work with the faithful to further formulate among the servicemen high spiritual-moral qualities in the interest of the combat abilities of the troops.[128]

Third, and finally, the ROC intensified its PR efforts to ensure broad support for the revival of the military clergy. Besides promoting his vision to the top leaders, Kirill cultivated among the senior and mid-level commanders at least a readiness to explore the subject. He linked the reintroduction of the military clergy to two important issues preoccupying society and the military during the mid-2000s. First, as the issue of dedovschina was becoming more prominent, Kirill presented the military clergy as a potential remedy for this civil-military disease. He argued that any dealing with dedovschina disconnected from the spiritual-moral foundations was doomed to failure. He was effective enough to establish this linkage even in the Russian bureaucratic consciousness. In 2006, when another tragedy at the Chelyabinsk armor school brought dedovschina to the fore of public debate, the chief military prosecutor submitted a proposal for a law on the military clergy that, according to him, would "strengthen discipline, increase patriotism, and solve the dedovschina problem." The Parliament rejected the proposal, but Kirill continued his campaign on all possible fronts. In 2006 Putin qualified the presence of religion in the military as being constructive and positive, and he advised elaborating on the pre-Soviet and foreign experience in this field. With this clear signal on the subject, the opposition to Kirill began to vanish.[129]

Second, to prepare a positive professional climate, the ROC activated its allies within the military. As Kirill began turning the renaissance of the military clergy into an organic part of the military reform,[130] senior brass began publishing in professional periodicals about the positive experience of the church-military cooperation in the ancient Russian, tsarist, and post-Soviet eras.[131] A steady stream of articles, including by experts from the GS think tank, called for an association with the ROC, to maintain the spiritual-moral aspects of the reform.[132] The discussion evolved against the backdrop of the introduction of the term *national security* into the Russian military lexicon. The articles argued that in light of the changing character of warfare, with soft, cultural, and informational aspects of national security looming ever larger, the importance of moral-patriotic education was heightened.[133]

As one of the GS officers put it, when IT turns a soldier "from a simple screw in the military machine" into an "intellectual reconnaissance-strike complex," his "spirituality becomes more significant." According to the author, once an operator had enjoyed the support and had been under the control, virtual and actual, of his commander and comrades. But now, due to the advancement of IT, he is left entirely to his own devices. "A momentary weakness and hesitation, resulting from faintheartedness—and the enemy will destroy the soldier and his entire unit. Only perfect psychological stability, based on the greatest sense of patriotism, which is a necessary part of spirituality, may ensure victory."[134] The author emphasized the importance of spiritual-moral motivation and education in the era of asymmetrical warfare, when strategists aim at the informational-psychological destruction of the enemy. Obviously, in such a zeitgeist, the reintroduction of the military clergy emerged as a desirable enterprise, and the ROC's position resonated with the expectations of the military seeking to boost the moral motivation of the servicemen as the reform intensified.[135]

Moreover, Kirill argued that without military clergy, the armed forces were exposed to the missionary efforts of foreign denominations. These were presented as subversive "efforts to weaken the morale-psychological state of the military personnel, to reset its motivational foundations, and by so doing to influence the combat readiness of the Russian military."[136] The words of a senior officer from the Main Educational Work Directorate well illustrate this:

> The growing importance of spiritual security relates to the active Russian political effort to formulate a multipolar world order. According to the National Security Concept, the Russian Federation is determined to systematically defend its cultural and religious identity. [. . .] Analysis of the religious situation in Russia, in the context of international relations, demonstrates that Western countries led by the USA purposefully stimulate a destructive phenomenon in Russian religious life. The driver of such efforts is clear— the U.S. aspiration to build a unipolar world.[137]

The cumulative effect of the above three efforts—churching, catechization, and the PR campaign—yielded the desired result in 2009. Kirill, by then already patriarch, sent, as the leader of the Inter-religious Council of Russia, a letter to the president suggesting that the institution of the military clergy be restored.[138] On 21 July 2009, President Medvedev approved the recommendation and ordered its establishment. The main arguments outlined in the patriarch's document referred to the successful cooperation with the armed forces for over a decade. Directly in relation to the nuclear triad, he argued that "realization of this decision will make it possible to increase the psychological stability of the servicemen, especially in the detachments under permanent combat readiness and also those actually performing real combat missions." According to the president's decision, the Department of the Work with Faithful Among Military Servicemen became part of the Main Educational Work Directorate (also known as the Work with the Personnel Directorate). The new body became the main vehicle for realization of the presidential decision in the coming years.[139]

CHAPTER 6

FAITH-NUCLEAR NEXUS

NUCLEAR INDUSTRY

When the nuclear industry, like the entire country, rose from its knees, it began paying the ROC back for the safety net provided in the 1990s. This was a genuine thankfulness mixed with a reverence for the political line, which increasingly co-opted religion for the sake of national enterprises. The boost in the nuclear-church bonding during that period owes a lot to Sergei Kirienko, the presidential envoy to the Volga Federal District (2001–5) and the head of the Russian State Atomic Energy Corporation (ROSATOM) (2005–16). Kirienko's proximity to Putin stemmed from his being a classical type of Russian state servant (*gosudarev chelovek*)—a patriotic technocrat able to switch to liberal or conservative in the interest of the higher cause. In addition, both shared a growing affection for the faith and an interest in Asian martial arts, and in the late 1990s, for a short while, Putin, as the head of the FSB, was even subordinate to Kirienko, then prime minister.[1]

The pro-religious climate emerging under the new president was immediately relevant to Kirienko, as his federal district included the city of Sarov, which in addition to being the heart of the nuclear weapons industry was turning into an important national religious center. As presidential envoy, he was about to host the 2003 celebrations of the one hundredth anniversary of Seraphim's canonization. The expected participation of Putin and the patriarch turned it into a major national event, and Kirienko became the central organizer of the festivities. The government established a special organizing committee headed by Kirienko and Metropolitan Filaret, which included the deputy ministers of finance, economic development, culture, and transportation, as well as several governors and Parliament members. It was probably the first time in modern Russia that such high-level government figures were working for the sake of the joint state-church venture on such a scale. Since the main ceremonies were planned to occur within the Seraphim church in the city of Sarov, which the patriarch would consecrate in the presence of the president, Radii Il'kaev, the VNIIEF head, became the main figure on the ground.[2]

Kirienko overviewed the event's contents, budget, logistics, and accommodation of pilgrims and coordinated among the federal and regional administrations, the ROC, the VNIIEF, and the local business sponsors.[3] Toward the celebrations, the ROC reacquired the building of the church that had been constructed over Seraphim's cell and consecrated during the 1903 canonization, in which since 1949 the city theater had resided. The plan was to prepare the church for full religious functioning and to reconsecrate it during the festivities. In 2001 the theater was given a new building, and Kirienko, the city administration, the VNIIEF, and the local metropolitan began a restoration of the temple. The aid coming from state enterprises and private companies included the bell gable. The biggest of the eight bells, of four tons' weight, was a personal donation from Putin. Within a year the temple had new golden domes.[4] In January 2003, the cross replaced the TV antenna over the renovated church, and in April the permanent priest arrived from Moscow. During Easter, the iconostasis and the interior were decorated.[5]

In summer 2003, the celebrations began with great fanfare. Hierarchs and senior clergy from fifteen world Orthodox churches arrived. A procession of about fifty thousand people brought the reliquary with the relics of Seraphim from Diveevo to the Sarov church, where they had originally been kept.[6] The patriarch and the president awaited them at the entrance. The setting of the event emphasized the church-state nature of the celebrations, highlighting the parallel with the 1903 experience. Commentators underscored the fact that Seraphim had been canonized on Tsar Nikolai's initiative, thus ensuring resonance with the role of Putin.[7] After consecrating the church, both the patriarch and the president conducted a supplication service in front of the saint's remains, exactly as the tsar and the metropolitan of Moscow had done in 1903. Then both addressed the audience.[8] In his speech, the patriarch linked the two canonizations and emphasized the continuity of history.[9] Evoking the same parallel, Putin, who was still establishing his status as a national leader, presented the patriarch with a lithograph depicting Tsar Nikolai during the 1903 canonization.[10] Putin's speech praised Seraphim's deeds as a prominent example of service to God and the Russian people and Fatherland and stressed that the celebrations had become possible thanks to the revival of the religious and spiritual liberties in Russia.[11]

Putin's visit to the VNIIEF, the first ever, followed the service at Seraphim's church. This coincided with the reorganization of the nuclear complex from the ministry to a state corporation, which made the future somewhat uncertain again for the seniors of the nuclear industry. Although Putin came from the *siloviki*,[12] he was not particularly close to the nuclear field, and the industry was unsure to what extent he was going to maintain the pronuclear momentum that had emerged under Yeltsin. The tone and content of Putin's remarks at the closed meeting with nuclear weapons designers allayed their apprehensions. He called the VNIIEF "a center of strategic importance" for Russia, for which "nuclear weapons have been and still are the foundation of our security," and he asked for an outline of the industry's problems.[13]

The issues raised by the industry seniors related to weapons' modernization under the CTBT, financial support, and the organizational future. Putin reassured them "that under any reorganization, whatever transformations the MINATOM [Ministry of Nuclear Affairs] goes through, the [nuclear weapons] complex will stay intact."[14] He praised the safety, security, and R&D level of the nuclear weapons despite the previous difficult circumstances, emphasized that the arsenal should be effective under various operational scenarios, probably in reference to the modernization of strategic and nonstrategic weapons, and assured them that "Russia should and would stay a great nuclear power."[15] According to Il'kaev,

Putin's visit communicated to all that "our Orthodox tradition, Russian science, and the Motherland's defense are not phenomena strange to each other, but interwoven."[16] The ROC, as the main facilitator, claimed credit again for delivering the president, as it had for saving the industry in the 1990s.

Following the 2003–4 celebrations, the organizing committee was not dismantled but institutionalized itself in 2005 as the Fund of St. Seraphim Sarovsky.[17] A coproduction of clergy, the Sarov authorities, and ROSATOM seniors, the fund became one of the main facilitators of the faith-nuclear nexus in the following years. Its goals included commemoration of the saint's heritage; revival and popularization of Orthodox values though pilgrimage, missionary activity, and catechization; and consolidation around them of the scientific community and Russian society. Kirienko headed the board of trustees, which included Il'kaev, and the local metropolitan led the executive committee, with a ROSATOM senior as his deputy.[18] Kirienko's initiatives at the federal district perfectly coincided with the fund's agenda. In 2005, exploiting his power as presidential envoy, he began "restoring historical justice"—returned the rare icons from the regional museums to the local parishes, and intensified restitution of church property and the restoration of the Diveevo and Sarov Monasteries.[19]

When in the same year Kirienko was nominated to head ROSATOM (a reincarnation of MINATOM), the ROC and the VNIIEF could not have wished for a better choice. The patriarch personally congratulated the new nuclear minister, not concealing his delight with Kirienko's attention to the religious aspects of Russia's political and social life.[20] There had been cooperation between the nuclear complex and the ROC before Kirienko, but it now received the strongest impetus from the top. As part of the zeitgeist, big business and state corporations were expected to support the pro-religious policies of the Kremlin, and Kirienko did exactly that in his new professional eparchy. Riding the economic boom, ROSATOM initiated huge nuclear energy projects all over Russia.[21] Many of the new installations acquired religious attributes, such as chapels next to the new reactor blocks or nuclear power stations, icons hanging above the emergency buttons of the reactor's control panel,[22] and patronage and restoration of the churches of the eparchies on whose territory the nuclear energy stations were located.[23] According to the director of the Rostov Nuclear Station, Kirienko's explicit intent "to construct a new temple with every new block of the nuclear station" accelerated construction.[24] Kirienko promoted the faith-atoms nexus also abroad, for example, in Iran and Brazil.[25]

In 2006 Kirienko urged the construction of new churches in the closed nuclear cities. He saw this as ROSATOM's operational task, aimed at ensuring the spiritual security of the nuclear experts.[26] Facilitated by the St. Seraphim Fund, restoration of the John the Baptist church and of the Blizhniaia Pustyn'ka church, and construction of a special installation over St Seraphim's tomb, all of them on the territory of the closed city and within the VNIIEF, began.[27] Responding to a question about whether the monastery's reopening would disturb the top-secret work, Kirienko, who since 2003 had been the organizer and patron as well as a pilgrim to the Sarov-Diveevo celebrations,[28] emphasized the national-level significance of Sarov—a location that encapsulates Russia's spiritual power and its strategic prowess.[29] According to him, the proximity of the state's spiritual and security centers was not coincidental. "The monastery life and the activities of the VNIIEF demand seclusion and a lack of vanity. Thus, the revival of the Sarov Monastery will not disturb the work of the nuclear center."[30] In 2006, in recognition of Kirienko's contribution to the revival of the saint's heritage, the patriarch awarded him the Order of Seraphim Sarovsky.[31] In 2008 ROSATOM allocated about USD 4 million for restoration of the Kazan Cathedral in the Diveevo Monastery and construction of a hotel for the growing number of pilgrims.[32] In parallel, work had been progressing in Sarov to remove all of the nuclear center's installations beyond the monastery walls.[33]

Against the backdrop of the strong impetus from the top, individual religiosity grew slowly but steadily among the industry experts and the residents of the closed cities. The conversion of Viktor Mikhailov, MINATOM head until the late 1990s, was indicative of the general attitude within the industry. In 2000, after handing over the ministry to his successor, Mikhailov moved back to the VNIIEF, became its honorary scientific director, and led the Institute of Strategic Stability—an internal think tank exploring strategic aspects of nuclear weapons. A confirmed Soviet atheist, Mikhailov, as one of the main beneficiaries of the cooperation with the ROC during the time of troubles, incrementally developed a personal sentiment toward the faith. At first, this was mainly about returning favors through administrative support—helping the ROC to reacquire, restore, and construct temples in Diveevo, Sarov, and Sanaksarsk.[34] In time, his attitude became more personal. In 2004 he presented a richly decorated icon of Seraphim Sarovsky, which he had received as a minister, to the monastery, and he shared publicly for the first time his memory of being baptized as a child. In the same year, he argued for the first time that Sarov was a holy place and that the "creation of the nuclear weapons there was not accidental," since "defense of the Motherland is a holy deed."[35]

The 2008 edition of his memoir, *I Am a Hawk*, revealed the metamorphosis he had undergone. In contrast to the previous editions, the introduction discussed the religious history of Sarov and St. Seraphim, the centrality of the place to the Orthodox faith, the symbolism of God's choice to locate the heart of the Soviet nuclear project there, the restoration of sacred sites, and the revival of religious consciousness in Russia. He emphasized the symbolism of the tsar leading the 1903 canonization and the president and patriarch co-leading its hundredth-anniversary commemoration, praised Putin's meeting with the VNIIEF, and dubbed its experts "pious angels of fire" and Christ-loving warriors. The same edition also for the first time featured on its cover the nineteenth-century gravure depicting the cross procession at Sarov.[36] When Mikhailov passed away in 2011, the patriarch and the Nizhni Novgorod metropolitan sent condolences and expressed appreciation for his contributions to the nuclear complex, cooperation with the ROC, and revival of Sarov's religious life.[37]

Supported from the top, the conversion of the nuclear complex reached a remarkable scale. In 2009, toward the celebrations of the Soviet nuclear test anniversary, ROSATOM and the Russian Federal Archive arranged an exhibition presenting a history of the Soviet nuclear weapons program. Kirienko headed the organizing committee, which included the VNIIEF head, leading Russian nuclear physicists, historians, and the archiepiscop of Nizhni Novgorod.[38] Several historical essays and declassified archival materials of the exhibition, titled *Atomic Project of the USSR: Sixty Years of Russia's Nuclear Shield*, were published as a book-catalog.[39] The archiepiscop's introductory essay followed welcoming notes by the heads of ROSATOM and the Federal Archive, promoting the already widespread mantra about the role of Seraphim in the Soviet nuclear project. Given such recognition in the addresses by the nuclear minister and chief state archivist, it acquired almost official status and as such was indicative of the faith-atoms bond:

> Remarkable scientists, engineers, and technicians have been creating the most formidable weapon in the famous monastery, where a hundred years before the hermit saint Seraphim labored. There, where this God's pleasurer taught about the Holy Spirit and forecasted the destinies of Russia, the nuclear shield, which stopped the aggressive aspirations of the Fatherland's adversaries, was created. Sarov, which once used to be the center of Russian monkhood, became the capital of Russian science and weaponry.[40]

The archiepiscop's contribution was not limited to words of welcome. His piece, "St. Seraphim and Nuclear Weapons," was the first of several historical essays followed by a collection of primary sources. Its place as the opening chapter highlighted the ROC's role, and its contents gave a tone to the volume and the exhibition and as such are noteworthy. The essay began by interpreting the verse from the St. Seraphim akathist—"Be joyful, shield and wall our Fatherland." The archbishop drew a parallel between the saint, whom the akathist presents as defending Russia by the power of his holiness, and the atomic weapons, featured in the title of the exhibition as the nuclear shield protecting Russia. The following paragraph argued that the inception of the Russian nuclear shield in the holy land of Sarov was divine predestination and claimed that as long as these weapons defend Russia and Orthodoxy they are moral and blessed.[41]

> Until a certain moment only American Los Alamos possessed nuclear secrets. Japan learned how easily a singly owned nuclear weapon can be employed. However, from the moment that Sarov stood up to Los Alamos, the endless fear turned into a balance of fear. [. . .] Maybe mutual nuclear

deterrence was given to the world as a unique chance to save itself from annihilation? [. . .] Naturally, the end of the nuclear monopoly was laid down here, in Sarov, in the cell of Father Seraphim, who commanded the faithful to seek a peaceful spirit. If St. Seraphim had not allowed the atomic bomb to be created, no nuclear center would be here. This point of view is not surprising anymore. Nuclear experts today directly relate the words from St. Seraphim's akathist to the obvious circumstance, that in the 1940s they started their difficult labor not elsewhere but exactly within the walls of the Sarov Monastery. Their secret labor is reminiscent of the spiritual retreat of the hermit-monks in their cells. Today, they often recall that the word "Seraphim" in Hebrew means "the burning" and see the great saint as a patron of nuclear scientists.[42]

The archiepiscop also noted that it was the ROC that in the 1990s urged the then "weak state to adopt a responsible attitude to preservation of the nuclear weapons complex," and he gave his assurance that St. Seraphim Sarovsky would continue to guard, bless, and assist the industry.[43] The last pages of the essay featured extracts from Patriarch Alexey's statement at the 1996 conference "Nuclear Weapons and Russian National Security," which positioned the ROC as a staunch supporter of the nuclear weapons complex and promoter of its interests among the leadership and public.[44] The essay straightforwardly communicated that divine intervention was involved in the inception of the Soviet nuclear project and that the ROC became the guardian angel of the nuclear weapons complex during the post-Soviet times of trouble and now provided pastoral care to its leaders. A picture of Metropolitan Kirill, who in 2009 was already designated as the next patriarch, illustrated the concluding note. The exhibition traveled for two years between cities related to the nuclear industry.[45] The celebrations of the anniversary were followed by a photographic exhibition organized by the VNIIEF at the Russian Parliament. Titled *The Land of Sarov—Custodian of Russia's Greatness*, it covered two themes: the history of the VNIIEF and the life and spiritual deeds of St. Seraphim.[46]

Toward the decade's end, in parallel with the introduction of Orthodox education in the secondary schools, the ROC expanded its missionary work at the higher education and scientific institutions, in particular in the nuclear sphere. As part of the restitution of the ROC's property, it was given back churches on the territory of the nuclear scientific centers. After their restoration, it tried to turn them into the house churches. This trend gathered momentum under Kirienko.[47] The story of the Moscow Engineering Physics Institute (MIFI)—the primary alma mater of the nuclear industry's cadre and an umbrella for all ROSATOM scientific-educational institutions across Russia—is indicative. Since 2004, a priest of the rank of protoierei began providing permanent pastoral care to the Orthodox professors and students of MIFI. In 2005 Patriarch Alexey blessed the rector's request for a house church to commemorate the fathers of the nuclear weapons project.[48]

In 2010, in the presence of the MIFI rector, the ROSATOM deputy head, and senior clerics, Patriarch Kirill consecrated the church at MIFI's main building.[49] Then, MIFI's scientific council granted Patriarch Kirill an honorary doctorate degree, for active efforts to spread Orthodox education among the closed cities' youth. In response, Kirill spoke about the role of science and religion in contemporary Russia and presented the decision to open the church not as "part of the fashionable trend, as some have tried to depict it," but as the reflection of a genuine quest for religiosity.[50] In parallel, a big wayside cross was erected in MIFI's central square. Symbolically, it replaced the abstract sculpture nicknamed "the eternal student," epitomizing the MIFI students' long-standing motto.[51] According to the official version, the cross commemorated the MIFI graduates and experts who "[fell] in the battles for the creation of the Motherland's nuclear shield."[52]

The churching of science, nuclear physics in particular, became such a major trend that it generated a wave of counterreaction.[53] In 2007 ten members of the Russian Academy of Sciences, more than half of them physicists, including two Nobel Prize winners, sent an open letter to the president, protesting the ROC's massive intervention in science, state educational policy, and public affairs. However, the initiative had limited, if any, impact. Both the senior clergy and pro-ROC academics, including the head of the Russian Academy of Sciences and the director of the VNIIEF, as well as Orthodox public activists and NGOs, initiated such a wide countercampaign that together with the silent support of the state it totally neutralized the "Letter of Ten."[54] In 2012 the Ministry of Education and Science would include the subject Foundations of Religious Culture and Secular Ethics in the school curriculum, and in 2015 it would approve Theology as a new scientific discipline.[55]

The ROC, which was gradually becoming one of the main pillars of the Kremlin's new ideology, continued to co-opt ROSATOM in its ideological activities. In 2010 the Orthodox Initiative, a grants competition begun by the St. Seraphim Sarovsky Fund, gathered such momentum in Russia that it transformed into a new and higher-ranking structure—the Coordination Committee for Encouraging Social, Educational, and Informational Initiatives, under the auspices of the ROC. Headed by the patriarch himself and with the head of ROSATOM as its executive director, the committee's main aim is to support initiatives that consolidate civil society on the basis of the traditional Orthodox values, through the annual allocation of grants. The committee has established missions in all the Russian regions and also in several former Soviet republics, in this way extending the Kremlin's effort to forge a new national identity.[56]

By the end of the decade, when public critique increased regarding the teaching of Orthodox culture at school, the restitution of property to the ROC, its position on exhibitions and performances, and the reintroduction of the military clergy, the ROC initiated several projects aimed at improving its social image. Seniors from the nuclear industry, which by that time benefited from strong public and political support, were always at the bridgehead of these efforts. In August 2010, the patriarch invited about forty leading figures from Russian arts, sports, and science to join the Council on Culture, aimed at establishing a dialogue with the public-cultural elite about the desired directions of the spiritual-intellectual development of the society and national culture. The head of the Sretensky Monastery, Archimandrite Tikhon, became the secretary of the council. The only scientist to serve on the council was Il'kaev, VNI-IEF's scientific director.[57]

STRATEGIC MISSION MISSILE FORCES (RVSN)
In the early 2000s, an intensive rejuvenation of the nuclear triad started. The ground leg—the RVSN—led in terms of both arsenal moderniza-

tion and conversion to faith. Toward the end of the decade, the construction of churches, pastoral care of the troops, and initialization of the annual cycle of religious rituals made it the most churched service within the nuclear triad. According to Patriarch Kirill, the uninterrupted support of the RVSN Military Council made it possible by 2006 to construct all the churches and chapels that were planned in the bases, garrisons, and testing ranges and to open Sunday schools and Orthodox military-patriotic clubs for youth.[58] Although exact numbers are unavailable, the situation in Vlasikha, the Main Staff garrison, may be indicative of the general trend within the bases and closed cities.

By mid-decade, the clergy of the Vlasikha garrison church included a protoierei, three priests, and a deacon—an RVSN major (and former Communist) who voluntarily undertook ecclesiastical obligations when not on duty at the Main Staff.[59] Allegedly, up to three hundred officers and soldiers regularly attended the services at the temple, dubbed within the congregation, and on its website, as the "RVSN Cathedral." In 2005 its assigned temple opened in the RVSN hospital.[60] The cathedral's compound became a catechization center of the servicemen and their families. The priests conducted conversations on religion, history, church-military cooperation, and current social-political issues.[61] In parallel, the Orthodox Sunday school and the "Iliia Muromets" patriotic club for youth "opened for officers' children.[62] Officers' wives, guided by the clergy, taught at the school; the church master, a retired colonel who had served in the RVSN security troops, headed the club.[63] It combined the teaching of military and Orthodox history with basic military preparation, under the title of "Primary Orthodox Military Training."[64] Out of six hundred youngsters who have attended it since its establishment, about a hundred joined the officers' corps.[65] Unsurprisingly, at the end of the decade icons were placed over the desks and computers of the junior commanders in the Main Staff,[66] and to the municipal heraldic emblem the city council added St. Varvara, heavenly patroness of the RVSN, holding a sword in one arm and a temple in the other.[67]

By mid-decade, in almost all the RVSN divisions and armies, in line with the cooperation agreements with local eparchies, priests were providing "permanent pastoral care to missile regiments deployed in their canonic territories." Thus, according to the patriarch, the RVSN already then developed a solid basis for the introduction of the military priests.[68] The main tendency during the decade was the extension of the systematic clerical and churching activities from the main garrisons and headquarters to the lower, tactical-operational levels of command. As different missile armies indicate, the ROC and the RVSN were busy streamlining their chains of command, as the clergy in eparchies, *blagochiniia*,[69] and parishes escorted missile armies, divisions, and regiments. Where there was no garrison church with a permanent cleric, pastoral work was conducted by assigning the missile units to the nearby parishes. Thus, several churches took care of one division or opened small praying rooms within its regiments.[70]

By 2008 almost all of the RVSN units either had permanent local pastors within the eparchies or received pastoral care through regular clergy visits from the RVSN section of the Synodal Department. Father Mikhail, the main nuclear priest, paid monthly pastoral trips to different divisions, thus covering annually several armies deployed all over Russia. He and other priests participated in the meetings dedicated to disciplinary issues and took an active part in socializing new draftees entering the corps. According to Father Mikhail, back then, when the national idea was still being crystallized and was not clear to all, the priests offered a motivational explanation for why recruits should volunteer for military service.[71]

When toward the end of the decade the intercontinental ballistic missile (ICBM) tests and exercises intensified, clergy began participating in the launches and conducting pastoral conversations with the mobile units during the patrol breaks (often deep in the forests) and with the missile silo operators in their underground modules. Among his pastoral missions, Father Mikhail included struggling with soldiers' acedia—apathetic listlessness leading to negligence—one of the deadly Christian sins. He sought to cultivate soldiers' desire "to carry their heavy cross, important for all of us, and soul-saving for each of them."[72] Calling for the consecration of every launch, he argued that only highly spiritual-moral people, who understood the consequences of their actions, should serve in the RVSN.[73] Although educational officers within the units served as liaisons, until the official introduction of the military clergy, all of these activities, even according to the main RVSN pastor, were somewhat illegal.[74]

During the decade, a cycle of ROC-RVSN joint rituals emerged. The annual Orthodox-nuclear calendar comprised three main celebrations: commemoration of the RVSN Academy's establishment on 4 December, the RVSN corps' patroness saint's day on 17 December, and the graduation ceremony of the RVSN Academy's FOC around Easter in spring. The first event begins with a joint supplication service at the Kremlin's Uspensky Cathedral, which the patriarch leads, assisted by the Synodal Department head, with the RVSN senior officers and academy cadets attending. Following the service, which coincides with one of the twelve main Orthodox holidays, the Entry of the Mother of God into the Temple, the patriarch offers pastoral words to the RVSN, linking operational and spiritual aspects of the nuclear service.[75] As he said in one of the ceremonies: "Next to such a formidable weapon should be not only a person excelling in education, upbringing, strength, discipline, and willpower, but also a person full of responsibility in the face of God. In your labor there can be such moments when no knowledge, no will or strength will be sufficient to make the right decision. But if God will be with you, you will never make fatal mistakes."[76]

After the supplication service, the celebrations move to the academy— the main incubator of the nuclear missileers. The RVSN commander, with the corps' seniors behind him, personally greets the patriarch at the entrance and escorts him inside. The event usually turns into a conference of the seniors from the nuclear triad and industry. The patriarch's speech is followed by professional reports, and then the military and clergy bestow medals and exchange gifts.[77] For example, in 2009, when the RVSN commander outlined the growing importance of the corps in Russian national security and elaborated on how they might be employed, the patriarch praised "the labor of the missileers maintaining strategic parity." He emphasized "the sacrificial nature of the service among the current generation of missileers," in reference to the previous hardships, and insisted that "missile weapons should be in clean hands," in reference to the ROC's indispensable role in the Russian nuclear buildup and employment.[78]

The second event is the most important RVSN annual nuclear-religious holiday—the day of the corps' establishment and of its patroness saint. The patriarch either conducts a supplication service in the main Russian church, Christ the Savior Cathedral in Moscow, or comes to the Main Staff in Vlasikha to lead the service at the RVSN cathedral. The RVSN commander, wearing parade uniform but without a peaked cap (contrary to military tradition but in keeping with Orthodox rite), greets the patriarch on the stairs of the temple and presents him with a bouquet of white roses. A female officer offers him bread and salt, while the garrison is drawn up in formation in front of the temple. Following the service, in praise of the corps' patroness saint, the patriarch addresses the assembled RVSN officers, soldiers, and veterans.[79]

In the first part of the decade, when the state was still unable to fully provide for the corps and their families, the patriarch usually took the opportunity to encourage the corps, which during difficult times had shown itself to be "a school of moral bravery and patriotic loyalty," and praised its spiritual-moral climate, which had "the most positive influence on all aspects of RVSN life and activities." The RVSN commander would respond: "Thanks to the patronage of the martyr St. Varvara and the spiritual support of the ROC, led by Your Holiness, the Strategic Rocket Forces have successfully accomplished all their missions during this year." The ceremony usually concluded with the bestowal of medals on officers and clergy.[80]

Toward the end of the decade, when the problems had subsided and the missions of the nuclear component became very central, the emphasis changed accordingly. The patriarch's address during the 2010 celebrations resonated with the Kremlin's messages of the same time: "Speaking of the RVSN, I would like to emphasize that this very corps is the main deterrent power of Russia. Thanks to the prowess that this corps possesses, Russia—which went through unprecedented destruction of its state life at the end of the twentieth century, unprecedented human losses during peacetime—has been protected. Thanks to these troops, which hold the shield and the sword of enormous force, our country has preserved great power status."[81]

After becoming patriarch, Kirill, in contrast to his predecessor, began inviting the RVSN High Command to conduct this annual ceremony not in the RVSN cathedral in Vlasikha but at Christ the Savior Cathedral in Moscow.[82] In keeping with the growing role of nuclear weapons, this gave the ceremony higher visibility and elevated the corps' status. No less importantly, however, it made the patriarch the host of the ceremony. The RVSN commander coming to him, and not the other way around, demonstrated the special but not symmetrical relationship between the pastor and his flock.

The third main annual event—the graduation of the FOC's distinguished students—takes place at the Kremlin's Uspensky Cathedral, always on Easter Monday, the second day of the Orthodox Bright Week.[83] The ceremony starts with a procession of the graduates carrying religious banners and icons around the temple, followed by the liturgy dedicated to the event and led by the patriarch. Kirill personally hands the diplomas to the graduates after they have received his and the dean's blessings and kissed the cross. By the middle of the decade, the FOC had graduated about twelve hundred servicemen, among them five generals, ninety-five senior officers, and more than four hundred junior officers. In ten years, the number of graduates would reach three thousand, many of them serving as educational officers in the nuclear triad.[84] Others, with direct combat duties, functioned as nonofficial assistants of the commanders for the work with religious soldiers, assistants to the clerics in the garrison churches, and Sunday school teachers.[85] Some of them, upon retirement, became priests at the RVSN garrison churches.[86] In 2010, for reviving the institution of the military clergy, the scientific council of the RVSN Academy awarded the patriarch the rank of honorary professor.[87]

The above nuclear-Orthodox holidays are supplemented by all sorts of activities at the RVSN bases, including baptizing conscripts at the garrison churches, counseling conscripts with problematic behavior and social backgrounds, joint celebrations of units' anniversaries, supplication services on the commemoration days of heavenly patrons, an oath of allegiance, the arrival of the junior officers to the RVSN after graduation, and excursions to patriotic-historical places and pilgrimage to sacred sites.[88] By the end of the decade, academy priests were conducting supplication services during official ceremonies of the school year opening, graduation, and the oath of allegiance.[89] Granting religious medals and saints' remains to the military became a norm.[90] Similar rituals extended to the Rostov and Serpukhov Military Institutes, regional bodies that prepared officers in addition to the RVSN Academy and that also opened

FOCs.[91] Local eparchies organized seminars for the educational officers working in the RVSN higher education bodies.[92] In addition to the two national military holidays, joint celebrations of the main Orthodox feasts became routine.[93] Every Christmas in the RVSN Main Staff, most of the officers and soldiers, from generals to the rank and file, participate in the traditional "Jordan bathing" ceremony led by the corps' priest.[94] On Easter, whole companies arrive at the garrison church for the liturgy, procession of the cross, and consecration of eggs and bread.[95]

It is difficult to assess exactly the impact of the rituals, pastoral care, and catechization efforts on the RVSN during this decade. In the words of Father Mikhail, the catechization and religiosity of the officers evolved incrementally. First they started to wear the cross, then they came to the services and observed the holidays, and then they began consecrating combat duties, new missiles, test launches and exercises, and the units operating all of the above.[96] This undoubtedly shaped and framed a state of mind in a certain way across the entire chain of command. By the end of the decade, supplication services at the beginning of exercises appeared for the first time.[97] In 2008 the RVSN general saw a positive impact of the pastoral work on discipline and the corps' overall state of combat readiness.[98] As the RVSN deputy commander for armaments put it in 2010: "The Russian army can't fully function and conduct its combat tasks without Orthodox faith. [. . .] The priest of our church in Vlasikha, Father Mikhail, always tells us: the good should be with feasts. God commanded: 'Do not kill,' however when there is a clear choice between the freedom and independence of your people and the aggressor's death, the soldier opts for the latter. His duty is blessed by the ROC."[99]

LONG RANGE AVIATION (LRA)

Like the other nuclear services, thanks to the growing funding and political attention, the LRA revived during the decade. In 2001, for the first time since 1991, it flew over the North Pole, renewed search and reconnaissance missions of the air carrier groups, and reintroduced regular staff exercises in training for deployment from the main to the operational bases. In 2002 pilots began to train in refueling in air, and the next year two Tu-160s and four Tu-95MSs conducted a sortie over the Indian

Ocean. By mid-decade the exercises intensified,[100] and in 2007, for the first time since the Soviet collapse, the average annual flight time of the pilots exceeded eighty hours, and it almost doubled the following year.[101] This rise in combat training culminated in 2008 when the LRA conducted nuclear missile launches (using conventional munitions), the first training of its kind, during an overflight to Venezuela.[102] Long-range patrols outside Russia became routine. The dramatic increase in combat activity coincided with the boost in conversion. Like the other services, the LRA undertook construction of the churches in its garrisons, de facto institutionalized the military priesthood even before its official introduction, intensified catechization activities, and invented its own religious-professional rituals and sacred relics. The relatively small size of the service, the smallest leg of the nuclear triad, and the centrality of its main priest within the ROC's hierarchy enabled it by the end of the decade to catch up with the conversion of the RVSN—the initial leader of nuclear Orthodoxy.

Father Konstantin based his proselytization tactics on a familiarity with the organizational culture of the service. He concentrated his conversion efforts on senior officers, on the assumption that if the LRA commander and command became practicing Orthodox, their subordinates would quickly emulate them.[103] This tactic proved effective. As one of the priests put it, when the LRA commanders became the avant-garde of the faithful, their subordinates adjusted themselves accordingly and began visiting churches, attending services, and adopting rituals.[104] The subordinates had been aware of the conversion from the beginning of the decade, when the LRA commander won approval for the service's long-sought temple in Moscow's center. In 2000 Patriarch Alexey gave his blessing for the construction of the chapel-memorial of St. Iliia, the patron saint of the service, at the LRA Main Staff.

In two years the chapel was completed, and the patriarch came to consecrate it during the LRA's ninetieth-anniversary celebrations. The Air Force (AF) deputy commander and the full LRA Military Council participated in the ceremony, co-led by the patriarch and the LRA commander. The complex included the chapel, the hall of the fallen aviators, and the LRA museum.[105] The chapel's decoration corresponded with the

LRA's professional ethos. At the center of the iconostasis was the Holy Trinity. On one side of it, the big icon depicted the biblical episode of the whirlwind lifting of the prophet Elijah into the sky in a chariot of fire. The other side featured the major Russian military saints, St. Prince Alexander Nevsky and St. Prince Dmitry Donskoy; St. Iliia Pechersky, the prototype of the folklore hero whose remains are in the Kievo-Pecherskaia Lavra in Kiev; Archangel Mikhail, commander of the heavenly forces; and St. Georgii the Victor, patron of Moscow and the Russian state.[106] The LRA commander took the patriarch to the C2 center of the Main Staff, introduced the members of the Military Council to him, briefed him on the LRA's history and future professional plans, and outlined avenues of cooperation.[107]

The consecration of the Main Staff chapel in August 2002 gave an impetus to LRA garrisons all over Russia.[108] In September a wooden chapel of Archistrategos Mikhail was consecrated in the Soltsy base (Tu-22M3 regiments) in western Russia, and the foundation of the St. Innokentii church was laid down in the Ukrainka base (Tu-95MS regiments) in Russia's Far East.[109] In October 2002, construction of the St. Prophet Iliia church began in the Shaikovka base (Tu-22M3 regiments) near Moscow, and in 2003 the chapel was constructed in the Siberian military town of Belaia (Tu-22M3 regiments). In 2004 construction of the St. Prophet Iliia church started in the Engels base (Tu-160) in central Russia, and the construction of the church with the same name began in 2005 at the Arctic garrison of Tiksi.[110] In the absence of state or ROC funding, the LRA officers donated to construction and were directly involved in the work.[111] As the commander of an LRA division put it, "We assist construction with what we can, [. . .] and hope that soon new churches will strengthen the aviators' spirit. It is so good when the road to the skies goes through the temple."[112] By 2010 all the LRA bases had churches or chapels,[113] newly built or existing ones converted into garrison temples, and conducted a congregational life.[114] To commemorate this achievement, the ROC and the LRA published in 2010 a special calendar featuring all the garrison temples of the aerial leg of the nuclear triad.[115]

Catechization within the LRA diversified. By 2004, regular clerical activities within the Main Staff included pastoral conversations about the foundations of Orthodox culture, meetings with Moscow priests, and excursions for officers and their families to historical-religious places, monasteries, and religious educational institutions.[116] Catechization expanded also to professional education. Father Konstantin established and became the dean of the FOC in the AF Academy.[117] A chapel opened and clerical activities began in Tambov High Air College—the main institution preparing the LRA officers cadre. Unsurprisingly, the title of the doctoral dissertation that the LRA Military Council's secretary, an active-duty colonel, defended in 2007 at the GS Academy was "Spiritual Security of the Russian Federation."[118]

Like the other services, the LRA introduced its own rituals: renaming of strategic bombers, veneration of unique relics, and aerial cross processions. The tradition of renaming nuclear bombers after persons or cities of historical-religious significance dates to the late 1990s.[119] During the conversion decade, this became a massive trend. Tu-160s were named after persons and Tu-95MSs after cities.[120] The renaming ceremony became an essentially religious ritual. Its central element—consecration of the jet—resonated with the baptism of the newborn.[121] By 2008, when new Tu-160s started to join the squadrons, the consecration of the jets and their crews by the priest and joint prayers became part of the official ceremony of joining combat duty.[122] Aviators saw this ceremony as a revival of the pre-revolution tradition, when chaplains consecrated the heavy bombers of the "Iliia Muromets" squadron as they left the factory.[123]

The veneration of unique, service-related, relics became another custom. First, in 2002 the patriarch granted the personal religious banner of the Chenstokhovskaia Mother of God to the LRA commander. According to the official press release, "the banner symbolizes the military commander's spiritual authority" and "is constantly in his office or taken to the places of his combat duties."[124] Then, in 2005, after Putin's sortie on a Tu-160, the patriarch brought to the Main Staff some of the remains of the recently canonized St. Fedor Ushakov.[125] Presenting this unique relic at the main C2 center of the nuclear aerial arm, the patriarch said that from now on St. Feodor Ushakov would spiritually guarantee the well-being of the Fatherland's defenders among the ranks of the LRA. Following the ceremony, he was given a tour of the central C2 room of the Main Staff and met with its officers on duty.[126] Finally, the new LRA commander decided that all the garrison churches should have relics of St. Iliia Pechersky, the patron saint of the service.[127] What he saw as defense of Russia's borders "from seen and unseen enemies" demanded a huge amount of the saint's flesh.[128] The LRA commander and the main priest turned for assistance to the metropolitan of Kiev. The Ukrainian hierarch cooperated, and in September 2009 the icons embedded with pieces of the saint's remains (*moscheviki*) arrived at all seventeen LRA garrison churches.[129] According to the LRA priest, in this way the saint "is protecting Russia's borders not only with his spirit but also with his flesh."[130]

In 2007 the LRA priests and commanders introduced another ritual—aerial cross processions (*vozdushnye krestnye khody*). In 2007 the philanthropic fund, headed by retired Soviet general Valentin Varennikov, initiated an "aerial cross procession" to commemorate the alleged overfly of Moscow in winter 1941 by the Tikhvinskaya Mother of God icon. The Ministry of Emergency Situations, then headed by the current DM, Shoigu, provided a helicopter to overfly Moscow and the Golden Ring cities. The aerial iconostasis included icons with the relics of St. Georgii, St. Alexander Nevsky, and St. Feodor Ushakov and an icon with pieces of Jesus's crucifixion cross.[131] *Krasnaia zvezda*, the MoD official newspaper, citing secondary sources, asserted that the current aerial cross procession was a revival of the GPW tradition, although that had never occurred.[132]

The LRA immediately co-opted the ritual. In the same year, sixty priests participating in the annual All Russian Gathering of the Military Clergy[133] decided to bless the strategic bomber bases of the Moscow region, overflying them aboard a refueling jet carrying icons and the LRA relics.[134] In December 2007, the LRA and the Tambov eparchy arranged an aerial cross procession, this time to overfly the region where the main air college preparing the LRA pilots and the main training base are located and the tanker regiments are deployed. Carrying all the regional relics and icons and reciting blessings, the priests overflew the installations in a Tu-134, the main training aircraft of the LRA, "to prevent the troubles from entering the region."[135] In the following years, during pro-

fessional holidays and celebrations of regiments' establishment anniversaries or at the request of commanders, aerial blessings of specific bases
to prevent troubles became widespread.[136]

As in the other services, by the end of the decade the LRA priests
began becoming involved in operational activities. Like the RVSN clergy,
the priesthood of the strategic bombers needed to share professional experience and refine their conduct. But in contrast to the RVSN, within
the LRA this activity became an integral part of the corps' routine. Annually, senior commanders of the LRA units gather at one of the corps'
bases to summarize the past year and to outline plans for the coming one.
In 2005, for the first time, dozens of clerics providing pastoral care to the
LRA all over Russia congregated as part of the corps' senior commanders' gathering.[137] A setting of this type, with military and clergy partak-
ing in the same professional activity, was unprecedented for the LRA, for
the nuclear triad, and for the Russian military. In the following years, such
gatherings became regular,[138] and they would later spread also to the other
legs of the nuclear triad.

On 17 August 2007, for the first time since 1992, Moscow officially
renewed the LRA's permanent patrols over the Pacific, Indian, Atlantic,
and Arctic Oceans. The ROC internalized that for the Russian strategic
community, and the LRA in particular, the operational and symbolic significance of the patrols was difficult to overestimate. Four days following
the Kremlin's announcement, to commemorate and bless this important
event, the patriarch sent one of Moscow's main archiepiscops to deliver
to the LRA Main Staff the icon of St. Alexander Nevsky with his relics
and to bless with the icon the senior command that was about to begin
combat duty. Following the prayers at the Main Staff, the cleric and the
deputy commander of the LRA read out the notes from the patriarch and
the LRA commander to the senior command and the pilots.[139]

In August 2008, the archiepiscop of Vladimir and Suzdal, in the presence of the LRA chief of staff, consecrated the main LRA C2 field post
at an undisclosed location in his eparchy. Following the joint prayers
within the installation, the priests and pilots conducted a cross procession
around the base.[140] The ceremony was followed by an unprecedented sortie in which this field post played a central role. For the first time, the

strategic bombers trained on performing nuclear launches during a sortie outside Russia. On 10 September, two Tu-160s from the Engels Air Base flew to Venezuela carrying non-nuclear missiles and trained over the neutral waters of the Atlantic Ocean and the Caribbean Sea, simulating launches of nuclear weapons.[141]

NUCLEAR NAVY

By the time the naval leg of the triad began standing firmly on its feet in the second half of the decade, it had already been converted. As in the other services, churching and expansion of the priesthood, the renaming and consecration of submarines, veneration of relics, naval cross processions, and clerics joining operational missions all became routine. Almost ten years before the official introduction of the military clergy, the Petrozavodsk and Petropavlovsk eparchies, on whose territories the Northern and Pacific Fleets are deployed, established departments of cooperation with the military and systematically interacted with the nuclear squadrons of both fleets.[142] Cooperation agreements signed by these squadrons and even by specific submarines with the local eparchies codified the existing reality and provided a legalization of sorts to activities already ongoing informally within top-secret garrisons and closed cities. Often these agreements summarized, reaffirmed, and expanded previous covenants, incrementally adding areas of cooperation and specifying responsibilities.[143]

The garrison churches that had emerged in the previous decade within the bases of the nuclear submarines in both fleets expanded their activities. In the NF, the congregation of the nuclear submariners' garrison church in Vidiaevo, established in 2000 and led by a permanent priest, grew incrementally as the crews of the non-nuclear submarines caught up with their nuclear colleagues, asking for their vessels to be consecrated and for icons to be put aboard, which the nuclear squadron's priest did.[144] In 2003 the Sevmash director approved the restoration of the Nikolsky church within the shipyard and the conduct of occasional services. Shipyard workers funded the restoration. When in 2005 the renovated altar and chapels were ready, the metropolitan consecrated the temple as the Sevmash house church. Since then, the services have taken place on Sundays and major holidays, and the shipyard workers baptize their kids there. In 2009 the church, located in the heart of the top-secret shipyard, acquired a new golden onion dome.[145] Similarly, in the PF the church of St. Andrei of the nuclear submarine squadron, established in 1999 and led by a retired nuclear submariner ordained as a cleric, was conducting regular services and missionary, catechization, and pilgrimage activities.[146] As the congregation grew, in 2006 the Seraphim Sarovsky church was established in Viliuchinsk. The bells of this temple were made using metal from decommissioned missile range measurement ships, which track submarines' ballistic launches.[147]

Religious influence steadily penetrated the Severodvinsk shipyard—the heart of the Russian nuclear shipbuilding industry, constructing submarines for both fleets. The renaming and consecration of the submarines, a trend that had started in the previous decade, became a norm. The newly commissioned vessels acquired names with religious connotations. During the 2000s, Sevmash was engaged in repairing one by one the Soviet nuclear strategic submarines of Project 667 BDRM, which then still served as the backbone of the maritime leg of the nuclear triad. Following the crews' requests, two nuclear submarines were named after cities of religious significance in the Ural region—Verkhoturie and Ekaterinburg.[148] In 2002 and 2004, the archbishop of both cities, who patronizes both submarines and their crews, flew in to Sevmash from Ural region to consecrate them.[149] In 2006 another two vessels of the project, *Tula* and *Briansk*, left the shipyard. Before smashing the bottle of champagne against the vessels' bows—an old naval tradition—the local archimandrite consecrated the submarines according to the Orthodox rite.[150] *Kareliia* and *Novomoskovs*, the last vessels of the project, were consecrated in the same way upon completion of repair.[151] Priests of the Arkhangelsk eparchy, in which Sevmash is located, conducted the consecrations, addressed the crews, and granted them small personal icons.

Since the mid-2000s, Sevmash has intensified work on the Borei-class nuclear-powered submarines armed with Bulava ballistic missiles. The first three submarines of that class received the names of grand princes of Russia—Iurii Dolgoruky, St. Alexander Nevsky, and Vladimir Monomakh—and were consecrated at the start of work.[152] The Soviet ballistic missile nuclear submarine TK-208, armed with Bulavas, was renamed after St. Prince Dmitry Donskoy. The fourth submarine of the new class was named *St. Nikolai*, later changed to *St. Prince Vladimir*—in tribute to the baptizer of Rus.[153] In 2009 the Severnaia Verf shipyard commissioned the 12th GUMO C2 cutter, *St. Seraphim Sarovsky*. The official announcement explained the name choice as a tribute to the patron of the nuclear shield.[154] While the nuclear submarines underwent repairs or were in the process of construction, the local eparchial department conducted regular spiritual-patriotic activities with the crews.[155]

The veneration of relics and the establishment of "red corners," precursors of the underwater churches, began aboard the nuclear submarines. In 2009 the VNIIEF and Sarov city administration representatives visited the submarine Sarov deployed in Severodvinsk and presented to the crew icons with pieces of the relics of St. Seraphim Sarovsky and St. Fedor Ushakov.[156] The archiepiscop of Nizhni Novgorod, whose eparchy covers Sarov and the VNIIEF, consecrated these relics, which since then have been kept at the submarine's mess deck.[157] In the PF, in 2006, during the celebrations of the Russian submarine fleet's one hundredth anniversary, the eparchy together with the squadron high command designed a commemoration badge featuring the patron saints of the squadron—St. Andrei, St. Nikolai the Miracle-Maker, and St. Georgii the Victor. On the day of the anniversary, the nuclear submarine dove to depth with Archiepiscop Ignatii aboard, so that the cleric could consecrate the badges that were later presented to the best squadron servicemen.[158]

Other professional-religious rituals included supplication services during the new squadron commanders' assumption of position and liturgies at the start and end of the training periods, with all squadron senior officers present,[159] and during the oath of allegiance ceremonies. In August 2009, for the first time ever in the Russian military, commanders suggested that the 150 cadets at the Viliuchinsk nuclear submarine base, who had just completed basic training, take the oath of allegiance on the cross and Bible. About 70 percent volunteered to become, as the official eparchial announcement said, "not simply military servicemen but Orthodox warriors," thus performing not only their military but also their Christian duties. After pronouncing the text of the official oath according to the field manual and signing it in front of the officer, each cadet kissed the Bible, as the priest touched his forehead with the cross and let him kiss it while sprinkling him with holy water.[160]

Almost in parallel with their LRA colleagues, the submariners began practicing cross processions. The first available account dates from December 2009, when the Port Arthur Mother of God icon, the patroness of the Far East defenders of the Fatherland, was delivered to the garrison church of the nuclear submarine squadron in the PF. It stayed in the church for a day, so that all the sailors not on duty and their families could touch it and pray next to it. On the next day the squadron priest delivered it to Krasheninnikov Bay, where the squadron submarines are deployed. They put this two-square-meter icon on the deck of the icebreaker, which carried it along the piers where the submarines were tied. The icebreaker stopped next to each one, so that the priest could bless the vessel and the crew.[161]

The conversion of the nuclear Navy demanded deeper involvement of clergy in operational activities than in the RVSN and the LRA. The specifics of the service defined this necessity. Since large numbers of the congregations were aboard their vessels most of the time and increasingly at sea, to conduct their missions the priests needed to go underwater. This was different from the RVSN and the LRA, where the congregations were accessible within the barracks.[162] The precedent for a priest joining a nuclear submarine on an operational mission at sea occurred in the 1990s, when the metropolitan of Petropavlovsk-Kamchatsky joined a submarine of the PF, which after repair at the Severodvinsk shipyard cruised from the North back to its base. When funding began to flow in the early 2000s, more submarines entered the docks for repairs. In 2003 the Zvezda shipyard completed repair work on the strategic nuclear submarine *St. Georgii the Victor* in four months. Assigned to the PF, the submarine was about to conduct its first operational trip—a clandestine cruise from Primorsk in the High North to its home base in Kamchatka in the Far East. When several months before the cruise commanders of the nuclear squadron requested Episcop Ignatii to assign a cleric to repeat the mission he had once conducted, he volunteered again. By special order, the Navy Main Staff approved this. During the cruise the episcop received twenty confessions, baptized eleven sailors, conducted services, and provided pastoral care.[163]

This underwater proselytism became widely known in the narrow circles of the naval nuclear community, and the NF's submariners began catching up. In summer 2006, following approval by the Gadzhievo base commander and the blessing of the local bishop, Protoierei Leonid Leontiuk, head of the Petrozavodsk department of cooperation with the military, a retired border guard officer, and a priest of the local church, was temporarily included among the crew of the nuclear submarine *Kareliia*, for the duration of its operational cruise to the training range. The submarine already had two big icons hanging at the officers' deck and in the canteen, so upon arrival the cleric started missionary activities by consecrating the submarine sections constituting the aggregates of the nuclear reactor. During the cruise he conducted services and catechization conversations, baptized six sailors, and took confessions from the willing. Since a majority of the sailors were on full readiness alert, the confessions and one-on-one sessions with the priest occurred in the sailors' combat duty stations. During the cruise, the deputy commander of the squadron was aboard. It is unclear how deeply he was involved in religious activities, which he obviously approved, but the priest closely cooperated with the educational officer.[164] In the next decade, clerics aboard the nuclear submarines during operational missions at sea would become a widespread practice in both fleets.

Finally, the faith-atoms nexus in the Navy featured another phenomenon. More than in any other setting, during the encounters with the nuclear submarine crews Patriarch Kirill was vocal about the current Russian deterrence policy and the role of nuclear weapons in national security. There were several possible reasons for that. In terms of media coverage, the naval audiences were always bigger than those of the RVSN and the LRA—the submarines' crews that congregated to meet him numbered in the several hundred. Technically, delivering an address from the upper deck was easier than arranging an event of equivalent impact with ICBMs or strategic bombers. Also, the spike in naval activity coincided with Metropolitan Kirill's efforts to support the Kremlin's geopolitical agenda. He had for long positioned the ROC and its nuclear pastors as the main contributors to Russian national security and strategic stability. Addressing nuclear submariners in 2005, Kirill said:

The Russian nuclear shield is the only guarantor of independence and sovereignty in today's daunting world. Russia—with all its capabilities, natural resources, colossal size, and intellectual resources—could not be a great power without your military labor. [. . .] Many would prefer Russia not to have protectors like you. The ROC, as the spiritual mainstay of our people, on the contrary, ensures that loyal and courageous sons will serve the Fatherland, that our military will be strong and not in need, and will multiply the traditions of its glorious forefathers, when the spirit of patriotism, combat camaraderie, and fraternal assistance reigns.[165]

In August 2009, a month after the president's approval of the introduction of the institution of military clerics, Patriarch Kirill visited the northern eparchies. At the center of the trip was the Severodvinsk Sevmash shipyard, where at that time the Borei-class submarines were being prepared for commissioning. The crews of the *Dmitry Donskoy* and *Iurii Dolgoruky* nuclear submarines, in full parade uniform but with their hats off, according to the Orthodox tradition, were arranged in two long lines on both sides of the shipyard's pier and on the upper deck of the nuclear submarine. The patriarch, with the NF commander on his left and the Sevmash director on his right, followed by the metropolitans, advanced through the lines. He went up to the open deck, the military orchestra played a march, and the crews greeted him in unison with the official military salute "Zdraviia zhelaiu" and added "Your Holiness."[166]

Standing over the launching silo of the Bulava ICBM, the patriarch addressed the crew arranged on the upper deck. He launched into his regular formula—the importance of the nuclear potential for Russian national security and the ROC's indispensable assistance to those operating these weapons in extreme morale-psychological conditions:

It's a great honor and a genuine happiness to meet you on the deck of this remarkable ship; to its functioning are linked the very high hopes of our country. [. . .] To protect the Motherland in an extreme situation, which is exactly what the submariners do, one should have excellent training skills, good education, tremendous internal discipline, but most importantly—strong spirit. Wars have been won mainly not by the strength of weapons, but by the strength of spirit. The power of spirit is stronger than the power of metal, the power of weapons, and the power of human reason. I wholeheartedly wish you this power of spirit. [. . .] For centuries the ROC has strengthened the spirit of the people. Today it pays considerable attention to its interaction with the military, because no money will compensate for the losses, which the person who took the oath of allegiance is ready to sustain. This is why the material factor, though very important and necessary, will never be decisive in state security. Only a spiritually strong person can rise, charge, and endanger his life. [. . .] Russia's great power status and its peaceful and bright future depend on the submariners' labor and loyalty to the Motherland. May God bless you all and let you forge here, on the banks of Severodvinsk, the undefeatable shield of the Motherland.[167]

Kirill presented the submarine with the big Mother of God icon and the submariners with personal small icons of Jesus.[168] The Sevmash director assured the patriarch that the next Borei-class submarine would be given the name of St. Nikolai.[169] Then he went on to Nikolsky Sobor, also on the territory of Sevmash, to lead the service. The church had been returned to the ROC and the services resumed since 2003, but since it was on the territory of the top-secret shipyard, access was restricted to only the Sevmash workers.[170] Following the service, the patriarch delivered a brief speech. His main message was that the nexus between the spiritual and the material, between labor and prayer, between military and church, between faith and science—a reference to the ROC and the nuclear community—makes Russia a strong state.[171] At the end, the senior guests—the Parliament vice-speaker, the governor of the Arkhangelsk District, the Severodvinsk mayor, Northern Fleet and Belomorsk base commanders, and Sevmash and Zvezdochka directors—received Communion from the hands of the patriarch.[172]

SPACE COMPLEX

Military Space

During the late 1990s, the cosmodromes, the RVSN space launch sites, were relatively less churched than other parts of the corps due to their faraway locations; however, the basic ecclesiastical drive was there as elsewhere within the RVSN. In 2001 the space component of the RVSN turned into a separate service—the Space Forces (SF). Exactly then a big leap forward in the new corps' conversion occurred. This coincided with the arrival of Protoierei Artemy Emke to serve as permanent priest at the Archistrategos Mikhail church in Mirnyi—the closed city adjacent to the Plesetsk cosmodrome, the main spaceport of the Russian military. This relatively young cleric (b. 1972), who became the driving force behind cat-echization of the SF, arrived in 2002. His activism did not go unnoticed, and in 2005 he was nominated as the head of the Eparchial Department for Interaction with the Military.[173] Three clerics subordinate to him in the cosmodrome units have previously served in the RVSN.[174]

About ten thousand soldiers serving in the Plesetsk cosmodrome are deployed in several bases and smaller units, some of them several hours' drive from each other. Naturally, the church in Mirnyi, which opened in 1998, was accessible to the residents of the closed city—mainly the servicemen of the main staff and adjacent bases; however, the rest of the units were out of reach. In 2003 Father Artemy initiated "mission-ary airborne landing" (*missionerskii desant*). This proselytism activity, outreaching the faraway deployed units, gave a tremendous boost to conversion of the service. Since 2003, *desanti* have occurred twice a year, usually around holidays, both religious (Christmas, Easter, and Configuration) and military (the RVSN, Cosmonautics, and the Father-land's Defender Days), and included several standard elements: liturgy, confessions and Communion, baptismal ceremonies, a pastoral talk, a question-and-answer session, a movie screening, and concerts of military and religious patriotic songs.[175]

For the first desant destination, Father Artemy chose the SF Prepa-ration Center, the cosmodrome's biggest unit, which trains around a thou-sand draftees every six months for the SF and the RVSN.[176] The liturgy was conducted in the base club. The improvised altar, featuring an ico-nostasis and candles, was located in the club's center, exactly beneath a several meters-long camouflaged plywood replica of the Topol ICBM, hanging on the central wall.[177] Desanti usually lasted for two weeks, dur-ing which they landed in ten cosmodrome units. Students and professors of St. Petersburg University's FOC often joined to assist.[178] Annually, on average, the desanti outreached to about fifteen hundred to two thousand soldiers, out of whom, on average, about three hundred confessed and took Communion and about a hundred were baptized.[179]

In parallel, the cosmodrome commanders who viewed these activities favorably started incremental construction of churches within bases. In 2004 the cosmodrome's commander approved the reconstruction of the eighteenth-century chapel of the Kazan Mother of God at the entrance to Mirnyi. The opening ceremony and consecration were linked to the fiftieth-anniversary celebrations of the cosmodrome. Since then twice a year, on the day of the Kazan Mother of God icon, cross processions have taken place from the Archistrategos Mikhail church within the city to the chapel.[180] In 2009 the first two garrison churches were erected. The club, which witnessed liturgies during the desanti, was consecrated as the temple of St. Varvara and became the house church of the SF Preparation Center. As in many other cases, construction was funded by the servicemen's donations.[181] In summer, construction of the St. Joan the Warrior church started at the Plesetsk military airport, a base of the special SF and RVSN aviation unit.[182] The unit commander, an AF colonel, and its educational officer, a major, were the main initiators of the project. They oversaw construction, carried out mainly by the soldiers, and arranged donations from the unit and from private sponsors.[183] Several months after the first services in the unit's church, Father Artemy consecrated all the unit's airplanes and helicopters.[184]

In the same year, the cosmodrome's commander initiated the building of the chapel and chapel column inside the Main Staff, to "spiritually strengthen the servicemen and empower their thoughts." In May 2010, Father Artemy, accompanied by the cosmodrome commander, his deputies, and the city head, led the supplication service to mark the start of construction of the St. Nikolai chapel.[185] In contrast to other religious activities aimed primarily at compulsory service soldiers, this chapel is devoted solely to the needs of the cosmodrome's high command. The cosmodrome's senior officers led the first prayers upon completion of construction.[186] Around late 2010, a decision was made to build an additional church next to the launch site. The cornerstone of the All Saints church was laid down in summer 2011, and in summer 2013 the services started.[187]

During the decade, religious ritual permeated all stages of space activity. In 2007 General Lieutenant Oleg Ostapenko, the cosmodrome's commander, introduced a tradition of consecration of the space launches.[188] Since then, with rare exceptions, all the launches from Plesetsk, on average one every two to three months, have been consecrated.[189] The priest places the table with the holy water several meters in front of the missile. Slightly in front of him, two soldiers hold up religious banners with the icons of Christ and St. Georgii, while the combat launching unit stands in a row in front. The priest addresses the unit, asking for God's help in bringing to fruition the enormous human labor invested in the preparation of the launch, and then he says a special blessing, while circling the missile and sprinkling holy water. He then returns to the launching unit and sprinkles holy water on the servicemen.[190]

In early 2010, Ostapenko, having been promoted to SF commander, invited Metropolitan Iuvenalii of the Moscow eparchy to visit and consecrate the Main Test and Space Systems Control Center. Located in the closed city of Krasnoznamensk, the center is the main Russian military and commercial satellite control post, which manages about 80 percent of the Russian orbital spacecraft constellation. The metropolitan consecrated the center in February 2010 and gave its commander, a general-major, an Archistrategos Mikhail icon as a "symbol of God's patronage over the Main Center and all the military personnel serving there." All the seniors of the SF were present at the consecration ceremony. All the officers of the center, close to a hundred of them, were drawn up in rows during the sprinkling of the holy water and consecration. This relatively lengthy ceremony did not interfere with the center's functioning, including communication sessions with the satellites of the Global Navigation Satellite System (GLONASS).[191]

By the end of the decade, the SF institutionalized a routine cycle of religious activities. Priests have participated in the official celebrations of Cosmonautics Day, the major professional holiday of the SF; organized cultural-educational activities, religious-patriotic movie screenings, and concerts; conducted pastoral conversations on the foundations of Orthodox faith during basic training; baptized all the willing at the garrison churches; given pastoral blessings and sprinkled holy water on the formations during the oath of allegiance upon the completion of basic training; consecrated launches, new weapon systems, and new units' banners; conducted conversations with young officers who have arrived at the cosmodrome; and led memorial services for the corps' soldiers killed in action.[192] Similar religious activities, as well as excursions and visits to space museums, started taking place in the SF units deployed across Russia during the discussed decade.[193]

The Anti-Missile Defense (PRO)

The PRO troops division, within the SF, constitutes part of Russia's strategic deterrence potential, although it is not often mentioned in conjunction with the nuclear triad. The Russian System of Missile Attack Warning (SPRN)[194] consists of two echelons—a space echelon, which pinpoints the enemy missiles from space, and a ground echelon, based on over-the-horizon radio-locating stations that spot missiles in flight. Mutually complementary, they channel information to the SPRN Main Command Center, which in turn issues an early warning to the political leadership, based on which the latter considers nuclear retaliation—launch on warning or a second strike. The same center also issues a warning to all the legs of the nuclear triad and to the anti-ballistic missile defense.[195]

Conversion of this segment of the strategic arsenal gathered momentum toward the end of the decade. Religious life in Sofrino-1—the headquarters of the 9th Air Defense division, the main Russian missile defense force operating A-135 anti-ballistic missile systems—started in late 1990, as part of the general religious revival within the closed cities linked to the RVSN. As early as 1996, Sofrino residents arranged a small congregation and sent a letter to the garrison commander requesting the construction of a church in the closed city.[196] A tiny wood chapel of St. Dmitry Donskoy was erected to address the immediate needs of local believers. However, the construction process, funded by the residents' very modest donations during the 1990s, took more than a decade. The official date of the church's establishment is 2006, and it was only in the following year that its bells arrived.[197] The religious life of the garrison actually gathered momentum in the second half of the decade.

The year 2004 saw the first encounter between clergy and the commanders of the PRO troops in Sofrino-1. The clerics met with soldiers and officers, conducted pastoral talks, and brought presents—a TV set, three guitars, and items of personal use. On their part, the unit commanders thanked the clerics and presented them with the album "The History of the SF," expressing the hope that cooperation would become regular.[198] Since the mid-2000s, the clergy of the Moscow eparchy has intensified pastoral care of the PRO units deployed around Moscow, mainly in Sofrino-1. On major religious holidays they visit the base to conduct services and bring presents, baptize soldiers, and conduct pastoral conversations on the importance of military service, brotherhood, mutual support, and discipline.[199] By the end of the decade, meetings on cooperation between PRO senior commanders and local clergy became regular.[200] Chapels and churches started to appear within the PRO units of the Moscow district, encouraged by the favorable attitude of the bases' commanders and of the troops' commander, General-Major V. N. Liaporov, who since 2009 has headed the division.[201]

No later than summer 2009, officers of the SPRN Main Command Center, located in Solnechnogorsk, invited a local priest to consecrate the operations room. Since then, the icon of St. Alexander Nevsky has hung on the wall, next to the combat banner of the center.[202] When in 2009 the new early warning radar station in Armavir (which provides long-distance monitoring of airspace against a ballistic missile attack emanating from the south) became operational, icons were hung on the walls of its central command post.[203] During 2009 the SPRN units, as elsewhere in the military, were exchanging the old Soviet banners for the new ones, with heraldry featuring more religious attributes, including crosses and portraits of St. Georgii the Victor. Starting at the Main Command Center, and then in all the other SPRN units, local eparchial priests responsible for cooperation with the military consecrated the new banners in the presence of the SF commanders.[204]

By 2010, as elsewhere in the SF, in the Solnechnogorsk blagochinie, where the central units of the SPRN troops are deployed, the annual cycle of activities was established. On Christmas and Easter, the SPRN units are officially drawn up in parade formation to be greeted by pastoral words from the priest, who also reads the patriarch's holiday blessing to the warriors, followed by prayer and the distribution to soldiers of Christmas cards and sweets. During Easter the priest delivers to the servicemen traditional Orthodox Easter bread, icons, and pocket prayers of the Orthodox warrior.[205] Similarly, the clergy has become part of the official celebration of the Fatherland's Defender Day, standing next to the high commanders and blessing the soldiers during this purely secular professional holiday introduced during Soviet times.[206] The clergy also bless and sprinkle holy water on the young draftees during the oath of allegiance ceremonies.[207]

Civilian Space

The conversion of the civilian segment of the space program received a boost as well during the decade. Sessions between the cosmonauts and the patriarch from the orbital station, the building of churches, pastoral care, and blessing of the crews and of the launches, as well as taking relics aboard and conducting space cross processions, all became a norm. The two main figures in converting the industry have been Father Sergei, since 1997 the priest of the Baikonur cosmodrome's congregation, the launch site of the civilian segment of the Russian space program located in Kazakhstan, and Father Yoav, the priest of the cosmonaut team, who has provided pastoral care since 2003 at the closed city of Zvezdnyi, where Russian cosmonauts live and train.

Construction of the St. Georgy church in Baikonur, the cornerstone of which was laid in 1997 by Father Sergei, a retired RVSN officer, was completed in 2005 on the fiftieth anniversary of the city. Baikonur residents and cosmodrome officers donated to the church's construction, which the city mayor, who encouraged the revival of religious life in Baikonur, supported.[208] Father Sergei, who was awarded an honorary badge for "Cooperation in the Space Field" by the Russian State Space Corporation (ROSCOSMOS), modified a used rocket protection case into the temple's baptismal font—a water basin used during the baptismal ceremony.[209] In 2007 the temple acquired from Patriarch Alexey its two main relics—an icon with pieces of St. Georgii's remains and the Kazan Mother of God icon, which was taken into space in 2004.[210]

Consecration of the launches that Father Sergei initiated at Baikonur has been fully institutionalized. At Father Sergei's request, Patriarch Alexey approved the rite of blessing for the spaceships. A modified version of the standard Orthodox traveler's blessing,[211] it became a canon for the Russian space priesthood. The ritual has also been established. Father Sergei starts blessing the rocket vehicles of the Soyuz type, which deliver the cosmonauts into space, from the bottom, and then takes the elevator up while reciting prayers. Blessing the rocket vehicles of the Proton type is more physically challenging. There is no elevator, so the cleric takes the stairs to get to the top of the rocket, which is seventy-two meters high. He stops at every stage to sprinkle holy water and to bless.[212]

Father Sergei argues that all the failed launches were not blessed. Although he does not claim that the ritual solves technical mistakes, he sees in all these cases divine intervention. As he puts it, "We are praying and asking God that the labor of thousands of people, who deal with the rocket and prepare the cosmonauts, from the general designer to the technician inserting the last bolt, be blessed."[213] The ROSCOSMOS leadership has continually been supportive of the prelaunch blessings, despite growing public critique of the ritual and of the clericalization of the space industry in general.[214] Following one of the failed launches, the ROSCOSMOS head asserted that the agency would continue with the blessing procedure, although it is not within the federal regulations.[215] According to him, only in three cases, involving one Russian and two foreigners, did the cosmonauts refuse to accept the blessing.[216]

During the decade, conversion of the space complex also reached to the heart of the civilian space program—the closed city of Zvezdnyi, where Russian, and previously Soviet, cosmonauts (and their families) live and train. In 2002, through a friend's connection, Father Yoav, a monk in Troitsa-Sergeev Lavra—the most important Russian monastery and the ROC's spiritual center located in Sergiev Posad, near Moscow—was invited to visit Zvezdnyi. Passionate about space since a young age, during his excursion at the Preparation Center the monk was introduced to the commander of the cosmonauts' team, Yurii Lonchakov, who would become head of the Preparation Center in 2014. Impressed, Lonchakov invited himself and several other cosmonauts from his team to visit the monk's monastery. The pilgrimage went well, connections were forged, the visits continued, and Lonchakov introduced the priest to the head of the Preparation Center.[217] Following several pastoral talks that touched on spiritual and professional issues, the Preparation Center seniors started to invite Father Yoav on a regular basis to consecrate the offices, departments, and airplanes. The circle of the priest's encounters with the cosmonauts and industry seniors grew wider.[218]

Since 2007 cosmonauts preparing for launch and willing to receive pastoral care have visited at Troitsa-Sergeev Lavra to confess to Father Yoav and to receive the blessing of St. Sergei Radonezhsky, one of the most important patron saints of Russia buried in the monastery, by venerating his relics. Thus, Father Yoav became the priest and confessor of the cosmonaut team.[219] Since then, the willing cosmonauts, before launch, have confessed and received a blessing either by visiting the monastery on the way to Baikonur or by having the monk come to the cosmodrome to escort them. In the monastery they touch the St. Sergei Radonezhsky relics, participate in the service, and, following the confession and sprinkling of holy water, receive portable small icons of Jesus and Mother of God and a small Bible. Alternatively, Father Yoav has arrived at Baikonur to do the same three days before the launch.[220] On several occasions, the monk even arrived to meet the cosmonauts immediately upon their landing from space.[221]

Conversion expanded to the space station. Bringing relics aboard and conducting rituals with them became a routine. Following a request from Father Yoav, Lonchakov took into space a piece of a relic of St. Sergei Radonezhsky, to bless the planet during the sixteen daily orbits around the earth that the station conducts. Father Yoav called these "cross processions" around the globe. The monk also asked a cosmonaut to take the relics with him into open space, which he did. Other cosmonauts during the decade took with them relics of the martyrs St. Fedor Stratil and St. Fedor Tiron, pieces of the relics of St. Nikolai from the Italian city of Bari, and relics of St. Peter and St. Philip, Moscow metropolitans, and

St. Georgii. Cosmonaut Maxim Suraev took with him a piece from the God's Cross, which was kept at the station for six months.[222]

In 2005, with the blessing of Patriarch Alexey, a cross was sent to the International Space Station and has been there since, together with several small icons, a Bible, and prayer books. It is located on the wall of the main room, right over an iconostasis containing two icons of the Mother of God, two icons of Jesus, and one each of St. Sergei Radone-zhsky and of St. Nikolai.[223] The iconostasis has been modified from one crew to another. On one occasion, in an exception to the rule, a cosmo-naut who arrived at the station took all the icons off the wall, arguing that he was an atheist.[224] By 2009, the iconostasis featured a mixture of religious icons and the "icons" of Soviet cosmonautics—Konstantin Tseilkovsky, Yurii Gagarin, and Sergei Korolev.[225]

Since the early 2000s, sessions between the clergy and the cosmonauts in the orbital station became a common practice. Contacts with the patriarch usually occurred on Christmas, Easter, and Cosmonautics Day.[226] According to Father Yoav, during the decade, several cosmonauts began reading evening and morning prayers on board,[227] and in some cases, be-fore going into outer space, several of them called to get his blessing and moral support and to confess.[228] Unsurprisingly, cosmonauts who have spoken about Father Yoav see him as the pastor who "goes with them to the front lines," referring to his participation in the everyday work of the cosmonaut cadre. According to them, having undertaken the entire course of cosmonauts' basic physical training, including underwater and weight-lessness drills, Father Yoav is better able to internalize the needs of the cosmonauts and adjusts his pastoral care accordingly.[229]

THE 12TH MAIN DIRECTORATE OF THE MINISTRY OF DEFENSE (12TH GUMO)

Conversion of the 12th GUMO, the relatively least churched segment of the nuclear community during the 1990s, accelerated during the decade. By 2010, the service overcame all the previous difficulties, accomplished organizational reform, and churched its main components—the Central Nuclear Testing Range (Polygon), the Main Interservice Training Cen-ter, the Central Scientific-Research Institute, and the Main Staff. The nuclear custodians institutionalized religious rituals similar to other corps, and in some cases the intimacy of the service seniors with the ROC left behind other segments of the triad. The pace of this service's conversion was meteoric. Although it started almost from scratch in the late 1990s, by the end of 2003 all the 12th GUMO garrisons, according to the Synodal Department report, either had their own house church or had a temple assigned to a nearby congregation, or they were in the process of arranging one or the other.[230] The Synodal Department, reporting to the ROC's highest management forum on cooperation with the military, mentioned regular interaction with the GUMO command on matters of pastoral care to the servicemen and their families in the garrisons and closed cities.[231] As elsewhere, even before the service signed an official cooperation agreement with the Fund of St. Seraphim Sarovsky in autumn 2007, local, bottom-up initiatives resulted in the establishment of churches next to the bases and involvement of the priests in the servicemen's catechization.[232] The stories of the nuclear congregations at the Central Testing Range in Novaia Zemlia and at the Main Training Center are illustrative.

The church and congregation of the nuclear polygon, the first in the 12th GUMO and the most northerly in Russia, opened in 1998 and have steadily grown since then. The polygon continued functioning under the CTBT, since, as its commander put it, "as long as nuclear weapons exist, there is a necessity to maintain them at a high level of readiness, verifying their safety and reliability."[233] During the eight years (1999–2007) that Ieromonk Innokentii served in Belushia Guba, the settlement of the polygon, the religious life of the base expanded slowly but steadily. Initially, the permanent members of the congregation, who observed all the rituals and attended all the services, numbered fifteen people, about 1 percent of the city's residents. By 2004, the monk managed to establish good social ties with the local residents, mainly officers. He regularly visited military units, participated in the oaths of allegiance, consecrated the buildings, and conducted pastoral conversations. Due to weather conditions, he regularly delivered his Sunday sermons through local TV.[234]

In the early 2000s, the polygon commander initiated construction of a new stand-alone church, instead of the small original one within the children's cafeteria. General Vladimir Verkhovtsev, future head of the 12th GUMO and then its chief of staff, approved the request and supported the work.[235] Donations of residents funded the project; Severspetsstroi, the special construction service for the 12th GUMO, conducted the work; and the VNIIEF contributed the bells.[236] In September 2006, during the celebrations of the anniversary of the polygon's establishment, Episcop Tikhon consecrated the Nikolsky church,[237] the garrison's territory, and its equipment. The MoD newspaper *Krasnaia zvezda* dubbed it the polygon's consecration.[238] As the eparchy put it, "Exactly here about half a century ago the state's nuclear shield was forged. Now, the all-defeating weapon of the Christians—the cross of the Christ—illuminates our northern borders."[239] On behalf of the patriarch, for their role in construction, the episcop gave awards to the polygon's commander and his chief of staff and to the deputy, for educational work.[240] In the same year, Ieromonk Gavriil (Bogdanov), a retired naval officer, succeeded the first priest and vigorously continued his activities.[241]

The first garrison church of the 12th GUMO opened in the 84th Main Interservice Training Center in 2002. Located near the small village of Sharapovo in the Moscow region,[242] the center is the main training facility for the nuclear arsenal's maintenance and assembly for soldiers and noncommissioned, commissioned, and senior officers from all the services, who, upon graduation, serve in the nuclear storage facilities across Russia.[243] The village has the fifteenth-century Mikhailo-Arkhangel'skaia church, and when in 2000 this half-ruined temple was returned to the ROC, residents asked that services be resumed. The authorities approved the registration of a congregation, and the local metropolitan sent a monk named Kirill (Egorkin) to lead it. As the priest began reviving religious life and restoring the temple, social-spiritual contacts were forged with the commanders of the nearby base, who occasionally joined the liturgies. Lacking finance and manpower, restoration progressed slowly. Due to weather conditions, the services were possible only during the summer, and the priest asked the garrison commander for assistance during the colder seasons. On Easter 2002, the garrison commander ordered the conversion of a neglected building within the base into the garrison church. Named after St. Nikolai the Miracle-Maker, it became the assigned temple of the Sharapovo church.[244]

In short order, the servicemen's intensive work equipped the church with the necessary religious attributes and prepared it for round-the-year services. The local archiepiscop consecrated it as the garrison church of the Main Training Center. The ceremony was attended by the commanders of the 12th GUMO and of the garrison, the local administration, and the personnel training at the time within the base—about three hundred soldiers, officers, and generals. Following the ceremony, the commanders arranged for the metropolitan and the clergy an excursion within the nuclear custodians' training center. By the end of the decade, catechization activities gathered momentum within the base, and the center was fully converted and became an integral part of the Sharapovo congregation.[245]

In 2003 the patriarch awarded, at the Kremlin's Uspensky Cathedral, the St. Daniil Order to the 12th GUMO commander and to his deputy for educational work, General Nikolai Moroz, for "developing, leading, and accomplishing the program of military churches' construction."[246] Similarly, in 2005 the Fund of Andrei the Apostle granted the commander its annual award for achieving the total churching of his service.[247] Swift conversion was not a miracle. In the Synodal Department, the 12th GUMO, as well as the SF, has been part of the RVSN sector,[248] which naturally produced cross-fertilization; the most intensive work of the RVSN priests projected on the pastoral care within the 12th GUMO. Moreover, the central apparatus of the service was well prepared for co-operation.[249] Traditionally, many of the 12th GUMO Educational Department officers have come from the RVSN, which already had been intensively churched, and, unsurprisingly, they brought with them to the GUMO a religious spirit from the RVSN.[250]

Conversion of the 12th GUMO accelerated when in 2006 Verkhovtsev, the chief of the GUMO Main Staff, became the service head. His pro-ecclesiastic activism and personal affection for the faith made him one of the ROC's most popular nuclear generals. In July, Patriarch Alexey invited Verkhovtsev to join a major liturgy at Uspensky Cathedral, congratulated him in conjunction with his promotion, and presented him with a religious banner featuring the icon of Jesus with a sword in the background.[251] Such personal and, at the same time, widely publicized exposure of a top-secret figure was unusual. Moreover, in 2007 two major events—the official designation of the patron saint of the service and the erection of the St. Nikolai statues in its main bases—illustrated the intimacy between the ROC and the Russian nuclear custodians.

In September 2007, the most publicized event ever related to the service occurred. The 12th GUMO for the first time openly celebrated its professional holiday—Day of the Nuclear Maintenance Specialist—which the president designated as an official holiday and which coincided in 2007 with the sixtieth anniversary of the service's Soviet predecessor.[252] An official ceremony, commemorating the day and the anniversary of the "Russian nuclear weapons complex," was arranged for all of the 12th GUMO's senior commanders, retired and active duty, in no less than Russia's main temple—the Cathedral of Christ the Savior.[253] The chief of the GS thanked the service for preserving strategic deterrence potential during the most difficult times. "The sign of respect and gratitude for your labor is the fact that the 12th GUMO servicemen, civilian personnel, and veterans are celebrating their holiday in the main temple of Russian military glory." The blessing of the most senior uniformed commander turned what followed into an official ritual of designating the heavenly patron for the service.

The patriarch's speech, which appeared on the front page of *Krasnaia zvezda*, elaborated on the choice:

> It is difficult to overestimate your sacrifice when serving the Fatherland, while the state, due to objective circumstances, could not provide decent living conditions for scientists, veterans, experts, and military servicemen developing nuclear weapons and maintaining them at the due level. It is a joy to admit that despite the difficulties, your initiatives have created conditions in the closed cities for the revival of spiritual life; Orthodox temples and chapels have been erected, and in Sarov, the cradle of the nuclear weapons complex, the all-Russian sanctuary—the St. Seraphim Sarovsky temple—has been restored. So let him, from now on, be the heavenly patron of all of you and of the entire Russian nuclear weapons complex. Congratulating you respectfully on your anniversary, I pray to God and St. Seraphim that the

weapons entrusted to you will always be in the hands of God and will stay only a weapon of deterrence and retaliation.[254]

During the service acknowledging the GUMO and honoring St. Seraphim, the patriarch urged the flock to "thank God for his mercy and assistance to Russia's nuclear shield and to ask for God's blessing and heavenly defense from the patron of the nuclear specialists—St. Seraphim."[255] Following the liturgy, the vicar of Moscow announced that a cooperation agreement had been signed between the 12th GUMO and the Fund of St. Seraphim Sarovsky, its aims being "to strengthen the spiritual foundations of military service to the Fatherland and to develop cooperation in the sphere of spiritual-moral enlightenment of the servicemen and their families."[256] The sixteen best units of the 12th GUMO then received a *khorugv'*, an Orthodox heraldic banner used for liturgies, with an icon of St. Seraphim.[257] The GUMO commander thanked the patriarch for his prayers and attention to the warriors and wished him good health.[258]

The ostentatious celebrations of the GUMO's anniversary continued. In December the patriarch visited the 12th Central Scientific-Research Institute (CSRI)—the brain of the service, which conducts fundamental and applied research on the effects of nuclear weapons' use. Established after the first Soviet nuclear test in 1949, the institute, similarly to the VNIIEF in Sarov, is located on the territory of the nineteenth-century Gethsemane-Chernigovsky Skete, an isolated community of hermit monks living in underground catacombs. The skete was part of the larger monastery—Troitsa-Sergeev Lavra, the most important Russian spiritual center—located about three kilometers away. The closed city, built in the 1950s on the skete's confiscated land, was known during the Cold War by the code name Zagorsk-7. In 1990 one temple from the original skete and several cells were returned to the ROC and again became part of the *lavra*.[259]

The patriarch came to the CSRI to consecrate the memorial for St. Nikolai the Miracle-Maker and the foundation stone of the institute's church.[260] The ceremony was attended by the commanders of the 12th GUMO and of the 12th CSRI, the director of the St. Nikolai the Miracle-Maker Fund, city administration, senior officers, and clergy.[261]

The covered statue stood in the central square of the institute, the former monastery, with its back to the main building and facing the main entrance—a red-brick gate with a golden dome and a cross on the top. A green carpet, the official color of the Moscow Patriarchate, led from the patriarch's limousine at the gate to the statue, and green carpets lay on the snow in front of it. The commander of the GUMO greeted the patriarch with a bouquet of white roses and escorted him through the ceremonial guards in winter parade uniform and toward the statue. As the military orchestra played and the monastery choir sang, the commanders of the service and of the institute uncovered the statue.[262]

It was a three-meter-high bronze figure of St. Nikolai Mozhaisky, with a sword in one hand and a temple in the other, standing on a two-meter-high black granite foundation.[263] The statue symbolizes the unity of the spiritual faith and military bravery. According to Russian Orthodox folklore, St. Nikolai assisted the residents of Mozhaisk during the Tatar-Mongol siege, when following their intensive prayers he appeared in the skies holding a sword in one hand and the fortress of Mozhaisk in the other and so intimidated the enemies that they were scared away.[264] At the back of the statue, a plaque in the form of a shield with a cross on top of it reads: "This memorial was erected in 2007 to signify the 60th year of the MoD 12th Main Directorate's establishment." A plaque of the same form at the front epitomizes the logic of deterrence: "To the creators of Russia's nuclear shield"; right beneath it, in bronze letters, it reads: "Those who come to us sword in hand will die by the sword. Alexander Nevsky."[265] This saying of the canonized prince is known to almost everyone in Russia, due to the historical movie drawing parallels between the heroic figure of the prince and Stalin, who commissioned the film and popularized it during the GPW.

Following a consecration ceremony that included prayers and the sprinkling of holy water on the monument, the patriarch thanked the Russian nuclear custodians for forging Russian strategic power. "We should remember all those who labored on the creation of Russia's nuclear shield, because it prevented a Third World War and spared mankind a nuclear catastrophe." Verkhovtsev's response emphasized the notion of divine predestination of the strategic arsenal:

> Historically, our developments in the nuclear field always went hand in hand with the Orthodox spiritual heritage. The state's nuclear shield was forged in Sarov—the place where Seraphim Sarovsky established his cell—and one of the centers of nuclear scientific development—the 12th CSRI—has been located on the Sergiev-Posad land [named after the most venerated Russian saint]. Today, we are reviving the connection between the military bravery and spiritual faith, and restoring the Orthodox traditions. This year, the 12th GUMO has acquired its own heavenly patron—Seraphim Sarovsky.[266]

On his part, the CSRI commander assured the patriarch that "the historical, cultural, and spiritual center of Troitsa-Sergeev Lavra is under the vigilant eye of the institute and will be further preserved."[267] After the statue was consecrated, the patriarch accompanied by both high commanders laid a note signed by the three of them under the fundament of the St. Nikolai the Miracle-Maker temple that was about to be constructed on the territory of the CSRI. As the monastery choir sang psalms, the patriarch consecrated the cornerstone. Junior officers of the GUMO put the vases with the flowers next to the just-consecrated statue and fundament, and then about two dozen honorary guards with their flags and rifles marched, saluting the patriarch.[268] In the following years, the fund erected about a dozen statues of the saint on the perimeter of the Russian borders to protect the state from all directions. Two were erected in 2008 within the garrisons of the 12th GUMO: one at the Central Testing Range in Belushia Guba in the central city square,[269] and another one in 2010 at the Main Headquarters of the GUMO in Moscow.[270]

By the end of the decade, the main segments of the 12th GUMO were receiving permanent pastoral care and conducting a cycle of rituals, as in the other parts of the nuclear triad. By 2010, every official welcoming ceremony of the new shift at the Main Training Center included an address from the garrison priest.[271] Meetings between the clergy providing pastoral care to the GUMO entities and the commanders of the service, its main units, and the educational work department became regular.[272] The banners presented to the sixteen best units were appearing at parades and official ceremonies, Verkhovtsev put a huge icon of Seraphim behind his office armchair, icons of the saint appeared next to the national symbols within the bases and at several weapons systems platforms, and new garrison temples continued to appear within the smaller bases.[273] Naturally, Verkhovtsev did not miss the first visit of Metropolitan Kirill in his capacity as patriarch to the RVSN Academy and greeted him there with the RVSN seniors.[274]

CHAPTER 7

STRATEGIC MYTHMAKING

GENERAL MYTHMAKING

As the ROC was converting the military, strategic mythmaking—the reading of religious connotations into history that emerged as a grassroots phenomenon of the 1990s—came in very handy. It offered an unparalleled capitalization opportunity, and the ROC skillfully co-opted it, demonstrating a causal link between the spiritual support of the church and battlefield successes. The mythmaking became handy to the military as well, since it naturally coincided with its need to fill an ideological vacuum, cultivate a new esprit de corps, reformulate its professional ethos, and establish a pantheon of heroes for the sake of indoctrination within its ranks.[1] During the conversion decade, general mythmaking comprised three interrelated narratives—ancient Russian, relating to the GPW, and relating to the Soviet space program.

First, from the beginning of the decade, "to upgrade servicemen's morale-psychological condition," the ROC started cooperating with the GS Educational Work Department on "familiarizing the military with the state-national idea," through a "revival of the genuine military-historical memory."[2] Pursuing this goal, the ROC sought to demonstrate, through various educational materials, that throughout Russian history no battle had been won without the participation of the church.[3] The official summary of the 2003 annual Christmas readings, conducted within the GS Academy and dedicated to "Orthodox Enlightenment in the military," is indicative:

> Russia is standing in the way of those who seek world hegemony. Forces of evil are approaching our southern and western borders. Despite the difficulties, the country preserved its two vitally important institutions—the military and the church. In the contemporary conditions, it is impossible to build the military and strengthen its morale-psychological component without reconsidering the Fatherland's history and the role of the church, which inspired the warriors in their acts of bravery. It is necessary to restore the Church in the souls of the warriors as an indispensable condition for victory over the forces of evil. Otherwise, the state, stripped of national-religious content, would cease to be Russia.[4]

Incrementally, the ROC began outlining the Orthodox military ethics and popularizing the concept of "Christ-loving warriors" (*Khristoliubivoe voinstvo*). In 2004 Vladimir Legoyda—a figure close to the current and previous patriarchs, founder and editor of the pro-Orthodox journal *FOMA*, which is read by millions, and head of the Synodal Department of Relations with Society—published a programmatic article on the Christian attitude to war. According to him, since Orthodox military ethics does not perceive war as an absolute evil if "Christ-loving warriors" are waging it, the images of the saint and the warrior are intertwined in Russian history and folklore. In the Russian pantheon of saints more than half have been warrior-princes or warrior-monks, and their images "formed the ideal for the Russian military" and "played a significant role in the formation of Russian culture." Since the blessing of the religious authority became a necessary condition for victory, according to Legoyda, ties between church, rulers, and warriors have been one of the oldest trends in national culture.[5]

This culture preserved itself under the anticlerical Peter the Great, "when the traditional way of life was almost destroyed" and the church was transformed into a state ministry, and even during the Soviet era. Although the Soviet historiography omitted direct references to the faith of renowned military commanders, it presented their deep piety as love for the Motherland and then linked patriotism, and the moral-spiritual energy that it generates, with military genius and combat effectiveness. According to Legoyda's main thesis, the ROC has always carried the burden of infusing the nobility and ordinary soldiers with an "awareness of their high cause" and training them in the spirit of Christ-loving warriors.[6]

The ROC chose the most important event in public memory to illustrate this thesis. The second and main trend in the non-nuclear myth-making related to the contribution of faith to the Soviet victory in the GPW. The ROC had popularized this theme since the 1990s.[7] This effort first culminated in 2005, with the celebrations of the sixtieth anniversary of the GPW victory.[8] Toward the festivities, a book called *God's Mercy and Assistance during the Great Patriotic War* compiled several dozen accounts of divine interventions, miracles, and the faith of regular soldiers and Soviet marshals. It became so popular that, in the following years, several editions were issued, *Krasnaia zvezda* published a passage from it, and the Moscow Patriarchate widely distributed it.[9] In parallel, movies about the GPW featured priests fighting next to the soldiers, taking confessions, or giving blessings for battle, divine interventions, or simply a high level of religiosity among soldiers and commanders. Often the historical inaccuracies of these movies bordered on total nonsense.[10]

According to Sergei Filatov, one of the leading Russian scholars of religion, toward the anniversary, the ROC dropped its criticism of Stalin's anti-ROC campaigns and instead praised the wartime state-church cooperation.[11] The patriarchate adopted an active position on this matter. In March 2005, it co-organized with the MoD a conference on the ROC's role in the GPW. After welcoming remarks by Moscow's governor, the DM, and the patriarch, the speakers—high military commanders,[12] senior clergy, and historians—talked about the wartime normalization of state-church relations, the ROC's pivotal role in the victory, the part of Patriarch Sergei and other hierarchs in consolidating the national identity and translating it into military effectiveness, the ROC's donations toward the purchase of armaments, priests joining the military and the partisan movement, and expressions of religiosity among soldiers and officers.[13]

The event featured a combination of solid scholarly reports, claims unsupported by primary sources, and politicized statements. The ROC widely disseminated the proceedings, as they enabled it to claim, together with the state, a major part in bringing victory—the event that the Kremlin co-opted as one of the main themes in promoting Russia's image as a great power. To provide a solid basis for its claims, and to somehow control the noncanonical mythmaking trend, the ROC compiled, with the assistance of the presidential and the FSB archives, a collection of more than two hundred archival documents illustrating its role in the GPW.[14] This positioning of its wartime activity enabled the ROC to present itself as the main partner of the state, then and now. In the same month, Patriarch Alexey and Metropolitan Kirill conducted the VRSN's annual meeting, titled "Unity of Nations and Cohesion of the People—a Pledge for the Victory over Fascism and Terrorism." The concluding communiqué argued that only the unparalleled unity and spiritual-material cohesion of the Soviet people had ensured the victory in the GPW.[15]

This robust popularization of the wartime history and positive emphasis on state-church relations emanated also from the Russian Civilization notion, which Metropolitan Kirill, already then the main ecclesiastical ideologist, introduced in the early 2000s. Against the backdrop of the state's search for a national idea, the ROC started to popularize the revival of the traditional values and social-cultural-political organization based on them. The ROC presented this as a natural extension of a thousand years of Russian history during which the lives of state and church had been merged into one, especially during the wars, when Orthodox faith became a common denominator of self-identity and national mobilization. The ROC emerged from this vision as the main custodian of Russian culture, history, and values.[16]

The ROC defined the essence of Russian Civilization by contrasting it to the West—the main source of Russophobia over history. Russia is presented as seeking peace and cooperation, the West as reluctant to accept its uniqueness and respect its needs. According to Filatov, this constant prewar situation with the West was among the factors that accounted for the apocalyptic Russian siege mentality, turning it into a narrative of "sacral struggle through history." "The heroes of this struggle become commanders who accomplished victories on the Western front, political leaders who prevented Western military, ideational, political, and cultural expansion," and the clergy who facilitated national cohesion. Likewise, military opposition to the West throughout Russian history is perceived as an "expression of the eternal struggle of Russian Civilization with the Antichrist."[17]

Since "the heroes of this struggle receive the sacred aura," even Stalin's regime, which was initially radically anticlerical and thus could not have been farther from being "Holy Rus," nonetheless appears so when situated in the context of sacral struggle with the West. In the words of Patriarch Alexey, "Soldiers, often without realizing it, continued a Russian spiritual tradition and became the heirs of the previous glorified Christ-loving warriors." Orthodox education, according to the patriarch, made it possible to prevail against a formidable enemy during the GPW and to put the country back on its feet.[18] In short, Russian Civilization adopted the Soviet epoch as part and parcel of the Russian national heritage.[19]

Russian Civilization extended the concept of "patriotic service" that Metropolitan Sergii had introduced during the war, when Stalin restored the patriarchate. The "patriotic service" concept—a variation on the "symphony" theme of state-church relations—perfectly suited the Soviet ideology. The church, according to the concept, "perceives itself as an ideological support of the authoritarian rule [. . .] and serves as an obstacle to internal subversion and Western destabilizing influence." According to Filatov, during the post-Soviet times Metropolitan Kirill revived "patriotic service" under a new title.[20] In 2010 Moscow's central GPW museum hosted a big exposition called "Blessing for the Victory" and a roundtable titled "The Contribution of Religious Organizations to the Victory," which brought together Parliament members, historians, public figures, and clergy. The speakers outperformed each other in emphasizing the ROC's contribution.[21] Similar events devoted to the ROC's role in the GPW were conducted in other eparchies around Russia.[22] Central newspapers started publishing historical articles outlining the propagandistic, financial, and moral support that the ROC provided to the Soviet authorities during the war.[23] In May 2010, talking after the service at the church memorial to the GPW on Poklonnaia Gora, Patriarch Kirill argued that, like Napoleon's invasion, the GPW was God's punishment for the transgression of the Russian nation.[24] "The victory in the GPW occurred with the participation of God's willing, and the war itself was the test that God by his mercy sent to the people to save them."[25]

By the end of the decade, the references to nonaccidental coincidences became common, as did the sync between divine and professional military calendars.[26] Some within the military become receptive to these ideas and started turning them into a sort of professional ethos.[27] The ROC "provided a key component of the ideological doctrine of 'Orthodoxy, Autocracy, and Nationalism,'" and that was also the foundation of Russian military loyalty.[28] During the decade, *Krasnaia zvezda* adopted the figure of speech *podvizhnichestvo*, in relation to the deeds of military commanders. In Russian the word relates to philanthropic labor for the sake of a higher goal and for the good of mankind and is used strictly in a religious sense. The newspaper started to apply it when discussing the deeds of the military, especially those reviving cooperation with the ROC.[29]

The third mythmaking trend involved the religious interpretation of the Soviet space history. It was fueled by, among others, cosmonauts serving and retired, such as Alexey Leonov, the first human to perform a space walk, who expressed their religious views in public.[30] Mainly, however, Father Yoav, who during the decade actively explored and popularized "the history of the cosmonautics presented from the Orthodox angle," promoted this trend. According to the accounts, which the monk gathered in his research, the producers of the first rockets were baptized; Sergei Korolev was a believer, had a personal confessor, and donated to the monasteries; and many Soviet cosmonauts prayed at the most dangerous moments.[31] One of the primary expressions of this trend was the representation of Yurii Gagarin as a true believer. Father Yoav claimed that Gagarin's mother had been close to the nun Makaria, whom Gagarin also met and assisted. Gagarin, according to the narrative promoted by the monk, was deeply faithful and clandestinely baptized his niece and his daughter. The monk argued that Gagarin even argued for the restoration of the Christ the Savior Cathedral.[32]

The Russian space establishment adopted the narrative. In 2010 the ROSCOSMOS TV and movie production studio, which promotes historical events related to the space industry, issued and widely circulated the documentary *Space as Obedience*. The word *obedience*, or *poslushanie* in Russian, in addition to its secular meaning of submission, also refers to duties imposed on monks. The first scene depicts Russian cosmonauts, in space uniform, kissing the cross, while the priest sprinkles holy water on them before the launch. Then, against the backdrop of the launch pictures, the voice-over explains: "According to the sacred tradition there are three skies: the lowest is the earth's atmosphere, the upper one is the Kingdom of God, and the cosmos in between them is the second sky. In this second sky, where the space orbits lie, invisibly reside the devils." Against these "evil spirits of the under-sky," continues the voice of Father Yoav, "there is a need to consecrate the spaceships, to take confession from the crew, and to give them Communion" and for them to "pray in orbit, so that God will save them."[33] The movie also referred to divine intervention during emergencies, and suggested that older cosmonauts had encouraged the younger ones, who were not baptized, to do that prior to the first launches.[34] The ROSCOSMOS leadership disregarded critique of the movie as being full of inaccuracies and the open letter from the association of atheists asking it to comment on the motivating reasons for the movie's creation.[35]

Strategic mythmaking acquired iconographic expression. In 2007 a priest of the SF garrison church suggested creating a special military icon comprising the heavenly patrons of all the corps of the Russian military. The icon, featuring forty-one saints and called "Sobor of the Patron Saints of the Russian Warriors," was produced in 2008 and consecrated by Metropolitan Iuvenalii. Following the consecration, its image was reproduced and sent to all the churches providing pastoral care to the military. In 2009 the same church issued a calendar with an icon, which included all the Orthodox and official professional holidays of all the corps and services.[36]

NUCLEAR ORTHODOXY

Political-economic stabilization and then improvement from the mid-2000s stimulated a search for a unifying national idea. The absence of one and the Kremlin's interest in it encouraged a public debate. A plethora of views competed over the political discourse, in a variation on the traditional exchange between Slavophiles, Westerners, Atlanticists, and Eurasionists.[37] The most notable notions, and those who advanced or popularized them, included the *Russian Doctrine*, by the nationalist-orthodox ideologists; *Project Russia*, by the intellectuals associated with the security services; *Island Russia*, by certain academics; *Sovereign Democracy*, by the Kremlin's ideologist Vladislav Surkov; *Sovereignty of Spirit* and *Political Orthodoxy*, by the circles associated with the patriarch; and *Nuclear Orthodoxy*, by Egor Kholmogorov, in addition to several other notions, less notable.[38]

None of these was adopted in full, but ideas and themes from them informed the regime's ideology. Among these, the notion of *Nuclear Orthodoxy* stands out. It co-opted previous nuclear mythmaking, adding sophistication and coherence.[39] The notion evolved during the decade in three stages. First, the nuclear mythology from the 1990s acquired critical mass toward Putin's 2007 statement on faith and atoms. Then, following the president's statement, Kholmogorov gave to this collection of beliefs more structure and popularized it among the general public. Finally, the notion was canonized when the Russian Doctrine project, led by the patriarch, absorbed it. What follows is a brief intellectual history of the Nuclear Orthodoxy concept.

Since the late 1990s, references ascribing a divine connotation to nuclear weapons had steadily increased. The myth progressed from a figure of speech into an effort to "scientifically" establish this fact. Toward the festivities in 2003, clerics popularized a symbolic interpretation of the verse in St. Seraphim's akafist: "Be joyful, the shield and protection of our Fatherland." According to the new reading, the word *shield* in it refers to the nuclear arsenal. In line with this new interpretation, since the Soviet bomb was produced in Sarov and the development of nuclear weapons was still ongoing there, the saint had forecast, and indeed enabled the creation of, Russia's nuclear potential—the ultimate "protection of the Fatherland." This was not a coincidence, but a fulfillment of prophecy.[40]

The interpretation resonated within the nuclear industry; it further legitimized its work, saturated it with sacral meaning, and elevated its prestige. Toward the 2003 celebrations, the industry seniors began adopting a similar tone. Even Mikhailov, a former minister, emphasized the divine predestination of the faith-atoms linkage.[41] Around the same time, Dmitry Sladkov, the VNIIEF's director for public relations, illustrated the then-emerging wisdom: "Deep prayer and professional work, the living memory of St. Seraphim, and an outstanding level of science merged in Sarov" and created protection "of the Fatherland by the formidable weapon. [. . .] If St. Seraphim hadn't allowed the nuclear bomb to be created, nothing would have happened. [. . .] We pray to him for the solidness of the Russian nuclear shield, [and] perceive Seraphim, [whose name] means blazing in Hebrew, as the patron of nuclear scientists."[42] In addition to the divine predestination theme, Sladkov and Igor' Zhidov, another VNIIEF senior, popularized the industry's need for pastoral-spiritual care. The title of their article in the journal *FOMA*—"Physicists Without Priests Are Modern Papuans"—was an allegory for humans in an uncivilized state and referred to the desire to entrust the church with the spiritual health and care of the nuclear weapons specialists. The authors spoke on behalf of the industry, undisturbed by the existence of opposing views.[43]

In 2004 the Russian government funded the publication of a biography of the central personalities of the Soviet nuclear project—Igor Kurchatov, Andrei Sakharov, Yulii Khariton, Yakov Zeldovich, Kirill Schelkin, and Nikolay Dukhov. The author, Schelkin's son, titled his book *Apostles of the Atomic Age*. The choice of a religious term both in the title and in the book's conclusion, titled "Sobor Soul of Russia," offered a straightforward bottom line—Seraphim Sarovsky, the patron saint of the developers of the nuclear weapons, had helped in an "unreal short period of time to create the all-punishing nuclear sword against Russia's enemies." According to the author, "The heavens gave us our [nuclear] apostles. The apostles of the atomic age, to whom this book is dedicated, had [. . .] a huge thirst for creativity [. . .] and a sense that their labor for the sake of Russia pleases the heavens. [. . .] This is why I decided to call these six Russian 'bombmakers' our apostles in the harsh realities of the atomic age."[44]

Half a year before Putin's conference, in a lengthy interview to one of the major Russian newspapers, the VNIIEF deputy repeated the mantra about the not accidental union between nuclear science and religion.[45] Thus, Putin's 2007 remark on nuclear weapons and Orthodoxy as the two pillars of statehood did not come as a bolt out of the blue for either the nuclear industry or the public. This atmosphere made both relatively receptive to interpretations of Putin's statement, which became the launching pad of the Nuclear Orthodoxy concept. Putin's statement indeed became a major landmark in the evolution of Nuclear Orthodoxy, as the forces propagating this notion immediately co-opted it.[46] The main popularizer of this unofficial yet widely circulated concept became Kholmogorov, a journalist, publicist, public figure, and ideologist of religious-conservative nationalism. Immediately following the president's statement, Kholmogorov published a programmatic article titled "Putin and Nuclear Orthodoxy" in the biggest Orthodox resource of the Russian internet, widely read by those interested in state-church relations. Other Russian media quickly republished it, turning Kholmogorov's interpretation into the widely popularized frame of reference, and the kernel, of the Nuclear Orthodoxy concept.[47]

Kholmogorov argued that the Kremlin had orchestrated the press conference, so that Putin's answer could communicate his political will—ideological guidance on the direction in which Russia should advance after the power succession. Putin's course was clear, argued Kholmogorov—Nuclear Orthodoxy. Putin, according to him, had distilled the main national security formula, holding that Russia rests on "the nuclear shield and sword, created by scientists and the military, and the spiritual Orthodox shield and sword, which St. Seraphim put in the hands of every Russian." "Putin not accidently linked Orthodoxy with the state's internal security, and nuclear weapons with its external security. This is a complex 'Russian protection'—a defense against evil spirits and against people led by them. [. . .] Nuclear Orthodoxy is an eschatological Russian strategy for all times [. . .] if we, the Russians, want to preserve our existence."[48]

It was the first time that the eschatological component appeared in conjunction with the concept:

> Orthodoxy is a religion of eschatology, a religion of the Second Coming. The peculiarity of the Russian way in Orthodoxy is the quest to make Rus witness to the Second Coming, to bring its existence to such an eschatological

threshold, where it meets its Savior. Nuclear weapons [. . .], which are developed in Sarov, [. . .] protect the world from premature apocalypse, from eschatological experiments of the 'dark side.' The possibility of the world's doom at any moment excludes the triumph of Satan's rule. For Russia nuclear weapons are the guarantee [. . .] that at the moment of the Second Coming the worldly Rus and the heavenly Rus will indeed meet and that the existence of the worldly Rus will not be terminated ahead of time. Thus, the development of nuclear weapons [. . .] serves for Russians as a material guarantee of success in [. . .] a spiritual age, inherited from the saint fathers, in particular St. Seraphim [. . .]. We have no way but Nuclear Orthodoxy.[49]

Kholmogorov merged previous public and professional discourses about predestination and the divine connotation of nuclear weapons under the umbrella term of *Nuclear Orthodoxy* and crystalized its first postulate: the state's mission is to provide for its citizens, and for all the Orthodox, conditions for getting closer to God and to preserve the Holy Rus for the Second Coming. To accomplish this mission successfully, being Orthodox is insufficient; Russia needs to be a strong power, so that no one can impose their political-spiritual will on its way of life. Consequently, nuclear weapons have not only the military-political mission of preventing a premature apocalypse, but also a spiritual mission—preserving the sovereignty of the Orthodox way of life against satanic forces.[50]

In June 2007, Kholmogorov went to Sarov, to preach to the converted at the VNIIEF. In his address he took the concept a step further and added the second postulate: to stay strong as a nuclear power, Russia must stay Orthodox and protect itself from ideological, cognitive-psychological subversion. Consequently, spiritual-pastoral care of the nuclear weapons designers acquires unparalleled importance:

Under conditions of mutual nuclear deterrence, the war of perceptions, subversion of the opponent's combat spirit, his political integrity, his self-identity, acquires a bigger role [than before]. It is about imposing on the adversary alien meanings and forcing him to make the wrong choice. As long as the nuclear clinch is intact, war will be waged through these tools [and] indirect blows. For this reason, in parallel with the traditional military defense, the state should provide the nation with protection of meanings from the mental threats. In the realm of [nuclear] military technologies, we simply should not lose the existing level; in the realm of protecting consciousness, however, we should basically work from scratch. Our most terrible catastrophe in the 1990s related to the fact that the Soviet state failed to protect the sovereignty of consciousness.[51]

Thus, the Nuclear Orthodoxy rests on two postulates: "to stay Orthodox, Russian should be a strong nuclear power," and "to stay a strong nuclear power, Russia should be Orthodox." Addressing the VNIIEF, Kholmogorov argued that despite not being officially acknowledged, "Nuclear Orthodoxy practically has become an official ideology in contemporary Russia."[52] Kholmogorov gave a final twist to his concept, positioned as an "ideology," when he linked to it the term *agiopolitics*—a neologism of his inspired by two Greek roots. Agiopolitics stands for the influence of God, the saints and the sacral places on the political processes.[53] He used this concept as some sort of scientific apparatus to argue that what might seem to be the accidental coexistence of faith and atoms is actually divine intervention, a case of predestination. According to this concept, the saints (monks, elders, warriors, and rulers) perform "political miracles" to realize the agiopolitical will of God. Seraphim Sarovsky patronizing Russian nuclear weapons is one example of this phenomenon. This twist enabled Kholmogorov to interpret Seraphim's eschatological prophecy as being related to the end of the world and the appearance of the Antichrist before the Second Coming. The life of Seraphim, according to the canonical account, included a meeting with the Mother of God, who revealed to him that a ditch had to be dug around the Diveevo Monastery, which became, according to the ROC's canon, the fourth lot of the Mother of God on earth, after Jerusalem, Mount Athos, and Kiev. Today this ditch is one of the main sanctuaries in Diveevo. The canon says that the ditch's height reaches to the skies, that the Mother of God took this land as her lot, that everyone praying near it acquires an additional three lots, and that when the Antichrist comes he will pass everywhere but the ditch.[54]

Kholmogorov injected a geostrategic meaning into this canon. He argued that Seraphim had taken patronage over the Russian nuclear weapons, in front of which in powerless fury all Russian enemies have fallen still, and which broke all their hopes of destroying Russia. These weapons are a sort of *military-political ditch*. However, for it to preserve its strength, it should be surrounded by the spiritual ditch of Orthodox faith. [. . .] In the wars of the new century Russia will not have a second chance if we do not surround ourselves with the double ditch—a ditch of undefeatable material weapons, which excludes the very possibility of using weapons against us, and the ditch of spiritual weapons. [. . .] Exactly for this reason Nuclear Orthodoxy has become the field where the state and the Church in contemporary Russia found each other and created a symphony.[55]

Jardar Østbø qualifies Kholmogorov's vision as a "blend of politicized Orthodoxy, imperialism and militarism," conveying a clear military and geopolitical message.[56] By September 2007, Kholmogorov, probably inspired by the developments of the previous year, argued that the ideology of "nuclear orthodoxy, despite the sarcasm and slowness of the bureaucrats, was successfully gaining ground."[57] Indirectly, the concept received an additional boost when Kholmogorov's energetic popularization efforts coincided with the highly publicized celebrations of the sixtieth anniversary of the 12th GUMO (described in the previous chapter). Public and professional communities saw the setting of the celebrations as an extension of Putin's statement and of Kholmogorov's narrative. According to the leading Russian newspaper, "The gala supplication service in the Christ the Savior Cathedral dignified the final formulation of nuclear orthodoxy." The article derisively suggested that the next step would be the introduction of "a compulsory consecration rite of the ICBMs on combat duty" and modification of the nuclear weapons employment protocol to include "Prior to use, receive the patriarch's blessing."[58] It is unclear whether the author realized how close the situation in the Russian nuclear triad already was to his sarcastic prognosis.

Religious twists in the *Krasnaia zvezda* article on the history of the 12th GUMO left little doubt about the official attitude. The piece argued that Kurchatov, the head of the Soviet nuclear project, prayed to the Mother of God icon before the first nuclear test. Sections outlining the esprit de corps of the service mentioned, among the special qualities of the nuclear custodians, "the asceticism of devoted eremites [*podvizhnicheskaia askeza*]"—a word strictly reserved for use in a religious context in colloquial Russian. It is no accident, argued the author, that "the officers' service is compared to that of monks, with their discipline, hierarchy, spirituality, and obedience. The officers [of the 12th GUMO] are an ascetic generation of eremites affiliated with the greatest state secret and its super weapon."[59]

In a section titled "Faith and Loyalty," the article explored the spiritual foundations of the nuclear directorate:

> What gave them the power to overcome the difficult conditions of life, overloads, and tension? What was the source of power among people of Kurchatov's type? Why did Korolev, after torture, create missiles of tenfold power? Not everyone lost the faith. [. . .] Even those who became atheists [. . .] still preserved the thousand-year-old loyalty to the Fatherland. Patriotism was always the religion of the Russian officer. [. . .] All of them withstood this god-sent super-test to demonstrate super-loyalty to Russia. [. . .] Every day in Arzamas-16, the builders of the nuclear center—columns of gloomy prisoners—passed by the monastery walls. The same columns dug out underground warehouses for the nuclear warheads. Once their mission was over, they were sent to Kolyma, never to come back. These prisoners are brothers in the misfortune of Korolev [. . .] and thousands of others. They are martyrs. Their consecration is ahead. [. . .] The West lacked this terrible but priceless experience.[60]

The author suggested that the leaders of the Soviet atomic project realized that the ROC was their main competitor on earth. They decided to prevail over it by deploying the nuclear project's main segments in the two main sanctuaries of Russia—the main nuclear weapons' design bureau in the Sarov Monastery and the 12th GUMO Central Scientific-Research Institute (CSRI) in the Gefsimany Skete of the Sergiev Posad Monastery. The author saw it as deeply symbolic that the GUMO had revived spiritual life within its ranks, taken care of the sanctuaries located on its bases and in its closed cities, celebrated its anniversary in the main Russian cathedral, and acquired Seraphim as its patron.[61] Such an article published in the central official newspaper of the MoD implicitly gave an official stamp to the emerging new ethos within the strategic community.

The following year, Mikhailov, then head of the VNIIEF's Institute of Strategic Stability, poetically argued in the new edition of his memoirs that "Orthodox tradition sees the Fatherland's defenders as saintly warriors. Thus, the pious warriors of the nuclear center have been creating the shield, upon which any formidable sword raised against our Motherland will break. They are the contemporary Seraphims, the fiery and burning hearts of Russia, the guardian angels of our land."[62] Mikhailov's metaphor revealed knowledge of the subject. The biblical seraphs, the heavenly beings at the top of the hierarchy of angels, guarded God's throne; their name is translated from the Hebrew as "the burning ones."

The peak of Nuclear Orthodoxy in 2007 coincided with the peak of the Russian Doctrine project in which Kholmogorov was one of the editors. This project, which absorbed the Nuclear Orthodoxy concept, came about as follows. In autumn 2005, several radical nationalist-Orthodox intellectuals from various political movements united around the "sacral meaning" of the Russian ethnic-national identity, as the main logic driving the state's development, and conducted the first Russian March—a mass demonstration on the streets of Moscow. The event, which since then has been repeated annually in several major Russian cities, was attached to the Day of National Unity.[63] The Kremlin sought to co-opt this blend of conservative patriotic-nationalistic groups, some driven by Soviet nostalgia, others promoting the notion of Great Russia, and some venerating the Orthodox values.[64] However, since it did not provide any solid ideological content to the new holiday, the radical nationalist movements hijacked the event. Among the organizers were Alexander Dugin and Kholmogorov. Both spoke at the meeting and led the first column of the procession.[65]

After the march, the leading activists-intellectuals decided to outline their visions, in order to find common denominators, resolve disagreements, and compile a document that would provide "structured and coherent answers" to the main questions pertaining to Russia's future. This 800-page document, covering major aspects of political, economic, social, educational, spiritual, and cultural life, written by about sixty contributors and edited by three main coauthors, became a sort of "Russian Nationalist's Bible."[66] It reflects on the contemporary and prospective challenges and opportunities and offers courses of action, based on an eclectic mix of ideas. The first part outlined the spiritual-political essence of the nation; the second dealt with the Russian spirit and the ROC's role; the third looked at internal and external aspects of statehood; the fourth explored the economic dimensions; the fifth covered social issues; and the conclusion outlined recommendations for decision makers.

The section dealing with the National Military Doctrine and the force buildup strongly corresponded with the ideas of New Generation Warfare and cross-domain coercion practiced by Moscow in the following decade.[67] With regard to the nuclear strategy, the document stated:

> RVSN will play a special role in psychological pressure on the potential aggressors (the USA and China). Under the conditions of the suppressing superiority of the potential enemy in PGMs and air force (the USA) and in ground forces (China), *nuclear weapons became for us the most important "force equalizer." Most important is the psychological education of the Russian ruling elite: it should show the whole world its resolve to use nuclear weapons at the critical moment, unafraid of any international tribunals* [italics in the original]. In contrast to the previous Soviet leadership [. . .], and the contemporary Chinese leadership, Russia today lacks such resolve. We should merge development and modernization of the nuclear-strategic arsenal with psychological operations, aimed at convincing the whole world of Russian decisiveness and mercilessness when repulsing aggression.[68]

The part of the doctrine outlining the desired Russian image elaborated on this notion:

> The ruling power should find a way to demonstrate its ability to use force, including, under certain circumstances (which should be clearly defined), nuclear weapons; this is an extreme argument, but it should be a feasible one, in case of a threat to our spiritual sovereignty and efforts to put a crimp on Russia's independent political course. [. . .] We should make our enemies face the fact that *in our ethical system, force is the source of good blessing, and a state that can't use force, can't be considered sovereign* [italics in the original]. The twenty-first century Russian can't be a passive observer, running away from reality's most complicated tasks, but must militantly express his ethical and spiritual ideal.[69]

The initial draft of the doctrine was discussed at a series of events. The first roundtable discussion occurred in 2005 on the Island of Corfu during the "Russian Week," organized by the Russian Fund of Entrepreneurs, the Russian Embassy, and the Federal Service of Military-Technological Cooperation. Similar roundtables in academic and public forums in Russia followed, including a major event at the Union of Scientists. Following addresses by the three coeditors and Kholmogorov, remarks were offered by Metropolitan Kirill, the vice speaker of the Russian Duma, the chief editor of the Military Publishing House, the vice president of the Senior Officers Union, and editors of several leading Russian newspapers. In parallel, press, radio, and television popularized the doctrine. Dmitry Kiselev, the Kremlin's chief propagandist, argued on a central TV channel that "in its aims and intonation" the doctrine coincided with Putin's all-national agenda. In August 2008, a website compiled all the information on the document, stimulating public discussion on the subject.[70]

The doctrine gained broad recognition when Metropolitan Kirill arranged for it to be heard at the annual All-World Russian Sobor.[71] In less than a month, a refined version of the document came out as a book with a popular publishing house, as part of a series named "Maksim Kalashnikov Recommends," to increase the sales and ratings. Kalashnikov, who coined the term *Nuclear Orthodoxy* in 1998, was one of the three main editors of the Russian Doctrine and by 2007 a widely read publicist and author. The subtitle of the book originally was *The Russian Chance in the Twenty-First Century to Break Through a Global Time of Troubles*. In the subsequent editions, from about 2010, the title was changed to *Russian Doctrine: The State Ideology in Putin's Era* and to *Strategy of Russian Doctrine: Through Dictatorship to the State of the Truth*.[72] The patriarch and the metropolitan, addressing secular and religious audiences, dubbed it "the leading project of national revival."[73]

The exact impact of the ideas promoted by the Russian Doctrine and Nuclear Orthodoxy on the Kremlin and the strategic community is unclear, although a certain influence was obvious.[74] For example, a critique from high-ranking figures of the nuclear community indicated the growing magnitude of clericalization within its ranks. In 2007 Alexei Obukhov, a prominent diplomat and arms control expert, published in one of the leading Russian nuclear affairs periodicals an article titled "Nuclear Weapons and Christian Ethics." He reviewed the ongoing churching of the nuclear community, and the mythology that mystically combined religious fervor with the development of nuclear weapons, and then strongly criticized it, arguing against the religious imperative of nuclear weapons. Obukhov's critique revealed the breadth and depth of the already existing faith-atoms nexus:

> Ascribing to St. Seraphim patronage of the atom bomb is tantamount to an attempt to change the past. [. . .] The intellectual and spiritual bridges with which some apologists try to connect Seraphim with the atomic and hydrogen bombs are unconvincing [. . .]. Something in the depths of one's soul resists lending an aura of sainthood to the atomic bomb, the use of which would usher in Armageddon. [. . .] The Soviet-Russian nuclear bomb does not need the church's blessing. [. . .] No one should be deluded by the coincidence of location. That St. Seraphim and KB-11 carried out their work on the territory of the Sarov monastery is a noteworthy historical fact occasioned by fate and, to a certain degree, the deliberate anti-religious policies of the state.[75]

The critique made little difference, as attested to by the response of the 12th GUMO's commander to the patriarch in December 2007 at the CSRI of the nuclear custodians,[76] by Kholmogorov's publication of the most coherent version of the Nuclear Orthodoxy concept in 2008,[77] by the décor of the nuclear weapons museums,[78] and by the highly publicized ROSATOM exhibition in 2009, reflecting on the Soviet nuclear history from the religious angle. Veterans of the nuclear industry publicly argued that to some the mushroom cloud following a nuclear explosion was remindful of the person on the cross; that within the laboratories located in Sarov's monks' cells "the struggle with the implacable enemy was going on, fueled by eternal strength and spiritual power"; and that the highly disciplined spirit of the service in the monastery and the labor of the nuclear designers resemble each other. Radii Il'kaev, then the VNIIEF's scientific director, took the same opportunity to argue that only the church, during the most daunting moments, had always been with the Russian people, spiritually supporting them. For this reason, now, for the sake of the salvation of the people in general and the designers in particular, in return for the spiritual support of the church, it is necessary to support it.[79]

In September 2009, addressing a crowd of several thousand youth in Nizhni Novgorod, Patriarch Kirill argued that "Russian nuclear weapons, produced in Sarov, are a factor of deterrence and of the preservation of the sovereignty of our country" and that the nuclear center's being located at the site of St. Seraphim's service is a case of "real materialization of divine providence."[80] In the same year, a special communications boat built for the needs of the 12th GUMO was named after Seraphim Sarovsky, who according to the designers "predicted the establishment of Russia's nuclear shield."[81] In 2010 even *Krasnaia zvezda*, in an article on the RVSN nuclear priests, in a paragraph under the heading "Strategic Mission Church"—a figure of speech merging the word *church* with the name of the RVSN in Russian (Strategic Mission Missile Forces)—referred to the topic of divine predestination:

> It is difficult to say whether it is an accident or causality, but if we look at the map, then as a rule, somewhere near the missile units there will be the great holy places of Russia. Let us recall the units in Kozelsk, Bologoe, Iuriev, which nestle in the shadow of Optina Pustyn, of the Iversky and Spaso-Preobrazhensky Monasteries. And in Ural, where several strategic bastions have been deployed, ten years ago an important event took place— the laying of the monastery foundation for the martyrs of the tsarist family.[82]

SUMMARY REMARKS ON
THE CONVERSTION DECADE

This part covered the "conversion decade"—the period from the early 2000s to 2010, during which nuclear churching became state policy. When religion began playing an increasing role in Russian politics, and when the leadership began flirting with faith, a top-down trend supplemented the initial grassroots impulse of the 1990s. During the decade of *conversion*—a period that coincided with Putin's first two terms—the Kremlin restituted church property, introduced the institution of the military clergy, and enhanced the ROC's role in educational, social, and foreign policies. These top-down initiatives caught up with the earlier bottom-up tendency. Putin's public and private religious persona and the evolution of his personal and instrumental religiosity left a strong imprint on all of the above. By the end of the decade, the ROC became part and parcel of the nuclear officialdom, and catechization and churching peaked in all the services of the nuclear triad. The commanders of the nuclear corps and seniors of the nuclear industry signed cooperation agreements with the ROC and established close contacts with the patriarch and clergy. The nuclear mythmaking evolved into the formulation of the Nuclear Orthodoxy doctrine—a widely circulated public belief, with which Putin himself concurs, arguing that in order to preserve its Orthodox character, Russia needs to ensure its being a strong nuclear power, and to guarantee its nuclear status, it has to be genuinely Orthodox.

CHAPTER 8

STATE-CHURCH RELATIONS

CHURCH AND SOCIETY

The clergy and ecclesiastical infrastructure grew enormously as the Russian population went through the most significant religious revival since the Soviet collapse (see table 8.1). While in 1991 only 37 percent of citizens identified themselves as Orthodox, by 2017 that share grew to almost 80 percent.[1] The majority of these declared Orthodox, however, have been nonpracticing (*rastserkvlennye*) and not actively translating faith into actual social behavior. Genuine practice—familiarity with dogmas and canons, performing rituals, and regular church attendance—has been below the extraordinarily high rates of self-reported religiosity and lower than in some "less religious countries." Only 17 percent prayed daily, and less than 15 percent attended services more than once per month.[2] Less than half of the self-reported Orthodox performed certain rituals during the year.[3]

This "believing without belonging" phenomenon has resulted from the intertwining of religion and national self-identity.[4] When nonobservant Russians came to consider being Orthodox among the defining elements of belonging to the nation, and of cultural-civil self-identification, naturally the ROC became one of the major and most trusted social institutions.[5] When one-third of the population requested that Orthodoxy be accorded the status of an official religion, the ROC's main task became turning declared "believers" into practicing "belongers."[6] To outreach the

TABLE 8.1

Year	Dioceses	Bishops	Parishes	Priests	Monasteries
1988	76	74	6,893	6,674	22
2008	157	203	29,263	27,216	804
2016	293	282	34,764	35,171	926

Data source: Gregory Freeze, "Russian Orthodoxy and Politic."

"pious but un-churched flock," the ROC has expanded its activities across the board and supplemented traditional lines of operation with new ones. For example, in addition to his weekly Sunday sermon on social-political topics of the day, "Pastoral Word," which is broadcast on state central TV channel, Patriarch Kirill has prioritized Web 2.0 Orthodoxy,[7] engaged the flock at rock concerts,[8] and even blessed the activities of the most famous bikers' club, whose leader, closely associated with Putin, regularly organizes public events,[9] including annual patriotic bike tours to Crimea.[10]

The ROC's unparalleled status and political-social achievements have also generated a wave of antagonism.[11] Criticism has focused on the ROC as being a business corporation, consisting of several dozen enterprises, including banking, that enjoy enormous tax exemptions.[12] Luxury cars, yachts, watches, and other extravagant possessions of the clergy have raised eyebrows. There has also been public disapproval of restitution of previously seized church's property and state-funded restoration of ecclesiastical estates.[13] The return of museum property, such as icons and church artifacts, which nonreligious activists consider to be part of the national heritage, has become another source of tension.[14] The liberal intelligentsia has criticized the ROC's position on secular culture, art, same-sex relations, and, especially following the Ukrainian crisis, patriotism.[15] In all of the above, the ROC and the Kremlin have fought each other's battles. The latter has shielded the former from the waves of criticism, both rhetorically and through laws that criminalize insulting the faithful. Following several trials, anticlerical forces internalized that excessive protest may result in a harsh attitude on the part of the authorities.[16]

The ROC, in turn, has publicly supported the Kremlin's political course in domestic and foreign policy. Despite the criticism, the ROC continued to enjoy public prestige and ideational influence, which during the decade the state began co-opting for its political purposes more than ever before. Katarzyna Chawrylo attributes the ROC's increasing presence in public life to the government policy during Putin's third term, when the Kremlin, to strengthen its legitimacy, began promoting conservative ideology and traditional values, of which the ROC has been the guardian.[17] For the former, the ROC offered a political constituency. The latter expected from the needy Kremlin an increased enthusiasm to promote its agendas.[18] When in the wake of the 2011–12 political crisis the incentives to cooperate of both the Kremlin and the ROC became enhanced, the Moscow Patriarchate already possessed a solid vision of state-church relations, which would guide the emerging dynamic. By the time of his installation as patriarch, Kirill was the main theoretician and implementer of this vision.

Patriarch Kirill's vision of state-church relations boiled down to three principles. First, the church should be loyal to the state regardless of regime type. The Byzantine model of a "symphony," implying state-church concord, was the ideal. In theory, the model implies constructive cooperation and consensual equilibrium between equals. Aware that the Byzantine emperor totally subordinated the church to his will, Kirill urged the implementation of the symphony's ideal type only, and not of the Byzantine practice. Second, although the Russian Constitution separates state and church, the ROC should have access to all spheres of social life and express its positions on the state's economic, internal, and foreign policies. Third, Kirill urged that Orthodoxy retain its privileged position. For him, in addition to being the faith of the majority of Russian citizens, Orthodoxy for centuries had shaped the Russian national identity and had been the state religion (*Gosudrastvoobrazuiuschaia religiia*), and therefore it deserved exclusive status. In contrast to Putin, Kirill refused to define Russia as a "multi-confessional state," calling it an "Orthodox country with national and religious minorities."[19]

The reality, however, has been more nuanced than "symphonic," where in return for privileges, the ROC delivers ideological support to the Kremlin.[20] There are several views. Some scholars suggest that the president is the dominant partner in the relationship. When the ROC's agenda collides with that of the Kremlin, the latter subordinates the former to its will, along the lines of "managed democracy."[21] Others outline a "competitive model," where areas of convergence coexist with competition and tensions. On the surface, the church and the state are on good terms, but the patriarch, according to this view, collaborates with the Kremlin only if "state policy serves *raison d'eglise*, not just *raison d'état*."[22] Kirill is aware of this delicate game and acts accordingly, especially on sensitive matters.[23] Likewise, "Putin's maneuvering room is limited," as "he must appear supra-confessional in a multi-confessional state" in addressing his diverse constituencies.[24] Thus, to portray the ROC as the Kremlin's obedient servant or speak about a symphony of equals would be an oversimplification. However, whatever the nature of the relationship, more keeps the ROC and the Kremlin together than drives them apart. Their views mostly converge, making them allies that share the same values rhetorically and in reality.[25] During the operationalization decade, closer relations between state and church resulted in the ROC's greatest ever engagement in domestic and foreign policy.

CHURCH AND DOMESTIC POLITICS

Domestically, Orthodoxy became the main pillar of Russian nationalism and the basis of state ideology. According to Marlene Laruelle, during the 2000s the Kremlin switched from a nonideological approach to seeking a national idea, defined then as conservatism—a centrist ideology that is opposed to extremes and ensures social-political stability. Since Putin's return in 2012, this posture has become more elaborated. The regime's ideological modus operandi began encapsulating anti-liberalism and anti-Westernism, while emphasizing Russian uniqueness, ethno-religious values, the revival of patriotic feeling, tsarist-Soviet imperial nostalgia, and Russia's great power status.[26] The Kremlin realized that conservatism unites the nation only if it avoids explosive contradictions. To ensure the lowest common denominator, it kept the national idea vague, avoided rigid definitions, and ensured the harmonic coexistence of a doctrinal plurality under the rubric of "traditional values." This made it possible to communicate with diverse audiences without creating unbearable tensions despite opposing narratives. Realizing that an overdose of nationalism could be counterproductive, the regime practiced its "state-controlled" version. It appealed to ethno-national sentiments to mobilize public support, but preserved a centrist position that embodied "Russia's multiple identities" to prevent any upsurge of dangerous separatism among alienated minorities.[27]

Still, despite the risk of estranging certain social-ethnic groups, Orthodoxy loomed large in the new national glue. When Putin began drawing on social conservatism,[28] the ROC turned, according to Fiona Hill and Clifford Gaddy, into the "ultimate repository of Russian values."[29] Orthodoxy became more than religion; it became the measure of national identity, exactly as it used to be before the revolution, when language and faith had been the criteria of belonging to the nation even for ethnic non-Russians.[30] This new role of Orthodoxy naturally spoke to Putin's fascination with religious philosophy, which since the second half of the 2000–2010 decade had inspired the Kremlin's ideology. Reportedly, the ideas of Ivan Ilyin, a Russian religious philosopher and one of the main intellectual forces within the Eurasianism movement, particularly inspired Putin and provided the conceptual bricks for the national ideology, which he devised during his third term.[31]

Putin has been impressed by Ilyin's social philosophy, way of reasoning, perception of Russia, and historical predictions. Ilyin envisioned the Russian state, embodied in the tsarist and Soviet empires, as "a unique geohistorical entity tied together by the spiritual unity of the Euro-Asian nations." In the 1950s, he argued that the current reincarnation of this entity would collapse due to internal contradictions, that fascination with the Western way of life and blind application of its political-social standards would follow, and that this emulation of the alien way of life would eventually result in costly disillusionment. Ilyin suggested that in order to weaken post-collapse Russia, the West would use spiritual-ideational subversion by injecting ideas of democracy, liberalism, and federalization, which were alien to Russian tradition. He rejected democracy as an appropriate configuration for Russia and saw no alternative to enlightened national authoritarianism. As Anton Barbashin and Hannah Thoburn put it, "In Ilyin's eyes, it was impossible to unite the geographic, ethnic, and cultural diversity of Russia without centralized power." Only a powerful leader at the top, benefiting from the subjects' support, could prevent internal chaos, and only the embrace of traditional Orthodox values and spiritual renewal "under the auspices of the ROC" would ensure the post-collapse geopolitical revival. Along the unique Russian path, Ilyin saw religion "as intricately connected with politics."[32]

Ilyin's philosophy intellectually informed and morally justified Putin's authoritarian style, his conservative discourse epitomized in the "vertical power" management of democracy, and his narrative about the causes and consequences of the humiliating post-Soviet times of trouble. On top of it all, inspired by Ilyin, Putin, according to Barbashin and Thoburn, "has spoken of the need for religious revival and the valuable role of the ROC" in forming the moral values of Russian society and "preserving [its] rich historical and cultural heritage."[33] When Putin became convinced that the West would be disinclined to treat Russia as a respected power,[34] and when repulsion of Western political-cultural aggression became the central theme, state ideology came to encapsulate many of the ideas promoted by Ilyin and other philosophers of the Euroasian movement.[35] Since Putin's first reference to Ilyin in his 2006 address to the Parliament, his speeches and the official political discourse and statements by Vladislav Surkov, the Kremlin's main propagandist, have used Ilyin's writings as "propaganda clichés" promoting the regime's ideological course. In 2014 Putin gave regional governors the assignment to read Ilyin's work, *Our Mission*, over the winter break.[36]

The rise of protest movements and falling public support approaching the 2012 elections accelerated the Kremlin's co-option of the ROC.[37] The latter offered support on several levels. First, it began legitimizing Putin's persona, just as the ecclesiastical hierarch used to legitimize the tsar. Patriarch Kirill, congratulating Putin on his birthday, praised his efforts to save Russia from political-spiritual disintegration[38] and increase its international status and applauded his care after the spiritual health of the nation.[39] Surkov said that Putin was a God-sent president at a difficult moment of history.[40] Moreover, the ROC began equating itself with the state. In September 2012, against the backdrop of the charged election atmosphere, Patriarch Kirill, in a lengthy interview he gave to central TV channel host Dmitry Kiselev, argued that protests against the ROC, epitomized among other things by the group Pussy Riot's performance, constituted aggression against the state and subversion of its internal cohesion, cultural nucleus, and civilizational code. Kirill defined it using the military term *reconnaissance by force*, implying that this was a probing of the state's ability to defend itself on the cultural-spiritual front.[41] During the inauguration ceremony following the controversial election, Kirill sensed a political opportunity and delivered exactly what was expected of him—approval of the president-elect in the eyes of the public.[42] Moreover, he presented God as the divine source of Putin's power and the ROC as not only the legitimizer of the president's rule but also its pastor.[43]

CHURCH AND NATIONAL IDENTITY

The adoption of Orthodoxy as one of the main organizing motifs of national ideology came to a climax when Putin introduced the term *spiritual staples* into the political-public discourse in December 2012. He announced this in his address to the Parliament as a generic reference to the substance that staples the Russian state into one, which empowers the nation and is the source of its pride and strength at home and abroad. The term, widely used since then, has been a vague and constantly evolving concept. In his first allusion to spiritual staples, Putin spoke of their deficit in society and referred to several generic religious virtues—mercy, compassion, support, and mutual assistance. In subsequent references to the spiritual staples, the recurring themes have been Russian language, a common thousand-year history, and Russian culture, saturated by Orthodox tradition. Putin has urged support of "social institutions, which embody and maintain these staples and have proven through history their ability to preserve and pass them across generations," and has called for enhancing moral religious instruction in public education.[44]

Some commentators have argued that Patriarch Kirill was the source of the president's inspiration. The concept, Putin's variation of sorts on the theme of "Orthodoxy, Autocracy, and Peoplehood," followed Kirill's usage of this term in a sermon half a year earlier. The sermon dubbed the ROC and Orthodoxy as the Fatherland's main spiritual staples and their destruction as leading to destruction of the state.[45] Analyzing the address, a top Russian newspaper's editorial suggested that the president had delegated to the ROC the right to develop the national idea and had substituted it for civil society, which had begun being too independent and problematic for the Kremlin. The concept made the ROC a social tool supporting the state's initiatives in the realm of family, motherhood, children's and youth's education, social problems, and strengthening the patriotic spirit of the military. The population, according to the editorial, saw such delegation of authority as natural, since Orthodoxy historically has been related to an ethno-national foundation. In today's Russia, argued the commentators, religion for the majority of the population had become a means of national and cultural self-identification. Putin accurately sensed the vibe—"If we support the church we support patriotism."[46]

In 2016, four years after the introduction of the term *spiritual staples*, Putin's congratulatory birthday note to Patriarch Kirill clearly illustrated how the Kremlin perceives the role of the ROC in relation to this concept and the national ideology.[47] Putin thanked Kirill for serving the Russian church, state, and people at home and abroad, calling him the high authority of the ROC, "which played a huge role in the establishment and evolution of the Russian state" and which "preached love of the Fatherland and has been its powerful moral defender, promoting principles of kindness, truth, and loyalty." Putin has defined the ROC as "the main spiritual pivot of our people and our statehood" and has thanked the patriarch for concrete support in the fields of public education, social initiatives, and the moral upbringing of the nation.[48]

In parallel with popularizing the spiritual staples concept, and against the backdrop of growing tensions with the West, Putin began presenting contradictions between the United States and Russia as emanating not only from different geopolitical views but also from cultural and value dissimilarities. The different philosophies of life—individualism and materialism as the foundation of U.S. identity and collectivism and spirituality as the basis of Russian being, and their respective accompanying values—made mutual understanding between the two countries, according to Putin, possible but difficult.[49] Several years later, this tone became harsher, and Putin criticized "secular Americans and Europeans for rejecting their roots, including the Christian values that constitute the ba-

sis of Western civilization."[50] In 2017 a majority of Russian Orthodox re-
spondents reported conservative views, favored traditional values on the
major social-political issues, and expressed doubts about democracy as the
best form of government.[51]

The revival of traditional values and enhancement of spiritual staples
demanded the reconciliation of Orthodoxy with the Soviet project.[52]
Father Tikhon, the head of the Sretensky Monastery, sometimes dubbed
"the Kremlin's department of ideology,"[53] published *The Non-Saints Saints*,
a compilation of the stories about the lives of monks in the Soviet Union.[54]
Elegant prose and the author's identity made the book a best seller. Like
Tikhon's earlier movie project, the book served the Kremlin's ideological
need to present Orthodox values as spiritual staples transcendent through
history. The book bridged the chasm between the ROC and the Communist period, presenting it as a God-sent test of the faithful epitomized
in the lives of everyday saints.[55]

Unsurprisingly, at around the same time, the phenomenon of the "Orthodox Stalinists" expanded,[56] despite the fact that Patriarch Kirill and
Metropolitan Hilarion, the ROC's main intellectual, overall avoided glo-
rifying the Soviet past and Stalin's role in it.[57] The ROC's leadership,
probably sensing the Kremlin's needs, became more reserved in their criticism, balancing the narrative of repression with the great state achievements.[58] This also served the patriarch, who during the decade had been
busy implementing the institution of the military clergy. He expressed
this notion well when talking to the nuclear submariners: "The Church
has always been with the armed forces, throughout history. Even when
for ideological reasons the Church was externally segregated from the
people in uniform, internally it was not—in every service it prayed for the
rulers and for the military."[59] Another manifestation of the new national
ideology was the splash of "gastronomic nationalism," both in the Kremlin
and on the streets of Moscow.[60]

RELIGION AND FOREIGN POLICY
Russian World
Against the backdrop of growing tensions with the West following
the Ukrainian crisis and Middle Eastern turmoil, the ROC became an

active foreign policy player, promoting Moscow's interests.[61] It not only legitimized the Kremlin's course abroad, but also became its policy arm, expanding its influence worldwide. Regardless of actual effectiveness, the ROC became, during the decade, a frequent tool of choice in the Kremlin's geostrategic gambits in three theaters of operation—the near and far abroad, Ukraine, and the Middle East. In Central and Eastern Europe, and in the near abroad, where large Orthodox populations reside, the ROC used local churches and clergy affiliated with Moscow to preach sympathy toward the Kremlin's course, orienting the flock away from the West.[62] Guiding these efforts across locations even without coordination from Moscow was made possible by the framework of the *Russian world.*

By the time of his enthronization, which coincided with the growing tensions with the West, Patriarch Kirill had already crystalized this concept. According to him, originally the term had pure religious-historical meaning and referred to the ancient Slavic nations of Russia, Ukraine, and Belorussia, which became one entity, "baptized in the Kiev baptismal font." Kirill provided this original definition with a new, geopolitical meaning. According to him, the "Russian world" today refers to the "spiritual-cultural-civilizational code of the historical Rus," of which the ROC has been the creator and the custodian, especially during times of trouble.[63] The concept encompasses not only residents of this "historical Russia" but also a huge diaspora worldwide, which emerged out of several waves of immigration over the previous centuries, but shares the Russian civilizational code. Affiliation with this global community is cultural-spiritual-historical and not ethnic-religious, although the ROC takes upon itself the responsibility of preserving it.[64]

For the needs of the Russian World doctrine, Kirill borrowed the concept of "passionarity" from Lev Gumilev, one of the central ideologists of the Eurasianist movement. In Gumilev's works, passionarity stands for an exceptionally high level of activity of a given ethnic-social group, which aims to change the status quo in several realms through an enormous collective readiness for exceptional endeavors and self-sacrifice. Passionarity results in geostrategic achievements and a change in the status of a given ethno-social entity. According to Gumilev, Russians became a "super-ethnos" through a series of conflicts with the Eurasian steppe peoples, which eventually consolidated the Russian ethos into a power, which since then has opposed its main threat—the influence of the West aiming to disintegrate the Russian civilizational entity. In the patriarch's interpretation, passionarity, which he saw as one of the most important spiritual qualities of the Russian people, refers to the "capacity of the ethnos for historical exploit [podvig], sacrifice, self-development, a quest to go beyond narrow national being." Such an interpretation naturally resonated with the view of Russia as the Third Rome—as a "light unto the nations"[65]—as well as with opposition to the West.

The concept became a nonofficial umbrella term under which the Kremlin's previous ideological efforts to crystalize a unifying national idea among various groups harmonically coalesced. Experts mention three interrelated meanings of the concept associated with different groups. The first meaning relates to the space where the Russian language and the joint Soviet and post-Soviet cultural codes and mentality, including nostalgia for certain aspects of the Soviet Union, have spread. This meaning became widespread in the nationalistic-patriotic intellectual circles. The second meaning relates to the sphere of the Kremlin's influence in the new Moscow-centric quasi union, mainly on the territory of the post-Soviet space, and widespread in the circles close to the Kremlin. The third meaning, created by the circles close to the ROC, sees the Russian World as the sphere of influence of the Russian version of Orthodoxy, encompassing the Russian language, culture, and religious tradition and a joint interpretation of history.[66] The Kremlin quickly realized that it could leverage this "world" into some sort of integrated geopolitical-cultural space, which includes several ethno-national groups residing in the post-Soviet space and worldwide.

The Russian World became especially handy to the Kremlin when it designated foreign soft subversion as one of the main national security challenges. The concept complemented the compatriot policy—the Kremlin's initiative from the previous decade aimed at supporting and cultivating pro-Russian patriotic feelings among its former citizens worldwide. The Russian World doctrine offered an opportunity to upgrade this notion in terms of content and scope, and the Kremlin turned it into a tool of soft power in the international arena, especially in the near abroad. The concept became part and parcel of the Kremlin's public diplomacy effort worldwide to "project Russia's voice on the global stage" and to reach out to and bond with former compatriots, both ethnic and nonethnic Russians. The state-funded "Russian World" and Rossotrudnichestvo engaged these audiences through cultural, language, and media programs, promoting a worldview in accord with the Kremlin's agenda.[67] The criterion of belonging is not ethnic but cultural-linguistic, under the assumption that people who "speak Russian" also "think Russian" and "act Russian."[68]

Russian officials were open about their intent to operationalize the concept. In 2010, reflecting on the Russian role in world politics, ROSATOM's deputy head argued that the ROC should position itself as the church not only of the Orthodox believers in Russia but of all Orthodox Christians worldwide. To him, Moscow, "the heart and the brain of the Russian center of gravity," had for the first time in history become the de facto heir of Rome and Constantinople. "Now, the state leadership should learn how to skillfully utilize this huge resource for the sake of consolidating influence in the world."[69] In 2011 President Medvedev for the first time publicly used the term *Russian World*. He praised the ROC's work with foreign diasporas and compatriots both in the near abroad and worldwide and urged it to increase its participation in public life, enhance national cohesion, and promote state interests abroad.[70] When, in Putin's view, in the following years the West began creating "fifth columns in Russia," Moscow responded in kind by fielding "social values, nationalism, religion, language, and history" on the battlefield.[71]

Ukrainian Crisis

During the decade, the Russian World, against the backdrop of the overall theocratization of politics, began influencing even the performance of professional analysts. The story of the Russian Institute of Strategic Research (RISI) during the Ukrainian crisis is indicative. A government think tank, which had been part of the Foreign Intelligence Service (SVR) until 2009, it provides the president's administration with analysis of international trends in support of foreign policy decision-making. The current head, Mikhail Fradkov, moved to RISI in 2017 after heading the SVR. The previous head, Leonid Reshetnikov, a professional intelligence officer, arrived in 2009 after retiring as a lieutenant general heading the SVR informational-analytical service. While still there, Reshetnikov became a practicing Orthodox and developed an affinity for religious philosophy and Eurasian ideology. Upon arrival at RISI, he gathered around him Orthodox experts who held similar views and he involved clergy in the scientific-intellectual life of the institute. Reshetnikov promoted restoration of the lost imperial Orthodox grandeur, and in such a climate RISI's credo became not only informational-analytical but also ideological-propagandistic. This intellectual predisposition prevented RISI's analysts from foreseeing the course of events during the Ukrainian crisis, which resulted in analytical blunders and intelligence surprises for the Kremlin. The blunders were a combination of what Uri Bar-Joseph and other scholars of intelligence affairs define as "intelligence to please" and "cognitive closure."[72]

When the crisis peaked in Kiev in late 2013, RISI, driven by its spiritual-intellectual predisposition, estimated that Ukrainian statehood and sovereignty were a fiction and argued that Ukraine had a pseudo-identity artificially created by the machinations of Russia's enemies in 1917 and in 1991 and that it always has been part of the Russian World. This analysis suggested that this quasi state and quasi nation could exist only as an integral part of the broader imperial project, and therefore these historical mistakes should be corrected.[73] The same logic suggested that Euro-integration would be disastrous to Ukraine in the economic, cultural, and spiritual-religious senses. RISI bombarded the Kremlin with memoranda arguing that the vast majority of the Ukrainians are pro-Russian, in terms of a common memory and national mentality, and that only a marginal minority manipulated by the West was opposed to the pro-Moscow orientation. Eventually, RISI failed to foresee Maidan and tried to convince its consumers of the impossibility of such a scenario. Later, RISI promoted the Novorossiia project and underestimated the mobilization and resistance potential of Ukraine, not to mention the sanctions regime.

According to an insider, RISI shared responsibility for decision-making processes resulting in the worst international crisis in Russia's contemporary history.[74] It is difficult to establish whether RISI's analysis shaped or supported the Kremlin's course, but Moscow's actual steps during the crisis were in accord with the above arguments. Moreover, following the integration of Crimea, Putin and Patriarch Kirill "repeatedly underscored the idea of Holy Rus" with regard to the peninsula and presented its importance not only as the "symbol of Russian military glory and unprecedented valor" but also as the site of the baptism of the baptizer of Rus, Holy Prince Vladimir, "who assumed Christianity on behalf of Russia."[75] Explaining the strategic importance of Crimea during his annual address in 2015, Putin emphasized this sacral aspect: "The peninsula is of importance as the spiritual source of the development of a multifaceted but solid Russian nation and a centralized Russian state. It was in Crimea, in the ancient city of Chersoneses [. . .] that Grand Prince Vladimir was baptized before bringing Christianity to Rus. [Thus, Crimea has] invaluable civilizational and sacral importance for Russia, like the Temple Mount in Jerusalem for the followers of Islam and Judaism."[76]

Emphasizing the baptismal site of the man who brought Christianity to Rus underscored the peninsula's "Russianness." Thus, bringing Crimea back had deeper and broader meaning than simply restoring the continuity with the Soviet past, making it an event of a higher order of magnitude.[77] The installation in 2016 of a huge bronze statue of St. Prince Vladimir on Borovitskaia Square right next to the Kremlin's entrance and facing Christ the Savior Cathedral was the next step in cultivating this religious heritage. The Orthodox Christianity that Vladimir the prince founded now informs the domestic and foreign policy of another Vladimir, the president. Dugin, Kholmogorov, and other mythmakers of political Orthodoxy interpreted the return of what they saw as "the cradle of Russian faith" as the state's return to being itself and "re-becoming the Third Rome."[78]

Middle East

Moscow's conduct in the Middle East demonstrated a similar trend. With increasing Russian activity in the region since the beginning of the Arab Spring, the majority of Western experts focused on geostrategic drivers of Russian behavior, overlooking the impact of religious and messianic beliefs on the Kremlin's decision-making and its quest, genuine and instrumental, to give Russia's mission a sacred connotation. Only a few scholars, Dmitri Trenin in particular, have argued from the start of the regional turmoil that a spiritual element has been among the factors shaping the Kremlin's approach to Syria and the Middle East. When the crisis emerged, the Orthodox narrative already had become a pillar of Russian national ideology, and it was naturally extended to foreign policy. From the start of the Arab Spring "in Syria, as in Egypt and Iraq, Russian officials have publicly expressed concern over the safety and rights of Christian minorities caught in the whirlwind of Islamist resurgence." In a situation where Moscow saw Europe as decadent and distanced from its Christian roots and the United States as reluctant to do anything in the region from which it was pivoting to withdraw, the Kremlin and the ROC picked up "the mantle of defenders of Christian faith."[79]

In February 2012, Metropolitan Hilarion, the head of the ROC's external relations department, presented evidence to Putin about the persecution of Christians in the region, "from church demolitions in Afghanistan and bombings of churches in Iraq to the violence against Christians taking place in rebellious towns in Syria." After delivering the facts, the metropolitan asked Putin "to make the protection of Christianity around the globe a major part of his foreign policy." In response, Putin assured him: "You needn't have any doubt that that's the way it will be."[80] This was not empty rhetoric. Even before the intervention in Syria, Moscow encouraged the ROC to expand its regional influence among and through local Christian communities. The Moscow Patriarchate reached out to Christian denominations beyond the Orthodox communities in Egypt, Israel, Jordan, Lebanon, the Palestinian Authority, Syria, and Tunisia, providing the Kremlin with the humanitarian pretext for further diplomatic initiatives and enabling it to promote itself as the only patron of persecuted regional Christians. Moscow pursued this line of diplomacy in thwarting Western intervention in Syria through an alliance with the Holy See, which envisioned Russia, not the United States, as a protector of Middle Eastern Christians. Regardless of the accuracy of these self-attributions, the Kremlin created and exploited several informational struggle opportunities, enabling Putin to aggrandize himself as a historical figure bringing order to the region, guarding Christian values, and accomplishing Russia's civilizational mission.[81]

Several factors led Russia to intervene in Syria, although experts, as a rule, overlook the role of religion in Moscow's decision. Those who did pay attention to it saw it as a smokescreen for Moscow's realpolitik expansionism. However, the messianic factor in Russian decision-making in the Middle East is not novel, but the continuation of a long tradition, driven by the Third Rome narrative, which positions Russia as the spiritual center responsible for the salvation of the Christian world and of all humanity. This self-perception has had its ups and downs in the Kremlin's considerations over history. At moments when Moscow saturated official ideology with this national narrative, the messianic driver found clear expression on the ground during the tsarist, Soviet, and post-Soviet epochs.[82] Middle Eastern turmoil and the Syrian civil war coincided with the rise of this myth in Moscow and offered a perfect opportunity to capitalize on its geopolitical potential. Moscow envisioned its great power status as coming with a responsibility to patronize the forces of light against the forces of evil, especially when the West left no alternative to salvation.[83]

From the start and throughout the Russian intervention, ROC seniors have publicly expressed their support for the military operation, legitimized it from a Christian ethics point of view, and qualified it as a just war serving the needs of national security, preventing genocide, and protecting regional Christians.[84] On several occasions, Patriarch Kirill even dubbed the operation in Syria a Holy War,[85] but then downgraded this rhetoric, to prevent the undesired image of crusaders that might have alienated Russian Muslims and regional allies. Still, he continued emphasizing that intervention in Syria is an "extension of the great historical tradition" of state and church standing up to defend the Orthodox people of the Middle East.[86] According to the RVSN cleric, a majority of the officers, reflecting on the military operation in Syria, felt solidarity with Patriarch Kirill's position: "We are participating in the salvation of oppressed and humiliated people in the Middle East."[87]

When the situation in Syria had relatively stabilized and Moscow moved on to the postwar rebuilding phase, the ROC claimed a role in these humanitarian and social efforts and extended its role as an arm of Russian foreign policy. Speaking about the historical role of the ROC in Russian politics in the Middle East and North Africa, Mikhail Bogdanov, deputy head of the Ministry of Foreign Affairs, in 2017 openly praised the ROC's activities aimed at "strengthening the geopolitical influence and authority of [the Russian] state" in this key region and promised further support for the efforts of religious diplomacy.[88] In 2017 foreign minister Sergey Lavrov, praising the role of the ROC in Russia's Middle Eastern policy, referred to it as a state-ecclesiastical co-enterprise of public and direct diplomacy.[89] When a new administration arrived at the White House in 2017, Metropolitan Hilarion, in unison with Russian diplomats, attempted to convince U.S. vice president Mike Pence that Washington and Moscow were counterterrorism allies and should better cooperate in the Middle East.[90] The ROC also secured cooperation with the Holy See in postwar reconstruction in Syria.[91]

PRIVATE AND PUBLIC RELIGIOUS PERSONAS

Personal manifestations of faith among state leaders persisted during the decade. Medvedev, during his tenure as president and prime minister, continued his predecessor's traditions. In addition to publicized appearances in churches and pilgrimages to holy places, including Diveevo and Sarov, on his working desk, between a statuette of Tsar Peter I and an Apple monitor, an icon of a guardian angel was displayed, and a big house church was constructed in his summer manor right next to the main residence.[92] Lavrov, foreign affairs minister, more reserved in his religious expressions, also visited churches and lit candles during services in the framework of official and unofficial occasions,[93] but sources suggest that he did it more on the pro forma side, as a nod to the zeitgeist. Sergei Ivanov, former DM, continued, as the head of the president's administration, to make the sign of the cross in public during important professional events.[94] Father Tikhon, alleged confessor of Putin, expanded his network of influence among the seniors of the national security and intelligence apparatus during the decade. Moreover, he became a central religious figure inside Putin's court, significantly influencing state policy in the realm of culture and ideology.[95]

Within Putin's entourage, the religiosity of DM Sergei Shoigu, whether genuine or a facade, stands out. It strongly contrasted with the attitude of his predecessor, Anatoliy Serdiukov, who expressed respect for the ROC in tribute to the zeitgeist, but had tense relations with the patriarchs. Shoigu, who in his previous capacity as minister of emergency situations closely cooperated with the ROC and often arranged Putin's vacations and pilgrimages, became the first DM to make the sign of the cross when commanding the Victory Day parade—the biggest annual military ceremony. Since 2015, when entering Red Square through Spassky Tower, the Kremlin's main ceremonial gate, which regained its sacral meaning under Putin,[96] his cabriolet stops, Shoigu takes off his peaked cap and makes the sign of the cross according to Orthodox tradition. Even if Shoigu's choice to do so annually is purely a public relations move, as some commentators have argued, it still illustrates the type of image he chooses to communicate.

Putin's public and private religious persona continued to evolve during the decade. In 2012, still as prime minister, he conducted a round-table in Sarov with key figures of the strategic community on the main themes on the military-industrial agenda.[97] The visit, which included meetings with the VNIIEF senior officials and a prayer at St. Seraphim church, reinforced his earlier public statement about faith and national security. In the same year, he visited Israel, as always starting his trip with prayer at the Church of the Holy Sepulchre.[98] Senior Israeli officials reported on the disproportional diplomatic energy that Putin expended on what they saw as purely symbolic topics, such as the return of the Russian compound in Jerusalem and other ROC property in Israel and permission to conduct religious-educational work within the ROC's installations among the locals.[99] Putin's behavior during his presidential inauguration differed strikingly from that of Medvedev. His body language, the way he made the sign of the cross (often ahead of time), and the way he determinedly took the cross from the patriarch's hands to kiss it seemed more confident, natural, and sincere than Medvedev's performance during the same ceremony four years before.[100]

In 2016 he visited Mount Athos in Greece again, accompanied by the patriarch and Metropolitan Hilarion, to celebrate one thousand years of

Russian monks' presence there. Following the supplication service at the main cathedral, where he stood on the throne of the Byzantine emperor, Putin emphasized the exceptionally meaningful role of Mount Athos for Russia in strengthening its Orthodox faith.[101] Addressing the hierarchs, he spoke as a monarch of an Orthodox state.[102] Upon resuming his speech, Putin collected his papers, waited until translation was accomplished, took a dramatic pause, and then, before leaving the pulpit, announced the traditional Orthodox Easter greeting—"The Christ is risen." The audience responded in kind—"He is risen, indeed."[103] Putin's interviews with American documentary director Oliver Stone during 2015–17, as well, demonstrated both his deep and genuine religiosity and his desire to share it with the public.

CHURCH-MILITARY RELATIONS

Following the official establishment of the military priesthood—the ROC's greatest achievement in the security realm—as priests began arriving to the troops, the ROC intensified its media campaign popularizing the innovation.[104] Sources within the military, including *Voennaia mysl'*, the leading military professional periodical, offered lessons from historical and foreign experiences, praising the new institution and offering constructive suggestions for its further development.[105] In the beginning, there was a certain level of criticism from within and outside the military.[106] It was not a principled objection to patriotic education among the servicemen, but a protest against the delegation of this authority to the clergy, as well as disagreement with the growing clericalization of the military. However, the more the political-military leadership demonstrated its support for the new institution and expressed its religiosity, the less vocal this antagonism turned out to be. This became especially visible when Putin resumed the presidency, and Shoigu stepped in as the new DM. In 2012 Putin publicly emphasized the need to further develop the military clergy, which he saw in the broader context of state-church relations.[107]

Despite the overall favorable political and bureaucratic climate, objective problems emerged, as neither the ROC nor the military leadership knew exactly how to deal with the new institution. The biggest issues were finding qualified candidates, training them adequately, arranging their dual subordination (to the commander of the unit and to the local archiepiscops), and defining areas of responsibility between them and the deputy commanders for educational work.[108] Eventually, the new institution came to rely on the earlier experience of nonofficial cooperation between the ROC and the military.[109] Many of the priests, who have provided pastoral care to the military during the past two decades, both within and outside the nuclear triad, have incrementally acquired new posts and become the backbone of the new institution. The ROC has been actively engaging the MoD to approve their status, thus fully legitimizing their previous activities.[110]

The beginning of this process coincided with the tenure of Serdiukov, whom the ROC strongly disliked and criticized for the slow pace of the introduction of the military clergy. Although Kirill had asked Serdiukov several times to increase the pool of the military clergy and accelerate the pace of candidates' approval, Serdiukov did exactly the opposite; he downsized the original allotment that the ROC suggested by almost two-thirds and slowed down the approval process. The patriarch appealed directly to Putin, and his criticism added to the already accumulating allegations against Serdiukov, which eventually led to his discharge. The golden era of the ROC-military relations began in 2012 with the arrival of Shoigu,[111] who several weeks after his nomination came to meet the patriarch in his residency at St. Danilov Monastery.[112] Since then, in addition to regular meetings with the DM and military brass in the GS Military Academy, the patriarch has frequently participated in the meetings of the MoD Board.[113]

In August 2016, when the number of positions designated for the military clergy in the Russian Armed Forces was approaching over three hundred,[114] in a highly publicized manner Kirill met with Shoigu to summarize four years of cooperation. Speaking from the position of pastor, the patriarch made two points: First, he argued that in contrast to the situation under his predecessor, there was a positive attitude within the military to Shoigu's policies and reforms.[115] Second, he designated Shoigu as personally responsible for the successful and intensive introduction of the military clergy and enabling them to conduct the spiritual education of Orthodox servicemen. Shoigu, on his part, assured the patriarch that the work of the clergy had significantly decreased the amoral behavior of the servicemen and had almost totally eradicated the phenomenon of *dedovschina*.[116] He also praised the intellectual and professional level of the clerics whom he personally had met before they were dispatched to the remote garrisons, and he thanked the patriarch for supporting high mo rale in those faraway units, especially in the High North and in Syria.[117]

Indeed, from the beginning of the military operation in Syria, priests have provided uninterrupted pastoral care to Russian troops there. In September 2015, several clerics, one field church, and one mobile church clandestinely landed with the first wave of the expeditionary force. These clerics have been the Russian commanders' assistants for work with the faithful, and when deployed with their organic formations they have continued their routine pastoral activities as permanent priests in Latakia and Tartus.[118] The field church of St. Nikolai has been deployed in the Khmeimim base, which hosted the bulk of the Russian Air Force. The field church of St. Admiral Ushakov has been operating in the port of Tartus—the main Russian naval facility in Syria. Daily liturgies, celebrations of Christmas and Easter, processions of the cross, pastoral conversations, and confessions became part and parcel of the Russian operation. On holidays, additional clerics arrived from Russia to reinforce the permanent order of battle and to bring presents from Patriarch Kirill.[119] Priests also visited Russian units and military advisers deployed all across Syria and, when accompanying forward deployed units, have extended their activities to Christian congregations.[120] Wearing uniforms with special cross insignias, they reported to the expeditionary force deputy commander.[121] When the first killed in action began to arrive, the ROC conducted services during the official military burying ceremonies.[122]

Russian pilots conducting sorties from Khmeimim have taken small paper icons along on their bombing missions, putting them on the maps and target lists, which they take into the cockpit.[123] This should come as no surprise; a year before the sorties, the commander of the LRA, the service that had conducted several bombing raids in Syria, claimed that before every combat mission his pilots received blessings from priests and that there were icons in many cockpits.[124] Benefiting from the pastoral care of the military clerics aboard were the vessels of the Caspian Flotilla, which launched missile strikes into Syria;[125] the Black Sea Fleet cruiser *Moscow*;[126] and the Northern Fleet aircraft carrier *Kuznetsov*, which provided fire support from the Mediterranean. They conducted daily liturgies, received confessions, baptized, and morally supported the sailors. According to the commanders, this contributed to the morale-psychological stability of the crews, reduced tensions, and increased unit cohesion and discipline.[127] A year after the beginning of the operation, Shoigu thanked the patriarch for the care provided to the expeditionary force and proudly mentioned the expensive Karelian pinewood from which a new, permanent Khmeimim garrison church was built.[128]

The main novelty of the operationalization decade has been the steady involvement of clergy in the lowest level of field activities within various corps. This was particularly visible in the Airborne Troops (VDV), the service that shares its main priest with the RVSN and is, outside the nuclear triad, the most clerically intensive part of the military.[129] For example, in 2011 the VDV clerics began parachuting together with the first-timers to morally support them during the airdrop.[130] Commenting on this trend, B. M. Lukichev, head of the department of the work with faithful servicemen within the Main Educational Work Directorate, compared the role of the military clergy to that of the Soviet *politruks/zampolits* (political officers). He envisioned them, in addition to conducting the services and being actively involved in educational work, as "morally" instructing and controlling the servicemen in the midst of their combat missions, like during the Soviet times.[131] The patriarch, striking a similar chord, repeatedly emphasized that the spiritual-intellectual education and religious "fear of God" cultivated by the new institution would contribute to servicemen's discipline, motivation, and readiness to conduct any operational mission.[132]

The topics of religious-military sermons became closely connected to current events. Patriarch Kirill repeatedly positioned the military clergy institution as related to national identity. This project, according to him, contributes to the formulation of the servicemen's consciousness based on traditional Russian values—a task of great importance when external forces are seeking to supplant Russia's "cultural tradition and spiritual identity."[133] In 2016 the keynote address of the GS Academy's deputy commander, titled "The Role of the Spiritual Component in Preparation of the Officers' Cadre,"[134] resonated with the programmatic speech of the chief of the General Staff, Valerii Gerasimov. Contemplating the evolution of operational art, Gerasimov outlined future tasks in the realm of nuclear and conventional modernizations and urged further improvement of the patriotic preparation of the servicemen—since victory, according to him, would be achieved not only through material means but also by "spiritual resources of the people" and their national cohesiveness in the face of aggression.[135]

During strategic annual exercises, mobile field churches have been deployed and clergy have conducted field supplication services for the opening of the exercises and consecrated the weapons, provided pastoral care, including baptism ceremonies, and ensured morale-psychological support in combat conditions.[136] Various corps and Navy units that for techno-tactical reasons were unable to deploy field churches began acquiring mobile iconostases for use in the field.[137] By 2014, the military clergy across the services were equipped with sets of year-round field uniforms and personal equipment with a special insignia of the Orthodox cross.[138] To ensure pastoral care in the field, several publishers issued multiple editions of the *Orthodox Military Prayer Book* in the small, pocket format convenient for a combat environment. In 2011–13 alone, four different editions were printed.[139] In 2015 the Moscow Patriarchate published ten thousand copies of the book.[140]

CHAPTER 9

FAITH-NUCLEAR NEXUS

NUCLEAR INDUSTRY

By the second decade of the twenty-first century, the clergy and religiosity had penetrated not only the rituals but also the professional worldview and modus operandi of the nuclear industry. Sarov turned into a spiritual-scientific-security think tank of sorts, which brings together public, religious, and defense intellectuals generating ideas related to domestic and foreign policy for Russian politicians. Also, leading scientific universities, which educate a young cadre for the Russian nuclear industry and scientific units in the military, established faculties of theology, integrated into academic life. The period witnessed the climax, thus far, of the ecclesiastical penetration into the nuclear industry—a direct progression from the previous decade of conversion.

Professional and religious lives in Sarov merged. The local clergy have participated annually in the closed VNIIEF professional celebrations and addressed the audience together with senior city and industry officials.[1] Gradually, the city monastery acquired all of the churches located in the VNIIEF territory.[2] In 2012, ROSATOM head Kirienko arrived in Sarov to participate in the consecration of the Zosima and Savvati church. Funded by ROSATOM, this huge cathedral was erected in less than two years.[3] As the local archiepiscop conducted the service, Kirienko, the city mayor, and the VNIIEF head and its scientific director stood in line under the icon of St. Seraphim, with a group of nuclear officials behind them, and prayed collectively. Kirienko's address indicated how faith and profession were interwoven:

> It is not accidental that the center of security and of state power was created where historically the center of [spiritual] strength used to be. They are apparently supporting each other, as both the sanctuaries in Sarov and the Federal Nuclear Center are developing at an equally rapid tempo. People are the main wealth of the nuclear industry, and they live not only by material but also by spiritual values. Thus, the re-creation of the temple and return of the original shape of the monastery contributes not only to the ROC and to Sarov, but also to the VNIIEF.[4]

In 2011, "to attract attention within the nuclear industry, primarily of the youth, to the patronage of St. Seraphim of those strengthening the Motherland's defensive shield," ROSATOM, the St. Seraphim Fund, Sarov city administration, and the Moscow Engineering and Physics Institute (MIFI) initiated two projects for the nuclear cities' residents. The first, "Orthodox Sanctuaries of the Atomic Cities," was a photographic competition related to the main themes of the saint's teaching. The second project, "Spiritual Heritage of Seraphim Sarovsky," was a video competition among the students of the nuclear industry's universities. In the following years, the finalists' works toured the ROSATOM cities.[5] During the decade, popularization of the saint continued beyond the nuclear industry. The Russian Postal Service commissioned stamps commemorating Seraphim's, the monastery's, and the VNIIEF's anniversaries,[6] a wave of videos about the saint included an animated film about his life. He became one of Russia's most admired saints. Almost every Russian Orthodox church worldwide has introduced his icon.

Since the mid-2000s, the ROC has been consolidating all educational-catechization activities within the nuclear community.[7] Putin's trip to Sarov in 2012 offered an opportunity. Following a roundtable on national security, the patriarch blessed the establishment of Sarov's scientific-spiritual center. Kirill saw it as a forum of clergy, scientific circles, state bureaucracy, and society that would explore issues pertaining to national security through conferences, roundtables, and seminars. In 2013

Metropolitan Georgy, several deputy ministers, and ROSATOM and city officials gathered to implement the patriarch's guidance. They nominated VNIIEF and Sarov Monastery as cohosts of the center, located it within the monastery, and defined "Science, Orthodoxy, and National Security" as its motto.[8] They envisioned it as an educational platform and a think tank of sorts that would bring together government experts and NGOs and operate at the social-personal, nuclear community, and federal levels.[9] Organizers saw influencing state policy on the social-political issues as the center's main mission.[10]

Indeed, since its establishment, the center's annual activities have been synchronized with the Kremlin's security and foreign policy. The subjects of the 2014 seminars, under the rubric "Spiritual Foundations of the Fatherland's Security," corresponded with policy discussions stimulated by the notion of New Generation Warfare, emphasizing soft aspects of modern war. The titles of the events speak for themselves.[11] One seminar—"Interaction of Scientific-Technological and Spiritual Foundations for National Security Strengthening"—was particularly illustrative. The session on the current challenges included the following reports: "New Types of Wars in the Twenty-First Century," by the president of the Geopolitics Academy; "Challenges in Cyberspace," by the director of the Scientific Research Institute of System Analysis (NIISI);[12] and "Weapons on New Physical Principles," by the head of the VNIIEF Laser Physics Institute. The session on soft and spiritual challenges highlighted the linkage between external and internal threats. It underscored how Russia's enemies are seeking to destroy the traditional values of the ruling elite and to evaporate social cohesion and national unity.[13]

In 2015 "Unity of the Russian World" was the center's annual theme.[14] A roundtable, "Russian Civilization and Restoration of National Identity," brought together state officials, public intellectuals, clerics, and nuclear scientists. Participants highlighted the contradictions with Western values and cultural orientation, the centrality of religion to Russian civilization, and coming to terms with the Soviet past; presented the Crimea episode as part of the "Russian World" restoration; and discussed its goals for the twenty-first century.[15] Another roundtable, "Russian Military-Technological Security," brought together the heads of leading security think tanks and military experts. Discussions focused on the changing character of war that underscores intellectual-spiritual battlespace; the strengths and weaknesses of the Russian military;[16] import-substitution in the cyber sphere and informational-technological independence from the West; computer modeling for a new generation of nuclear weapons; and the need to define "spiritual staples" and national goals to enable strategic planning. As always, Metropolitan Gregorii and the VNIIEF scientific head chaired the meeting, which included joint prayer at the Sarov sanctuaries.[17]

The main event of 2016 was a roundtable, "Faith and Science— Interaction for Russia's Sake." It was synchronized with the patriarch's visit to Sarov to celebrate the twenty-fifth anniversary of the reacquisition of Seraphim's relics and the VNIIEF's seventieth anniversary. Following in the footsteps of his predecessor, Kirill first arrived at Diveevo, where Patriarch Alexey reburied the relics in 1991. The coffin with the saint's remains was brought to the monastery's square, where Kirill conducted the liturgy. All of the Russian metropolitans prayed together with him and the honorary guests: ROSATOM's head, heads of several parliamentary committees, the Nizhni Novgorod governor, VNIIEF senior officials, and the commander of the 12th GUMO, who, as opposed to his predecessor, rarely appears in public.[18] Following the service, everyone moved to Sarov to consecrate the Uspensky Cathedral—the monastery building where the remains of the saint were buried in 1903 and which was undergoing restoration. The father-superior and a cohort of officials—the deputy prime minister and Military-Industrial Commission head, ROSATOM's head, VNIIIEF's director and scientific head, the rector of Moscow State University, and Sarov's mayor—greeted the patriarch at the entrance. Upon consecration, the clergy, state officials, and roundtable participants prayed together at the saint's cell, which had been restored within the renovated Seraphim Sarovsky church.[19]

After presenting the VNIIEF director with a St. Seraphim icon featuring episodes from his life and from Russian nuclear history, specially painted for the occasion,[20] Kirill opened the scientific-spiritual roundtable.[21] He congratulated the VNIIEF, praising its contribution to the state's strategic might and to the cooperation of science and religion. The patriarch saw this collaboration as relevant not only in the nuclear realm but also in other fields where scientific work involves moral responsibilities and has dangerous implications, such as biological and information technologies that enable control over people's lives.[22] In response, Radii Il'kaev thanked Patriarch Kirill for the ROC's vital support that had saved the nuclear weapons industry by influencing policy and for neutralizing antinuclear public sentiment, arguing that scientists "sophisticating formidable nuclear weapons" still need moral-spiritual assistance from the ROC.[23] In the spirit of this roundtable, the center's subsequent meetings during the year explored "spiritual-moral foundations of the modern state," discussed the "symphony of spiritual and secular powers," and sought to ensure that managerial elites consisted of "spiritually solid people."[24] It is unclear yet to what extent the center influenced the political course. Clearly, however, the center's activities provided national-level legitimization of the Kremlin's foreign and domestic policy and produced concepts and ideas informing both.

In parallel, the center conducted various catechization activities for the nuclear cities' youth and for the students of nuclear institutes. In terms of clericalization of higher education, during this decade MIFI, the alma mater of the nuclear-weapons industry's cadre, again left other universities far behind. In 2012 MIFI's scientific council unanimously approved the opening of the faculty of theology and its inaugural dean— Metropolitan Hilarion, the ROC's External Relations Department head, a holder of an Oxford doctorate in theology, and one of the leading candidates to become future patriarch. According to Hilarion, the faculty enables young nuclear physicists to broaden their education, expand their religious worldview, and develop their personal attitude toward Orthodox culture.[25] By then, the monk, an MIFI graduate himself, had become the priest of the institute's house church and done catechization work.[26] At around the same time, social science articles started to appear, exploring parallels between the metaphysical and mystical aspects of nuclear physics and religion and arguing for a more solid spiritual enlightenment of nuclear industry experts.[27] Under an influential dean, the theology faculty expanded its activities significantly, gradually turning into the main body of interaction between religion and science within the higher education community.[28] By the end of the decade, for MIFI students, the wayside cross, the house church, and the faculty of theology became something natural.[29]

STRATEGIC MISSION MISSILE FORCES (RVSN)

During the "operationalization decade," the RVSN preserved its leading status within the nuclear triad in terms of width and breadth of religious activities. It also led in turning garrison churches into spiritual-social centers cultivating a national identity among the servicemen and their families. In 2013 the Synodal Department stated that it "is an obvious fact that this corps, justly named Russia's nuclear shield and sword, is the most churched service" and dubbed its priests "strategic pastors"—a play of words alluding to the title of the service.[30] The service had staffed the newly introduced military cleric positions, involved them at the lowest possible levels of tactical activities, and fully integrated them within the chain of command. The clergy became part and parcel of routine RVSN operations. The annual cycle of Orthodox activities and rituals intensified in terms of participants,[31] and garrison churches within the closed cities became centers of cultural-social-patriotic life for the families of the RVSN servicemen.[32] For example, the main church in Vlasikha became more than a place of worship but also a "center of spiritual and cultural life," attracting middle-aged, elderly, and young people.[33]

In keeping with the Russian political discourse, religiosity and patriotism merged within the nuclear forces as well. Patriotic clubs within the bases were turning into garrison churches while preserving their original missions, becoming "spiritual-patriotic" centers.[34] Banners newly introduced to all RVSN divisions featured prerevolutionary heraldry with religious symbols instead of the old Soviet ones, underscoring this trend.[35] The clerics also merged religiosity and patriotism in their sermons. Speaking in 2016 at the RVSN Academy graduation ceremony, the head of the Synodal Department said:

> I would like you all [. . .] to remember that we are defending the dearest thing—our Motherland, spiritual interest, our cultural indigenousness. We defend the monasteries, churches, and sacred places of our Russia. Pray God

that in your service there will be no use of deadly weapons. This is a weapon of deterrence and warning. [But] your service should guarantee that no one, no leader of any country, will doubt that we are able to respond in the proper way.[36]

The priests also linked this symbiosis of faith and patriotism with a Russian military theory of that time, which underscored the merging of soft and hard aspects of warfare. According to the RVSN Academy priest, since Russian nuclear deterrence had successfully prevented military coercion, Russia's adversaries now wage subversive information war aiming at perception. They try to manipulate the servicemen's conscience, in order to prevent them from conducting their nuclear duties. For this reason, the priest attributed the highest importance to the pastoral care that he provides to the RVSN servicemen before their operational duties and combat missions.[37]

Through the year, as in the previous decade, the Synodal Department's representatives conducted regular pastoral trips to missile regiments, held conversations with draftees at the training centers, and lectured on Orthodox themes to the RVSN cadets, to the youth within the closed cities, and to veterans and active-duty servicemen at RVSN hospitals and their families. Through these short visits, nuclear pastors from Moscow covered all of the RVSN divisions and higher education institutions.[38] These activities supplemented the routine pastoral care conducted by permanent priests within the units. Following the introduction of the military clergy, these permanent priests have gradually changed their informal status within three RVSN armies to official positions as commanders' assistants for work with faithful servicemen. The RVSN High Command has sought to nominate retired military, preferably RVSN officers, who have been assigned as priests to the new posts. Commanders have assumed that such clerics, capitalizing on their knowledge of the RVSN specifics, would more quickly find common language with servicemen during religious and everyday activities.[39]

The first priests staffed new positions at the Yoshkar-Ola and Tagil divisions in 2011. Both clerics at the rank of protoierei, a retired RVSN major and a lieutenant colonel, had previously served as eparchial priests providing pastoral care to the missile units next to their congregations.[40] In 2012 the Novosibirsk missile division received its nominee at the rank of *igumen*, a retired company sergeant major, who had previously served at the church in the closed RVSN city.[41] Although by 2016 about sixteen hundred missileers had graduated from the FOC,[42] and in principle could serve as a reservoir for the relevant cadre, the ROC preferred to send candidates from its own ranks, and it considered the pace of staffing new positions, in the RVSN and in other services, to be slower than desired. Local archiepiscops began assigning clerics "on credit" to military units, voluntarily and nonofficially, expecting the MoD to approve them later. Yet, three years after the introduction of the military clergy to the divisions, about two-thirds of the RVSN priests still provided pastoral care within the bases without official nomination.[43]

Extending pastoral care down the chain of command, to the level of divisions, had been one of the tendencies in the previous period. During the "operationalization decade," clerical penetration reached down to the most tactical level—the crews operating weapon systems in the field and the barracks of the missile regiments. Although the trend had begun earlier, now the priests got more frequent access and came into closer proximity to the weapon systems, and commanders, following the introduction of the new institution, perceived the priests as part of the order of battle.[44] More often than before, clerics consecrated the missiles and participated in preparations for launch.[45] Prayer rooms have been steadily appearing within the barracks of the missile regiments where there is no garrison church or chapel, which usually were constructed on the upper level—within the missile divisions.[46] The Seraphim Sarovsky Fund sponsored the design of these rooms[47]—a reincarnation of the "red corners" in the Soviet Army barracks. In parallel, in 2012 the Vlasikha garrison was the first to introduce a mobile church to be used during field maneuvers and combat training outside the base.[48] Other units began emulating it and the VDV experience, where Father Mikhail, the main priest of both services, had steadily equipped airborne divisions with these new mobile churches.[49] Mobile churches became handy when priests began participating more often in field maneuvers and missile division exercises. Now, they not only conducted a supplication service at the start of the exercise but also participated in the maneuvers of the mobile missile complexes and conducted pastoral conversations with and provided religious care to the servicemen in the field.[50]

The "operationalization decade" brought another novelty—a professional symbiosis between the RVSN Educational Directorate and the "nuclear clergy." The importance that Russian military tradition attributes to this directorate, interchangeably called the Directorate for Work with Personnel, is difficult to overestimate. The directorate's head is a member of the RVSN Senior Council and reports directly to the RVSN commander.[51] His subordinates, deputy commanders for work with personnel, are embedded at all levels of command within the armies, divisions, and regiments and, in some cases, even battalions and companies.[52] An organ of RVSN management, it is responsible for "education and morale-psychological maintenance of the combat activity, mobilization readiness, combat duty, nuclear safety, preparation, and employment of the RVSN."[53] A reincarnation of the Soviet Main Political Directorate, it "ensures a unified understanding and solid implementation of national security policy," cultivates the desired climate within the units, "maintains the personnel's high morale-psychological level, and formulates among servicemen the qualities of a professional citizen-patriot." It also develops commanders' "psychological-pedagogical skills."[54] It comprises three departments and a psychological service and is responsible for the "psychological preparation of servicemen for conducting combat missions."[55]

The RVSN conducts harsh screenings of its servicemen, in terms of social-psychological background and professionalism. The selection process aims to ensure total reliability of each one and to determine "whether one can or cannot accomplish the mission."[56] The directorate commander could not wish for better allies than the military clergy, especially after almost two decades of deep cooperation with the ROC. Institutionalization of informal liaisons between the directorate and the ROC has resulted in the deep and wide integration of the priests into even the most sensitive fields of work.[57] The priests and the directorate have formulated a modus operandi whereby the military clergy become neither substitutes for nor subordinates of the educational officers, but their comrades in arms, with complementary missions.[58] The RVSN began involving clergy in the annual study-methodological gatherings of the missile armies' high command.[59] Commanders summarize the previous year, exchange experiences, outline the next year's projects, and participate in workshops for training in new work methods. Usually the RVSN commander either comes to present his vision or communicates it through his deputy, and the directorate commander heads the gathering. In 2011, senior officers from all of the directorate's units arrived at the RVSN headquarters for the annual gathering. About three dozen deputy commanders of the missile armies and division levels and commanders of the polygons, C2 centers, higher education institutions, training centers, and nuclear arsenals attended. For the first time in the history of these gatherings, RVSN military clerics and representatives from the Synodal Department participated.

The number of military clerics was still very small, as the new posts had just been introduced, but they immediately were involved in the most sensitive issues on the RVSN agenda. In addition to standard topics, several new issues were added.[60] One was logical—a workshop on "cooperation of units' commanders with their assistants for work with the faithful in the interest of spiritual-moral education of the military servicemen." Other issues included sharing experiences of using polygraph and IT testing systems to explore the moral-personal qualities of the ORBAT (order of battle) and conducting with all the participants a practical workshop on the theme "organization of the morale-psychological maintenance of the combat duty of the missile regiment on the highest level of combat alert."[61] Since then, the deep involvement of the nuclear clergy in these gatherings has continued. As the gatherings are a microcosm of the actual functioning of the corps, they probably represent well the depth of clerical penetration in the routine. In a similar RVSN gathering in 2013, the number of clerics increased.[62] The priests were fully integrated in the sessions and sat together with other participants—lieutenant colonels and colonels from the missile armies.[63]

In the 2015 gathering, there were already priests from ten missile divisions, and the overall number of participants had grown to forty, thirteen clerics among them. The tools and skills of military-patriotic education became the main theme of the gathering, strongly resonating with the ideological-political climate in Russia. One of the novelties was involving the nuclear priests in a workshop conducted at the Central Command Post and dedicated to "organization of the morale-psychological maintenance of the combat duty shifts in the central command and control posts."[64] Another novelty that emerged at around the same time was the involvement of the clergy in the study-methodological gatherings of the RVSN psychologists. Various seminars, training sessions, and roundtables provided participants with the practical and technological tools of the psychological work with servicemen. For the first time, they also discussed cooperation of the units' psychologists with the commanders' assistants for work with the faithful for the sake of providing spiritual-psychological support for the servicemen performing combat readiness duties. A separate section dealt with work with the polygraph, and another summarized the lessons learned from "creating the composition of the duty shifts based on the psychological compatibility of the members of the crew and on their ability to conduct joint tasks in a lengthy time frame."[65]

LONG RANGE AVIATION (LRA)

In 2011, a year following the introduction of the military clergy institution, the MoD designated the LRA as the best corps in terms of cooperation with the ROC. According to the announcement, the service had staffed all planned military clergy positions, in every garrison a church was functioning, and priests provided pastoral care to the servicemen in every regiment.[66] In reality, only two priests within the LRA's main air bases, Engels and Ukrainka, had been officially nominated to the LRA. The rest, indeed operating in more than a dozen churches at the LRA regiments and units, had been functioning voluntarily.[67] Although the official nomination process went as slowly as elsewhere, still, due to the LRA's small size, commanders at the top had sustained religious practice among the pilots and conscripts and provided the clergy with unlimited space for maneuvering.[68]

By the middle of the "operationalization decade," consecration of the airplanes, technique, weapons, and residences; blessing of the servicemen conducting operational missions; collective and individual pastoral conversations with the servicemen; and their attendance at church services were all deeply ingrained in the everyday life of all LRA garrisons.[69] Religious rituals became tightly interwoven with the LRA's combat activities. Liturgies at the start and end of the exercises and icons in the cockpits of strategic bombers, which previously had been episodic occurrences, now became more frequent in all the garrisons from which crews left for exercises, combat missions, and patrols.[70] According to the LRA commander, by 2014, before every operational mission the pilots received a priest's blessing and many of them brought icons into their cockpits.[71] The pastor to the main LRA training and tankers' base underscored the importance of these ceremonies, which assure pilots "that in the consecrated airplane God's grace is assisting the person in the cockpit."[72]

As in the RVSN, professional and religious ceremonies merged. For example, in 2012, when consecrating a new banner at the Engels base, the local episcop, instead of using the official term of combat banner, called it a "khorugv'"—a religious military flag—and positioned it as a symbol of faith, patriotism, and profession.[73] This apparently benign figure of speech accurately depicted the LRA's state of mind as religious rituals became organic parts of professional settings. At the same base the next year, during the weekly gathering of all units on the assembly ground, following the anthem and the raising of the national flag, the commanders outlined the weekly combat mission. A joint prayer blessing these forthcoming duties and the sprinkling of holy water on the formations followed.[74] Other LRA garrisons gradually introduced similar practices.[75] In 2016, summarizing the annual work, the LRA main priest concluded:

> All the garrison churches are properly functioning, priests conduct the weekly liturgy on the plaza, within the regiments services are taking place, and pilots receive blessings of the combat sorties. [. . .] In addition [during the year], there have been meaningful events in the lives of pilots, which priests actively supported—prayers before combat actions and consecration of missiles that were used in Syria. In the words of the pilots themselves, the priests have a beneficial influence on the servicemen's spirit, assisting [them] to overcome fear when accomplishing their missions.[76]

As in the previous decade, the LRA clergy have joined the periodical meetings of the corps, which summarize the results of the work of the staffs, bases, and services and outline plans for the following year. The clerics conduct their own meeting with the same aims as a subsection of this most important LRA professional gathering. Such a setting enables them to interact with all the corps' senior officers at the same time and present their work to them, as well as receive an audience with and the guidance of the corps commander. The work of the section has started and ended with a joint prayer with the pilots.[77] In all cases, regimental commanders and their priests have arrived together, as an organic formation.[78] In parallel, since the middle of the decade, the priests have closely cooperated with LRA military psychologists in assisting conscripted servicemen in moments of hardship.[79] By the end of the decade, the ties of the corps' senior officers with the ROC's central figures grew stronger, especially with the head of the Sretensky Monastery, Archimandrite Tikhon, an influential figure in the Kremlin court.[80]

NUCLEAR NAVY

The Navy commander in chief and all the fleet commanders entered the "operationalization decade" as converted admirals, publicly expressing their religious devotion and supporting the ROC's activities.[81] Patriarch Kirill's 2010 visit to the PF nuclear submarine squadron in Viliuchinsk aptly illustrates the then state of ROC relations with the nuclear Navy. Kirill had been to the base before, but this was his first visit as patriarch and after the official introduction of the military clergy. Accompanied by the local governor, he started by visiting the *St. Andrei* squadron's garrison church—the oldest church of nuclear submariners. Commanders of the Forces in the Russian North-East, of the nuclear submarines squadron, its chief of staff, all of them rear admirals, and the garrison priest, a retired nuclear submarine captain, greeted the patriarch and joined him in the service.[82] Following the prayer, he proceeded to the base. On the shore, all the squadron crews were arranged against the backdrop of their vessels—three Borei class and several other nuclear submarines anchored along the piers of Krasheninnikov Bay. As the squadron commander took the patriarch through the formations, the dynamic of the ceremony resembled official parades where the military commander, from a subordinate position, introduces the forces to the higher authority.[83] Kirill addressed the crews as a spiritual custodian talking to custodians of strategic power. He expressed his deepest gratitude to the submariners who during the post-Soviet period "did not tremble, did not leave their combat posts, remained faithful to the oath of allegiance under the most difficult conditions that many saw as humiliating, and with humility, grit, and loyalty to the Fatherland kept on accomplishing their military duty."[84]

As on other occasions, the subtext of the patriarch's remarks attributed to the ROC credit for improvements in the Russian nuclear triad, the Navy in particular. The rest of his speech promoted three messages: the importance of Russian nuclear weapons, the ROC's role in preserving them through spiritual care of the servicemen, and turning the newly introduced institution of the military clergy into the main tool for this task. If "the spiritual power of our military will be augmented by modern military-technical power," concluded the patriarch, then Russia would "posses a reliable shield and defense." He expressed the hope that in the near future more priests "will serve side by side with the servicemen, spiritually strengthening them."[85] Kirill's vision materialized completely during the decade. The rituals and ceremonies had expanded and become more sophisticated; naval processions of the cross and venerations of special "naval relics" had multiplied; religious, professional, and patriotic activities had merged into one; and increasing numbers of clerics joined nuclear submarine crews during their operational missions, providing pastoral care and conducting services in the specially constructed submarine sanctuaries. More than ever before, the sermons attached religious connotations to geopolitical events.

In both fleets, nuclear submarines continued to receive uninterrupted pastoral care. In the NF, in addition to the eparchial clerics pastoring the base, the Sevmash and Zvezdochka shipyards and the special submarine construction and repair brigade hosting crews awaiting their vessels all acquired their own clerics—a priest of the Nikolsky cathedral within Sevmash and a monk, who was the brigade commander's assistant for work with the faithful. A brigade, a squadron subunit, constructed for its needs the house church of St. Prince Vladimir, and Zvezdochka established a church-chapel of St. Feodor Ushakov near its pier. As the pace of ships' commissioning, including Borei-class submarines, has increased, the clerics have conducted consecration ceremonies at the beginning of construction work, when the vessels and crews leave the shipyards for pre-commissioning tests, and upon completion of construction.[86] In the PF, the newly appointed metropolitan Artemy, in addition to routine pastoral visits to the crews and guiding the military priests of the eparchy, has regularly met with the commander of the fleet's submarine forces to discuss cooperation. During the decade, the base acquired a new chapel at the military cemetery and a new church in the city of Rybachii, within the residential area of the submariners' families.[87] As the cleric and commander stated, "The peculiarities of the submariners' service, especially the long raids, produce psychological tension and intensify family problems. Thus, it is important not only to produce comfortable conditions for conducting service, such as residences, schools, and medical care for the families, but also not to forget about the spiritual and moral state of our defenders."[88] Construction of new churches within the residential areas of the closed cities for the needs of the servicemen's families continued during the decade in both fleets.[89]

Naval processions of the cross and the worship of unique naval relics became routine in both fleets among the residents and servicemen of the nuclear submarine bases and were indicative of the religious zeal in Russia and the passion for venerating miracle-inducing relics that characterized the decade.[90] In the NF, since 2012, annually the submarines' crews have conducted processions of the cross on the streets of Severodvinsk on the day of the passing of St. Fedor Ushakov, marching with icons and religious and civilian naval banners and in full parade uniform.[91] However, it was the PF, located far away from the main Russian sanctuaries, religious centers, and monasteries, that introduced the standard set of rituals and left its northern colleague behind in terms of veneration of the most sacred relics. Usually, residents of the closed city and the servicemen would touch the relics within the garrison church or venerate them during parades in the central plaza of the base, with the entire squadron command present at the supplication service and blessing ceremony. The priests also conducted a naval procession of the cross with the relics aboard an icebreaker, which had passed through the bay near the piers where the nuclear submarines were anchored with their crews standing on their decks, and a helicopter flew over the naval installations blessing them from above. In 2010 the Mother of God icon from Christ the Savior Cathedral spent two days at Viliuchinsk, the closed city of nuclear submariners.[92] In 2014 the icon of St. Sergei Radonezhsky—the most ancient and famous patron saint of Russia from Troitsa-Sergeev Lavra—arrived.[93]

In 2015, after unification with Crimea, a delegation from the Feodosia eparchy visited the PF. The clerics brought the relics of St. Georgii, St. Dmitry Solunsky, and St. Varvara to the base.[94] That same year, to underscore the importance of reacquiring the territory where the baptism of Rus occurred, the patriarch dispatched the relics of St. Prince Vladimir, the Baptizer of Rus, to Kamchatka. The nuclear submarine base there was the first stop of the visit. Grand Duchess Maria Vladimirovna, of the House of Romanov, arrived together with the relics and joined the metropolitan and the squadron commanders at the ceremony. Following the already routine ritual of blessings, marches, salutes, and kissing of the icon, the senior officers addressed the crews. Their points highlighted the parallels between civil-military relations at the time of the two Vladimirs, the Saint Prince and President Putin.[95] In 2016, when the relics of St. Feodor Ushakov arrived at the base, all the squadron servicemen, either by order or by choice, touched the relics and kissed them.[96]

Incrementally, in both fleets, military and religious events, both low-key and at the highest level, merged. Organic integration of religious ceremonies into the secular did not produce a dissonance, as it built on a solid basis. For more than a decade, the clergy has promoted within the Navy a religious interpretation of the main heraldic symbol of the service—the Andreevsky cross banner of the Russian Navy.[97] In 2010 *Severodvinsk*, the first of the newest Yasen-class nuclear-powered attack submarines, armed with fourth-generation cruise missiles, was commissioned from the shipyard. President Medvedev, DM Anatolii Serdiukov, and Navy commander in chief Vladimir Vysotsky led the ceremony, but it was the Arkhangelsk archiepiscop who opened the event with a consecration ritual and supplication service praising the constructors and blessing the crew. During the ceremony, including the president's address, the big St. Nikolai icon leaned against the submarine, with the clerics lined up and standing next to the crew in front of the speakers.[98] Even in less ceremonial but entirely official and closed events, such as the signing of the decree commissioning submarines from the shipyard to the Navy upon the completion of repair work, it became a norm for clerics to be present, bless the event, and sit among the senior officers in the first row behind the table on which the document was signed.[99] Clerical addresses during these events have blended faith, patriotism, and professionalism.[100]

Following the introduction of the military clergy, like the other services, the naval arm of the nuclear triad began turning its existing priesthood into the commanders' assistants for work with the faithful. The PF received eight new positions, and given the long-lasting nexus between the ROC and the nuclear submariners, they were the first to acquire the new nominees, some of them retired nuclear submariners.[101] In 2015 more than 50 percent of the military clergy consisted of retired officers.[102] As in other services, the naval nuclear clerics often have been former mid-level retired servicemen. Commanders encouraged this trend and sought candidates of this kind, whom they saw as the best fit. Indeed, priests–former officers knew how to address commanders; were familiar with the organizational culture, the sailors' state of mind, and service difficulties; possessed security clearances; knew the equipment; and were trained to function underwater.[103] The story of Father Veniamin, whose career went full circle—from retired nuclear submarine captain, to a monk at the Sanaksarsk Monastery, and then, in 2012, to an assistant to the Belomorsk submarine base commander for work with the faithful in the NF—illustrates this trend well.[104] According to him, monks are better suited to serve in the military priesthood on submarines than regular "white clerics," since long missions with crew underwater demand separation from wife, children, and congregation.[105] In parallel, another monk of the Arkhangelsk eparchy, a former nuclear submarine officer, began providing pastoral care in the NF.[106]

As elsewhere, so too in the nuclear Navy, the introduction of military clergy raised many issues. There was no clear division of labor and responsibility between commanders, educational officers, and military priests. Departments for cooperation with the military within the eparchies were now charged officially with providing regular care to the units, but this was often beyond the capacity of the local clergy. Candidates' selection processes were often lengthy and demanded approval by five levels of the ROC and the MoD. Some priests even argued that it was easier to function on a voluntary basis, not being constrained by so many administrative regulations.[107] The situation was improving gradually, but the intensity of activities among the nuclear submariners increased. Eparchies volunteered additional clerics to serve within the bases and the garrison churches; although formally these priests were not on the official staff of the squadron, they fully coordinated their activities with the commanders and clergy at the bases.[108]

Priests became involved, more often than ever before, in the operational activities of the nuclear submarine fleet. For example, in 2011, when Episcop Artemy became the new Kamchatka metropolitan, in the spirit of the times, his acquaintance with the nuclear flock of the PF began with a guided tour by the squadron commander aboard a nuclear submarine.[109] It included an excursion to the main command post, ballistic missiles storage, and the submarine's nuclear reactor. "I was amazed and encouraged," said the cleric, "seeing what weaponry our Russia possesses."[110] Pastoral care of the servicemen assigned to the naval testing range, where all Russian nuclear submarines undergo ballistic and cruise missile tests before commissioning by the Navy, became permanent. Priests have been accompanying fully armed nuclear submarines during prolonged test-raids at sea.[111] In keeping with the MoD regulation on the military clergy, regarding the priest's duty to participate in naval cruises, shore maneuvers, and exercises, clerics sought to join as many raids with the nuclear submarines as possible.[112] The participation of the clergy together with the base command and families in welcoming the submarines returning from raids also became routine during the decade.[113]

Father Veniamin, a monk who has often joined the raids of various nuclear submarines of the NF, is convinced that catechization of the crew is more effective at sea than within the base. Ashore, the priest interacts with the servicemen only when day duties are completed, during their leisure time. Aboard, on the contrary, the crew are available to him around the clock, both when on duty and afterward. Moreover, commanders have encouraged pastoral conversations with the crew on duty also out of instrumental considerations. During the long shifts, when computers control most of the submarine functions and the crew's physical activities are limited, even brief conversations with the priest better enable sailors to stay awake and diversify a monotonous routine that diffuses focus.[114] Also, close interaction during the raids enables priests to better explore sailors' backgrounds and personal qualities and to screen those on whom they can lean during the prospective catechization work ashore.[115]

A priest's typical day aboard the submarine begins when he arrives at the command post to sprinkle holy water and bless the shift on duty. During the changes of shift, the commander on duty outlines combat missions to the sailors, officers, and engineers-mechanics. If the shift falls on a particular religious holiday or saint's day, the priest says a couple of words on the event, explains to whom and how to address prayer today, and tells what made a specific saint famous. During the night, he goes through the ship and talks to the sailors on duty. As a rule, recalls Father Veniamin, the sailors have been happy to talk to him, since when the whole crew is asleep and the sailors on duty are awake and cannot leave their post, talking to a priest becomes an entertaining episode. In addition to social and intellectual fun, it also keeps sailors awake and focused. In addition, the priest reads passages from Orthodox literature on the submarine's radio, which broadcasts via loudspeaker.[116]

Underwater temples (*podvodnye pokhodnye khramy*), an equivalent of the RVSN field churches, became another feature of the operationalization decade. At the beginning, sailors lacked specially designated places to conduct services on submarines. They prayed either in the missile storeroom or inside the officers' mess deck, where the crew gathers on specific occasions and where officers dine and discuss professional issues. Several submarines, in addition to prayer corners, improvised altars and unique relics or had icons inside the command post, next to displays of missile weaponry.[117] However, the more priests became involved in tactical-operational activities during the lengthy missions at sea, the higher the demand became for more elaborate services aboard. The Omofor Fund, an Orthodox-patriotic charity for military veterans, offered a solution—portable temples for submarines. During the previous decade, it had donated portable temples to the cruiser *Moscow* and to the aircraft carrier *Kuznetsov* and had then adapted its design to make it suitable for submarines.[118]

In 2015, when the Omofor Fund equipped the flag battleship of the Baltic Fleet with a field temple, there were already forty such sanctuaries across the Navy, about half of them on the submarines of the PF and NF;[119] the intent is to equip the entire Russian underwater fleet with them.[120] The temples are equipped with a cloth, folding-screen iconostasis, about two meters high and four meters wide, featuring icons adorned with golden threads. It can easily be unwrapped and positioned on board. From the start of the decade, during submarine repair work and construction, the Sevmash administration and clerics began designating special locations for these folding-screen iconostases within the submarines. Consequently, the fleets received submarines with built-in temples, which had been blessed during the construction process. In other cases, the Omofor Fund representatives and clerics have gone to the bases where the submarines have been deployed and brought the iconostases to the crews.[121]

The consecration ceremonies of the underwater temples became a symbiosis of military and religious rituals. The crews were arranged in parade formation either in the central plaza of the base or at the piers right next to the nuclear submarines. The base, squadron, or submarine commander together with the cleric, often the local metropolitan, and the president of the Omofor Fund, a retired vice admiral, led the ceremony. The cleric consecrated the folding screen iconostases in front of the crews, and then the three of them addressed the audience, explaining the practical and spiritual importance of the event.[122] A parade followed. When the marching formations passed the temple, the officers saluted the icon, and the sailors turned their heads up and to the right, exactly as they would during a military parade. The priest meanwhile sprinkled holy water on the passing lines of servicemen.[123]

Finally, during the decade, the clergy became more vocal in referring to geopolitical issues of the moment and strategic aspects of nuclear deterrence, in their sermons to crews. It started with general references at the beginning of the decade and progressed to the need for spiritual support of the nuclear operators, given the moral-psychological tensions emanating from the danger of the nuclear submariner's profession.[124] Then, incrementally, the more involved the priests became in operational activities, the more—in the priests' own words—the pastoral care of the officers of the nuclear submarines demanded familiarity not only with "the techno-tactical aspects of the service, but also with the main political directions, goals, and missions that the political leadership and senior command have outlined for the Navy and for the military in general."[125]

By the middle of the decade, against the backdrop of nuclear weapons' increasing role in national security, the clerics were linking their generic patriotic-spiritual mantras to the current geostrategic realities. They emphasized "the importance of the nuclear weapons for defending the Motherland," "for guaranteeing Russian independence," and for the promotion of political goals.[126] In 2014, right after the unification with Crimea, speaking to the senior command of the Pacific nuclear submarine squadron at the celebrations of Submariner Day, the local metropolitan presented the ROC's view on the role of the nuclear triad as being relevant to recent events:

> The Motherland provided you with very powerful weapons—the nuclear sword, which is the undisputable argument for enemies of Russia, who do not want to see it strong, independent, and integrated. Recent events [. . .] in Ukraine constitute the clear supporting evidence. If we had not possessed this power, probably no one would have heard and paid attention to the will of the majority of the Crimean people. But, thank God, there is a strong Russia. You and your service are providing this strength. We are thankful to you for the act of heroism that you have been carrying out. On this day I wish you strength of spirit, the assistance and protection of God during combat missions in the depth of the ocean, and that you work to provide peace and security to our country, and to those nations that enjoy Russian patronage.[127]

Speaking the next year at the same event, he reemphasized his point: "Today we celebrate the day of reunification, the fair entrance of Crimea and Sevastopol, the Russian sailors' city of pride, into the Russian Federation. This happened, and happened peacefully, without bloodshed, because you professionally and firmly hold the nuclear sword of our Motherland."[128] Moreover, speaking about the roles of the nuclear naval priests against the backdrop of a charged international atmosphere, senior clerics straightforwardly argued: "If the necessity arises, we will go together with you into battle."[129] Finally, another trend emerged during the decade. Probably to some extent due to organizational competition over shrinking resources within the nuclear community or inside the Navy, the naval nuclear clerics began emphasizing the submariners' leading role within the nuclear triad.[130]

SPACE COMPLEX

During the decade, PRO and early warning (EW) units began catching up with other segments of the SF in terms of churching and catechization. To accommodate the increasing activities of the independent service by 2011, the Synodal Department established a section of the SF headed by a protoierei, and military clergy started to arrive at the SF units in various eparchies.[131] As in the other services of the nuclear triad, the clergy concentrated on the catechization of the servicemen, in order to deal with the all-Russian issue of "believing without belonging."[132]

The annual round of activities that had emerged within the SF during the previous decade became more entrenched during this one.[133] Clergy held regular celebrations of religious and secular holidays within the garrisons (Christmas, Fatherland's Defender Day, Easter, and Victory Day), baptized conscripted servicemen, and conducted pastoral conversations with new shifts of officers and services during operational activities, training, and parades.[134] As elsewhere, priests who had conducted these activities on a voluntary basis incrementally were turning into official commander's assistants for work with the faithful.[135] As in other parts of the nuclear triad, during the consecration of the new banners clergy have been part and parcel of the ceremonies.[136] Supplication services also preceded the beginning of construction work for the new early warning missile radar stations.[137] In 2012, during the celebrations dedicated to the fiftieth anniversary of the establishment of the PRO corps, Metropolitan Iuvenalii, in the presence of the SF and PRO corps commanders, consecrated the church-chapel of the Derzhavnaia Mother of God in Sofrino-1 base—the headquarters of the main anti-ballistic missile defense division.[138]

The blessing of launch activities continued in both the military and civilian space industries. Failed launches did not deter the cosmodrome priest from conducting consecration ceremonies, but rather made him even more determined to accomplish what he sees as a sensitive mission that puts at stake "the prestige of the state, enormous funds, and the labor of many people." "I hope that soon our Russian Glonass will substitute for the U.S. GPS (global positioning system) over the territory of our country," said Father Artemy following the consecration ceremony of the GLONASS satellite launch and right after consecrating the Soyuz-U missile that sent the Kosmos optical surveillance military satellite into orbit.[139] Within the civilian part of the Russian space program, blessing ceremonies continued and even took on a global reach. In 2012 the priest of the Los Angeles Spaso-Preobrazhensky Church consecrated the space rocket Zenit-3SL. Most of the rocket parts were produced in Russia, but the Boeing Corporation had produced some of the components and assembled the rocket.[140]

The operationalization decade projected into space as well. On several occasions during Christmas, the patriarch conducted sessions with the International Space Station to congratulate the cosmonauts.[141] In March 2011, following a liturgy at the Christ the Savior Cathedral, he presented to the ROSCOSMOS head the icon of the Kazanskaia Mother of God and requested that it be taken into orbit during the flight commemorating the fiftieth anniversary of the first space launch. In the following weeks, Kirill met with two cosmonauts preparing for the launch and asked them to keep it in the Russian area of the station.[142] In April 2011, the Soyuz TMA-21 shuttle was launched from Baikonur with the crew members connecting to the International Space Station, and the cosmonauts accomplished the patriarch's wish.[143] On Easter, they left the following note in the orbital diary: "We celebrated Easter modestly—had some meals and watched a movie in our part of the station. During the day father Yoav spoke to us. In the evening the patriarch was online; he congratulated us, talked to us, and blessed us. It was a comfort talking to him."[144]

As elsewhere during the decade, the trend of venerating unique relics within both the military and civilian segments of the space program gathered momentum. The ROC brought famous relics from central Russian sanctuaries to the faraway garrisons and closed cities of the SF, enabling soldiers and civilians to bow before them and pray. For example, during

2012, it circulated among the SF garrison churches parts of the relics of St. Alexander Nevsky and St. Sergei Radonezhsky.[145] In 2014 clerics brought the icon of St. Sergei Radonezhsky for the servicemen to venerate at the Kliuchi-20 garrison church in Kamchatka, a testing range of the SF, previously part of the RVSN, where all of the ICBM warheads, including the Topol and Bulava, land during tests and exercises.[146]

In 2010 the first service was conducted in a thirty-nine-meter-high wooden Church of God's Transfiguration in the closed town of Zvezdnyi—the holiest place of the Russian space program. Envisioned as the main church of the Russian space program, it aggregated all the unique space-related relics: pieces of God's cross, which had spent half a year in orbit; a piece of St. Nikolai's relics; and the relics of St. Sergei Radonezhsky, which cosmonauts had taken twice into outer space and with which they had conducted a procession of the cross around the globe.[147] Finally, as in the other services, clerics more and more frequently linked historical, current, and religious affairs when addressing both SF and civilian space program audiences. For example, in his speech during a consecration ceremony in Zvezdnyi, attended by ROSCOSMOS senior officials, active and retired cosmonauts, and regional administration officials, Patriarch Kirill used verses from the Bible to interpret scientific space exploration and exploitation as one of the most important and God-pleasing activities in which humans can engage. He presented it as a divine dictum to the cosmonauts.[148]

THE 12TH MAIN DIRECTORATE OF THE MINISTRY OF DEFENSE (12TH GUMO)

During the decade, meetings to discuss cooperation for the coming year became routine between the head of the 12th GUMO and commanders of the service's main units with the clergy who provided pastoral care to the servicemen. In the biggest garrisons of the service, such as the Main Interservice Training Center in Sergiev Posad and the Central Polygon in Novaia Zemlia,[149] as well as at the smaller bases and arsenals, clerics addressed the new conscripts upon arrival and at the oath of allegiance ceremonies; conducted conversations with the servicemen; blessed tactical-operational activities, such as exercises and field training; baptized the willing; and conducted supplication services on the memorial day of St. Seraphim Sarovsky, the patron saint of the service.[150] Several new churches were constructed, and prayer corners and rooms were established in the barracks of the smaller garrisons.[151] Like other services during the decade, GUMO had been exchanging its banners in what had turned into a purely religious ceremony. Interestingly, as in other official ceremonies, religious banners with the icon of St. Seraphim, which the patriarch had presented to all the GUMO units several years earlier, were employed in the ritual.[152] GUMO clerics also started to practice aerial processions of the cross, flying over nuclear arsenals and blessing them from above.[153]

Rituals established during the previous decade remained intact. In various GUMO garrisons, as elsewhere in the nuclear triad, priests participated in the official ceremonies and celebrations of the major official military holidays, as well as religious ones, conducted either within the garrison churches or in the nearby churches of the local eparchies. During these events, the garrison or unit commander, priest, and deputy commander of educational work were the central figures addressing the officers and soldiers.[154] Clergy were actively involved in the professional celebrations of the service, too. In 2014, on the sixtieth anniversary of the Central Polygon, the deputy DM , the GUMO commander, and the local bishop participated in the opening of the monument dedicated to the "creators of the Russian nuclear shield," which started with a consecration ceremony.[155] During the anniversary celebrations of the 12th GUMO Main Interservice Training Center and those of its garrison church, which were conducted on base, the unit commander repeatedly presented garrison priests with letters of official gratitude for pastoral care of the soldiers and members of their families.[156] The fact that military commanders were giving the priests letters of gratitude for their catechization efforts, and not the other way around, is indicative of the place of religion during the operationalization decade.

Not much information is available on the new clerics' nomination to official positions within the nuclear custodians' service. Apparently, the majority of the nominees continued their previous pastoral care, but now in a new official capacity, and as in other parts of the triad, several GUMO clerics were retired officers,[157] and often with double responsibilities—

toward the military unit and toward the local congregation.[158] Two main features of the operationalization decade were deeper cooperation of the clergy with deputy commanders for personnel, responsible for, among other things, screening and maintaining the proper morale-psychological state of the nuclear custodians, and growing clerical involvement with youth in GUMO-related schools and universities. The service commanders, in their own words, have paid special attention to the selection, preparation, and morale-psychological state of the servicemen who deal directly with nuclear armaments.[159] To this end, among other things, in 2016 the service introduced a new polygraph system ensuring the "psychological and psycho-physical exploration of the candidates, first in the GUMO and then in all the services operating nuclear weapons." As elsewhere, the deputy GUMO commander for work with personnel, whose subordinates cooperate with the clerics within the service, has been responsible for this task.[160]

Unsurprisingly then, the service began conducting joint study-methodological gatherings for the deputy commanders for work with personnel and assistant commanders who work with the faithful operating in GUMO units all over Russia. Apparently, the first meeting of this kind occurred in 2014 and since then meetings have been conducted annually. The workshops and simulations of the event have dealt with morale-psychological assessments of the servicemen, maintaining order and military discipline, and the spiritual-morale education of servicemen and their families. Most of the attention has been paid to upgrading work with the contract servicemen. The clerics and the officers have exchanged experiences and outlined a model of cooperation for the following years.[161] Apparently, such deep involvement of the clergy with the personnel department suggests that they are intimately familiar with, and in some cases probably co-responsible for, the most sensitive issues of the service.

Garrison priests also became actively involved in the patriotic education of the youth within the school systems and in the framework of the Yunarmiia, the Youth Army—a state-sponsored, all-Russian, military-patriotic youth movement established in 2015 in an effort to cultivate the pro-Kremlin youth. A reincarnation and mixture of sorts of the Soviet-era Pioneers, Komsomol, and DOSAAF organizations, it is somewhat more militaristic than its predecessors and has been widely popularized and supported by the state. In 2017, Yunarmiia cadets participated for the first time in the V-Day military parade. The clergy has taken an active part in this endeavor within the GUMO garrisons and closed cities, assuming responsibility for the spiritual-patriotic education of the youth, while the commanders have provided them with the basic military skills.[162] Given that the deputy commander of the GUMO has personally curated these events in several garrisons and has involved the military clergy in them, it is safe to assume that a similar trend will gather momentum on other bases across Russia in the coming years.

Another novel development relates to the "scientific companies"—the project that the Russian MoD introduced in 2015 to maintain a reservoir of well-trained reservists in the advanced and demanding scientific-technological disciplines from the leading Russian universities. The main tool of their training during their service and before the draft has been military faculty (*voennaia kafedra*). MIFI—the main nuclear research university, which trains the cadre for the 12th GUMO and the nuclear triad and has close ties with the service—has been actively involved in this MoD initiative. In 2016, out of 104 graduates, 37 became officers and sergeants in the reserves and received their military IDs personally from the commander of the 12th GUMO. "Hundreds of the graduates of your remarkable university," he told them, "serve in our directorate" in scientific and managerial positions. The course takes about two years, depending on the specialization, and upon graduation the student receives a military rank. In the words of the rector, "One can't imagine MIFI today without cooperation with the 12th GUMO, where our graduates serve basically in all of its departments." Some of the graduates eventually join the 12th GUMO as professional servicemen or serve as its reservists.[163]

Studies in the course include monthlong field military tactical training that takes place at the main training base of the 12th GUMO in Sergiev Posad, exactly where the Nikolsky church and the GUMO's main church have been located for more than a decade.[164] In parallel, MIFI has been extensively penetrated by the ROC, has established a faculty of theology, and has conducted active catechization work on campus among the Orthodox students. Given the convergence of religious and patriotic upbringing in today's Russia and a certain level of patriotic feeling among those who join the program, one may assume a certain level of religious influence on this course. In 2015, during the summer conscription, the new head of the Synodal Department, Protoierei Sergii, participated in the first ceremony marking the dispatch of the conscripts from the main commission center in Moscow to the scientific companies in the Russian Armed Forces. His blessing and sanctification of the conscripts followed the speech of a one-star general who was leading the event. Among the services that received the conscripts was the 12th GUMO Central Scientific-Research Institute (CSRI) in Sergiev Posad.[165]

This CSRI, the brain of the 12th GUMO, established its first scientific company in the same year with the assistance of ROSATOM "for the interests of the nuclear weapons complex and state security." VNI-IEF has been closely involved throughout the process, from selecting the candidates to curating their work during the service.[166] After about a year and a half of compulsory service in the GUMO central institute, the scientific company, which brought together thirty graduates of the leading scientific universities, conducted applied science research for the needs of the 12th GUMO. Upon completion of their service, eight servicemen decided to become officers, and the rest joined the military-industrial complex. In December 2016, the 12th GUMO commander arrived to personally summon lieutenants to the ranks and addressed them in the same monastery compound, next to the statue of St. Nikolai the Miracle-Maker, which the patriarch had sanctified nine years earlier.[167] The level of religiosity of these young officers, who had been catechized to some degree by the FOC in their universities and also were exposed to the religious activities in which the 12th CSRI was involved, is as yet unclear. But a patriotic state of mind and affinity with national ideology is highly likely to be a consideration among the majority of those who joined the program, as well as parameter for those who screened them. In 2016 there were already twelve scientific companies in the Russian military, with about four hundred conscripts serving in them.[168]

CHAPTER 10

STRATEGIC MYTHMAKING

DURING THE OPERATIONALIZATION DECADE, the three main motifs of strategic mythology, which had emerged in the previous years—relating to the GPW, relating to space, and relating to the nuclear project—continued to be visible. Some myths acquired such grotesque form that even clerical sources made an effort to refute the noncanonical interpretations. In 2013, on the pages of the Orthodox journal *FOMA*, one of the leading Russian historians of ROC-state relations refuted the main GPW myths one by one.[1] Another research demonstrated that Stalin's flirtation with the ROC had been instrumental, unrelated to the leader's spirituality, but aimed at mobilizing internal and external support.[2] Other secular researchers explained why the narrative about divine miracles assisting the Soviet leaders and warriors was nonsense.[3] These efforts seemed not to matter, as by then the myths had taken on a life of their own.

Those ROC sources that positioned Stalin's turn toward the church as a purely pragmatic move, nonetheless continued to mention wartime divine interventions that had brought victory.[4] *Krasnaia zvezda*, the main official military newspaper, referred to these myths as historical facts. In the case of St. Matrona, several facts from the original book, including her meeting with Stalin, strongly contradicted not only the common vision of secular history, but even Orthodox dogmas. The ROC officially criticized the narrative and produced a canonical version of her life.[5] However, the myth had the upper hand. Icons featuring Matrona's blessing of Stalin remained in most churches, and new icons continued to appear in Moscow, St. Petersburg, Pskov, and Kursk. New books described the role of faith and divine interventions in pre-Soviet and Soviet military history and during the wars in Afghanistan, Chechnya, and Georgia.[6] Even children's books popularized the accounts about the miracles in ancient and modern Russian military history.[7] In such an atmosphere, the absorption and circulation of these myths continued. Their exact imprint on the worldview of the Russian strategic community and general public is unclear. Apparently, they fertilized the soil for dissemination of the Nuclear Orthodoxy, Russian Doctrine, and Russian World concepts. They probably also made the general public more receptive to the Kremlin's spiritual staples ideology, which has peaked since 2012. Like the Soviet agitprop, political mythmaking has merged faith, nationalism, and patriotism and utilized the eventual hybrid for social mobilization against an external enemy.[8]

In 2011 the RVSN and VDV main priest argued in *Krasnaia zvezda* that at the most daunting moments in history—when the Poles, Napoleon, and Hitler, respectively, had threatened Russia—providence saved the state and that divine interventions would preserve it if "faith infects the servicemen's hearts."[9] Senior officers echoed him. General-Major Aleksandr Cherkasov, professor of the Military University (the former Military-Political Academy) and former head of the GS Educational Department, discussed the spiritual foundations of Russian military culture in the same newspaper. In addition to the material aspects of warfare, he designated a spiritual basis as a necessary condition for victory. He saw its strengthening as a pressing mission in light of foreign aggression aimed at demoralizing the population and sapping the motivation to serve. Revival in the military of the "Christ-loving warriors" atmosphere would, according to him, make it possible "to adequately react to the changing character of war" in the "moral-spiritual and informational-psychological spheres" and to repulse aggression.[10]

On V-Day 2011, the patriarch addressed the GS Academy professors and graduates. In a nutshell, his interpretation of the GPW argued that the Soviet victory against all odds occurred only due to God's will, the people's faith, and spiritual cohesion.[11] On 22 June 2011, he argued again that the massive heroism and sacrifice that eventually brought victory had derived from the spiritual power and faith of the Russian people and that then, as now, the ROC was responsible for maintaining this virtue.[12] The reactions of the military were mixed; the ROC explained the unwillingness of the commanders to accept such an interpretation as a function of "insufficient spiritual education."[13] Catechization efforts doubled.[14] When Kirill made the same point during the 2015 V-Day celebrations, the military received it more readily, probably given the leadership's growing inclination toward religiosity:

> The GPW Victory is God's miracle. It suffices to recall that several kilometers away from here the enemy was standing, but could not enter Moscow. It was excellently equipped and trained and had conquered all of Europe. We venerate the heroism of our soldiers and our people, who stood up for the defense of Moscow and all Russia. However, it is impossible to explain this victory only from the human point of view. [. . .] The victory in the GPW was God's miracle.[15]

The mix of the Soviet, Orthodox, and pre-Soviet became evident in the Kremlin's ideology,[16] and its narrative of Russia as a great power became "a combination of Soviet nostalgia, yearning for revenge, and historical mysticism based on Byzantine and Orthodox heritage."[17] The mix of faith, patriotism, and nationalism perfectly coincided with the emerging geopolitical context. In 2014, speaking on the anniversary of the start of World War I, Patriarch Kirill interpreted the tsar's decision to go to war in patriotic-religious terms and paralleled support of the "brotherly Serbian people," which he equated with saving Orthodoxy, to current events in Ukraine.[18]

In July of the same year, following the liturgy on the Day of the Baptism of Rus, which is also the day of St. Prince Vladimir, Patriarch Kirill outlined his vision of the spiritual foundations of Russia's national security. His speech corresponded with three contemporary developments: Gerasimov's programmatic article, which emphasized the linkage between soft and hard power under the umbrella notion of New Generation Warfare; the 2015 National Security Doctrine, which emphasized the linkage between external and internal threats; and, finally, popularization of the image and role of St. Prince Vladimir, producing a resonance with Vladimir Putin's role in history.[19]

Starting with a rhetorical question about the relevance of the prince in the twenty-first century, the patriarch outlined the impact of the saint on Russia's national security:

> What did we receive from Prince Vladimir?—Orthodox faith. [. . .] Preservation of this civilizational kernel was not easy. [. . .] At certain moments it happened that enemies saw this kernel as dangerous for them, and tried to destroy or reformat it according to their own standards. [. . .] In the battles waged by Alexander Nevsky, and by Dmitry Donskoy, and in many other wars, our nation defended this kernel. The slogan "For the Faith, the Tsar and the Fatherland" put faith in the first place, because if it is destroyed then the tsar will not endure and the Fatherland will lose its sovereignty, if not physically then spiritually.[20]

The subtext and reference to the lessons learned from the Soviet collapse were evident. When reflecting on both the Soviet and the post-Soviet eras, he used the term *Orthodox* as synonymous with *Russian*, giving the latter adjective cultural-civilizational meaning and using the notions of faith, patriotism, and ideology interchangeably:

> In the twentieth century we faced an even greater danger, when [the enemies] decided to destroy the Orthodox faith not only by the power of weapons, but by combining violence with conviction. [. . .] Today again many would like to transform our kernel, by employing military and ideological means. [. . .] They threaten us externally and use other means internally, in order to convince our people that the Orthodox faith, our proud spiritual tradition [. . .] is some sort of prejudice, that it has nothing in common with the modern human being, with his strength, culture, and understanding of what is good and bad.[21]

Kirill alluded to the current Western hybrid subversion aimed at presenting an alien way of life as a universal one and then imposing it on Russia, which would eventually lead to the implosion of the state from within.

This soft subversion, according to him, is more dangerous than hard national security threats:

> Probably, current ideological pressure on the faith is more terrible than that which was accompanied by violence. [. . .] If they wrap a person with soft power, lure him with the sweet life, contrasting his poorness to wealth, which they posses only because they are different—then someone, especially among the young, may tremble. [. . .] If such thoughts obsess our people [. . .] we will lose Russia. [. . .] Thus we should remember that today, living in a time of military rumors and threats, we will stay strong and unbeatable if we preserve our faith. [. . .] May God save Russian power and its armed forces. [. . .] May God save the historical Rus, our brother Slavic nations . . . [and] the kernel that holds our life and our security.[22]

In parallel to the general mythology outlined above, two trends loomed large in the space-related discourse. Further promotion of the earlier narrative about the Soviet cosmonauts and space scientists as pious individuals continued with redoubled strength.[23] In addition, a new myth emerged. It attributed sacral meaning to the choice of the date for the first space launch. As in the case of military history, when the surge of mythology gathered momentum during the approach of the fiftieth V-Day anniversary in 2005, a similar wave of mythology surged toward the fiftieth anniversary of the first Soviet space launch in 2011. Father Sergei, the Baikonur cosmodrome priest, offered the most straightforward version of it. According to him, the Soviet decision to launch Gagarin on 12 April was not accidental, but providential. On that day, the Orthodox Church celebrates the memory of St. Ioann Listvichnik (St. John Climacus, also known as John of the Ladder), the seventh-century Mount Sinai monastery monk. His famous work, *Ladder of Divine Ascent*, deals with the rise of one's soul to God through thirty spiritual steps, each of them concerning another moral virtue. Father Sergii argued that Korolev purposefully planned to conduct the launch on that date.[24] Nearing the anniversary celebrations, Protoierei Smirnov, the head of the Synodal Department, delivered a sermon linking Cosmonautics Day and the deeds of St. Ioann Listvichnik. According to him, just as the saint had spiritually ascended his ladder, Soviet scientific-engineering thought had ascended into space.[25]

Both myths merged during the celebrations. For example, in April 2011, the Synodal Department arranged, for the scientists and veterans of the rocket-space industry and SF, cosmonauts, students, and representatives of the Orthodox youth movements, a conference to commemorate the fiftieth anniversary of Gagarin's space launch. The head of the Synodal Department argued that "Russia made the grand leap in cosmonautics solely thanks to the spiritual power of the people" involved in the aerospace industry[26] and that the current lag in the field was due less to financial difficulties than to the lack of spirituality.[27] In parallel, Cosmonautics Day, a holiday that during Soviet times had epitomized atheism and which propaganda had utilized in anti-religious efforts,[28] acquired a new meaning. Annually, on the anniversary of Gagarin's death, Father Yoav, the cosmonauts' team priest, and several cosmonauts visit the town of Kirzhach, near where Gagarin crashed. Together with the local priest, they conduct a memorial service, followed by a gathering, commemorative speeches, and a procession of the cross from the church to the site of Gagarin's death.[29] Similarly, since the beginning of the decade, the SF clerics have arranged Cosmonautics Day celebrations for the servicemen.[30]

The nuclear strand of mythology became less visible as compared to previous periods. The main trend during the decade became direct references to the geostrategic developments in which nuclear forces were involved. The main clerical message was to highlight their role in preserving Russia's indigenous and sovereign way of life. In 2012, talking to the graduates of the FOC, Patriarch Kirill said that the Russian nuclear shield, while "defending the Fatherland and historical peoples who are close to us spiritually, at the same time is the source of peace, maintaining the most important balance, which does not give anyone the right or opportunity to use deadly nuclear weapons and remain unpunished."[31] The patriarch's last sentence, linking Orthodox culture, as the central national value, to the nuclear weapons that preserve it, corresponded with Putin's 2007 "nuclear Orthodoxy" remark and his "spiritual staples" notion. In 2016 one of the major Russian newspapers commented on the opening of the spiritual-scientific centers within the closed nuclear cities, arguing that ultimately Nuclear Orthodoxy had acquired its target audience.[32]

In August 2016, addressing an audience in Sarov, Patriarch Kirill re-emphasized predestination when commenting on the Soviet decision to establish the nuclear laboratory in the monastery:

> Probably, those destroying the temple could not imagine what great implications it would have for the state's destiny. Due to pragmatic considerations, unrelated to our national heritage, here was laid down the foundation of the institution, which would produce the Fatherland's nuclear shield. Thanks to the scientists, engineers, technicians, and workers who labored here, in the cell of Saint Seraphim, but were not connected with the great spiritual tradition, wrong deeds turned into good implications. With the power of divine blessing, it happened that exactly in the cell of Saint Seraphim was created the force, which has protected our country and the whole world from terrible thermonuclear war.[33]

SUMMARY REMARKS ON THE
OPERATIONALIZATION DECADE

This part of the book has covered the period from 2010 onward, describing how the bottom-up and top-down tendencies have merged, reaching a peak in the clericalization of state-church relations. During the "operationalization decade" the nuclear arsenal has become one of the major instruments of national security, while religion has gained extraordinary prominence in national ideology. Putin's religious-ideological-philosophical views seem to have matured and become fully integrated into his geopolitical vision and policy choices. The religiosity of Putin and of his immediate entourage, which seems genuine, created the most favorable conditions for the ROC to expand its influence in all dimensions of social and political life. Religion has assumed a high profile in Russian domestic and foreign policy and become a measure of national identity for a majority of the Russian population. Faith and religion have manifested themselves on the battlefields and in foreign policy, both in Ukraine and in the Middle East. During the past decade the ROC, supported by the state, suppressed the last pockets of resistance to the military clergy, both within the armed forces and in the broader Russian social-political community. The clergy became part and parcel of the military, primarily within the nuclear triad, where the priests have penetrated all levels of command, have fostered patriotism and morale, and have resumed certain responsibilities within human reliability programs. The clergy have become integrated at the lowest tactical-operational levels across the corps: nuclear chaplains have been present in immediate proximity to the weapons, participated in exercises and operational combat duties, and assumed responsibility for the morale-psychological state of nuclear operators during operational routine.

CHAPTER 11

CONCLUSION

THIS BOOK HAS EXPLORED the interplay between religion, politics, and strategic affairs in Russia. It has focused on Russian Nuclear Orthodoxy, a unique nexus between the ROC and the Russian nuclear community, highlighted the drivers that have pushed religion and nuclear weapons toward each other, and outlined the consequences for theory and practice of international security. Tracing this phenomenon, which has evolved through the first three post-Soviet decades, the book has labeled each period according to the main characteristics of the state-church-nuclear dynamics at the time: *genesis* (the first post-Soviet decade), *conversion* (the second post-Soviet decade), and *operationalization* (the third post-Soviet decade).

FAITH, POLITICS, AND STRATEGY

The first part of the book described the inception of the church-nuclear nexus in the early 1990s. During this period the quest for religiosity emerged as a grassroots phenomenon within the nuclear complex, and the latter entered into a covenant with the ROC. The book defines it as the "genesis decade." A quest for a new national and professional identity marked the exodus of the Russian strategic community, and Russia as a whole, out of the Soviet era. Within the military-industrial complex, the Union's collapse most threatened the nuclear community. For the ROC, seeking to expand its base of influence, the disoriented military-nuclear complex became a target of opportunity. The former assisted the latter on many fronts: shielding it from political-social ostracism, lobbying for funding, and helping it to overcome value disorientation and a miserable social attitude toward it, reinvent its self-identity, and inject new meaning into its professional life. The genesis decade bore witness to the introduction of religious ceremonies into the everyday functioning of the nuclear community, the designation of patron saints for nuclear institutions, and the construction of churches in the nuclear weapons industry and in the garrisons of the triad's corps. Initially, the faith-atoms nexus enjoyed only marginal state financial-administrative support. In contrast, from the beginning, the ROC's proselytism was evident from the patriarch down to the priests interacting with the nuclear forces' commanders and the industry's officials within the local parishes. The decade also gave birth to religious-political mythmaking—the reading of divine meaning into Russian-Soviet military and nuclear history, which in turn shaped the ethos and narrative of a community in search of an identity.

The second part of the book covered the period from the early 2000s to 2010, during which nuclear churching became state policy. The book defines it as the "conversion decade." Russian Nuclear Orthodoxy initially emerged as a bottom-up phenomenon. However, when religion began playing an increasing role in Russian politics, and when the leadership began flirting with faith, a top-down trend supplemented the initial grassroots impulse. During the decade of *conversion*—a period which coincided with Putin's first two terms—the Kremlin restituted church property, introduced the institution of the military clergy, and enhanced the ROC's role in educational, social, and foreign policies. These top-down initiatives caught up with the earlier bottom-up tendency. Putin's public and private religious persona and the evolution of his personal and instrumental religiosity left a strong imprint on all of the above. By the end of the conversion decade, the ROC became part and parcel of the nuclear officialdom, and catechization and churching peaked in all the services of the nuclear triad. The commanders of the nuclear corps and seniors of the nuclear industry signed cooperation agreements with the ROC and established close contacts with the patriarch and clergy. The nuclear mythmaking evolved to its peak, namely, the formulation and dissemination of the Nuclear Orthodoxy doctrine—a widely circulated public belief, with which Putin himself concurs, arguing that in order to preserve its Orthodox character, Russia needs to ensure its being a strong nuclear power, and to guarantee its nuclear status, it has to be genuinely Orthodox.

The third part of the book, covering the period from 2010 onward, describes how these bottom-up and top-down tendencies have merged. The book defines this period as the "operationalization decade." During the decade, clericalization in state-church relations reached its peak. The nuclear arsenal has become one of the major instruments of national security, while religion has gained extraordinary prominence in national ideology. Putin's religious-ideological-philosophical views seem to have matured and become integrated into his geopolitical vision and policy choices. The religiosity of Putin and of his immediate entourage, which seems to a certain extent genuine, created the most favorable conditions for the ROC to expand its influence in all dimensions of social and political life. Religion has assumed a high profile in Russian domestic and foreign policy and has become a measure of national identity for a majority of the population. Faith and religion have manifested themselves on the battlefields and in foreign policy, both in Ukraine and in the Middle East. During the past decade the ROC, supported by the state, suppressed the last pockets of resistance to the military clergy, both within the armed forces and in the broader Russian social-political community. The clergy became part and parcel of the military, primarily within the nuclear triad, where the priests have penetrated all levels of command, have fostered patriotism and morale, and have resumed certain responsibilities within human reliability programs. The clergy have become integrated at the lowest tactical-operational levels across the corps: priests have been present in immediate proximity to the weapons, participated in exercises and operational combat duties, and assumed responsibility for the morale-psychological state of nuclear operators during operational routine.

It is important not to overblow the proportions of Russian Nuclear Orthodoxy. The focus of this book, the rich empirical evidence that has been presented, and the elaborated discussion may create a disproportionate impression of the magnitude of religiosity within the Russian strategic community. Some Russian defense intellectuals and security experts, when presented with the book's findings, were surprised to learn about this phenomenon of which they were unaware. Some of them, speaking off the record, qualified the clericalization of Russia as merely a passing fashion, a farce, and a facade. According to them, this is just an organizational and personal tribute to the zeitgeist, and when it comes to essential questions of strategy and operations, this pro forma religiosity will not matter. This book seeks to offer a more nuanced picture. It does not intend to overblow the level and intensity of religiosity in Russia, but equally it does not want to underrepresent the significance of the theocratization of the Russian strategic community. The analysis and arguments offered here build on a significant number of primary sources and seek to demonstrate the magnitude of the phenomenon, which for a long while has flown under the radar.

Although more time and research are needed to establish the impact of clericalization on operational behavior, it is already clear that the Russian case corresponds with some features of Ron Hassner's typology of military organizations shaped by religious characteristics.[1] Hassner defines "sacred time" as periods bearing religious meanings, which may fuel combat fervor on the battlefield,[2] and suggests that "in the absence of other constraints," decision makers may exploit these dates to generate force-multiplying effects.[3] The merging of professional and religious calendars, introduction of patron saint days, and reading of divine connotations into the dates of secular military and nuclear history, and even turning specific locations into nuclear-spiritual sanctuaries, have become widespread in Russia during the discussed period. As of this writing, there have been no indications of a willingness to initiate any operational move due to a particular "sacred" day. However, it is conceivable that in the future Russian decision makers, when choosing a time for a particular national security move based on operational considerations, might also highlight a possible religious connotation to generate public mobilization and a motivational effect.

"Sacred objects"—rituals and practices with the relics that "allow believers to communicate with the divine, and to receive favors"[4]—are on display in all of the nuclear triad's legs and within the nuclear industry. Service icons and religious banners and relics of the service-related saints and their statues have become widespread in the garrisons, staffs, C2 centers, and nuclear platforms. Veneration of these relics, as well as ground, air, and naval processions of the cross with them, has become routine. Sanctification of nuclear and space launches and platforms and naming them after saints can also be seen as part of this phenomenon. Nuclear corps' servicemen, individually and in groups, venerate relics, seek blessings of their duties, sanctify their weapons before operational missions, conduct religious rituals before operational activities, and carry protective sacred relics with them on combat missions.[5] Popularization of the narrative about the divine presence on the battlefield embodied in sacred objects, which have served as force multipliers and sources of success, has been part of the same trend. More research is needed, however, to establish how these "sacred objects" condition, if at all, the theory and practice of nuclear operations.

The presence of chaplains, whom Hassner dubs "sacred leaders," in modern militaries worldwide emanates from a strong confidence in a causal link between faith and military effectiveness.[6] Although it is far from being scientifically proven, there is a widespread professional belief that faith and military clergy have a positive effect on mobilization, recruitment, motivation, discipline, unit cohesion, combat functioning, battlefield courage, and servicemen's ability to cope with physical-psychological hardships, stress, and moral dilemmas, which all together increase combat resilience and resistance to shock.[7] All of these are precisely the responsibilities that the Russian military clergy attributes to itself and exactly the expectations that Russian commanders have of it. The functions of Russian military clerics resemble those of chaplains elsewhere worldwide, who offer counsel on personal and professional issues, enabling soldiers to gain "the peace of mind necessary for focusing on combat and training."[8]

The Russian military clergy, the nuclear priests in particular, could be seen as a reincarnation of Soviet political officers. This is especially true since 2018, when the military priesthood became one of the main departments within the reestablished Main Political Directorate of the Russian

General Staff, the same organ that once oversaw the work of political commissars.[9] However, in contrast to the Soviet political officers, who were frequently detested, mainly due to disillusionment with Communist ideology, the religiosity of the servicemen ensures that the military clergy are held in relatively higher esteem. Military clerics indoctrinate and maintain the patriotic-morale climate within the units in accordance with the state's political agenda and popularize the current version of Russian national identity. The scale and scope of their pastoral activities fostering patriotism and loyalty exceed the responsibilities of Western chaplains. Their sermons are not abstract theological observations, but religious concepts interwoven with operational and political agendas. Nuclear clerics in their sermons during the Ukrainian and the Syrian conflicts not only legitimized the political discourse, but also linked patriotic, military, and religious duties, interpreting the operations as the sacred duty of the faithful. In contrast to the Russian case, where this patriotic preaching is the default option, Western military chaplains have seldom "blurred the distinction between religious and political symbolism."[10]

Russian Nuclear Orthodoxy is likely to endure as a phenomenon. The penetration of faith into politics has been so wide, deep, and continuous, with so many vested interests across the political landscape and strategic community, that it is likely to outlive Vladimir Putin, even in the event of a different persona arriving at the Kremlin. Gravitation to religiosity began several decades ago and runs much deeper than the current political state of affairs. Putin, of course, promotes this religious agenda, but this phenomenon has been independent of the president and thus is likely to outlive him. If Putin continues to rule, the role of the ROC, of religion in national security policy in general, will be at least as prominent as it is today and is likely to increase. The critics of growing ROC penetration into political and social life may channel their discontent toward rolling back the role of the church in politics and in the strategic community. One of the conditions for this conceivable but highly unlikely eventuality would be a complete change of the current political regime, of the system supporting it, and the dissipation of the political culture that has evolved since the Soviet collapse.

It is unlikely that the Kremlin has not noticed the growing power of the ROC, in particular within the strategic community, or that it is unaware of the potential downsides of this trend, even if these lie far in the future. Presumably, the Kremlin realizes that its utilization of the ROC is a double-edged sword, as under certain circumstances "a priest or a patriarch might make the leap from the spiritual realm to the realm of politics,"[11] meaning that after a certain point, over-theocratization may become counterproductive.[12] Consequently, more than ever before, the Kremlin might seek a useful symbiosis with the ROC and at the same time try to control it, possibly by influencing internal ecclesiastical dynamics and promotion tendencies. The greater the potential challenges from the growing power of the ROC, the more likely the Kremlin is to tighten its ties with it for better control and co-optation. Paradoxically, a by-product of the "bear's hug" might be further involvement of the ROC in Russian strategic affairs.

FUTURE PROSPECTS AND IMPLICATIONS

What comes next? In terms of future prospects and implications, five arguments emanate from the analysis offered in this book. First, if the ROC's role continues to expand, it may become a tool of influence in bureaucratic rivalries among organizations competing for resources within and outside the strategic community. The pinnacle of state-church relations has coincided not only with the peak of military and nuclear modernization but also with an era of austerity.[13] Sequestration could intensify competition for funds within the nuclear community, in its turf wars with non-nuclear services, as well as in the "guns versus butter" rivalry between the military-industrial complex and other parts of government. The ROC may become a tool in this competition, enabling the nuclear community to outperform its non-nuclear and non-military competitors. In the competition within the Russian political elite between the forces promoting defense budgets and the forces advising the reallocation of funds away from the military-industrial complex,[14] the ROC may become a natural ally of the former and may also legitimize allocations to the defense sector to the public. Moreover, it may also become a vehicle of rivalry between specific legs of the nuclear triad. Symptoms of all of the above have already been on display.[15]

Second, the ROC is likely to continue serving as a mobilization tool ensuring both the quality and quantity of the draft. Even if Russia is shrinking demographically, as some argue, the ROC may assist in sustaining sufficient levels of motivated soldiers through pre-conscription patriotic education. This relates in particular to attracting qualified youth for the elite units of the nuclear forces and to the elite technological units, such as scientific regiments. Moreover, commanders of the nuclear units may increasingly seek Orthodox draftees, viewing them as being more reliable, motivated, and thus preferable candidates. For example, during Soviet times, ethnic background and party membership were among the control factors and selection criteria for the nuclear corps. Although these factors did not "automatically confer reliability," they represented "one more opportunity to evaluate an individual's political, social, and psychological attitudes on a recurring basis."[16]

Third, in the current political-ideational reality in Russia where faith has become mixed with national identity and patriotism, being a practicing Orthodox may become a promotion multiplier and equivalent to what membership in the Communist Party used to be. This analogy is enhanced by the fact that nuclear priests together with education-personnel officers strongly resemble a contemporary reincarnation of political officers. During the past years, in all three legs of the nuclear triad, priests have been directly involved in monitoring the moral-psychological reliability of the nuclear operators and are officially responsible for cultivating and maintaining the overall operational stability and functioning of the servicemen in general, the nuclear operators in particular. If this trend and the current zeitgeist continue, then the political leadership and senior commanders might seek to nominate pious officers to the leading nuclear command positions. Thus, not inconceivably, association with influential senior clerics within the Kremlin's court may positively affect career and promotion paths within the nuclear community.

Fourth, theocratization may have an effect on conflict duration and escalation dynamics. Religion "encourages or discourages participation in conflict" and conditions what participants "are and are not willing to do" in its course.[17] Scholars of IR have already been researching the imprint of religion on the duration, intensity, and resolution of conflicts and wars.[18]

The Russian case is in full accord with the lack of empirical evidence from elsewhere in the world that military clergy seek to "moderate the conduct of war" and terminate conflict due to moral-ethical considerations.[19] Partially, such a stand has also been amplified by the Russian nuclear clergy's self-selection, which often brings to these positions candidates with very specific backgrounds—converted former nuclear officers becoming priests and monks. Such a clergy is less likely to constrain conflict and might ensure a relatively easier path to escalation. Clergy legitimizing a belligerent political course may prolong conflict and potentially contribute to its intensification by ensuring stable public support of it.

Fifth, and finally, another possible but under-explored implication is the impact of religious beliefs on the effectiveness of deterrence. Does religious observance on at least one side of the deterrence equation hinder or empower this strategy? Are strategic choices of the observant different from those of the secular when it comes to dealing with the most crucial life and death issues?[20] Scholars argue that religion is relevant in crisis since it "maintains people's ability to act in situations in which they run against their own limits."[21] In situations of deterrence and warfare, leaders have exploited religious beliefs to motivate their people toward "a decisive victory against all odds guided by divine intervention."[22] Are observant politicians and nuclear operators less receptive to coercion?[23] Generalization on this matter seems possible only after thorough comparative research across different cases. However, it should come as no surprise if the current Russian strategic approach exploits an image of faith and religiosity attributed to the Kremlin in order to shape the strategic behavior and perception of its opponents. The image of the observant strategic actor, ready to go against all odds, grants more credibility to Russia's signals, threats, and perceived balance of interests. Thus, in keeping with the canons of deterrence strategy, as outlined by Lawrence Freedman and other classics of the field, the Kremlin may further promote its image as an observant strategic actor in the eyes of its counterparts and utilize it for more effective coercion across domains.[24]

CHAPTER 12

EPILOGUE

THE IMPACT OF RELIGION on strategy and operations in contemporary state militaries is a relatively new topic of inquiry. Scholars of international security have only begun to scratch its surface. The big data on the matter is still unavailable, and methods for theory development are insufficient.[1] This book contributes an in-depth discussion of the Russian case to the subject's research program. It also calls for several follow-up efforts, inspired by the Russian example, but aimed at being generic. Primarily, in addition to a further idiosyncratic exploration of the Russian case, the major avenue of research would be to situate the discussion in a comparative context. Such analysis may enable the formulation of a generic typology of faith and strategic affairs and progress toward a parsimonious model of religious belief–driven modern militaries.

COMPARATIVE CONTEXT

A comparative analysis is beyond the scope of this book. However, the first steps in this direction are possible. Penetration of organized religion into the professional life of state militaries is not a uniquely Russian phenomenon. In addition to the North American, European, and Asian cases, only in the Middle East, beyond the obvious cases of Iran and Saudi Arabia, has the resurgence of religion been on display in the Israeli,

Turkish, and Egyptian militaries during the past decade.[2] The drivers, depth, and width of theocratization vary, but all of the above have become more religious organizations than before. The synthesis of empirical evidence across these cases is sufficient to offer an initial generic typology.

The resurgence of religiosity in state militaries is not a binary situation, and each case can be placed along a continuum spanning three ideal types. The first ideal type may be defined as "Enabling Faith." This type refers to cases in which a state military enables faithful service members to practice their personal religious obligations while conducting their military duty. It is similar to providing for other basic needs and service conditions, such as food, supplies, and rest, and it equally applies to all denominations. The second ideal type is "Faith as Enabler." This type refers to state military organizations where religion has penetrated the national ideology and is equated with patriotism. In these cases, one dominant faith is singled out and becomes *primus inter pares* within the military. Organizations of this type modify their operational and combat procedures along religious lines, not only to enable the practice of the "national religion," but to use it for generating higher levels of military effectiveness. The third ideal type is "Military Theocratization"—a situation where religion shapes the strategic thinking and operational behavior of a military organization, including planning and execution. This is not only a utilitarian belief that the national religion is a force multiplier toward, during, and following the battle, but a situation when religious considerations shape the strategic means, ways, and ends of a given actor.

At this stage of theorization, it is difficult to clearly determine the dividing lines between the different ideal types. Transition from one category to another is incremental and probably progresses through several intermediate phases. It is also conceivable that military organizations might skip certain phases in different empirical cases and progress through them in different sequences. However, available empirical evidence already suggests that the majority of the previously mentioned state militaries have steadily gravitated away from the first and toward the third ideal type during the past decade. The pace of transition and the peculiarities have varied across the cases, but the overall tendency has been evident. As of this writing, the majority of cases are clustered around the second ideal type.

HYPOTHESES GENERATION

One could argue that the more a military organization moves away from the first ideal type, the greater the probability of the following interrelated outcomes: (1) the emergence of religious jurisprudence related to military affairs; (2) operators' demand for the counsel of theological experts; and (3) the potential emergence of parallel command authorities. Where is the Russian case in relation to these possible outcomes? Russia today, as the empirical evidence suggests, seems to be in the "Faith as Enabler" category and possibly in the initial stages of the path toward the "Theocratization" ideal type. Thus, questions about religious jurisprudence, theological counsel, and the emergence of a parallel command authority might become relevant, especially within the realm of the Russian faith–atoms nexus. Hard and circumstantial evidence makes it possible to offer several informed speculations on this matter. The conceivable scenarios and educated guesses offered subsequently are not definite answers. They aim to be careful theoretical and policy hypotheses that are to be tested in subsequent work and, as such, are merely a starting point.

Nuclear Jurisprudence and Theological Counsel

The ROC has been in total agreement with the Kremlin on the questions of nuclear acquisition, arms control, and nuclear use policy. Apparently, on various occasions, the clergy have publicly supported the state-driven pronuclear stance, and they have never favored either nuclear abolition philosophy or pacifist views. What is the state of Orthodox jurisprudence on nuclear affairs? Is there an official, canonical, theological position of the ROC on the main questions pertaining to nuclear strategy and managing nuclear operations? How does the ROC view the strategies of nuclear use, and does it have any reservations about them? Does Orthodoxy have a concept of extended deterrence? How does this nuclear ethic relate to Orthodox messianic and apocalyptic views—and to the concepts of holy war and martyrdom? Does the Orthodox eschatology affect the nuclear clerics' interpretations of current geopolitical events? Does their proximity to nuclear systems stimulate any eschatological contemplation? Do similar thoughts cross the minds of observant operators? Will the latter feel a need to discuss it with the former? If such discussions occur, do the clergy comply with state policy on these questions, or do they offer their own interpretations? If the latter is true, is there a dominant dogma and unanimous acceptance of it, or are there several schools of thought within the ROC?

It seems that an elaborated Orthodox nuclear jurisprudence dealing with the above questions is, as of now, nonexistent. Apparently, in Russia there has been no systematic theological discussion yet of the strategic-operational issues pertaining to nuclear weapons, including exploration of the causes and consequences of nuclear use. No available evidence suggests that the nuclear priesthood has been exploring these questions in depth or that serious discussions on these issues have been ongoing within the ROC. During the past several decades, references to the canonical Orthodox Christian just war theory have been made, but unrelated to the nuclear subject per se. Partially, this may be due to the fact that in Orthodox theology, in contrast to the Roman Catholic, *jus ad bellum* is a less elaborated concept, while the *jus in bello* corpus of knowledge has received even less attention. It is fragmented and inconsistent,[3] although immediately relevant for thinking about nuclear operations.

That said, the organizational-conceptual conditions and settings for joint explorations of these issues do exist, both within the nuclear community and within the ROC. Joint discussions by clergy and civilian experts about the changing character of war and contemporary security issues described in this book have made some passing reference to these issues. Moreover, within the military, priests and commanders of the nuclear corps conduct joint methodological seminars on questions of mutual professional interest. Within the nuclear industry, related questions have been co-explored since the 1990s. Within the ROC, for more than two decades, sections responsible for each leg of the nuclear triad function within the Synodal Department. Ongoing tenures of "chief nuclear priests" of the RVSN, LRA, and Navy, and their regular professional cooperation and exchanges with the educational officers from the related service, definitely have produced some interest and specialization on the subject matter. Decades of strategic mythmaking probably have generated a good starting point for the development of nuclear jurisprudence.

Thus, one could argue that given the current level of theocratization of the nuclear establishment and operationalization of the nuclear clergy, the latter, compelled by the potential demand from the former, will be interested in exploring these questions in depth and in a more elaborate manner than has been done until recently. An effort to produce a corpus of doctrinal and catechization literature on the subject of Orthodox nuclear ethics is likely to emerge. This book was unable to discover whether such a corpus of knowledge already exists or is about to emerge, but the subject demands further scrutiny. Closely following the ROC's doctrinal work on the issues of nuclear strategy is one of the major avenues of future research. Whose religious philosophy and whose sermons will appeal to whom within the strategic community? Whether there is a canonical view or several competing interpretations, it will be equally important to explore which priests and interpretations are more influential, if the audiences listening to the nuclear priests take them seriously.

Until recently, the nuclear clergy had been preoccupied with institutionalizing the routine of pastoral care and did not feel such a pressing necessity. One could argue that circumstances are likely to force them to think through and discuss among themselves the moral-spiritual aspects of various nuclear operations. The more the priesthood becomes involved in operational issues and the keener its professional contacts with the operators, the greater the likelihood that a demand for nuclear Orthodox jurisprudence will emerge. Such a corpus of jurisprudence will provide the priesthood with some sort of scheme and frame of reference for dealing with doctrinal questions in nuclear affairs. If such a nuclear jurisprudence emerges, and if the involvement of the ROC in the scientific and doctrinal activity of the nuclear sector continues, it should come as no surprise. It is not inconceivable that, in the coming years, ROC representatives may play, either at their own initiative or compelled by their formal status, a greater role in the conceptual discussions addressing the conundrums in classical nuclear strategy, such as: nuclear threshold, legitimacy of first use, targeting, the morally desirable size of the arsenal, and the questions of Orthodox extended deterrence.

The sermons of the nuclear clergy demonstrate their role as preachers discussing current geopolitical events and the importance of the service of the nuclear corps from a theological point of view. Like military clergy around the world,[4] Russian Orthodox priests have been assuring the nuclear corps' servicemen of a divine providence, which shields them from potential harm and judgmental mistakes, as long as they are spiritually oriented in the right direction and have religion in their hearts and minds. The self-assigned mission of the ROC in these situations is to provide the servicemen with the inner strength and moral-spiritual stamina to accomplish their mission. Consequently, the priests will be interested in exploring these issues in depth to better prepare for shepherding their nuclear flock. Eventually, like the Soviet political officers and contrary to other chaplains worldwide, it is not inconceivable that the Russian military clergy may shape nuclear strategy and operations.

Similarly, the findings of this book suggest that nuclear operators might seek the counsel of the nuclear priesthood. Contemporary Russia is no different from Western militaries, where commanders often pray for "the strength to bear the burden of command and the wisdom to make the right decisions."[5] Thus, in keeping with this phenomenon, Russian commanders, at various levels, in both peacetime and time of crisis, are more likely than not to seek advice from the spiritual pastors deployed with them, either on staff or in the field, to guide them toward the right course of action. Given the current level of involvement of the nuclear priests and the level of religiosity of the senior commanders, they are likely to involve the priests in these deliberations, and their opinion is likely to matter, more than ever.

The Cold War offers several examples of Soviet crisis behavior, when accidental technical circumstances turned small groups of tactical-level commanders into strategic decision makers. If during such a crisis, a Russian nuclear unit loses contact with central command, the priest providing pastoral combat care may become part of the narrow circle of decision makers and be next to the senior commanders when the decision is made. It is impossible to assess the level of receptivity to the nuclear priests' position or to categorically assess what their preferences or inclinations may be. However, it is possible to assume with a high level of probability that their advice and opinion would be solicited. Understanding "nuclear jurisprudence," and diagnosing the receptivity toward it among the operators, might be helpful in thinking about peacetime situations, especially for the scenario of "uncertainty," when operators lose connection with the highest command authority and are left to their own devices and the priests.

Human Reliability

In case of a bolt-out-of-the-blue attack, when reaction time is limited, the role of the nuclear priests might be minimal—there will be no time left for them to express their position to commanders and operators. However, the closer the situation is to a gradually escalating, protracted geopolitical crisis and to the scenario of prolonged conventional fighting, the more prominent the role and involvement of the nuclear priests in the decision-making might become. This might be especially true if nuclear forces are on prolonged combat alert. In such a setting, commanders, educational officers, and nuclear priests are likely to contemplate and interpret the geopolitical situation to the troops. Presumably, these three will also informally discuss potential nuclear use in light of the elevated levels of alert and expected orders from the political leadership. Discussions may intensify, especially if there is also a concurrent heated public debate, especially among political elites, and no national unity on the subject.

The classical dictum of managing nuclear operations is to keep the systems always ready for launch when ordered and never when not. How do priests and faith project upon this dictum, if at all? Does the Orthodox faith do anything for the human reliability of the Russian nuclear chain of command? Does it increase or inhibit the stability of the nuclear systems? Is an Orthodox nuclear operator more or less obedient than his secular peer? Are soldiers "more likely to follow orders fully and enthusiastically if the commander issuing the order has shared in their religious experiences?"[6] The answer is unclear.[7] On the one hand, religiosity may enhance obedience and commitment to turning the key when the order arrives, and not turning it when there is no order. On the other hand, however, it is not inconceivable that under certain circumstances nuclear operators, driven by faith and encouraged by the clergy, may establish pockets of disobedience. Consider the following arguments.

OBEDIENCE ARGUMENT   U.S. practitioners have emphasized the moral-psychological reliability of operators as one of the most important and troublesome components of nuclear management. The human reliability programs have been and are seen as important as the training in missile operational procedures. The biggest concern of General Russell Dougherty, commander of the Strategic Air Command (SAC) and director of the Joint Strategic Target Planning Staff during the Cold War, was that one of his subordinate operators, "upon receipt of a properly authenticated and valid execution order [. . .] would have any doubts and hesitation concerning his ability to 'turn keys'" and launch a nuclear attack. From his point of view, a formidable danger to proper functioning of the nuclear machine would be if a nuclear operator conditions his affirmative answer to launch the attack on subjective personal considerations.[8] For him, any operator who applies his "own subjective conditions to the decision to act on a valid order from proper authority" was fundamentally unqualified to be on nuclear weapons duty. The human reliability programs filtering out problematic candidates have been "applicable to all those assigned nuclear responsibilities" and have extended "to all aspects of personal behavior and social habits." Despite screening procedures, the SAC commander was gravely concerned with the obedience of nuclear operators,[9] and the issue of human reliability summarizes in a nutshell "the psychological climate of the nuclear command" during the Cold War.[10] Russian managers of nuclear operations are likely to share similar professional concerns, and their human reliability programs are similarly likely to screen unreliable candidates. Even during Soviet times, especially with respect to the work on Perimeter, a semiautomatic nuclear retaliation system for the scenario of decapitation, Soviet strategists were concerned with whether, under personal moral deliberations, individual nuclear operators, "young lieutenant colonels," would execute orders or defy them to "unleash a spasm of destruction."[11]

According to Hassner, religion in military organizations influences, among other factors, "the zeal with which units execute their mission, and the ability of individual soldiers to face challenges of war."[12] Professional belief today in several militaries worldwide holds that "religious patriotism" is more effective in this regard than the secular variety. Russia is part of this trend. According to this view, something about religion, as opposed to secular ideology, makes it a more effective force multiplier when it comes to mobilization, motivation, discipline, unit cohesion, battlefield risk-taking, and overall military effectiveness.[13] Driven by faith and seeing war as a religious duty, the observant are more eager to pay the highest price, to kill, and to accept deadly risks. If this is God's commandment, then there is no compromise. Thus, faith enhances the probability of obedience. Although causality has not been scientifically proven, this belief has become widespread.

In extension of this assertion, one may hypothesize that observant nuclear operators might be in better shape morally-psychologically to conduct their missions than their secular peers. Faith and permanent pastoral-patriotic care by the nuclear priesthood may provide operators with a better way to cope with psychological stress and moral dilemmas—and to have more confidence in the rightness of their performance. Moreover, if one rationalizes nuclear use as God's dictum, one becomes an instrument of God, which makes it easier to take responsibility for killing millions. As Hassner suggests, "Interaction with chaplains, whether a formal confession or an informal conversation, offers a range of psychological benefits to soldiers seeking to reconcile themselves with death, confront trauma, or overcome the guilt of killing."[14] For example, when during the Cold War "RAF [Royal Air Force] cadets expressed reservations about flying bombers loaded with nuclear bombs, their chaplain launched into an explanation about the 'morality of deterrence' and organized a program of special training for other chaplains who might encounter similar reservations."[15] Personal initiatives of this kind would be redundant in the case of the Russian nuclear forces. Obedience, discipline, motivation, fulfilling patriotic duty and orders, and service to a higher cause have been the dominant narratives that the nuclear clergy has promoted since the Soviet collapse.[16]

Such a role of the nuclear priesthood would be an extension of previous practices. During Soviet times, political officers were the KGB's chief collaborators in preventing unauthorized use and ensuring the execution of orders. The political organs of the RVSN, through their mandate to monitor the political reliability of the military, as elsewhere in the Soviet Armed Forces, made their officers part of the nuclear control process, with combat duties equivalent to the RVSN launch crews. In the other legs of the Soviet nuclear triad, in particular the SSBNs, political officers had been "a component of a multiple-key nuclear launch process."[17] In sum, in peacetime and during force buildup, training, and modernizations, members of the nuclear priests are most likely to serve as multipliers of discipline, order legitimation, and execution. They are likely to be in agreement with political initiatives and military modernizations. By extension, one could argue, that when it comes to the potential order of nuclear battlefield use, under the influence and encouragement of the ROC, strategists and operators will more easily overcome moral and ethical self-restraints and will execute missions exactly as ordered.

DISOBEDIENCE ARGUMENT   So far, on professional matters, the Russian military clergy, like military chaplains elsewhere in the world, have "put their full trust in the judgment of military authorities."[18] Is it possible for pastoral advice to interfere with political orders? It is not inconceivable. Consider the role of the clerics if (a) the leadership's orders run counter to the commanders' and operators' professional intuition or if (b) they are not in agreement with the patriarch's view and with the theological dogmas of nuclear jurisprudence.

The most daunting situation would be if in the course of a protracted geopolitical crisis, or an incremental escalation of conventional violence, an order from the political leadership, be it to execute restraint or to retaliate, runs counter to the professional-emotional inclinations of the operators.[19] During wartime, military professionals instinctively tend to do what they have been trained to do during peacetime. However, doubt and contradiction between an emotional or rational impulse and orders may still emerge. Circumstantial evidence suggests that discussions about dealing with the dilemma of executing a morally inappropriate order are not foreign to Russian officers.[20] In such a situation, the inclination to seek clerical counsel may grow. Consequently, dogmas of nuclear jurisprudence and the patriarch's views acquire unparalleled importance. Can political orders run against these two? Again, it is not inconceivable.

As Hill and Gaddy put it, the concept of tsar in the Russian tradition comes "in a political and spiritual package with the ROC," meaning that his authority is "unlimited by any but divine law." Both they and others apply this assertion to the current situation in Russia, even though "the presidential base of power is secular" and "the president is not divine or holy."[21] Although one might have difficulty imagining the patriarch opposing the nuclear initiatives of the political leadership for theological reasons, disagreements and tensions in state-church relations have been on display in modern Russia. The argument here is that the current highly cooperative and close nature of the state-church relationship is not predetermined. Theoretically, voices from within the church may question certain aspects of nuclear policy, since President Putin, even if he has indeed acquired a holy aura today in Russian public consciousness,[22] is not tsar from the ecclesiastical point of view. The ruler who is not tsar is not divinely anointed (*pomazannik Bozhii*) and, as such, does not have direct contact with God's will, as opposed to the patriarch.

If, in theory, the ROC loses confidence in the tsar, assuming that he betrays his people and the faith, the patriarch may take the initiative into his own hands. Although not very probable today, this scenario is still more likely than before, given the political power and social influence that the ROC has accumulated. Since the nuclear issue is so all-encompassing, due to its ability to change the fate of the world and mankind, it may be that the highest religious authority will decide that rendering unto Caesar what is Caesar's, unto God what is God's, does not apply to such a monumental issue and that he knows better. The clash between King Saul and the prophet Samuel, which illustrates the wartime disagreement of religious and secular authorities on the matter of strategic affairs,[23] is a biblical precedent. Tensions, disputes, and violent conflicts between tsars, patriarchs, and metropolitans on matters of state management have occurred in Russian history.[24] Moreover, in late 2017, violent public protests across Russia against the *Matilda* movie demonstrated that, in certain circumstances, emboldened radical Orthodox activists may get out of the Kremlin's control and begin playing by their own rules.[25]

Both scenarios, which are interrelated, raise a long list of questions. How will the priests respond if a nuclear commander or operator consults with them about hesitation to follow an order that runs counter to his basic moral-spiritual, emotional, or professional instincts? How do nuclear priests see their role in this situation? How do educational officers and commanders see the role of the priests? Do they have any routine peacetime training in preparation for such situations when they may be left to their own devices or encounter doubt and contradiction? Will the nuclear priesthood offer an alternative set of values that predisposes the operators to oppose the political leadership's orders?

These questions demand separate research, but three initial insights are already available. First, if the political leadership's order runs counter to both the operators' professional intuition and nuclear jurisprudence, the nuclear clergy multiplies the probability of disobedience. Second, presumably the probability of the military following the religious authority increases if the state is unable to fulfill its social, economic, and political responsibilities. Third, and in any case, if during a crisis nuclear commanders and operators seek a priest's guidance to deal with moral and ethical questions that emanate from the political leadership's order, this may mean that, de facto, there are two parallel lines of command authority—and a possible tension between the two. This would be a major break not only with military tradition but also with the spirit of the current Russian political system that rests on the unity of command emanating from the top of the power vertical.

These hypothetical scenarios are part of thinking about the unthinkable and may never materialize. However, if the contours of these speculations begin to emerge, the above questions offer a useful starting point for systematic thinking on the subject. One thing is clear—in crisis situations, accompanied by uncertainty, instability, and potential civil-church and civil-military tensions, the nuclear priesthood is likely to become part of the decision-making. Thus, the most basic takeaway from this book is a need to incorporate religion into any future analysis of strategic affairs in general, in the Russian case in particular. It is impossible to understand the current version of Russian political mentality and strategic culture, and consequently its security theory and practice, without the clerical and theological components. It is thus essential to follow the metamorphosis of the state-church contract in Russia and to explore how it projects onto national security policy, in particular in the nuclear realm. This is a major discontinuity from the past. Scholars of IR in general, of international security in particular, should be alerted to this phenomenon and follow it closely.

ABBREVIATIONS USED IN THE NOTES

EOPF	Entsiklopedia otechestvennogo odvodnogo flota
KhsAMM	Khram sviatogo Arkhangela Mikhaila, g. Mirnyi
KZ	Krasnaia zvezda
ME OVVSPU	Moskovskaia eparkhiia, Otdel po vzaimodeistviiu s Vooruzhennymi silami i pravookhranitel'nymi uchrezhdeniiami
MEV	Moskovskie eparkhal'nye Vedomosti
MFA	Ministry of Foreign Affairs
MK	Moskovskii komsomolets
NIIAU MIFI	Natsional'nyi Issledovatel'skii Iadernyi Universitet Moskovskii Inzhenerno Fizicheskii Institut (National Research Nuclear University Moscow Engineering Physics Institute)
NVO	Nezavisimoe voennoe obozrenie
OVTsS RPTs	Otdel Vneshnikh Tserkovnykh Snoshenii RPTs (Department of External Church Relations of the ROC)
OVVSiPU	Otdel po Vzaimodeistviiu s Vooruzhennymi Silami I Pravookhranitel'nymi Organami
RBK	Rossiiskii Biznes Kur'er
RF MoD	Russian Federation, Ministry of Defense
RVSN AAA	RVSN Academy Alumni Association Facebook page
SOMP VVSiPO	Sinodal'nyi Otdel Moskovskogo Patriarkhata po Vzaimodeistviiu s Vooruzhennymi Silami I Pravookhranitel'nymi Organami
ViZh	Voenno-istoricheskii zhurnal
VM	Voennaia mysl'
VPK	Voenno-promyshlennyi kur'er
VRNS	Vsemirnyi russkii narodnyi sobor (World Russian People's Council)
VVD	Vestnik voennogo dukhovenstva
VViMD	Vestnik voennogo i morskogo dukhovenstva
ZhMP	Zhurnal Moskovskoi patriarkhii

NOTES

CHAPTER 1

1. James Billington, *The Icon and the Axe: An Interpretive History of Russian Culture* (New York: Vintage Books, 1978), p. 36.

2. Hassner, in his work on faith and military organizations, defines religion as "a system of practices through which participants seek to ward off misfortune, acquire blessing, and obtain salvation. These can include prayers, ablutions, feasts, fasts, honors, and status symbols, or prohibitions on particular actions, speech, clothing, or attitudes." Ron Hassner, *Religion on the Battlefield* (Ithaca, NY: Cornell University Press, 2017), p. 15.

3. Monica Duffy Toft, Daniel Philpott, and Timothy Samuel Shah, *God's Century: Resurgent Religion and Global Politics* (New York: W. W. Norton, 2011); Eva Bellin, "Faith in Politics: New Trends in the Study of Religion and Politics," *World Politics* 60, no. 2 (2008): 315–47; Carolyn Warner and Stephen Walker, "Thinking about the Role of Religion in Foreign Policy: A Framework for Analysis," *Foreign Policy Analysis* 7, no. 1 (2011): 113–35.

4. Fabio Petito and Pavlos Hatzopoulos, eds., *Religion in International Relations: The Return from Exile* (Basingstoke: Palgrave Macmillan, 2003); Daniel Philpott, "Explaining the Political Ambivalence of Religion," *American Political Science Review*, 101, no. 3 (2007): 505–27.

5. Jonathan Fox and Shmuel Sandler, *Bringing Religion into International Relations* (New York: Palgrave, 2004); Robert Seiple and Dennis Hoover, *Religion and Security: The New Nexus in International Relations* (Lanham, MD: Rowman and Littlefield, 2004).

6. Mark Juergensmeyer, *Terror in the Mind of God: The Global Rise of Religious Violence* (Berkeley: University of California Press, 2003); Michael Horowitz, "Long Time Going: Religion and the Duration of Crusading," *International Security* 34, no. 2 (2009): 163–93.

7. Pippa Norris and Ronald Inglehart, *Sacred and Secular: Religion and Politics Worldwide* (Cambridge: Cambridge University Press, 2004); Vesselin Popovski, Gregory Reichberg, and Nicholas Turner, eds., *World Religions and Norms of War* (Tokyo: United Nations University Press, 2009).

8. Ron Hassner and Michael Horowitz, "Debating the Role of Religion in War," *International Security* 35, no. 1 (2010): 201–8; Ron Hassner, ed., *Religion in the Military Worldwide* (New York: Cambridge University Press, 2014); Hassner, *Religion on the Battlefield*; Stuart Cohen, *Israel and Its Army: From Cohesion to Confusion* (London: Routledge, 2008).

9. Horowitz, "Long Time Going"; Cohen, *Israel and Its Army*; Hassner, *Religion in the Military Worldwide*.

10. Assaf Moghadam, *The Globalization of Martyrdom* (Baltimore: Johns Hopkins University Press, 2009); Max Abrahms, "What Terrorists Really Want: Terrorist Motives and Counterterrorism Strategy," *International Security* 32, no. 4 (Spring 2008): 78–105.

11. Wallace Daniel, *The Orthodox Church and Civil Society in Russia* (College Station: Texas A&M University Press, 2006); Zoe Knox, *Russian Society and the Orthodox Church: Religion in Russia after Communism* (London: Routledge, 2005); Maija Turunen, "Orthodox Monarchism in Russia: Is Religion Important in the Present-Day Construction of National Identity?," *Religion, State and Society* 35, no. 4 (2007): 319–34; Irina Papkova, "Contentious Conversation: Framing the Fundamentals of Orthodox Culture in Russia," *Religion, State and Society* 37, no. 3 (2009): 291–309.

12. John Garrard and Carol Garrard, *Russian Orthodoxy Resurgent: Faith and Power in the New Russia* (Princeton, NJ: Princeton University Press, 2008); Daniel P. Payne, "Spiritual Security, the Russian Orthodox Church, and the Russian Foreign Ministry," *Journal of Church and State* 52, no. 4 (2010): 712–27; Alicja Curanovic, *The Religious Factor in Russia's Foreign Policy* (London: Routledge, 2014).

13. Garrard and Garrard, *Russian Orthodoxy Resurgent*; John Burgess, *Holy Rus': The Rebirth of Orthodoxy in the New Russia* (New Haven, CT: Yale University Press, 2017); Irina Papkova, *The Orthodox Church and Russian Politics* (New York: Oxford University Press, 2011).

14. Hassner, *Religion in the Military Worldwide*; Hassner, *Religion on the Battlefield*.

15. This call corresponds with Hassner's argument in favor of developing "religious intelligence" proficiency when analyzing religiously observant militaries. Equal proficiency in religious and military affairs may improve the diagnosis of the ends of strategy and ways of operational art, proclivities, vulnerabilities and force multipliers, and indicators of broader trends within a given society, of which the religiously observant military is a microcosm. Hassner, *Religion on the Battlefield*, pp. 133, 153–60.

16. For examples of this methodological approach, see Hassner and Horowitz, "Role of Religion in War"; Ron Hassner, "Religion and International Affairs: The State of the Art," in *Religion, Identity, and Global Governance*, ed. Patrick James (Toronto: University of Toronto Press, 2011), pp. 37–56.

CHAPTER 2

1. Anatolii Cherniaev, "Spirituality Destroyed," *Russian Politics and Law* 45, no. 5 (2007): 39.

2. Arkhiepiskop Kirill, "Tserkov' v otnoshenii k obschestvy v usloviiakh perestroika," *ZhMP*, no. 2 (1990): 34; Arkhiepiskop Kirill, "Nam neobkhodim aktivnyi dialog," *ZhMP*, no. 8 (1989): 52.

3. Clerics found their way into the first Congress of People's Deputies of the Union of Soviet Socialist Republics (USSR) and took up the work with the faithful across the country in all possible settings. Cherniaev, "Spirituality Destroyed," p. 31.

4. B. M. Lukichev, *Patriarkh Kirill i voennoe dukhovenstvo* (Moscow: FIV, 2016), p. 19.

5. John Garrard and Carol Garrard, *Russian Orthodoxy Resurgent: Faith and Power in the New Russia* (Princeton, NJ: Princeton University Press, 2008), p. 51.

6. Garrard and Garrard, *Russian Orthodoxy Resurgent*, p. 47.

7. "The war that you are waging is the war for liberation, a just war. May the courageous image of our great forbears inspire you in this war—Alexander Nevsky, Dmitry Donskoy, Kuzma Minin, Dmitry Pozharsky, Alexander Suvorov, Mikhail Kutuzov! May the victorious banner of great Lenin overshadow you!" Joseph Stalin, speech during the Moscow parade, 7 November 1941. A patriotic-propagandistic film titled *Alexander Nevsky*, which Stalin commissioned from the Soviet filmmaker Sergey Eisenstein, became one of the most popular movies of the war. Nevsky's address to his troops in the movie—"He who comes to us with the sword, shall perish by the sword"—became viral in the Red Army, which also, like Nevsky's soldiers, fought the Germans. In 1943 Stalin introduced a military order under Nevsky's name.

8. Garrard and Garrard, *Russian Orthodoxy Resurgent*, p. 51.

9. Lukichev, *Patriarkh Kirill*, pp. 8–9.

10. "For this reason, moral and ideological spoilage of the adversary's military has always been the most important task of the warring sides." "Vystuplenie Mitropolita Kirilla na Vsearmeiskom soveschanii 17 ianvaria, 1992 goda," *Put'*, no. 2 (15) (1992).

11. "Recently I visited the Baltic Fleet and I should tell you from the bottom of my heart: it has been a touching and deep spiritual experience for me. On the fleet's vessels I have seen hermits, who in the most difficult conditions, in poverty, disconnected from their families, without sufficient food supplies, deprived of normal living conditions, carry out the most difficult service. The only thing they have not lost is love of their people and of their Motherland. What will happen [. . .] to our nation, if they lose this high moral stimulus to carry out their hermitical military, moral service full of sacrifice?" "Vystuplenie Mitropolita Kirilla," p. 15.

12. "Vystuplenie Mitropolita Kirilla," p. 15.

13. "Editorial," *KZ*, 18 January 1992.

14. The deterioration reached a climax in 1994, when 60 percent of the new conscripts did not report to their units. Garrard and Garrard, *Russian Orthodoxy Resurgent*, pp. 207, 219.

15. Lukichev, *Patriarkh Kirill*, pp. 11–12.

16. Sergei Mozgovoi, "Vzaimootnosheniia armii i tserkvi v Rossiiskoi Federatsii," *Journal of Power Institutions in Post-Soviet Societies*, no. 3 (2005): 3.

17. The Joint Declaration established the Coordination Committee, consisting of the senior officers from the Main Educational Work Directorate and priests from the ROC's External Relations Department. The committee published its first white paper—*Concept of Relationships Between Organs of Military Management and Traditional Religious Congregations of Russia*. Lukichev, *Patriarkh Kirill*, pp. 12–17. Other segments of the Russian strategic community later used this template to formalize their ties with the church. Following the agreement, Kirill initiated meetings with other senior commanders to promote cooperation: the Internal Affairs Ministry (2 October 1994), the Federal Border Service (28 December 1994), the Ministry of Emergency Situations (29 December 1994),

and Federal Agency for Government Communications and Information (16 January 1995). Upon signing the agreement, Sergei Shoigu, the current Russian DM, said to the patriarch: "We are colleagues—you save people's souls and our role is to save their lives." Garrard and Garrard, *Russian Orthodoxy Resurgent*, p. 222.

18. Garrard and Garrard, *Russian Orthodoxy Resurgent*, pp. 217, 220.

19. Mozgovoi, "Vzaimootnosheniia armii i tserkvi," pp. 4–5.

20. Lukichev, *Patriarkh Kirill*, pp. 12–17; Mozgovoi, "Vzaimootnosheniia armii i tserkvi," pp. 4–5.

21. Mozgovoi, "Vzaimootnosheniia armii i tserkvi," pp. 16–18.

22. Mozgovoi, "Vzaimootnosheniia armii i tserkvi," p. 2; Garrard and Garrard, *Russian Orthodoxy Resurgent*, p. 207; Nikolai Mitrokhin, *Russkaia Pravoslavnaia Tserkov': Sovremennoe sostoianie i aktual'nye problemy* (Moscow: Novoe literaturnoe obozrenie, 2006), p. 329.

23. Lukichev, *Patriarkh Kirill*, pp, 16–17; Mozgovoi, "Vzaimootnosheniia armii i tserkvi," p. 16.

24. "There are different views in our society on the role and importance of the military. There are forces that purposefully discredit the Armed Forces in the eyes of the compatriots. At this uneasy time for the warriors, it is a duty of the Church to declare straightforwardly—the Armed Forces is unique among the state institutions that the society should morally support." Lukichev, *Patriarkh Kirill*, pp. 120–25.

25. "It's our duty to assist people in overcoming stress, to help them feel self-confident, to assist them in having material and spiritual motivation. [. . .] With no ethical motivation there will be no combat heroism." Lukichev, *Patriarkh Kirill*, pp. 120–25.

26. Lukichev, *Patriarkh Kirill*, pp. 128–29.

27. Garrard and Garrard, *Russian Orthodoxy Resurgent*, p. 209.

28. Garrard and Garrard, *Russian Orthodoxy Resurgent*, pp. 209–16.

29. In 1994 Patriarch Alexey expressed his hope that new pastors would arrive from within the military. By the early 2000s, more than a dozen retired and active-duty officers were ordained as priests upon graduation from Moscow's St. Tikhon Orthodox University and went on to function in the units. Mozgovoi, "Vzaimootnosheniia armii i tserkvi," pp. 11–12.

30. Lukichev, *Patriarkh Kirill*, pp. 17–18.

31. Lukichev, *Patriarkh Kirill*, pp. 17–18.

32. For priests establishing relations with military commanders, see Mozgovoi, "Vzaimootnosheniia armii i tserkvi," p. 3.

33. Lukichev, *Patriarkh Kirill*, pp. 129–30.

34. Mozgovoi, "Vzaimootnosheniia armii i tserkvi," p. 4.

35. Lukichev, *Patriarkh Kirill*, pp. 17–18.

36. Nominally they were subordinate to the Synodal Department, but given the rather broad autonomy of the local parishes then, the guidance and control were not really tight. Mitrokhin, *Russkaia Pravoslavnaia Tserkov'*, p. 329; Nikolai Mitrokhin, "Liubov' bez udovletvoreniia," *Journal of Power Institutions in Post-Soviet Societies*, no. 3 (2005): 3.

37. Lukichev, *Patriarkh Kirill*, pp. 68, 103–4.

38. For example, as a demonstration of this bond, the World Russian People's Council in 1996 arranged a hearing called "Nuclear Weapons and Russian National Security." Lukichev, *Patriarkh Kirill*, p. 21. On the ROC's defense of the military, see Arkhiepiskop Smolenskii i Kaliningradskii Kirill, "Za voinstvo nashe," *Armiia i kul'tura*, nos. 6–7 (1992).

39. Lukichev, *Patriarkh Kirill*, pp. 19, 130–31.

40. "U nashego khrama novyi nastoiatel'," *Khram prep. Andreia Rubleva*, 14 October 2011.

41. Construction on the cathedral started in 1992 and lasted for eight years. To complete the project, the patriarch mobilized the Kremlin; the federal bureaucracy; the mayor of Moscow, who was then one of the main power brokers of modern Russia; the gas, oil, and banking industries; and a cohort of oligarchs. In 2012 the band Pussy Riot would conduct their performance there. On establishing the cathedral as a force in the new state, see Garrard and Garrard, *Russian Orthodoxy Resurgent*, p. 86.

42. The 1812 decree envisioned the cathedral as a collective tomb, a cenotaph, to all fallen Russian soldiers, and on its walls are inscribed the names of all the officers who fell in all battles in Russia and abroad against Napoleon before and after 1812. During the Soviet era, the collective cenotaph for the unknown fallen soldiers was erected near the Kremlin wall following the Great Patriotic War. Together with the eternal fire next to it, it is one of the most sacred places for the Russian military and citizens. On the Post-Soviet rebranding of the cathedral, see Garrard and Garrard, *Russian Orthodoxy Resurgent*, pp. 81–91.

43. Since the cathedral commemorated the military victory, one of its two side chapels is dedicated to Russian prince St. Alexander Nevsky, who achieved victory over foreign invaders under the Orthodox banner. Garrard and Garrard, *Russian Orthodoxy Resurgent*, pp. 81–91.

44. Often, however, the local civilians rather than the uniformed people were the majority of the congregation. Mitrokhin, *Russkaia Pravoslavnaia Tserkov'*, p. 335.

45. *Domovaia tserkov' / domovoi khram*—a church building or part of the dwelling designated for performing religious services and ceremonies by members of a household or an institution.

46. In 1989, inspired by the celebrations of the baptism of Rus, General V. Ia. Shatokhin, dean of the missile and rocket forces faculty in the academy, initiated a visit of a group of professors to the Troitsa-Sergeev Lavra. The local archimandrite hosted them and suggested organizing a joint conference dedicated to Alexander Nevsky. During the conference, which took place in 1990, the participants suggested the establishment of the academy's temple. Eighty percent of the academy staff supported the idea. In 1992 the commander of the academy received approval from the GS to build the house church, and construction and decoration work started. "U nashego khrama novyi nastoiatel'."

47. "VAGSh okormliatsia domovym khramom vo im. Arkhangela Mikhaila," *Orthodox TV Channel "Soyuz,"* 2 October 2008 (quotation). The first church that was constructed on a military base was the temple of St. Georgii the Victor in 1994 at the Academy of Radiological, Chemical, and Biological Defense. Iurii Polarshinov, "Pervomy

armeiskomy khramu nuzhna pomosch'," *KZ*, 20 March 2009; "V strareishem khrame postroennom pri voennom uchebnom zavedenii, sostoialsia prestol'nyi prazdnik," *VViMD*, 11 May 2010. Before the Russian Revolution, the GS Academy, then located in St. Petersburg, included a small wooden church that Alexander Suvorov, the famous military commander, built with his own hands. To commemorate the one hundredth anniversary of his death, Tsar Nikolai II ordered the temple to be brought to the academy. After the revolution, the authorities disassembled the church for firewood. "20-letnii iubilei khrama arkhistratiga," *Khram prep. Andreia Rubleva*, 22 January 2016.

48. "20-letnii iubilei khrama arkhistratiga."

49. In those years the majority was still secular, hardly visited voluntarily, and converted incrementally. It would take about a decade until the congregation grew. The ROC was still thrilled that "at the heart of the most important and high-ranking military education institution the church is active and prayer is taking place." "VAGSh okormliatsia domovym khramom vo im. Arkhangela Mikhaila."

50. Oleg Nevzorov, "Tserkov' osvaivet pastvu v pogonakh," *Rossiiskie vesti*, 4 November 1996.

51. Mitrokhin, *Russkaia Pravoslavnaia Tserkov'*, p. 333.

52. Mozgovoi, "Vzaimootnosheniia armii i tserkvi," p. 6.

53. Mitrokhin, *Russkaia Pravoslavnaia Tserkov'*, p. 333.

54. Lukichev, *Patriarkh Kirill*, pp. 16–17.

55. Lukichev, *Patriarkh Kirill*, pp. 16–17. The military particularly appreciated the social-psychological-spiritual support of "special operations fathers" who during the Chechen campaigns accompanied fighting units. Lukichev, *Patriarkh Kirill*, p. 40. Priests also collected donations to be delivered to the soldiers in the combat zone. Mozgovoi, "Vzaimootnosheniia armii i tserkvi," pp. 6–7.

56. Mitrokhin, "Liubov' bez udovletvoreniia," pp. 2–3.

57. For the cooperation of mid-level officials, and for cooperation based on commanders' personal religiosity, see Mitrokhin, "Liubov' bez udovletvoreniia," p. 9; Mozgovoi, "Vzaimootnosheniia armii i tserkvi," p. 3. In addition to the case of the nuclear corps outlined in subsequent chapters, the personal factor explains the continuity of the ROC's influence in the GS Academy and beyond. Igor Rodionov, who was deputy and then head of the academy (1989–96), and who approved the construction of the house church there, became the DM in 1996. He positioned himself as a patriotic-Orthodox politician, and it was during his short tenure that the ROC and the MoD signed on 4 April 1997 an agreement that further extended and deepened cooperation.

CHAPTER 3

1. John Garrard and Carol Garrard, *Russian Orthodoxy Resurgent: Faith and Power in the New Russia* (Princeton, NJ: Princeton University Press), p. 53.

2. Garrard and Garrard, *Russian Orthodoxy Resurgent*, p. 65.

3. "Desert person"—*pustynnik* in Russian. This Orthodox ascetic tradition emanates from the early Christian practice of monks and nuns in the desert of Egypt, also known as Desert Fathers and Mothers.

4. S. Iu. Vitte, *Vospominania: Tsarstvovanie Nikolaia* (Moscow, 1923), vol. 1, p. 221; Garrard and Garrard, *Russian Orthodoxy Resurgent*, pp. 53–54; "Propoved' Patriarkha Kirilla v prazdnik obreteniia: Predstoiatel' Russkoi Tserkvi sovershil Liturgiiu v Diveevskom monastyre," *Patriarchia.ru*, 1 August 2016. Also see *Pravoslavnyi Sarov* (pravsarov. su); *Fond prepodobnogo Serafima Sarovskogo* (bfss.ru).

5. Garrard and Garrard, *Russian Orthodoxy Resurgent*, pp. 62–62.

6. Garrard and Garrard, *Russian Orthodoxy Resurgent*, pp. 55–57; "Propoved' Patriarkha Kirilla v prazdnik obreteniia." Also see *Pravoslavnyi Sarov*; *Fond prepodobnogo Serafima Sarovskogo*.

7. D. V. Sladkov (assistant to the VNIIEF director), "Vystupleniia," in *Problemy vzaimodeistviia RPTs i veduschikh nauchnykh tsentrov Rossii (7–10 marta 2000)* (Sarov: RFIaTs-VNIIEF, 2000).

8. RFIaTs VNIIEF—Russian Federal Nuclear Center, the All-Russian Research Institute of Experimental Physics of the Russian State Atomic Energy Corporation (ROSATOM). It was founded in 1946 as KB-11 to implement the Soviet Atomic Project in Arzamas-16, now Sarov.

9. RFIaTs VNIITF—Russian Federal Nuclear Center, the All-Russian Research Institute of Technical Physics of ROSATOM. The second main nuclear weapons design center.

10. Editorial, "Osveschenie vizita Patriarkha Aleksiia v Sarov," *Gorodskoi kur'er*, no. 63 (14 August 1991).

11. Garrard and Garrard, *Russian Orthodoxy Resurgent*, pp. 56–57, 62–65.

12. Garrard and Garrard, *Russian Orthodoxy Resurgent*, pp. 59–60.

13. I. G. Zhidov, ed., *Stanovlenie otnoshenii Rossiiskogo federal'nogo iadernogo tsentra VNIIEF i Russkoi Pravoslavnoi Tserkvi* (Sarov: RFIaTs-VNIIEF, 2008), pp. 6, 12.

14. Garrard and Garrard, *Russian Orthodoxy Resurgent*, pp. 62–65.

15. Garrard and Garrard, *Russian Orthodoxy Resurgent*, pp. 62–65.

16. Arkhiepiskop Gor'skovsky i Arzamasky Nikolai, "Tserkov' i gosudarstvo mogut sotrudnichat' v vospitanii dukhovnosti," *Gazeta VNIIEF "Impul's,"* April 1988.

17. Under the imprint of his childhood experiences beside his pious grandmother, with her icons and sanctuary lamps, Takoev did not become an aggressive atheist during Soviet times and even as Komsomol city secretary did not reveal facts about clandestine baptisms or church weddings. Alla Shadrina, "Valerii Takoev: Sarovu ne khvataet stolchnosti," *Vesti goroda*, 6 June 2012.

18. Zhidov, *Stanovlenie otnoshenii*, p. 11; I. G. Zhidov (senior scientist in the VNIIEF), "Vystupleniia," in *Problemy vzaimodeistviia RPTs*.

19. G. Kuligina, "Poseschenie Arzamasa-16 Arkhiepiskopom Nikolaem," *Panorama*, November 1990.

20. In 1989 the authorities dropped the secret Soviet title Ministry of Medium Machinery Production and renamed it the Ministry of Atomic Energetics and Industry. For Takoev's invitation, see Shadrina, "Valerii Takoev"; Tatiana Volodina, "Kakie liudi zdes' khodili!" *Gorodskoi kur'er*, 6 October 2011.

21. Editorial, "Osveschenie vizita Patriarkha Aleksiia."

22. Shadrina, "Valerii Takoev"; Tatiana Volodina, "Kakie liudi zdes' khodili!"

23. V. N. Takoev (interview), "Otchet o press konferentsii predsedatelia gorsoveta po itogam vizita Patriarkha Aleksiia II v nash gorod," *Gorodskoi kur'er*, no. 64 (16 August 1991).

24. Shadrina, "Valerii Takoev"; Tatiana Volodina, "Kakie liudi zdes' khodili!"

25. Zhidov, *Stanovlenie otnoshenii*, p. 5.

26. G. Lomanov, "Gorod kotorogo net na karte," *PV*, no. 49 (78) (December 1990); See also: V. Umnov, "Zdes' zhivut molchalivie liudi," *Sovershenno sekretno—Komsomol'skaia pravda*, 25 November 1990.

27. Zhidov, *Stanovlenie otnoshenii*, pp. 5–7.

28. Sergei Brezkun, "Akademik umer: Da zdravstvuet Sredmash!" *VPK*, 6 July 2011.

29. Zhidov, *Stanovlenie otnoshenii*, p. 8.

30. Takoev, "Otchet o press konferentsii."

31. Takoev, "Otchet o press konferentsii."

32. "Arzamas-16," *600 sekund*, 30 July 1991. The social-economic disaster was not only within the nuclear complex, but it was particularly felt there.

33. During Soviet times, this was the place where city believers quietly gathered to pray. Zhidov, *Stanovlenie otnoshenii*, p. 6.

34. Zhidov, *Stanovlenie otnoshenii*, p. 12.

35. Editorial, "Osveschenie vizita Patriarkha Aleksiia."

36. V. N. Takoev (deputy governor of the Nizhegorodsky District; head of the Arzamas-16 city council until 1993), in *Stenogramma sobornykh slushanii "Iadernaye vooruzheniia i natsional'naia bezopasnost' Rossii*," VRNS, 12 November 1996.

37. Tatiana Volodina, "Kakie liudi zdes' khodili!"

38. Takoev, in *Stenogramma sobornykh slushanii*.

39. Tatiana Volodina, "Kakie liudi zdes' khodili!" The patriarch did not take the model with him, and just as the city authorities were about to send it to Moscow, the coup d'état occurred. When it was all over, on 22 August, the senior city, VNIIEF, military, MVD, and KGB representatives took the model up to the roof of the city council building and made a photo in which the model, in their hands, is pictured against the background of the actual monastery bell tower—the most recognizable feature of the Sarov skyline. Shadrina, "Valerii Takoev"; V. Tenegin, "V Sarove i v dali ot nego," *Gorodskoi kur'er*, 18 August 2016.

40. Zhidov, *Stanovlenie otnoshenii*, pp. 12–13.

41. Viktor Mikhailov, *Ia iastreb* (Moscow: FGUP ISS, 2008), pp. 68–69, 252–54, 258, 474–75.

42. Mikhailov, *Ia iastreb*, pp. 260, 265.

43. Zhidov, *Stanovlenie otnoshenii*, pp. 13–14.

44. His note in the guestbook read: "We explored with interest the Sarov Museum of Nuclear Weapons, and saw the movies about the explosion of the atomic bomb and about what the nuclear center can produce for agriculture, medicine, and the other fields of peaceful life. May God ensure that that explosion, which was created here for the defense of our Motherland, is never used against people, but that the products of the outstanding minds of the center for creation and well-being will generously increase." Alexey,

the patriarch of Moscow and all Rus, 4 August 1993. See also pictures from Alexey's 1993 visit to the Museum of Nuclear Weapons, VNIIEF museum website.

45. Zhidov, *Stanovlenie otnoshenii*, p. 14.

46. E. Krestovsky and V. Klykov, "Kazhdyi dlia chegoto," *Sarov*, 7–13 October 1994; "Obraschenie uchastnikov kongressa 'Kul'tura i buduschee Rossii,'" *Gorodskoi kur'er*, no. 37 (14 May 1994); "Kruglyi stol 'Iadernyi schit Rossii: Nravstvennost', ideologiia, politika,'" *Gorodskoi kur'er*, no. 90 (17 November 1994); "Vstupitel'noe slovo nastoiatelia Sarovskogo khrama Vsekh Sviatykh o. Vladimira," *Atom*, no. 1 (1994): 2–3.

47. The VRNS is a public organization established in 1993 and headed since then by Patriarch Kirill. Its aim is to enable civil society and compatriots of the "Russian World" abroad to overcome the political, cultural, and spiritual split caused by the Union's collapse. The council serves as an annual forum for government and municipal officials, senior military officers, leaders of nongovernmental organizations (NGOs), scientific and cultural figures, representatives of Russian communities from abroad, and clergy to discuss the present and future problems of Russia. Since its establishment, it has conducted annual plenary meetings, operated regional departments throughout the year, and hosted political leaders. "O sobore," *VRNS* (vrns.ru).

48. The Sarov branch of the VRNS was officially established as an NGO in May 1996. The superior nun of the Diveevo Monastery and the deputy director of the VNIIEF, Radii Il'kaev, became its coheads. Zhidov, *Stanovlenie otnoshenii*, p. 18.

49. On linking the problems to the all-Russia agenda, see Zhidov, *Stanovlenie otnoshenii*, pp. 36–59. Survival included threatening to sell nuclear know-how. "If you are not going to feed us, all of us will move to Iraq." Zhidov, *Stanovlenie otnoshenii*, p. 54.

50. On the emergence of other such forums, see Zhidov, *Stanovlenie otnoshenii*, pp. 15–18; L. Kovshova, "Zachem sobor to sobirali?," *Panorama*, no. 4 (196) (22–28 January 1996). As one of the VNIIEF seniors put it in 1996: "Why exactly scientists, military, and church? Because their activity rests on serving something that is higher than you, than your personal comfort. The contacts of the VNIIEF and the church are in the realm of reconstructing the 'ethics of service.'" E. Vlasova, "Vozrodit' etiku sluzheniia," *Gorod*, 21 November 1996.

51. I. N. Sudarev (senior Ministry of Foreign Affairs official), in *Stenogramma sobornykh slushanii*; R. I. Il'kaev (acting director of the VNIIEF), in *Stenogramma sobornykh slushanii*.

52. The work started in late 1995 in the framework of the interagency committee coordinated by the National Security Council and aimed to prepare recommendations for the Kremlin regarding a series of decisions on the subject, which were taken between 1996 and 1999. A. A. Kokoshin, *Strategicheskoe upravlenie* (Moscow: ROSSPEN, 2003), pp. 315–19.

53. "Privetstvie Sviateishego Patriarkha Moskovskogo i vseia Rusi Aleksiia II" and "Mitropolit Smolenskii i Kaliningradskii Kirill," in *Stenogramma sobornykh slushanii*.

54. Zhidov, *Stanovlenie otnoshenii*, pp. 54–55.

55. Sudarev; Il'kaev; Iu. I. Faikov (first deputy of the VNIIEF, chief engineer of the VNIIEF, and professor in the Missiles and Artillery Department of the GS Academy); General Lieutenant V. Ia. Shatokhin (head of the Missile and Artillery Forces Faculty at the GS Academy); General Lieutenant N. S. Leonov (Moscow State Institute of

International Relations [MGIMO] professor [head of the KGB Information-Analytical Directorate, until 1991]); V. P. Lukin (chairman of the Duma International Affairs Committee); Iu. A. Kvitsinsky (councilor to the head of the Federation Council of the Parliament), in *Stenogramma sobornykh slushanii.*

56. Takoev; P. V. Boyarsky (president of the Polar Exploration Foundation); E. M. Ivanova (president of the Conversion and Women Association), in *Stenogramma sobornykh slushanii.*

57. General Major I. S. Danilenko (professor at the GS Academy); Il'kaev, in *Stenogramma sobornykh slushanii.*

58. Shatokhin, in *Stenogramma sobornykh slushanii.*

59. On the disarmament stratagem, see E. F. Volodin, in *Stenogramma sobornykh slushanii.* On the tactic to discredit Russia, see Shatokhin, in *Stenogramma sobornykh slushanii.*

60. Leonov; S. S. Sulashkin (chairman of the Duma Committee on the Military-Industrial Complex); Boyarsky, in *Stenogramma sobornykh slushanii.* For example, Mikhailov saw Greenpeace antinuclear initiatives in Russia as the arm of the oil lobby and perceived ecological activism as antistate subversion. Mikhailov, *Ia iastreb*, pp. 163, 254–55, 268–69.

61. Mikhailov, *Ia iastreb*, p. 164.

62. On funding salaries, see N. P. Voloshin (head of the Main Directorate for Nuclear Weapons Development in the Ministry of Nuclerar Energy of Russian Federation); B. V. Litvinov (chief engineer of Chelyabinsk-70); Il'kaev, in *Stenogramma sobornykh slushanii.* On food supplies, see Faikov, in *Stenogramma sobornykh slushanii.*

63. Litvinov; Sulashkin, in *Stenogramma sobornykh slushanii.*

64. Sulashkin, in *Stenogramma sobornykh slushanii.*

65. Elianora Ivanova, "Opening Webpage Statement," Conversion and Women Association, 15 March 1993, www.owl.ru/win/women/aiwo/convers.htm; see also Mikhailov, *Ia iastreb*, p. 67.

66. "The industry workers need a system of psychological-moral-social adaptation to the new realities." Zhidov, *Stanovlenie otnoshenii*, pp. 48–50.

67. Alexander Raskin, "Akademik ustal ot bezvihodnosti," *Kommersant*, 1 November 1996.

68. On the pastoral care of the nuclear community, see Konstantin Tatarintsev (ierei of the church in Tushino), in *Stenogramma sobornykh slushanii.*

69. Kirill, "Final Address," in *Stenogramma sobornykh slushanii.*

70. "The Final Proclamation," in *Stenogramma sobornykh slushanii.*

71. Zhidov, *Stanovlenie otnoshenii*, p. 18.

72. See, e.g., A. Shapovalov, "Glass ne tol'ko sviatoi obiteli," *Rossiiskaia gazeta*, 14 November 1996; D. Perevalov, "Nel'za dopustit' razvala iadernogo schita Rossii," *Moskovskii tserkovnyi vestnik*, 12 November 1996; E. Popov, "Doklad ot imeni Nichaia," *Sovetskaia Rossiia*, 14 November 1996; P. Felgenhauer, "Pravoslavnoe iadernoe oruzhie," *Segodnia*, 13 November 1996; M. Rebrov, "Zapovedi Gospodni i iadernaia bomba," *KZ*, 28 November 1996; V. Chukanov, "Nadezhen li schit u strany?," *Pravda*, 13 November 1996;

N. Gorbachev, "Iadernyi schit mnogostradal'nogo otechestva," *Glasnost*, no. 20 (1996); P. Gal'chenko, "Imeiuschii uzhi da suslishit: O role iadernogo oruzhiia v sud'be Rossii," *Gorodskoi kur'er*, no. 70 (21 November 1996).

73. A. M. Goncharov (councilor of the Duma Committee for Industry, Construction, Transport, and Energy), in *Stenogramma sobornykh slushanii*.

74. Zhidov, *Stanovlenie otnoshenii*.

75. Kokoshin, *Strategicheskoe upravlenie*, pp. 314–19, 478n31.

76. The title of his 1997 *Pravda* piece—"What a Happiness It Is to Live and to Create"—speaks for itself. Viktor Mikhailov, "Kakoe eto schast'e—zhit' i tvorit," pp. 190–208, and "10 let v bor'be za vizhivanie," p. 253, in Mikhailov, *Ia iastreb*.

77. Kokoshin, *Strategicheskoe upravlenie*, pp. 314–19, 478n31.

78. In conjunction with the crisis, "state television ran a broadcast segment in which the then chairman of the State Duma, Gennady Seleznev, held a direct phone conversation with the commander of a missile base outside of Moscow, during which they discussed the status of targeting U.S. facilities with Russian missiles. [. . .] A few days later, President Boris Yeltsin, then in China, unexpectedly confirmed Russia's robust nuclear capacity in the presence of television journalists." Alexei Obukhov, "Nuclear Weapons and Christian Ethics," *Security Index* 13, no. 1 (81) (2007): 98.

79. Radii Il'kaev, in Zhidov, *Stanovlenie otnoshenii*, pp. 3–4.

80. R. I. Il'kaev, "Otkrytie konferentsii," in *Problemy vzaimodeistviia RPTs*.

81. Radii Il'kaev, "Vystupleniia," in *Problemy vzaimodeistviia RPTs*. Also see Zhidov, "Vystupleniia."

82. Il'kaev, "Vystupleniia."

83. Mitropolit Kirill, "Vystupleniia," in *Problemy vzaimodeistviia RPTs*.

84. Zhidov, *Stanovlenie otnoshenii*, p. 19.

85. "Itogovyi dokument sobornykh chtenii VRNS 'Vera i znanie,'" *Tserkov' i vremia* 5, no. 2 (1998): 16–20.

86. "Itogovyi dokument nauchno-prakticheskoi konferentsii," in *Problemy vzaimodeistviia RPTs*.

87. Zhidov, *Stanovlenie otnoshenii*, p. 273.

88. The document also emphasized that "pacifist critique of the Russian nuclear weapons scientists" emanated from the circles that either underestimated Russian nuclear disarmament or were interested in Russia's weakening. "Itogovyi dokument nauchno-prakticheskoi konferentsii."

89. Zhidov, *Stanovlenie otnoshenii*, p. 20; Il'kaev, "Vystupleniia."

90. "Itogovyi dokument nauchno-prakticheskoi konferentsii."

91. Zhidov, *Stanovlenie otnoshenii*, p. 20.

92. Zhidov, *Stanovlenie otnoshenii*, p. 20.

93. Il'kaev, "Vystupleniia."

94. Il'kaev, "Vystupleniia"; D. V. Sladkov, "Vystupleniia"; A. V. Kondrashenko (head of the laboratory in the VNIIEF); A. V. Nedostup, "Vystupleniia," in *Problemy vzaimodeistviia RPTs*.

95. Zhidov, "Vystupleniia."

96. Nedostup, "Vystupleniia."

97. Ierei Konstantin Tatarintsev, "Vystupleniia," in *Problemy vzaimodeistviia RPTs.*

98. Zhidov, "Vystupleniia." In 1999 the mayor of Moscow accepted the ROC's demands and agreed to remove the icon of the Vladimirskaia Mother of God, probably the most famous Russian icon, from the Tretiakov Gallery to the Nikolskaia house church, located within the museum. In the following year, one of the MINATOM plants produced for it a special bulletproof decorated icon case. Elena Lebedeva, "Khram sviatogo Nikolaia Chudotvortsa v Tolmachakh," *Pravoslavie.ru*, 18 December 2006.

99. Kondrashenko, "Vystupleniia."

100. Aleksandr Sladkov, *Voennaia programma*, *TV Channel "Rossiia 1,"* 28 April 2008, (1:02 min.).

101. "Pervyi shag k vozrozhdeniu dukhovnykh osnov," *RVSN AAA*, 1 June 2010.

102. B. M. Lukichev, *Patriarkh Kirill i voennoe dukhovenstvo* (Moscow: FIV, 2016), p. 198.

103. "Pervyi shag k vozrozhdeniu dukhovnykh osnov."

104. Baikonur, Plesetsk, and Kapustin Iar were the sites of the three main testing ranges. The two divisions were in Bologoevo and Barnaul. On garrison churches and Sunday schools, see Lukichev, *Patriarkh Kirill*, p. 198.

105. Aleksandr Sladkov, *Voennaia programma.*

106. The icon was a copy of Andrei Rublev's famous work. "Ikona nebesnoi pokrovitel'nitsy strategicheskih raketchikov," *RVSN AAA*, 1 June 2010.

107. "V glavnom zale TsKP," *RVSN AAA*, 16 January 2014.

108. "45 let ispolnilos' zastupleniiu na boevoe dezhurstvo Tsentralnogo komandnogo punkta RVSN," *RF MoD*, 6 June 2012.

109. "Protoierei vnosiat ikonu," *RVSN AAA*, 30 August 2010; Ilya Bulavinov, "Iadernyi saliut pod Moskvoi," *Kommersant*, 25 April 1997; Mikhail Aniskin (author and producer), *TsKP RVSN—45 let* (28.12 min.), Press Sluzhba RVSN, 2005. By 2017 the icon was moved to a separate wall and is now on the left-hand side of the duty shift. "Tsentral'nyi komandyi punkt otmetil svoi iubilei," *TV Chanel "Schit nashego Otechestva,"* 14 June 2017.

110. "Osnovateli khrama prepodobnogo Ilii Muromtsa," *RVSN AAA*, 27 May 2010.

111. *Moskovskii tserkovnyi vestnik*, no. 24 (2000); A. S. Borzenkov, *Orenburgskaia strategicheskaia: Khronika osnovnykh sobytii istorii Orenburgskoi raketnoi armii* (Perm: Permskoe knizhnoe izdatel'stvo, 2001), chap. 1.

112. Aleksandr Sladkov, *Voennaia programma.*

113. *RMoD News*, 25 April 2008; Lukichev, *Patriarkh Kirill*, p. 199.

114. Alexander Dolinin and Anatolii Belousov, "Prikazano, blagoslovleno, priniato," *KZ*, 5 October 1996.

115. "Patriarshemu poddvoriu v RVSN—15 let," *RF MoD*, 26 April 2013.

116. This sparked some suspicion from within the garrison, which rapidly evaporated. Aleksandr Sladkov, *Voennaia programma.*

117. Construction lasted from August 1997 to April 1998. "General armii Vladimir Nikolaevich Iakovlev," *RVSN AAA*, 8 September 2010.

118. On the consecration and service, see "V den' prazdnovaniia Paskhi v nuneshnem godu otemtit svoiu 10-iu godovshchinu khram VMCh. Varvaru i prep. Ilii Muromtsa v glavnom garnizone RVSN (Odintsovo 10)," *RMoD News*, 25 April 2008. On the RVSN High Command, see Aleksandr Sladkov, *Voennaia programma*.

119. Aleksandr Sladkov, *Voennaia programma*.

120. "Ikona prepodobnogo Ilii Muromtsa," *RVSN AAA*, 1 June 2010.

121. Together with the interior of the GS Academy temple.

122. The fresco pictures Zhenia Radionov wearing a traditional tunic, in the style of Greek iconography, over a camouflage military uniform and carrying a small cross in his hand. It commemorates his decapitation when, in captivity, he refused to take the cross and convert to Islam. Aleksandr Sladkov, *Voennaia programma*.

123. "Patriarshii moleben v khrame vmts. Varvary vo Vlasikhe (pri shtabe RVSN)," *Moscow Patriarchy News*, 18 December 2006.

124. "Patriarshemu poddvoriu v RVSN—15 let."

125. Protoierei Mikhail Vasiliev functions as the main priest of the RVSN and of the Russian Airborne Troops' (VDV) main churches and also as the chief pastor of both corps. P. Korobov and S. Petukhov, "Ofitsery Gospoda," *Voennyi vestnik Iuga Rossii*, 1 January 2010. As the main pastor of the RVSN, he has an office near the Vlasikha church, next to the RVSN Main Staff. As the main pastor of the VDV, he has an office in the Main Staff of the VDV in Moscow. Aleksandr Sladkov, *Voennaia programma*.

126. "The level of the soldiers selected there is above average, thus working with them is intellectually comfortable." Anastasiia Iakovleva, "Dukhovno-iadernnye sily Rossii," *VViMD*, 17 December 2010.

127. Iakovleva, "Dukhovno-iadernnye sily Rossii."

128. R. Shkurlatov, "Blagovest: Est' takoi fakul'tet," *Krasnyi voin*, 2 February 2002; Lukichev, *Patriarkh Kirill*, p. 199.

129. Dolinin and Belousov, "Prikazano, blagoslovleno, priniato."

130. Shkurlatov, "Blagovest."

131. Dolinin and Belousov, "Prikazano, blagoslovleno, priniato."

132. Sergei Mozgovoi, "Vzaimootnosheniia armii i tserkvi v Rossiiskoi Federatsii," *Journal of Power Institutions in Post-Soviet Societies*, no. 3 (2005): 8.

133. Dolinin and Belousov, "Prikazano, blagoslovleno, priniato" (quotation); "Iurii Ivanovich Plotnikov," *RVSN AAA*, 28 May 2010.

134. Shkurlatov, "Blagovest."

135. The modules were "Formulation of Personal, Family, and Societal Worldview"; "Spiritual Foundations of Russian Culture"; "Personal, Family, and Societal Spiritual Life"; and "Spiritual, Moral, and Combat Foundations of the Military Service." Shkurlatov, "Blagovest."

136. "Vypuskniki FPK, 21.04.2014" and "Sv. Patriarkh Kirill vruchaet svidetel'stvo," *RVSN AAA*, 21 and 22 April 2014. On time spent in services and seminars, see "FPK Voennoi akademii RVSN osuschestvil ocherednoi vypusk," *RF MoD*, 8 May 2013.

137. Shkurlatov, "Blagovest."

138. "Patriarshee pozdravlenie kollektivu Voennoi akademii RVSN im. Petra Velikogo," *Moscow Patriarchy*, 3 October 2006.

139. Shkurlatov, "Blagovest."

140. "Sostoialsia ocherednoi vypusk FPK Voennoi akademii RVSN," *RF MoD*, 16 April 2012.

141. "Voennoi akademii RVSN im Petra Velikogo 195 let," *RVSN AAA*, 4 December 2015.

142. Lukichev, *Patriarkh Kirill*, p. 199.

143. On the cooperation agreements, see Iakovleva, "Dukhovno-iadernnye sily Rossii." On the consecration of posts during combat duty, see Mozgovoi, "Vzaimootnosheniia armii i tserkvi," p. 7; as performed by the patriarch, see Inna Batalova, "Nauchit' liubvi k Bogu i Otechestvu," *Pravoslavnyi khristianin*, September 2011.

144. "Nikolai Maksimovich Moroz," *RVSN AAA*, www.facebook.com/11130321 8912386/photos/a.114275028615205.6229.111303218912386/115015195207855/?type =3&theater.

145. Konstantin Sergeev, "V Voennoi akademi RVSN pomianuli pogibshikh raketchkov," *VVD*, 26 October 2012.

146. "Istoriia prikhoda," *Khram vmch. Panteleimona*, Iasenskoe Povecherie (blgchin.ru).

147. In Sergeev's last letter to the Kremlin, which was written in 2006, before his death, and was also published in the *Red Star*, he recommended reviving the institution of military chaplains. Iakovleva, "Dukhovno-iadernnye sily Rossii." The patriarch, in his letter of condolence, praised Sergeev's leading role in the spiritual revival of the Russian military, especially within the RVSN. "V Moskve prostilis' s byvshim ministrom oborony RF marshalom Sergeevim," *Moscow Patriarchy*, 15 November 2006. His grave is adorned with a big Orthodox cross, something not very typical of former Soviet senior commanders. "Nadgrobnyi pamiatnik," *RVSN AAA*, 29 May 2010.

148. Iakovleva, "Dukhovno-iadernnye sily Rossii."

149. For example, in the Orenburg Missile Army garrison churches, Sunday schools of Orthodox culture opened in the Perm (1998) and Omsk (2000) missile divisions. Borzenkov, *Orenburgskaia strategicheskaia*, chap. 1.

150. Nikolai Mitrokhin, "Liubov' bez udovletvoreniia," *Journal of Power Institutions in Post-Soviet Societies*, no. 3 (2005): 15

151. Iurii Sukharev, "Rozhdestvenskie vstrechi: Pravoslavie schit Rossii," *KZ*, 28 February 2003. In 1988–89 Soviet Tu-22M3s armed with conventional munitions conducted combat sorties in Afghanistan. RUFOR (web forum dealing with Russian military affairs), http://rufor.org/showthread.php?t=2142; Vladimir Rigmat, "840-i Krasnoznamennyi tiazhelii bombardirovochnyi polk," *Aviatsia i kosmonavtika*, no. 11 (2004). The author does not offer evidence to support his claim regarding the consecration, presumably the first in the Soviet military. Sukharev, "Rozhdestvennskie vstrechi." But if his claim is correct, it probably was driven by the overall religious awakening after the highly publicized celebrations of the one thousandth anniversary of the baptism of Rus in May and June 1988.

152. The LRA commander who approved the request was General Colonel Igor' Kalugin.

153. Anastasiia Iakovleva, "Novye gorizonty DA," *KZ*, 3 June 2011; "Sviaschenniki v voiskakh DA," *VViMD*, 3 May 2011; Oleg Ternovoi, "S Rozhdestvom Khristovym," *VVS segodnia*, 30 December 2005.

154. Ternovoi, "S Rozhdestvom Khristovym."

155. Sukharev, "Rozhdestvennskie vstrechi."

156. Sergei Arkhipov, "Armiia povernula moiu zhizn'," *Pravoslavie.ru*, 25 July 2006. The LRA commander was General Lieutenant Mikhail Oparin, of the 37th Air Army.

157. Oleg Litvinov and Andrei Ianchinsky, "Sluzhit' otechestvu veroi i pravdoi," *VVS segodnia*, 16 September 2002.

158. Arkhipov, "Armiia povernula moiu zhizn'."

159. Irina Pavliutkina, "Chasovnia v shtabe DA," *KZ*, 27 August 2002; Litvinov and Ianchinsky, "Sluzhit' otechestvu."

160. Arkhipov, "Armiia povernula moiu zhizn'."

161. Arkhipov, "Armiia povernula moiu zhizn'."

162. Arkhipov, "Armiia povernula moiu zhizn'."

163. Oparin, in N. N. Sokolova, *Dar liubvi* (Moscow: Obschestvo pamaitai igumenii Taisii, 2005).

164. Ternovoi, "S Rozhdestvom Khristovym."

165. Oparin, in Sokolova, *Dar liubvi.*

166. Vladimir Malyschev, "Sorabotnichestvo vo imia zhizni," *KZ*, 25 February 2005; Litvinov and Ianchinsky, "Sluzhit' otechestvu."

167. Litvinov and Ianchinsky, "Sluzhit' otechestvu."

168. Arkhipov, "Armiia povernula moiu zhizn'."

169. Ternovoi, "S Rozhdestvom Khristovym."

170. Litvinov and Ianchinsky, "Sluzhit' otechestvu." This divine ascension is also symbolic to other Russian military professions associated with the skies—the Air Force and the Airborne Troops, which also designated Iliia as their patron saint. Pavliutkina "Chasovnia v shtabe DA."

171. "Patriarkh Aleksii posetil shtab Dal'nei aviatsii," *Pravoslavie.ru*, 21 December 2004.

172. "Sviaschenniki v voiskakh DA."

173. "K-51 Verkhotur'e," in A. S. Nikolaev, *EOPF* (deepstorm.ru). On the center, see Liudmila Selivanova, "V more za Slovom Bozhiim," *VViMD*, 20 September 2013.

174. A. G. Diakonov, "Praktika vzaimodeistviia organov voennogo upravleniia Severnogo flota s religioznymi organizatsiiami," *VM*, February 2005.

175. The priest of the Uspenskaia church from the city of Vladimir came to consecrate it. "K-117 Briansk, proekt 667BDRM," in Nikolaev, *EOPF.*

176. For example, following several emergencies that the B-414 atomic submarine experienced, the crew asked the patriarch to rename it after a saint for divine protection. In 1996 the patriarch renamed it after St. Prince Daniil Moskovsky (the youngest son of St. Alexander Nevsky). In 1997 the Krasnogorsk archbishop consecrated it and granted the crew St. Daniil's icon. "Osviaschenie atomnoi podloki i privoenie ei imeni sviatogo kniazia Daniila, 19 marta 1997," *Galereia na Kotlovke* (kotolovka.ru); "K-414, B-414, Sv.

Daniil Moskovskii, proekt 671 RTMK," in Nikolaev, *EOPF*; "Torzhestava posviaschennye 700 letiu so dnia blazhennoi konchiny blagovernogo kniazia Daniila Moskovskogo," in *Khram sviatitelia Nikolaia Chudotvortsa v Biriuleve* (orthodoxy.stnikolas.ru).

177. Diakonov, "Praktika vzaimodeistviia."

178. Nikolai Filatov, "Kogda muzh ukhodit v more," *Pravoslavie.ru*, 12 August 2015.

179. "K-18, Kareliia, proekt 667BDRM," in Nikolaev, *EOPF*; "Vladimir Putin Aboard Arkhangelsk Atomic Submarine," *Pravda.ru*, 17 February 2004.

180. Iegumen Mitrofan, *Neugasimaia lampada "Kurska"* (Murmansk: Ladan, 2013); "Dukhovenstvo" and "O khrame," in *Khram Nikolaia Chudotvortsa v Vidiaevo* (hramvidiaevo.cerkov.ru).

181. "Patriarkh Kirill blagoslovil rossiiskikh podvodnikov," *Vesti.ru*, 22 August 2009; "Kratkaia istoriia Nikolo-Korelskogo monastyria," *Pravoslavnaia stranitsa Nikolaia i Eleny Andrushenko* (orthonord.ru) (accessed 7 September 2016).

182. "Patriarkh Kirill blagoslovil rossiiskikh podvodnikov"; "Kratkaia istoriia Nikolo-Korelskogo monastyria."

183. "Kratkaia istoriia Nikolo-Korelskogo monastyria."

184. "10 let apostolskoi propovedi v Osinom gnezde," *Pravoslavnaia Kamchatka* (pravkamchatka.ru), 14 December 2008.

185. "Predstoiatel' Russkoi Tserkvi vstretilsia s moriakami-podvondikami Tikhooneskogo flota," *Pravoslavie.ru*, 19 September 2010.

186. "10 let apostolskoi propovedi"; "Piatnadtsataia godovschina osviascheniia garnizonnogo khrama," *Pravoslavnaia Kamchatka*, 15 December 2013; "Predstoiatel' Russkoi Tserkvi vstretilsia s moriakami-podvondikami."

187. "10 let apostolskoi propovedi"; "Piatnadtsataia godovschina osviascheniia"; "Predstoiatel' Russkoi Tserkvi vstretilsia s moriakami-podvondikami."

188. "K-150, Tomsk, Proekt 949A," in Nikolaev, *EOPF*.

189. "Proekt 667BDR," *Forum klub Falersitika*, 27 March 2011.

190. "Dvadtsatiletie Petropavlovskoi i Kamchatskoi eparkhii," *Pravoslavnaia Kamchatka*, 14 October 2013.

191. "10 let apostolskoi propovedi"; "Piatnadtsataia godovschina osviascheniia."

192. *Kosmos kak poslushanie* (Moscow: Studia ROSKOSMOS, 2010).

193. Virgiliu Pop, "Space and Religion in Russia: Cosmonaut Worship to Orthodox Revival," *Astropolitics*, no. 7 (2009): 159–60.

194. *Kosmos kak poslushanie*.

195. Pop, "Space and Religion in Russia," p. 158.

196. Aleksander Milkus, "'Kosmicheskii' batiushka otets Sergii," *Komsomol'skaia pravda*, 10 April 2015.

197. *Kosmos kak poslushanie*.

198. Natalia Burtseva, "V kosmos s blagoslovelniem," *Vesti TV*, 13 December 2008; Milkus, "'Kosmicheskii' batiushka"; Pop, "Space and Religion in Russia," p. 158.

199. Bases are known by their code names, Object 413 and Golitsyno-2.

200. Evgenii, "Khram sviatogo Arkhangela Mikhaila," *KhsAMM*, 27 November 2013.

201. Dmitrii Andreev, "Derzhim porokh sukhim," *KZ*, 9 December 2009.

202. Dmitrii Andreev, "Garanty iadernogo schita," *KZ*, 3 September 2012.

203. Andrei Andreev, "Sistema nadezhnaia i efektivnaia," *Rossiiskoe voennoe obozrenie*, no. 8 (34) (2008).

204. Andrei Andreev, "Sistema nadezhnaia i efektivnaia," pp. 28–29.

205. National Intelligence Council, *Annual Report to Congress on the Safety and Security of Russian Nuclear Facilities and Military Forces* (February 2002).

206. Dmitrii Andreev, "Garanty iadernogo schita."

207. In the words of the current commander: "As long as nuclear weapons exist, there is a need to maintain it [the nuclear arsenal] at a high level of readiness, verifying its safety and reliability. Therefore, the nuclear polygon will continue to exist." Viktor Iuzbashev, "Moleben iadernomu oruzhiiu," *NVO*, 7 September 2007; Dmitrii Andreev, "Garanty iadernogo."

208. Olga Sidlovskaia, "Sv Nikolai—pokrovitel' morskoi voennoi bazy," *Karelia*, no. 38 (637) (17 May 2000); "Na Novoi Zemle osviaschen samyi severnyi pravoslavnyi khram Rossii," *Pravoslavie.ru*, 18 September 2006.

CHAPTER 4

1. Østbø uses the Third Rome narrative as a case study. Jardar Østbø, *The New Third Rome: Readings of a Russian Nationalist Myth* (Stuttgart: Ibidem Press, 2016), p. 54.

2. Østbø, *New Third Rome*, p. 49.

3. Østbø, *New Third Rome*, pp. 219–20.

4. Sergei Nepodkosov, "Bog voiny," *Sovershenno sekretno*, 8 December 2014; Nikolai Mitrokhin, "Liubov' bez udovletvoreniia," *Journal of Power Institutions in Post-Soviet Societies*, no. 3 (2005): 6–7.

5. Sergei Bolotov, "Stalin i Tserkov': Piat' faktov," *FOMA*, 5 March 2013.

6. Protoierei Vasilii Shvets, "Chudesa ot Kazanskoi ikony Bozhei Materi," in S. V. Fomin, *Rossiia pered vtorym prishestviem* (Moscow: Izdanie Sviato-Troitskoi lavry, 1993).

7. Shvets, "Chudesa."

8. Shvets, "Chudesa."

9. Nepodkosov, "Bog voiny."

10. Z. V. Zhdanova, *Skazanie o zhitii blazhennoi staritsy, matushki Matrony* (Moscow: Sviato-Troitskii Novo-Golutvin monastyr', 1993).

11. Maria Zhukova, *Marshal Zhukov—sokrovennaia zhizn' dushi* (Moscow: Izdatel'stvo Sretenskogo monastyria, 1999); Zhukova, *Marshal Zhukov—moi otets* (Moscow: Izdatel'stvo Sretenskogo monastyria, 2009).

12. Zhukova, *Zhukov—sokrovennaia zhizn' dushi*; Zhukova, *Zhukov—moi otets*. Also see Arkhimandrit Kirill, "Sokrovennaia zhizn' dushi," *Pravoslavie.ru*, 13 May 2003.

13. Viktor Mikhailov, *Ia iastreb* (Moscow: FGUP ISS, 2008), pp. 68–69, 252–54, 258, 474–75.

14. Mikhailov, *Ia iastreb*, p. 105; also see p. 148.

15. "Vstupitel'noe slovo nastoiatelia Sarovskogo khrama Vsekh Sviatykh o. Vladimira," *Atom*, no. 1 (1994): 2–3.

16. The term *act of bravery* (*podvig* in Russian) in its secular connotation refers to an act of heroism; in its religious connotation the same term refers to the labor of a religious person for the sake of God or the other faithful.

17. "Mitropolit Smolenskii i Kaliningradskii Kirill," in *Stenogramma sobornykh slushanii "Iadernaye vooruzheniia i natsional'naia bezopasnost' Rossii,"* VRNS, 12 November 1996.

18. "Obraschenie uchastnikov kongressa 'Kul'tura i buduschee Rossii,'" *Gorodskoi kur'er*, no. 37 (14 May 1994).

19. I. G. Zhidov, ed., *Stanovlenie otnoshenii Rossiiskogo federal'nogo iadernogo tsentra VNIIEF i Russkoi Pravoslavnoi Tserkvi* (Sarov: RFIaTs-VNIIEF, 2008), p. 48.

20. E. F. Volodin, in *Stenogramma sobornykh slushanii*.

21. General Major B. T. Surikov (expert of the Parliament Committee of International Affairs), in *Stenogramma sobornykh slushanii*.

22. General Lieutenant V. Ia. Shatokhin (head of the Missile and Artillery Forces Faculty at the GS Academy), in *Stenogramma sobornykh slushanii*.

23. V. N. Takoev (deputy governor of the Nizhegorodsky District; head of the Arzamas-16 city council until 1993), in *Stenogramma sobornykh slushanii*.

24. P. V. Florensky, in *Stenogramma sobornykh slushanii*.

25. Konstantin Tatarintsev (ierei of the church in Tushino; VVSPU member), in *Stenogramma sobornykh slushanii*.

26. Mikhailov, *Ia iastreb*, p. 181.

27. "Itogovyi dokument nauchno-prakticheskoi konferentsii," in *Problemy vzaimodeistviia RPTs i veduschikh nauchnykh tsentrov Rossii (7–10 marta 2000)* (Sarov: RFIaTs-VNIIEF, 2000).

28. Protoierei Vladimir Vorob'eb, "Vystupleniia," in *Problemy vzaimodeistviia RPTs*.

29. Maksim Kalashnikov, *Slomannyi mech Imperii* (Moscow: Krymskii most, 1998), p. 92.

30. The project included an anthem of the new state, written by Dmitry Shostakovich, the grandchild of the Soviet composer, and staged photographs featuring the residents of the city.

31. Fedor Romer, "Skazanie o Zemle Novonovosibirskoi—donesut do prezidenta Putina," *Kommersant*, 12 May 2001. Also see "Novo Novo-Sibirsk," *Limonka*, no. 196, cited in Max Frai, *Art-azbuka: Slovar' sovremennogo iskusstva* (accessed 4 March 2017).

32. Aleksei Beliaev-Gintovt, "My. Oni nemy," *Khudozhestvennyi zhurnal*, no. 54 (2004); "Proekt Novosibirsk: 23 February–10 March 2001," *Russkii muzei* (accessed 9 September 2016).

33. Beliaev-Gintovt, "My. Oni nemy."

34. "Interviu: Magiia i propoganda," *Doktrina* (website of Aleksei Beliaev-Gintovt, doctrina.ru) (accessed 9 September 2016).

35. Romer, "Skazanie o Zemle Novonovosibirskoi."

36. Sonia Metelkina, "Khudozhnik-evraziets Beliaev-Gintovt," *Evraziiskii soiuz molodezhi*, 17 April 2012.

37. "Interviu: Magiia i propoganda."

CHAPTER 5

1. Irina Papkova and Dmitry Gorenburg, "The Russian Orthodox Church and Russian Politics: Editors Introduction," *Russian Politics and Law* 49, no. 1 (2011): 3–7.

2. Papkova and Gorenburg, "Russian Orthodox Church."

3. Andrei Sebentsov, "Religion in the System of State Power," *Russian Politics and Law* 49, no. 1 (2011): 46–56; Irina Ivoilova and Sergei Kuksin, "They Did Not Take It on Faith," *Russian Politics and Law* 49, no. 1 (2011): 91–93.

4. Sergei Filatov, "Socio-Religious Life in Russia in the Fall of 2009," *Russian Politics and Law* 49, no. 1 (2011): 24–45.

5. Sergei Filatov, "Socio-Religious Life."

6. Andrei Mel'nikov, "Iadernyi schit protiv kul'ta pribyli," *Nezavisimaia gazeta*, 24 August 2009.

7. Genadii Druzenko, "Geopolitics from the Patriarch: The Heavenly Kingdom Versus the Russian World," *Russian Politics and Law* 49, no. 1 (2011): 65–74.

8. Promoting the greater role in the world "through the spread of Russian Orthodox Christianity" merged with the mercantile interest—reacquiring the tsarist property worldwide. Daniel P. Payne, "Spiritual Security, the Russian Orthodox Church, and the Russian Foreign Ministry," *Journal of Church and State* 52, no. 4 (2010): 712–27.

9. Brian Whitmore, "Russia's Patriarch Increasingly Becoming Major Force in Politics," *Radio Free Europe*, 6 September 2009.

10. "Russia: Special Report," *Economist*, 22 October 2016, p. 15.

11. "Russia: Special Report," p. 16.

12. Peter Finn, "Saints in Demand in Russia as Church Asserts Tie to State," *Washington Post*, 20 April 2007.

13. Anatolii Cherniaev, "Spirituality Destroyed," *Russian Politics and Law* 45, no. 5 (2007): 33.

14. Dmitri Trenin, "Russian Nuclear Policy in the 21st Century Environment," IFRI Proliferation Paper (2005), p. 7.

15. "Bol'shaia press-konferentsiia Vladimira Putina," *Lenta.ru*, 1 February 2007.

16. "Vladimir Putin pozdravil vsekh pravoslavnykh kristian s Rozhdestvom," *Kremlin.ru*, 7 January 2007; "Vladimir Putin pozdravil pravoslavnykh khristian, vsekh grazhdan Rossii, otmechaiuschikh Svetloe voskresenie," *Kremlin.ru*, 8 April 2007.

17. N. S. Leonov, *Zakat ili rassvet? Rossiia 2000–2008* (Moscow: Russkii dom, 2008), p. 352. Part of the compound hosts the headquarters of the ROC mission in the Holy Land, but the major part of this real estate in the center of Jerusalem is still owned by the Israeli government.

18. Richard Stengel, "Person of the Year 2007—Putin Q&A: Full Transcript," *Time*, 19 December 2007.

19. "Vladimir Putin: Moral'nye tsennosti ne mogut bit' nikakimi durgimi, krome religioznykh," *Patriarchia.ru*, 19 December 2007.

20. John Anderson, "Putin and the Russian Orthodox Church: Asymmetric Symphonia?," *Journal of International Affairs* 61, no. 1 (Fall/Winter 2007): 189.

21. For the formative impact of the Asiatic political-managerial tradition, see Boris Akunin, *Istoriia Rossiiskogo gosudarstva* (Moscow: AST, 2013–16), vols. 2–3.

22. Reciprocating for the icon of Jesus that he received from the patriarch, Putin presented the latter with a rare present—a piece of the Holy Robe of Jesus, a present from the Iranian shah to the Russian tsar. Leonov, *Zakat ili rassvet?*, pp. 350–52.

23. B. M. Lukichev, *Patriarkh Kirill i voennoe dukhovenstvo* (Moscow: FIV, 2016), pp. 92–93.

24. Charles Clover, *Black Wind, White Snow* (New Haven, CT: Yale University Press, 2016).

25. Medvedev entered office exactly when the movie was aired. Irina Papkova, "Saving the Third Rome," in *Reconciling the Irreconcilable*, ed. Irina Papkova (Vienna: IWM Junior Visiting Fellows' Conferences, 2009).

26. Papkova, "Saving the Third Rome"; Charles Clover, "Putin and the Monk," *Financial Times*, 25 January 2013.

27. Østbø calls the distortion of the initial Feofanian concept for current Russian political purposes "a false Third Rome." Jardar Østbø, *The New Third Rome: Readings of a Russian Nationalist Myth* (Stuttgart: Ibidem Press, 2016), p. 228.

28. Clover, "Putin and the Monk."

29. Not accidentally, the patriarch, following the official blessing of the new president, turned to Svetlana Medvedeva and wished her power in supporting her husband's service. No such gesture was ever made toward Putin's wife. This probably acknowledged Svetlana's active Orthodox position. "Moleben po sluchaiu vstupleniia v dolzhnost' Prezidenta Rossii Dmitriia Medvedeva," *Patriarchia.ru*, 7 May 2008.

30. Leonov, *Zakat ili rassvet?*, p. 352.

31. "Den' krescheniia Rusi," *VViMD*, 28 July 2011.

32. Anderson, "Putin," pp. 185, 188–89.

33. See, e.g., Iurii Khristianzen, "Pravoslavnaia vera dlia Putina ne bole chem shirma," *UA-INFO*, 17 July 2016.

34. Conversations with Yacov Kedmi, Israel, 2016–18.

35. Leonov, *Zakat ili Rassvet?* Beforehand, Leonov was responsible for intelligence operations in the North American continent and headed the KGB analytical service.

36. Leonov, *Zakat ili rassvet?*, pp. 341–42; Cherniaev, "Spirituality Destroyed," p. 39. The creed refers to the shared formula summarizing the core tenets of the Orthodox faith.

37. Fiona Hill and Clifford Gaddy, *Mr. Putin: Operative in the Kremlin* (Washington, DC: Brookings Institution Press, 2015), p. 48.

38. Anderson, "Putin," p. 185.

39. Anderson, "Putin," p. 188.

40. Anderson, "Putin," p. 185.

41. This monk of the Pskovsko-Pecherskii Monastery was known for his clairvoyance and wonder-working and was Tikhon's confessor. The note was on the occasion of his ninetieth birthday.

42. Anna Veligzhanina, "Dukhovnyi sovetchik Putina byl poslednim prorokom Rossii," *Komsomol'skaia pravda*, 9 February 2006; Dzheraldin Feigan, "Putin sleduet po tsarskim stopam," *Kenstonaskaia sluzhba novostei*, 6 May 2000.

43. Anderson, "Putin."

44. Excepting the first two years, when he went to the Christ the Savior Cathedral. See search results for "'Rozhdestvenskoe bogosluzhenie' v dokumentakh podpisannykh prezidentom Rossii," *Kremlin.ru* (accessed 10 November 2016).

45. Exceptions were in April 2000, when he went to the main cathedral of St. Petersburg, the Isaakievsky, and in 2003, while on a business trip to Tajikistan, when he went to the Orthodox cathedral in Dushanbe. See search results for "'Paskhal'noe bogosluzhenie' v dokumentakh podpisannykh prezidentom Rossii," *Kremlin.ru* (accessed 14 March 2017).

46. A pious neighbor in the communal apartment encouraged his mother, unbeknownst to his father, a secretary of the factory party cell, to baptize him. N. Gevorkian, A. Kolesnikov, and N. Timakova, *Ot pervogo litsa* (Moscow: Vagrius, 2004).

47. "Putin rasskazal o tom, kak ego krestili," *Interfax-Religiia*, 7 January 2012. Putin acknowledged in the documentary *The Patriarch* that his baptizer in Preobrazhenskii Cathedral was Father Mikhail Gundiaev; the film was aired on central Russian TV for Patriarch Kirill's seventieth birthday. "Putin rasskazal, chto rebenkom ego taino kretil otets patriarkha Kirilla," *Ivan-chai Russkii informatsionnyi portal*, 21 November 2016.

48. Gevorkian, Kolesnikov, and Timakova, *Ot pervogo litsa*. The wife of Anatolii Sobchak, the then mayor of Leningrad, who participated in the trip, concurred that Putin was wearing a cross then, but argued that it was also during that trip that he was baptized in Jerusalem, since, by his own words, he had been unable to before. Elena Masiuk, "Eto moe politicheskoe zaveschanie: O dniakh triumpha i predatel'stva v interviu vdovy, materi i eks-senatora," *Novaia gazeta*, 8 November 2012.

49. "Russian President Vladimir Putin Discusses Domestic and Foreign Affairs," *CNN Larry King Live*, 8 September 2000. President George W. Bush asked Putin about the story during their first meeting in 2001 in Slovenia, when he looked deep into Putin's soul. George W. Bush, *Decision Points* (New York: Crown, 2010).

50. Dmitrii Abramov, "Kto krestil Putina," *Ekho Moskvy* (blog), 24 March 2013.

51. Leonov, *Zakat ili rassvet?*, p. 342. Commenting on Putin's first year in office, Leonov, then one of the editors of the main Orthodox nationalistic-patriotic publishing house, called him a disciple of his enterprise. Hill and Gaddy, *Mr. Putin*, p. 48.

52. Leonov, *Zakat ili rassvet?*, p. 342.

53. "11 fotografii," in "Prezident prinial uchastie v prazdnichnykh torzhestvakh po sluchaiu 100-letiia kanonizatsii prepodobnogo Serafima Sarovskogo," *Kremlin.ru*, 31 July 2003.

54. "SMI: Putin provodit vykhodnoi na ostrove Valaam," *Gazeta.ru*, 10 July 2016.

55. Leonov, *Zakat ili rassvet?*, p. 349.

56. "Vladimir Putin: Moral'nye tsennosti."

57. He saw "little evidence that Putin's thinking is fundamentally influenced by a theological perspective." Anderson, "Putin," pp. 187–88.

58. "Maybe in religiosity he seeks salvation from many of his sins, the scale and price of which only he and the Almighty God know." Leonov, *Zakat ili rassvet?*, p. 348.

59. Leonov, *Zakat ili rassvet?*, p. 348.

60. Leonov gives the example of Ivan the Formidable, who combined true faith with terrible un-Christian deeds, for which reason, toward the end of his life, he wished to become a monk. Leonov, *Zakat ili rassvet?*, pp. 349–50.

61. The elder Kirill, the confessor of the Russian patriarchs, the head of the Valaam Monastery, and Putin's classmate who became a monk and priest in one of Moscow's churches were also named as possible confessors of Putin. Rimma Akhmirova, "Kto znaet vse tainy dushi prezidenta?," *Sobesednik*, 25 October 2006.

62. Papkova, "Saving the Third Rome."

63. Clover, "Putin and the Monk."

64. Akhmirova, "Kto znaet."

65. Leonov, *Zakat ili rassvet?*, p. 342.

66. Akhmirova, "Kto znaet."

67. Patrushev received several awards for promoting cooperation with the ROC. "Sviateishii Patriarkh Aleksii osviatil khram Sofii, Premudrosti Bozhei, na Lubnianke," *Mospat.ru*, 5 March 2002; "Patriarkh Aleksii nagradil glavu FSB ordenom Dmitriia Donskogo," *Interfaks*, 11 July 2005. Like the FSB, other actors within the Russian strategic community received their heavenly patrons and house churches by the end of the decade. Nikolai Ziborov, "Kto pokrovitel'stvuet silovikam," *Kommersant*, 23 September 2008.

68. Clover, "Putin and the Monk"; see also Clover, *Black Wind, White Snow*, pp. 301–2.

69. Anderson, "Putin," p. 188.

70. Clover, *Black Wind, White Snow*, pp. 301–2; see also Clover, "Putin and the Monk."

71. Akhmirova, "Kto znaet." (In Russian: *Pravoslavie, samoderzhavie, narodnost'*.)

72. Hill and Gaddy, *Mr. Putin*, pp. 64–65. Accordingly, the traditional Russian military slogan went "For Faith, Tsar, and Fatherland."

73. Hill and Gaddy, *Mr. Putin*, pp. 67–68.

74. Akhmirova, "Kto znaet"; Veligzhanina, "Dukhovnyi sovetchik Putina"; Feigan, "Putin sleduet po tsarskim stopam."

75. Maksim Shevchenko, "Kto derzaet rassuzhdat' o dushe prezidenta?," *Nezavisimaia gazeta*, 11 December 2001; Akhmirova, "Kto znaet."

76. Akhmirova, "Kto znaet."

77. Clover, *Black Wind, White Snow*, p. 301; see also Clover, "Putin and the Monk."

78. Hill and Gaddy, *Mr. Putin*, p. 68.

79. Anderson, "Putin," p. 188. According to some reports, Patriarch Kirill views Tikhon with some jealousy. Mikhail Rubin and Elizaveta Surnacheva, "Putin posetit svoego dukhovnika," *TV Dozhd'*, 22 May 2017.

80. Shevchenko, "Kto derzaet."

81. Clover, *Black Wind, White Snow*, p. 300. Akhmirova, "Kto znaet."

82. Clover, "Putin and the Monk."

83. Leonov, *Zakat ili rassvet?*, p. 343. Leonov, who knew Putin while still in the KGB, reveals an intimate knowledge of his religious life. His argument about Putin's faith sounds convincing, since the book is not a panegyric and is often critical. For example, he qualified Putin as being an "inconsistent, indecisive, and weak politician," when commenting on his decision to approach the Western Wall, during his visit in Jerusalem, and his reluctance to meet with the ethnic Russians residing in Israel. Leonov, *Zakat ili rassvet?*, pp. 345–47.

84. "Prezident vydelil iz svoego rezervnogo fonda sredstva na restavratsiju Kirill-Belozerskogo monastyria," *Kremlin.ru*, 20 May 2004; "Vladimir Putin podpisal raspori-azheniia o vudelinii sredstv iz reservnogo fonda prezidenta," *Kremlin.ru*, 1 August 2002; "Vladimir Putin posetil Kirillo-Belozerskii muzei-zapovednik," *Kremlin.ru*, 28 April 2001.

85. Putin approved the allocation of funds for the reconstruction of the neglected monasteries and churches and found time to meet with local businesspeople and construction companies charged with the restoration. Leonov, *Zakat ili rassvet?*, p. 343.

86. Putin, in his own words, has liked the country since his first trip, and he visited Israel again with his family as a tourist. "Putin Discusses Domestic and Foreign Affairs." Victor Zolotov, current director of the National Guard of Russia, once Putin's sparring partner for judo and boxing, his former bodyguard, and then head of the Federal Protection Service, accompanied Putin on all his visits to Israel and was right behind him at the Holy Sepulchre in 2005 and in 2012. "Prezident Rossii V. V. Putin pribyl v Sviatuiu zemliu," *Russkaia dukhovnaia missiia v Ierusalime* (rusdm.ru), 27 April 2005; "Prezident Rossii Vladimir Putin poklonilsia sviatyniam khrama Groba Gospodnia," *Rusdm.ru*, 26 June 2012.

87. *Maskirovka* is a Russian military term for the range of deception, camouflage, and denial mentods. Leonov, *Zakat ili rassvet?*, p. 344.

88. "Prezident Rossii V. V. Putin pribul v Sviatuiu zemliu."

89. According to Leonov, for "Orthodox Christians when entering this space saturated with a religious-mystical presence, there is no way of playing a certain role. Inside, it is impossible not to be sincere, as one stands alone before the face of God." Leonov, *Zakat ili rassvet?*, p. 345.

90. Leonov, *Zakat ili rassvet?*, p. 345.

91. "Poseschenie Ierusalima Prezidentom Rossii V. V. Putinym," *Patriarchia.ru*, 27 April 2005; "Prezident Rossii V. V. Putin pribul v Sviatuiu zemliu."

92. "Prezident posetil mesto Krescheniia Gospodnia na reke Iordan," *Rusdm.ru*, 15 February 2007.

93. "Otkrytie Strannopriimnogo doma na meste Krescheniia Gospodnia," *Rusdm.ru*, 27 June 2012; "Istoriia Strannopriimnogo doma," *Strannopriimnyi dom na meste Krescheniia Gospodnia* (hoteljordan.rusdm.ru) (accessed 16 March 2017).

94. "Vizit prezidenta RF v Palestinu," *Rusdm.ru*, 26 June 2012.

95. Leonov, *Zakat ili rassvet?*, p. 349.

96. "Vladimir Putin posetil Sviatuiu Goru Afon," *Kremlin.ru*, 9 September 2005.

97. During the 2000s, Evgenii Primakov, Sergei Shoigu, Sergei Stepashin, Iurii Chaika, Georgii Poltavchenko, and Vladimir Iakunin, among others, made this pilgrimage. "Vzoshel na goru: Komy palomnichestvo Putina pokazalos' intronizatsiei," *Lenta.ru*, 28 May 2016.

98. Vladimir Malyschev, "Sorabotnichestvo vo imia zhizni," *KZ*, 25 February 2005.

99. Holy Fire (*Blagodatnyi ogon'*) according to the Orthodox tradition is a miracle that occurs annually on Great Saturday, the day preceding Easter, at the Church of the Holy Sepulchre in Jerusalem, when a light emanates spontaneously from within Jesus Christ's tomb and turns into a form of fire, with which clergy and pilgrims light candles.

100. "Prosite mira Ierusalimu," *Fond Andreia Pervozvannogo* (fap.ru) (accessed 17 March 2017).

101. Lukichev, *Patriarkh Kirill*, pp. 40, 50.

102. For example, in December 2004, before putting the Topol-M missile on combat duty in the Tatishev Division, the test launch took place in the presence of DM Sergei Ivanov, the heads of the design bureau, and the RVSN High Command. Immediately after the successful launch, Ivanov, wearing a military uniform, crossed himself. Mikhail Aniskin (author and producer), *TsKP RVSN—45 let* (28.12 min.), Press Sluzhba RVSN, 2005.

103. Lukichev, *Patriarkh Kirill*, p. 27.

104. The numbers from the early and later reports were somewhat lower. Nikolai Mitrokhin, "Liubov' bez udovletvoreniia," *Journal of Power Institutions in Post-Soviet Societies*, no. 3 (2005): 4. Also see Lukichev, *Patriarkh Kirill*, pp. 47–48.

105. Mitrokhin, "Liubov' bez udovletvoreniia," p. 13.

106. The donations came from Rosoboronexport, Vneshtorgbank, and Ingosstrakh. "V VAGSh porshli torzhestvennye meropriiatiia," *Sinadal'nyi otdel*, 14 January 2016.

107. "20-letnii iubilei khrama arkhistratiga," *Khram prep. Andreia Rubleva*, 22 January 2016.

108. "VAGSh okormliatsia domovym khramom vo im. Arkhangela Mikhaila," *Orthodox TV Channel "Soyuz,"* 2 October 2008.

109. On the Order of Victory, see "Bogosluzhenie v domovom khrame Akademii Genshtaba RF," *Moscow Patriarchy*, 7 December 2007; "Poseschenie Sviateishim Patriarkhom Kirillom akademii General'nogo shtaba VS RF," *Moscow Patriarchy*, 31 May 2011.

110. The medal, modified in 1992, was called Hero of Russia and is still the highest military decoration. Other Soviet-era decorations on the columns included those of Suvorov and Nevsky for excellence in strategic-operational planning, both introduced during the GPW. By 2008 a majority of the officers attending the academy defined themselves as Orthodox but were not strictly practicing. Still, all the children born to academy cadets have been baptized in the church. Also, the priests have consecrated the housing that cadets receive during their period of study. "VAGSh okormliatsia domovym khramom vo im. Arkhangela Mikhaila." Since 2009, the academy has been commanded by General Yakovlev, a staunch supporter of the ROC's influence in the RVSN and in the military.

111. Katarzyna Zysk, "Russia's Naval Ambitions," in *Twenty-First Century Seapower*, ed. Peter Dutton, Robert Ross, and Øystein Tunsjø (London: Routledge, 2012).

112. For the first time in contemporary Russia, the religious ceremony of canonization was merged with the ritual of a military funeral, conducted with the uniformed guards of honor.

113. Lukichev, *Patriarkh Kirill*, pp. 29–34.

114. Lukichev, *Patriarkh Kirill*, pp. 26–27.

115. He allegedly visited Kiev, Novgorod, and Volkhov.

116. Lukichev, *Patriarkh Kirill*, pp. 26–27; Mozgovoi, "Vzaimootnosheniia armii i tserkvi v Rossiiskoi Federatsii," *Journal of Power Institutions in Post-Soviet Societies*, no. 3 (2005): 15.

117. An NGO, the fund was established in early 1990 to preserve Orthodoxy in Russia. Yakunin, then minister of railways, headed its board of trustees. In 2005 the fund bestowed its annual award on the head of the VNIIEF, Radii Il'kaev, and on the head of the 12th GUMO, Vladimir Verkhovtsev (on which more in the next chapter). "Obiavlenny lauriaty premii za veru i vernost'," *Pravoslavie.ru*, 14 December 2005.

118. Mozgovoi, "Vzaimootnosheniia armii i tserkvi," p. 8.

119. Conference titles included "Fatherland, Military Church," "Military Chaplaincy in Russian History," and "The ROC in the Great Patriotic War." Manuals had titles such as *The Spiritual-Moral Foundations of the Military Service* and *The Foundations of the Pastoral Service in the Troops—Tradition and Nowadays*.

120. Mozgovoi, "Vzaimootnosheniia armii i tserkvi," pp. 9–10.

121. Lukichev, *Patriarkh Kirill*, pp. 47–48.

122. Mozgovoi, "Vzaimootnosheniia armii i tserkvi," p. 13. Mitrokhin, "Liubov' bez udovletvoreniia," p. 4.

123. Lukichev, *Patriarkh Kirill*, pp. 48–49.

124. *Vera i vernost'* (2005); *Khristoliubivoe voinstvo: Pravoslavnaia traditsiia Russkoi armii* (Moscow: Russkii put', 2006); *Nauka pobezhdat: Za veru i Otechestvo* (Moscow: Danilovskii monastyr, 2008).

125. Lukichev, *Patriarkh Kirill*, pp. 49–50.

126. V. G. Mikhailovsky, *Voennaia didaktika* (Moscow: Ministerstvo oborony, 2006).

127. Lukichev, *Patriarkh Kirill*, p. 200.

128. "Kharakteristika religioznoi situatsii v VS RF v 2010 godu," *RF MoD* (accessed 10 November 2016).

129. Lukichev, *Patriarkh Kirill*, pp. 41–46.

130. Lukichev, *Patriarkh Kirill*, p. 54.

131. For the tsarist era, see, e.g., V. M. Kotkov, "Armiia i tserkov': Oput sotrudnichestva," *VM*, September 2009, pp. 37–41. for the post-Soviet period, see, e.g., A. G. Diakonov, "Praktika vzaimodeistviia organov voennogo upravleniia Severnogo flota s religioznymi organizatsiiami," *VM*, February 2005, pp. 39–47.

132. E. A. Kiselev and M. V. Shimanovsky, "Dukhovno-nravstvennoe obespechenie stroitel'stva VS RF: Problem i puti ikh resheniia," *VM*, January 2005, pp. 37–40.

133. See, e.g., A. Iu. Golubev, "O dukhovnom vospitanii v Rossiiskii armii," *VM*, April 2004, pp. 68–74; Golubev, "K voprosu o roli dukhovnosti v sovremennoi voine," *VM*, January 2008, pp. 52–56; V. A. Rodin and O. Iu. Efremov, "Dukhovnye osnovy

voinskogo vospitaniia," *VM*, August 2003, pp. 26–30; A. I. Burkin, "Obschestvo i natsional'naia bezopasnost' Rossii," *VM*, October 2003, pp. 75–80; A. Iu. Golubev and A. A. Akhmedov, "K voprosu o vvedenii instituta voennykh imamov v Rossiiskoi armii," *VM*, February 2008, pp. 59–66; A. Iu. Golubev, "K voprosu o patriotcheskom vospitanii v Rossii i ee VS," *VM*, February 2007, pp. 47–56.

134. Golubev, "K voprosu o roli dukhovnosti."

135. V. N. Buslovsky, *O vremeni, o sluzhbe, o sud'be* (Moscow: Triumphalnaia arka, 2010), pp. 237–38.

136. Lukichev, *Patriarkh Kirill*, pp. 43–45. The ROC saw the penetration of other denominations, mainly Catholic, and sects as posing a national security threat, since according to this view, any non-Orthodox servicemen could potentially be recruited to work for the enemy. Mitrokhin, "Liubov' bez udovletvoreniia," pp. 7–8.

137. Mitrokhin, "Liubov' bez udovletvoreniia," pp. 5–6.

138. The council comprised the principal mufti, principal rabbi, and principal lama.

139. Lukichev, *Patriarkh Kirill*, pp. 53–59. Between 2010 and 2013, Lukichev headed the department.

CHAPTER 6

1. Valerii Beresnev, "Sergei Pereslegin: Ia vse-taki Sergeia Vladlenovicha znaiu lichno; On ne liberal!," *Biznes Online*, 13 October 2016.

2. "Serafim Sarovsky predskazal sozdanie 'iadernogo schita' Rossii," *Pravda.ru*, 2 July 2003.

3. "Zasedanie Orgkomiteta po podgotovke k prazdnovaniu 100-letiia proslavleniia prepodobnogo Serafima Sarovskogo," *Nizhegorodskaia mitropoliia*, 9 June 2003.

4. Mikhail Chumak, "Podgotovka k torzhestvam 2003 goda," in *Sarov pravoslavnyi* (Sarov: VNIIEF, 2009).

5. Alexei Obukhov, "Nuclear Weapons and Christian Ethics," *Security Index* 13, no. 1 (81) (2007): 104; "Letopis vozrozhdeniia dukhovniu zhizni v Sarove—2003," *Pravoslavnyi Sarov* (accessed 22 February 2017).

6. Mikhail Chumak, "Svetlyi prazdnik prishel v Sarov," in *Sarov pravoslavnyi*; Radii Il'kaev, in *Stanovlenie otnoshenii Rossiiskogo federal'nogo iadernogo tsentra VNIIEF i Russkoi Pravoslavnoi Tserkvi*, ed. I. G. Zhidov (Sarov: RFIaTs-VNIIEF, 2008), p. 2.

7. "Serafim Sarovsky predskazal sozdanie."

8. "Prezident prinial uchastie v prazdnichnykh torzhestvakh po sluchaiu 100-letiia kanonizatsii prepodobnogo Serafima Sarovskogo," *Kremlin.ru*, 31 July 2003.

9. Chumak, "Svetlyi prazdnik prishel v Sarov."

10. "Prezident prinial uchastie v prazdnichnykh torzhestvakh."

11. "Vystuplenie na tseremonii blagoslovleniia krestnogo khoda," *Kremlin.ru*, 31 July 2003.

12. Russian politicians from the security and military services, usually of the Soviet era.

13. "Vstupitel'noe slovo na vstreche s uchenymi Rossiiskogo federal'nogo iadernogo tsentra," *Kremlin.ru*, 31 July 2003.

14. "Zakliuchitel'noe slovo na vstreche s uchenymi Rossiiskogo federal'nogo iader-nogo tsentra," *Kremlin.ru*, 31 July 2003.

15. "Vladimir Putin vstretilsia s rabotnikami Rossiiskogo federal'nogo iadernogo tsentra," *Kremlin.ru*, 31 July 2003.

16. Il'kaev, in Zhidov, *Stanovlenie otnoshenii*, p. 2.

17. The celebrations marked the one hundredth anniversary of the saint's canonization and the two hundred and fiftieth anniversary of his birth.

18. "O fonde" and "Pravlenie fonda," *Fond prepodobnogo Serafima Sarovskogo* (bfss.ru) (accessed 19 February 2017).

19. "Kirienko schitaet peredachiu ikony prp. Makariia Zheltovodskogo RPTs vosstanovleniem spraveldivosti," *Sedmitsa.ru*, 1 August 2005; "Kirienko otmechiaet aktivizatsiiu sovemstnoi raboty gosudarstva i RPTs po vozrozhdeniu dukhovnykh sviatyn'," *NEWSru.com*, 1 August 2005.

20. "Patriarshee pozadravlenie S. V. Kirienko s naznacheniem na post geniral'nogo direktora goskorporatsii ROSATOM," *Patriarchia.ru*, 12 December 2007.

21. The 2006 development program for the next decade planned to bring the share of the nuclear-generated energy to 16–20 percent and prospectively to 25–30 percent.

22. Igor' Mel'nikov, "Atomnyi kompleks Rossii vozrozhdaetsia," *Natsional'nye prioritety*, 19 April 2010.

23. "NIAEP pri stroitel'stve Nizhegorodskoi AES vosstanovit razrusehnnye pravo-slavnye khramy v Navashinskom raione," *ROSATOM*, 16 August 2010.

24. According to the director of the nuclear station, "nuclear specialists cannot be excluded from the spiritual life of the eparchy," as the Orthodox faith has been "very important for maintaining the safe usage of the nuclear station." Ekaterina Ostritsova, "Sotrudnichestvu AES i Volgodonskomu blagochiniu Rostovskoi-na-Donu eparkhii RPTs 10 let," *Ekologia i atomnaia energetika*, 11 February 2008

25. During his 2006 visit to Iran, Kirienko came to the Nikolaevsky church at Tehran to learn about the pastoral care and services that had been arranged in the temporary church at the Bushehr nuclear energy station for the Russian nuclear specialists. "Sergei Kirienko posetil Nikol'skii sobor v Tegerane," *Patriarchia.ru*, 27 February 2006. In 2008, during the Russia Days in Brazil, Kirienko opened the exhibitions *Orthodox Rus* and *Contemporary Russia*, to enable the counterparts to better learn about Russia, "which were formulated as a state thanks to Orthodox faith and the ROC." "Dni Rossii v Brazilii ukrepili dvustoronnee partnerstvo—Kirienko," *RIA Novosti*, 31 October 2008.

26. "Sergei Kirienko predlagaet stroit pravoslavnye khramy v zakrytykh atomnykh gorodakh," *OVTsS RPTs* (mospat.ru), 30 November 2006. During the decade, other big corporations—ROSNEFT, GAZPROM, and Russian Railways—constructed house churches and their seniors made pilgrimages to Sarov. "V podmoskovnom sele Usovo otkut khra, postroennyi na sredstva NK ROSNEFT," *ROSNEFT Press Center*, 6 July 2010; "V Votkinske sostoialas' tseremoniia osviascheniia Sviato-Georgievskogo khrama," *ROSNEFT Press Center*, 15 August 2008; Andrei Kalashnikov, "Bol'shoi biznes prodolzhaet dukhovnye traditsii," *Profil'*, 25 August 2008; "Sarovskuiu pustyn' posetil prezident RZhD Vladimir Iakunin," *Nizhegorodskaia eparkhiia RPTs*, 26 October 2010.

27. "Sviateishii Patriarkh Aleksii nagradil S. V. Kirienko ordenom Serafima Sarovskogo," *Patriarchia.ru*, 1 August 2006.

28. "ROSATOM v techenii goda napravil bolee 100 mln. rublei na vosstanovlenie khramov Serafimo-Diveevskogo monastyria," *Portal-Credo.ru*, 1 August 2008; "Sergei Kirienko posetil palatochnye gorodki palomnikov," *Nizhegorodskaia mitropoliia*, 31 July 2004.

29. Kirienko also mentioned the cultural center of Boldino, near Sarov, a place associated with one of the most prolific periods in Alexander Pushkin's writing. According to Kirienko, "It is clear to any person that there could be no strong state without such objects of honor and of the spiritual power. [. . .] This is what Russia obviously needs today." "Zasedanie Orgkomiteta po podgotovke k prazdnovaniu 100-letiia."

30. "Sviateishii Patriarkh Aleksii nagradil S. V. Kirienko."

31. "Sviateishii Patriarkh Aleksii nagradil S. V. Kirienko."

32. "ROSATOM vydelil bolee 100 mln. rublei na vosstanovlenie Kazanskogo khrama v Diveevskom monastyre," *Patriarchia.ru*, 1 August 2008.

33. "ROSATOM v techenii goda napravil bolee 100 mln. rublei."

34. Viktor Mikhailov, *Ia iastreb* (Moscow: FGUP ISS, 2008), p. 22. The Sanaksarsk Monastery holds the remains and the tomb of St. Admiral Feodor Ushakov.

35. Mikhailov, *Ia iastreb*, pp. 237, 348, 355.

36. Mikhailov, *Ia iastreb*, pp. 22–24. Previous editions were published in 1993, 1995, and 1996.

37. "Soboleznovaniia arkhipastyrei RPTs," *Pravoslavnyi Sarov*, 29 June 2011.

38. *Atomnyi proekt SSSR: Katalog vystavki* (Moscow: ROSATOM, 2009).

39. The contents included intelligence reports on the U.S. nuclear project and Igor Kurchatov's responses to them; a report of Lavrenty Beria to Joseph Stalin on the progress of the Soviet nuclear project; President Harry Truman's approval of the use of nuclear bombs against Japan; reports of the U.S. Air Force about the first Soviet nuclear test; materials on the role of the German scientists and the Gulag prisoners; pieces of ground from the Soviet nuclear testing range; and the chronicle made during the Soviet 1949 test explosion. On the religious side, the exhibition included relics related to the personal life of St. Seraphim and materials from the Sarov Monastery. "V Moskve prokhodit istoriko-dokumental'naia vystovka 'Atomnyi proekt SSSR'" (Sobytiia i meropriiatiia), *ROSATOM*, 27 July 2009.

40. *Atomnyi proekt SSSR*, p. 11.

41. The half-page picture of Putin and the patriarch surrounded by the clergy at the entrance to the St. Seraphim Sarovsky Cathedral in Sarov during the 2003 celebrations served as an illustration of the archiepiscop's point. *Atomnyi proekt SSSR*, p. 14.

42. *Atomnyi proekt SSSR*, p. 15.

43. A picture of Kirienko standing in Sarov surrounded by the metropolitan and the archbishop and examining materials pertaining to the life of the saint illustrated this passage. *Atomnyi proekt SSSR*, p. 15.

44. *Atomnyi proekt SSSR*, pp. 16–17.

45. "Vystavka 'Atomnyi proekt SSSR,' otkryls' v Voronezhe," *Rossiiskoe atomnoe soob-schestvo*, 10 December 2009; "V Rostovskom informatsionnom tsentre otrkylas' vystavka 'Atomnyi proekt SSSR,'" *Rossiiskoe atomnoe soobshestvo*, 23 August 2010; "V Stenakh DGU prokhodit vystovka 'Atomnyi proekt SSSR,'" *Rossiiskoe atomnoe soobschestvo*, 2 September 2010.

46. The deputy heads of the United Russia Party and of the VNIIEF and the heads of the parliamentary committee for foreign affairs and of the liaison with the compatriots abroad opened the exhibition. "Fotovystavka 'Zemlia Sarova—khranitel velichiia Otechestva'—proshla v Gosudarstvennoi Dume," *Rossiiskoe atomnoe soobschestvo*, 19 October 2009.

47. For example, Kirienko approved the restoration of the Znamenie church within Moscow's secret Alikhanov Institute of Theoretical Experimental Physics and turning it into the institute's house church. "Istoriia," *Pripisnoi khram ikony Bozhei Materi "Znamenie"* (evfrosinia.ru) (accessed 18 February 2017).

48. "O khrame," *Khram pir NIIAU MIFI* (hram-mephi.ru) (accessed 18 February 2017).

49. Donations of the faculty, students, and ROSATOM funded construction of the temple, which featured a big icon of St. Seraphim Sarovsky on its iconostasis.

50. "Sviateishii Patriarkh sovershil chin osviascheniia domovogo khrama v Natsional'nom issledovatel'skom iadernom universitete," *Patriarchia.ru*, 4 March 2010; "Podpisanno soglashenie o sotrudnichistve mezhdy Sinodal'nym," *Pod Andreevskim flagom* (Izdanie garnizonnogo khrama St. A. P. Viliuchinska), *Pravkamchatka.ru*, 18 December 2009; "Osviaschenie domovogo khrama v MIFI," *Patriarchia.ru*, 4 March 2010; "Predstoiateliu RPTs vruchen diplom pochetnogo doktora MIFI," *Patriarchia.ru*, 4 March 2010.

51. In Russian, *Dorogu osilit iduschii*. In Latin, *Viam supervadet sadens*, or in English, "The person walking the path will overcome it."

52. "Krest vozle glavnogo korpusa," *Entsiklopedia MIFI* (wiki.mephist.ru) (accessed 18 February 2017); Dmitry Anokhin, "Fizika, lirika, i bogoslovie," *ZhMP*, 5 November 2013.

53. "Prezident RAN Iurii Osipov prizval tserkovnykh i svetskikh uchenykh k ukrepleniiu sotrudnichestva na blago obschestva," *Rossiiskaia akademiia nauk*, 27 May 2005. On the churching of nuclear science in particular, see Elena Komleva, "Ot pravoslaviia k fenomenu iadernoi energii," *Pravo i bezopasnost'*, nos. 1–2 (44) (2013): 48–53.

54. "Tserkov' zanimaetsia i budet zanimat'sia vsem, chto volnuet liudei," *Pravmir.ru*, 24 July 2007; "Tserkov' i nauka—est' li konflikt? Mneniia akademikov," *Pravmir.ru*, 25 July 2007.

55. "Teologiia stala nauchnoi spetsial'nostiu v Rossii," *Interfax*, 23 January 2015.

56. "Pravoslavnaia initsiativa: O konkurse," *Pravkonkurs.ru* (accessed 16 February 2017); "Sergei Kirienko vystupil s dokladom na pervom zasedanii Koordinatsionnogo komiteta po pooschreniiu initsiativ pod egidoi RPTs MP," *Portal-Credo.ru*, 1 December 2010.

57. Olga Filina, "Krestnyi podkhod," *Ogonek*, 9 August 2010.

58. B. M. Lukichev, *Patriarkh Kirill i voennoe dukhovenstvo* (Moscow: FIV, 2016), p. 199.

59. Aleksandr Sladkov, *Voennaia programma*, TV Channel *"Rossiia 1,"* 28 April 2008 (1:02 min).

60. *Sobor RVSN* is a website of the Church of St. Varvara and St. Iliia Muromets (sobor-RVSN.ru).

61. Aleksandr Sladkov, *Voennaia programma*.

62. The kids numbered about 120.

63. *Sobor RVSN*.

64. Aleksandr Sladkov, *Voennaia programma*.

65. *Sobor RVSN*.

66. Aleksandr Sladkov, *Voennaia programma*.

67. "O gorode," Vlasikha Official City Website, http://vlasiha-zato.ru/o-poselenii/ (accessed 7 July 2017).

68. Lukichev, *Patriarkh Kirill*, pp. 199–200.

69. The ROC's administrative division merging several parishes of one eparchy, a blagochinie is equivalent to a deanery in the Roman Catholic Church. A *blagochinii* is subordinate to an *arkhierei*.

70. See, e.g., "Sovremennoe sostoianie Orenburgskoi eparkhii," *Istoriia Orenburzhia* (kraeved.opck.org) (accessed 30 August 2016); "Vstrecha Serpukhovskogo dukhovenstva s nachal'nikami voennykh chastei Serpukhovskogo garnizona," *Pravoslavnyi Serpukhov*, 3 March 2006; "Pervaia godovschina," *Ioshkar-Olinskaia eparkhiia*, 18 December 2010; "Blagoslovlenie na ratnyi trud," *Ioshkar-Olinskaia eparkhiia*, 21 June 2005; "Spisok dukhovenstva eparkhii," *Orenburgskaia i Buzulukskaia eparkhii RPTs MP* (accessed 30 August 2016); "U raketchikov svoi khram," *Ioshkar-Olinskaia eparkhiia*, 7 December 2007; "V den' pamiati sviatogo velikomuchennika Georgia Pobedonostsa," *Ioshkar-Olinskaia eparkhiia*, 6 May 2010. On the opening of small prayer rooms, see "Armiia gotova ispol'zovat' opyt tserkvi v rabote po dukhovno-nravstvennomy vospitaniiu voennosluzhaschikh," *Ioshkar-Olinskaia eparkhiia*, 1 March 2006.

71. Aleksandr Sladkov, *Voennaia programma*; Anastasiia Iakovleva, "Dukhovno-iadernnye sily Rossii," *VViMD*, 17 December 2010.

72. Iakovleva, "Dukhovno-iadernnye sily Rossii."

73. "Voiny ot Boga," *VViMD*, 20 September 2011.

74. Aleksandr Sladkov, *Voennaia programma*.

75. "Raketchiki pomolilis' vmeste s patriarkhom," *VViMD*, 6 December 2010; "V prazdnik Vvedeniia vo khram Presviatoi Bogoroditsy Predstoiateli RPTs i Pravoslavnoi Tserkvi v Amerike sovershili liturgiiu," *Patriarachia.ru*, 4 December 2014.

76. "Raketchiki pomolilis' vmeste s patriarkhom."

77. "Sviateishii Patriarkh Kirill posetil Voennuiu akademiiu RVSN im Petra Velikogo," *Patriarchia.ru*, 8 December 2009.

78. Iu. Malenkin, "Voiska postoiannoi boevoi gotovnosti," *Na strazhe Rodiny*, 18 December 2009.

79. "Sviateishii Patriarkh Aleksii posetil garnizon Glavnogo shtaba RVSN," *Mospat. ru*, 17 December 2004; "Patriarshii moleben v khrame vmts. Varvary vo Vlasikhe (pri shtabe RVSN)," *Moscow Patriarchy News*, 18 December 2006.

80. "Sviateishii Patriarkh Aleksii posetil garnizon Glavnogo shtaba RVSN."

81. "RVSN—osnova bezopasnosti Rossii," *VViMD*, 17 December 2010.

82. "V den' pamiati velikomuchenitsy Varvary Sviateishii Patriarkh Kirill vozglavil sluzhenie Bozhestvennoi liturgii v khrame Khrista Spasitelia," *Patriarchia.ru*, 17 December 2010.

83. "Patriarkh Moskovskii i vseia Rusi Kirill vstretilsia s voennosluzhaschimi Voennoi akademii RVSN imeni Petra Velikogo," *RF MoD*, 26 April 2011.

84. The program diploma says, "Managing the processes of formulation of spiritual values orientation in the sphere of general culture taught in the military educational institutions." "V Voennoi akademii RVSN imeni Petra Velikogo sostoialsia 20-i iubeliinyi vypusk," *RF MoD* 5 May 2016; "Sviateishii Patriarch sovershil Bozhestvennuiu liturgiiu v Uspenskom sobore Kremlia i udostoil patriarshikh nagrad riad moskovskikh klirikov," *Patriarchia.ru*, 24 April 2006.

85. "FPK Voennoi akademii RVSN osuschestvil ocherednoi vypusk," *RF MoD*, 8 May 2013.

86. Lukichev, *Patriarkh Kirill*, pp. 201–2.

87. "Vypusk FPK Voennoi akademii RVSN," *RVSN Rossii—LiveJournal*, 16 April 2012; "Sviateishii Patriarkh Kirill stal pochetnym professorom Akademii RVSN," *VViMD*, 7 April 2010; "Liudi v riasakh i v kamufliazhe," *VViMD*, 9 April 2011. Kirill had a genuine and long-lasting interest in military technique and weapons. In 1999 he received a certificate certifying his participation in the test flight of the MiG-29. In 2006 he received the badge "Honorary Submariner of the Navy." Lukichev, *Patriarkh Kirill*, pp. 24–25.

88. See, e.g., on the baptism of conscripts: "Blagodaria sotrudnichestvu so sviaschennikami v voennoi chasti raketnykh voisk kazhduiu nedeliu sovershaetsia Tainstvo Krescheniia," *Nizhegorodskaia mitropoliia*, 5 December 2007. On counseling conscripts: "Nizhegorodskii episkop sovershil bogosluzhenie v voinskoi chasti Dal'nekonstantinovskogo garnizona," *VViMD*, 3 June 2010. On units' anniversary celebrations, "Arkhiepiskop Georgii pozdavil s iubileem arsenal RVSN," *Nizhegorodskaia mitropoliia*, 26 November 2010; "Arsenal Surovatikha RVSN otmetil 56 godovschinu so dnia sozdaniia," *Prikhod prepodobnogo Serafima Sarovskogo p. D. Konstantinovo* (dk-5.prihod.ru), 23 November 2011; "Ioshkar-Olinskoe raketnoe soedinenie: 50 let na boevom dezhurstve," *RVSN Rossii*, 14 February 2012. On supplication services: "Nebesnyi pokrovitel' zemnogo voinstva," *Ioshkar-Olinskaia eparkhiia*, 7 May 2009. On the oath of allegiance: "V voinskikh chastiakh Federal'nogo upravleniia po bezopasnomy khraneniiu i unichtozheniiu khimicheskogo oruzhiia proshal tseremoniia priniatiia prisiagi," *VViMD*, 11 April 2011. On junior officers' arrival to the RVSN: "V raketnoi divizii popolnenie," *Ioshkar-Olinskaia eparkhiia*, 19 September 2006. On excursions and pilgrimage: "Raketchiki sovershili palomnichestvo v Diveevo, *VViMD*, 23 July 2010. In this last example, during the methodological gathering at the RVSN C2 Dalnekonstantinovsky

base, the high engineering command (about sixty generals and colonels headed by the deputy RVSN commander for armaments) from all over Russia visited the Diveevo Monastery. The pilgrimage included an excursion, veneration of the relics, and bathing in the holy spring of St. Seraphim Sarovsky.

89. On supplication services at the start of the school year, see "1 sentiabria v Akademii RVSN," *SOMP VVSiPO*, 5 September 2011; "V Akademii RVSN uchebnyi god nachalsia s molitvy," *VVD*, 2 September 2013. On services at graduation, see "V Voennoi akademii RVSN im. Petra Velikogo sostoialsia 180-i vypusk," *SOMP VVSiPO*, 27 July 2011.

90. For example, on Easter 2004, to commemorate the forty-fifth anniversary of the RVSN's establishment and the 250th birthday of St. Seraphim Sarovsky, Patriarch Alexey gave his blessing to granting a piece of the remains of the saint to the RVSN's St. Iliia church in Vlasikha. "Perenesenie chastitsy moschei prepodobnogo Serafima Sarovskogo," *Nizhegorodskaia mitropoliia*, 6 April 2004; P. Korobov and S. Petukhov, "Ofitsery Gospoda," *Voennyi vestnik Iuga Rossii*, 1 January 2010.

91. Iakovleva, "Dukhovno-iadernnye sily Rossii"; "Novosti," *Pravoslavnyi Serpukhov*, 20 June 2004 (accessed 29 August 2016).

92. "Vladyka Ioann vstretilsia s ofitserami RVSN," *Ioshkar-Olinskaia eparkhiia*, 18 September 2007.

93. The two national military holidays are Victory and the Fatherland's Defender Days.

94. Aleksandr Sladkov, *Voennaia programma*; "V Shtabe RVSN v podmoskovnoi Vlasikhe otmechaiut Kreschenie Gospodne," *RF MoD*, 19 January 2012.

95. "V garnizone RVSN vo Vlasikhe gotoviatsia k Paskhe," *Zvezda TV*, 23 April 2011.

96. Aleksandr Sladkov, *Voennaia programma*.

97. "Voennosluzhaschie Tsentral'nogo poligona Rossii poluchili blagoslovlenie na sluzhbu," *VViMD*, 7 June 2011; "Blagoslovlenie voinov na uchebu," *Ioshkar-Olinskaia eparkhiia*, 30 June 2006; "Blagoslovlenie na ratnyi trud."

98. Aleksandr Sladkov, *Voennaia programma*.

99. "Zamestitel' komanduiushego RVSN Vitalii Linnik posetil nizhegorodskii Aleksandro-Nevskii kafedral'nyi sobor," *Nizhegorodskaia eparkhiia*, 10 February 2010.

100. "Istoriia DA Rossii," *Muzei DA—Riazan Diagilevo garnizon* (avia-ryazan.ru) (accessed 30 December 2016).

101. Iu. Vladimirov, "Strategi rasshiriaiut geografiiu poletov," *Rossiiskoe voennoe obozrenie*, no. 12 (59) (2008).

102. "Istoriia DA Rossii."

103. Sergei Arkhipov, "Armiia povernula moiu zhizn'," *Pravoslavie.ru*, 25 July 2006.

104. "Pervyi iubilei: Voennye sviaschenniki o sluzhbe i sluzhenii," *VVD*, 21 July 2014.

105. "Patriarkh Aleksii posetil shtab Dal'nei aviatsii," *Pravoslavie.ru*, 21 December 2004; "Uchetnaia kartochka—Chasovnia Ilii Proroka pri shtabe DA VVS RF," *Khramy Rossii* (accessed 1 September 2016).

106. Irina Pavliutkina, "Chasovnia v shtabe DA," *KZ*, 27 August 2002; Oleg Litvinov and Andrei Ianchinsky, "Sluzhit' otechestvu veroi i pravdoi," *VVS segodnia*, 16 September 2002.

107. "Patriarkh Aleksii posetil shtab."

108. Oleg Ternovoi, "S Rozhdestvom Khristovym," *VVS segodnia*, 30 December 2005; "Patriarkh Aleksii posetil shtab."

109. "Soltsy-2, chasovnia vo imia Arkhistratiga Mikhaila," *Soletskoe blagochinie Novgorodskoi eparkhii* (soltsy.orthodoxy.ru) (accessed 29 December 2016).

110. Ternovoi, "S Rozhdestvom Khristovym."

111. Marina Vasil'eva, "Granitsa pod dukhovnoi zaschitoi," *KZ*, 3 July 2010; "Zavershilos' stroitel'stvo pervogo na Dal'nem Vostoke voinskogo khrama," *VViMD*, 3 June 2010.

112. Aleksandr Schetnikov, "Doroga v nebo vedet cherez khram," *Armeiskii sbornik*, no. 7 (July 2006).

113. "Khram. Nebo. Raketonosets," *Ural'skie voennye vest*, 12 August 2007; Vasil'eva, "Granitsa pod dukhovnoi zaschitoi"; "Sviaschennik osviatil strategicheskii raketonosets," *VViMD*, 1 September 2010.

114. According to the LRA's main priest, "The LRA leadership loves our church, attends regular and holiday services, and participates in confessions and Communions." Anastasiia Iakovleva, "Novye gorizonty DA," *KZ*, 3 June 2011. By the late 2000s, the LRA commanders' requests in writing to the garrison church to pray for the peace of the souls of deceased relatives became a norm. Marina Vasil'eva, "Ot Soltsov do Tambova," *KZ*, 27 April 2007.

115. Iakovleva, "Novye gorizonty."

116. "Patriarkh Aleksii posetil shtab."

117. Iakovleva, "Novye gorizonty."

118. Vasil'eva, "Ot Soltsov."

119. "Patriarkh Aleksii posetil shtab"; Vladimir Bekhter, "DA-85!" *Na voevom postu*, 31 December 1999; Iegumen Innokentii, "Strategicheskii bombardirovschik okroplen sviatoi vodoi," *Suvorovskii natisk*, 2 October 1999.

120. On Tu-160s, see Aleksandr Schetnikov and Genadii Roschin, "Geroi ostaiutsia v stroiu," *Armeiskii sbornik*, 31 December 2003; Editorial, "Osviaschen raketonosets," *KZ*, 30 May 2008. On Tu-95MSs, see Leonid Khairemdinov, "Armiia i dukhovenstvo," *KZ*, 21 June 2007; Artemy Emke, "Sviaschennik dolzhen bit dlia soldata ne tolko otsom," *Vesti kosmodroma*, 24 July 2007; Bekhter, "DA-85!"; Innokentii, "Strategicheskii bombardirovschik."

121. "Patriarkh Aleksii posetil shtab."

122. "Novyi Tu-160 postupil na vooruzhenie Rossii," *Aviatsiia i kosmonautika*, no. 6 (2008); "Sviaschennik osviatil strategicheskii raketonosets."

123. "Patriarkh Aleksii posetil shtab."

124. In the following years, the banner was passed on to the new commanders. Ternovoi, "S Rozhdestvom Khristovym"; Vasil'eva, "Ot Soltsov." Each 19 March, this icon's celebration day in the Orthodox calendar, the Main Staff arranges a special prayer session.

125. On Putin's sortie, see Ternovoi, "S Rozhdestvom Khristovym."

126. "Patriarkh peredal shtaby DA ikonu s chastitsami moschei Ushakova," *RIA Novosti*, 26 September 2005; Sergei Babichev, "Nebesnyi pokrovitel'," *Interfax-Religiia*, 28 September 2005; Ternovoi, "S Rozhdestvom Khristovym." In response, the commander

of the LRA proclaimed that for the LRA, which preserves the nuclear parity in the world, "the whole life of St. Fedor Ushakov is an example of the endless love for the Fatherland." "Patriarkh peredal shtaby DA ikonu"; "Aleksii II posetit shtab 37-i vozdushnoi armii VVS RF," *RIA Novosti*, 26 September 2005.

127. Iakovleva, "Novye gorizonty"; Vasil'eva, "Granitsa pod dukhovnoi zaschitoi."

128. "Okhraniaia rubezhi otechestva," *VViMD*, 7 July 2010.

129. "Moschi prepodobnogo Ilii Muromtsa dostavleny v garnizonnye khramy DA," *VViMD*, 5 October 2010; "V garnizony DA po granitsam Rossii dostavit ikony s moshkami Ilii Muromtsa," *VViMD*, 29 September 2010.

130. Iakovleva, "Novye gorizonty"; Vasil'eva, "Granitsa pod dukhovnoi zaschitoi." Several pieces of the relics have been given to the churches in Moscow that provide pastoral care to the LRA officers: the Tushino Transfiguration church, which functioned as the first temple of the corps in the mid-1990s; the Church of God of the Serpukhovsky Gates, which Father Konstantin, the main pastor of the LRA, heads and where many seniors moved after him; the church of St. Nikolai at the Tretiakov Gallery, to which pilots come to pray before the Vladimir Mother of God icon; and the Sretensky Monastery, which continuously provides spiritual support to the pilots. Iakovleva, "Novye gorizonty"; Vasil'eva, "Ot Soltsov."

131. Iakovleva, "Novye gorizonty."

132. "The first overfly of the Russian cities occurred on 2 December 1941, ahead of the preparations for the counterattack of the German forces. An LI-2 airplane conducted a flight with the Tikhvinskaya Mother of God icon. Stalin's personal pilot, Aleksandr Golovanov, conducted the mission." Marina Vasil'eva, "Krestnyi khod v nebe Rossii," *KZ*, 31 May 2007.

133. Artemy Emke, "Sviaschennik."

134. Khairemdinov, "Armiia i dukhovenstvo"; Marina Vasil'eva, "Sluzhit' otechestvu veroi i pravdoi," *KZ*, 26 July 2007.

135. "Pervyi krestnyi khod po vozdukhu," *Novosti Morshanska*, 20 December 2007.

136. "Zaveduiuschii sektorom VVS sovershil zaupokoinoe bogosluzhenie," *VVD*, 20 September 2013.

137. Ternovoi, "S Rozhdestvom Khristovym."

138. "Sbory Dal'nikov," *KZ*, 24 November 2006.

139. Editorial, "DA zastupaet na boevoe dezhurstvo," *KZ*, 30 August 2007.

140. "Osviaschenie KP DA," *KZ*, 5 August 2008.

141. "Tu-160 nesli na bortu uchebnue raketu," *Vesti TV*, 11 September 2008; "Rossiiskie strategicheskie bombardirovschiki prizemlilis' v Venesuele," *Aviaport.ru*, 11 September 2008.

142. Irina Tatarina, "Pomoch blizhnemu svoemu," *Informatsionnyi portal Petrozavodskoi i Karelskoi eparkhii* (accessed 3 January 2017); "Dvadtsatiletie Petropavlovskoi i Kamchatskoi eparkhii," *Pravoslavnaia Kamchatka* (pravkamchatka.ru), 14 October 2013.

143. For example, the agreements signed in 2008 and in 2009 between the eparchy of Petropavlovsk and Kamchatka and the Red Banner Submarines Squadron. "10 let apostolskoi propovedi v Osinom gnezde," *Pravoslavnaia Kamchatka*, 14 December 2008; "Piat-

nadtsataia godovschina osviascheniia garnizonnogo khrama," *Pravoslavnaia Kamchatka*, 15 December 2013; "Podpisanno soglashenie o sotrudnichestve." Another example was in July 2005, when Metropolitan Kirill signed on behalf of five Far East eparchies an agreement with the Squadron of Nuclear Submarines in Viliuchinsk, according to which the eparchies assumed patronage over the nuclear missile submarine *St. Georgii the Victor.* The ROC would bear "material responsibility for maintaining a necessary level of spiritual enlighten and moral upbringing of the personnel [and] assist in forging moral-psychological conditions of the service in the nuclear missile submarine." Also, according to the agreement, Orthodox youth from the Far East eparchies, possessing the necessary physical and spiritual-patriotic qualities, would have an option of serving on the nuclear submarine. Lukichev, *Patriarkh Kirill*, pp. 35–36; "Tserkov' beret shefstvo nad atomnym podvodnym kreiserom na Kamchatke," *Patriarchia.ru*, 7 July 2005. The idea of drafting Orthodox youth into specific units was incepted in the early 1990s. Since then, there have been two experimental units of this kind—one in the Air Defense and another in the Engineering Corps. Pavel Gerasimov, "Simfoniia dushi," *KZ*, 3 August 2011. There is one report about a platoon of seminary graduates serving in the Kozelsk RVSN division. Viktor Litovkin, "Batiushka Matros," *NVO*, 2 September 2011; "Zampolity po vere ili otsy rodnye?," *VVD*, 22 February 2012. An agreement was signed at the pier of the base, right next to the nuclear submarine itself, on a table covered with red velvet, strongly reminiscent of the Soviet setting. The squadron commander was in parade uniform, but the submarine's commander was in field uniform, as the nuclear vessel was probably on full operational duty. "Fotoreportazh: Buduschii patriarkh na Kamchatke," *Pravoslavnaia Kamchatka*, 29 January 2009.

144. "V Murmanksoi oblasti soverschenno osviaschenie atomnoi podvodnoi lodki 'Kostroma,'" *Mospat.ru*, 18 April 2008. Similar activities took place among submariners of the Baltic and Black Sea Fleets. "Nizhegorodskii sviaschennik sovershil osviaschenie podvodnoi lodki v Sevastopole," *Patriarchia.ru*, 22 September 2006.

145. "Kratkaia istoriia Nikolo-Korelskogo monastyria," *Pravoslavnaia stranitsa Nikolaia i Eleny Andrushenko*, http://orthonord.ru/ (accessed 7 September 2016).

146. "10 let apostolskoi propovedi."

147. "Khram v chest' prepodobnogo Serafima Sarovskogo, g. Viliuchinsk," *Pravkamchatka.ru* (accessed 1 March 2017).

148. Verkhoturie, due to its monastery, one of the biggest in Russia, is the spiritual capital of the Ural region, and the name of Ekaterinburg, the fourth-largest city in Russia, is attributed by the local archiepiscop to St. Ekaterina, though the city was actually called after the wife of Tsar Peter I.

149. "Arkhiepiskop Vikentii osviatil atomnuiu podvodnuiu lodku 'Ekaterinburg,'" *Pravoslavie.ru*, 2 April 2004; "K-54, Ekaterinburg, proekt 667BDRM," in A. S. Nikolaev, *EOPF* (deepstorm.ru).

150. "10 oktiabria sostoialas' tseremoniia vvyvoda iz ellinga PRK SN K-117 Briansk," *Advis.ru*, 11 October 2006.

151. "Podvodnyi kreiser 'Karelia' spuschen na vodu," *Vesti.ru*, 22 November 2008; "Sviaschennik naputstovoval ekipazh APL 'Novomoskovsk,'" *Arkhangel'skaia eparkhiia*, 6 August 2012.

152. "V Severodvinske osviaschena zakladka atomnoi podvodnoi lodki 4 pokoleniia 'Vladimir Monomakh,'" *Patriarchia.ru*, 20 March 2006.

153. "Novyi podvodnyi raketonosets poluchit imia 'Nikolaia Chudotvortsa,'" *Vesti. ru*, 22 August 2009.

154. "V armii i na flote," *Rossiiskoe voennoe obozrenie*, no. 11 (2009): 57–58; "Pokrovitel' iadernogo schita," *VPK*, no. 29 (28 July–3 August 2009).

155. "Sviaschennik provel besedu s voennymi moriakami," *VViMD*, 1 June 2011.

156. "Delegatsia predstavitelei RFIaTs-VNIIEF i rukovodstva Sarova s shefskim vizitom posetila Severodvinsk," *ROSATOM*, 25 March 2009. This submarine (B-90) may receive in future a small nuclear reactor, which explains the patronage of the VNIIEF. "Novaia podvodnaia lodka VMF Rossii," *Oruzhie Rossii*, 11 August 2008.

157. "Dukhovnaia podderzhka," *Flag Rodiny*, 29 October 2008; "Sviatoi voin Feodor—simvol silnoi Rossiiskoi derzhavy," *Pravoslavnyi Sarov*, 5 August 2011.

158. "Pamiatnik imperatoru Nikolaiu II ustanovlen na Kamchatke," *Patriarchia.ru*, 21 March 2006; "10 let apostolskoi propovedi."

159. "10 let apostolskoi propovedi."

160. "Prinimaia prisiagu," *Pravoslavnaia Kamchatka*, 12 August 2009.

161. Upon its being carried aboard from the icebreaker, several officers and submarine commanders approached the icon to kiss it. "Port Arturskaia sviatynia v Rybachem," *Pod Andreevskim flagom*, 28 December 2009.

162. In the next decade, the clergy of the missiles and strategic bombers would catch up with their naval colleagues.

163. "Podvodnaia lodka 'Sviatoi Georgii Pobedonosets' venrulas' iz remonta," *Pravoslavie.ru*, 25 November 2003; "Proekt 667BDR," *Forum klub "Falersitika,"* 27 March 2011; "K-433, Sviatoi Georgii Pobedonosets, pr. 667BDR," in Nikolaev, *EOPF*.

164. "Pravoslavnyi sviaschennik prinial uchastie v pokhode na podvodnom raketnom katere," *Patriarchia.ru*, 11 August 2006; "V morskoi pokhod so sviaschennikom," *Informatsionnyi portal Petrozavodskoi i Karelskoi eparkhii* (accessed 3 January 2017).

165. Lukichev, *Patriarkh Kirill*, pp. 143–44.

166. "Patriarkh Kirill blagoslovil rossiiskikh podvodnikov," *Vesti.ru*, 22 August 2009; "Poseschenie Sviateishim Patriarkhom Kirillom predpriiatiia OAO 'Sevmash,'" *Patriarchia.ru*, 22 August 2009.

167. "Sviateishii Patriarkh posetil Sevmash," *Patriarchia.ru*, 22 August 2009; "Patriarkh Kirill blagoslovil rossiiskikh podvodnikov."

168. "Patriarkh Kirill blagoslovil rossiiskikh podvodnikov."

169. "Novyi podvodnyi raketonosets poluchit imia 'Nikolaia Chudotvortsa.'"

170. "Patriarkh Kirill blagoslovil rossiiskikh podvodnikov."

171. "Predstoiatel Russkoi Tserkvi vozglavil sluzhenie utreni v Nikolskom sobore byvshego Nikolo-Korelskogo monastyria," *Patriarchia.ru*, 22 August 2009.

172. "Vizit Patriarkha Moskovskogo i vseia Rusi Kirilla na Sevmash," *Sevmash.ru* (accessed 7 September 2016). The patriarch's visit occurred, probably by design, on 22 August—the national Flag Day. This post-Soviet holiday was introduced in 1994 to celebrate the revival of the tricolor, which had been used by the Russian tsardom since

the seventeenth century, at first to designate merchant ships, and until the revolution as the national flag. Since the early 2000s the Kremlin has carefully crafted its national symbolism as part of the new national identity, and the patriarch on this day, and on later occasions, made himself an integral part of this effort. Most of the reintroduced symbols had religious connotations and thus elevated the role of the ROC. Commenting on the issue of the national Flag Day in an address to the youth of Arkhangelsk—a city with a religious name and a history linked to the Russian merchant and military fleets and also one of the main religious centers of the Russian North—the patriarch urged them "to preserve our symbols, because they encapsulate a lot of what links each and every one of us to the history of our country, with its spiritual and cultural essence." "Sviateishii Patriarkh Kirill: 'My dolzhny oberegat' nashi simvoly,'" *Patriarchia.ru*, 22 August 2009.

173. In 2011 Father Artemy became protopope (blagochinii) of the Mirninskoe Blagochinie, a subunit of the ROC eparchy that consists of several parishes. Dmitrii Andreev, "Derzhim porokh sukhim," *KZ*, 9 December 2009; "Dukhovenstvo—Protoierei Artemii Emke," *Arkhangel'skaia eparkhiia* (website) (accessed 4 September 2016).

174. Evgenii, "Domovoi khram v chest' sv. vlkm. Varvary v Uchebnom tsentre kosmicheskikh voisk," *KhSAMM*, 27 November 2013.

175. Svetlana Pimenova, "Den' zaschitnika Otechestva na kosmodrome," *KhSAMM*, 23 February 2012; Evgenii, "Otets Artemii: Material gazety 'Krasnaia zvezda,'" *KhSAMM*, 26 November 2013.

176. Evgenii, "Domovoi khram."

177. Evgenii, "Domovoi khram."

178. Pimenova, "Den' zaschitnika Otechestva"; Evgenii, "Otets Artemii."

179. Evgenii, "Otchet nastoiatelia khrama sv. Arkhangela Mikhaila protoierei A. Emke o rabote s voennosluzhaschimi kosmodroma Plesetsk v 2009, 2010, 2011, 2012, 2013 gg.," *KhSAMM*, 17 December 2013.

180. Evgenii, "Chasovnia v chest' Kazanskoi ikony Bozhei Materi," *KhSAMM*, 29 November 2013.

181. Evgenii, "Domovoi khram."

182. As in the case of the St. Varvara church, the liturgies have been conducted only in coordination with the unit commander, usually on the major holidays; however, the temple is open to the soldiers whenever they want to come, pray, and light a candle.

183. Anna Emke, "Khram sviatogo muchenika Ioanna Voina," *KhSAMM*, 27 November 2013.

184. Svetlana Pimenova, "Nastoiatel' khrama sovershil chin osviascheniia samoletov i vertoleta," *KhSAMM*, 4 March 2011.

185. "U shtaba kosmodroma budet vozdvignut' chasovoi stolp," *KhsAMM* (accessed 4 September 2016).

186. The first service took place in December 2013. Svetlana Pimenova, "Briket novostei," *KhSAMM*, 25 December 2013.

187. Evgenii, "Khram vchst' vsekh sviatykh," *KhSAMM*, 30 June 2013.

188. Ostapenko served since the 1970s in the RVSN. He became first deputy of the SF in 2004, then headed the Plesetsk cosmodrome, and commanded the SF from 2008

and the newly established Aerospace Defense Forces in 2011–12. In 2013–15 he headed ROSCOSMOS, which partially explains the boost in churching of the civilian space industry (more on this later in the chapter). Svetlana Pimenova, "Osviaschennaia raketa-nositel' 'Soiuz-2' uspeshno startovala," *KhsAMM*, 5 May 2011.

189. Svetlana Pimenova, "Startovavshaia s kosmodroma Plesetsk raketa," *KhsAMM*, 3 October 2011.

190. Svetlana Pimenova, "27 iunia s kosmodroma Plesetsk uspeshno startovala," *KhSAMM*, 27 June 2011; "Osviaschennaia raketa-nositel' so sputnikom voennogo naznacheniia uspeshno startovala," *KhSAMM*, 20 May 2012. Father Artemy has repeatedly emphasized the importance of his mission, since every launch bears several potential risks—financial losses, loss of space power prestige, and loss of life and health among the launching unit. Svetlana Pimenova, "Est' takaia rabota osviaschiat' raketo nositeli," *KhSAMM*, 15 November 2012.

191. "Mitropolit Krutitskii i Kolomenskii Iuvenalii osviatil Komandnyi punkt GITs KV," *VViMD*, 19 March 2010; Website of the Veterans of the Space Flight Control Service (KIK—Komandno Izmeritel'nyi Kompleks), "Tseremoniia osviascheniia KP GITs KV," www.kik-sssr.ru/00.2_Osviascenie_KIK.htm.

192. See, e.g., on Cosmonautics Day: "Novosti Odintsovskogo blagochiniia: V chest' dnia kosmonavtiki," *ME OVVSPU*, 6 May 2011. On cultural-educational and religious-patriotic activities: Svetlana Pimenova, "Na svetloi sed'mitse v uchebnom tsentre RVSN," *KhSAMM*, 26 April 2011. On baptisms: "Kursanty uchebnogo tsentra kosmicheskikh voisk v Mirnom priniali kreschenie," *VViMD*, 1 June 2011; Svetlana Pimenova, "Kursanty priniali kreschenie pered vypuskom," *KhSAMM*, 21 May 2011. On consecrations: Evgenii, "Otchet nastoiatelia khrama"; Svetlana Pimenova, "326 kursantov uchebnogo tsentra kosmicheskikh voisk priniali prisiagu i poluchili blagoslovlenie," *KhSAMM*, 11 June 2011. On conversations with newly arrived officers: Evgenii, "Otchet nastoiatelia khrama." On memorial services: Svetlana Pimenova, "Na Radonitsu protoierei Artemii Emke sovershil zaupokoinuiu," *KhSAMM*, 3 May 2011.

193. "Poezdka soldat srochnikov v Muzei kosmonavtiki," *ME OVVSPU*, 9 June 2011; "Radost' o Voskresshem Khriste," *MEV*, nos. 5–6 (2010).

194. SPRN—Sistema preduprezhdeniia o raketnom napadenii.

195. Anna Potekhina, "Za semiu zamkami," *KZ*, 30 September 2009.

196. On the Sofrino congregation, see *Khram Vsekh Sviatykh VRP, pos. Sofrino*, http://troitsa-pushkino.ru/temples/detail.php?ID=31.

197. "O khrame," *Khram Dmitriia Donskogo* (onhram.ru) (accessed 12 July 2016).

198. "Novosti Pushkinskogo blagochestiia," *Moskovskaia eparkhiia RPTs*, 6 November 2004.

199. See, e.g., on holiday visits: "Rozhdestvo v garnizone kosmicheskikh voisk," *Moskovskaia eparkhiia RPTs*, 11 January 2005. On baptisms: "Vesti iz blagochinii; Pushkinskii okrug, 6 oktiabria" *MEV*, nos. 11–12 (2011). On pastoral conversations: "Vesti iz blagochinii," *MEV*, nos. 3–4 (2010); "OVVSiPU," *Moskovskaia eparkhiia RPTs*, 2009.

200. "Vstrecha v Sofrinskom garnizone kosmicheskikh voisk," *Moskovskaia eparkhiia RPTs*, 25 January 2010.

201. "Pervoe bogosluzhenie v khrame-chasovne garnizona kosmicheskikh voisk," *VViMD*, 29 March 2011; "Prestol'nyi prazdnik v Sofrinskom garnizone," *Moskovskaia eparkhiia RPTs*, 15 March 2011; "Vstrecha s voenosluzhaschimi KV," *Moskovskaia eparkhiia RPTs*, 31 January 2011.

202. Potekhina, "Za semiu zamkami"; Viktor Panchenko, "Sisteme preduprezhdeniia o raketnom napadenii 40 let," *Vozdushno-kosmicheskaia oborona*, 28 May 2011.

203. *Nebesnyi schit*, documentary, *TV Channel "Rossiia 1,"* 2014 (2.33 min.).

204. "Osviaschenie boevogo znameni v Solnechnogorske," *Moskovskaia eparkhiia RPTs*, 31 July 2009; "Vruchenie boevogo znameni v Chernetskom," *Moskovskaia eparkhiia RPTs*, 9 December 2009.

205. "Prazdnovanie Rozhdenstva Hristova v Solnechnegorskom blagochinii," *Moskovskaia eparkhiia RPTs*, 7 January 2010; "Paskha v Solnechnegorskom blagochinii," *Moskovskaia eparkhiia RPTs*, April 2010.

206. "Den' zaschitika Otechestva v Solnechnegorskom blagochinii," *Moskovskaia eparkhiia RPTs*, 23 February 2010.

207. "Prisiaga v Solnechnegorskom blagochinii," *Moskovskaia eparkhiia RPTs*, 17 January 2010.

208. Aleksander Milkus, "'Kosmicheskii' batiushka otets Sergii," *Komsomol'skaia pravda*, 10 April 2015. On the mayor's support, see "Skonchalsia glava administratsii Baikonura," *ROSKOSMOS*, 11 September 2013; "Pravoslavnyi khram sv. vlkm. Georgiia Pobedonostsa," *Ofitsial'nyi sait admin. goroda Baikonur* (accessed 5 September 2016).

209. "Ikonostas khrama sv. vmch. Georgiia Pobedonostsa, poligon Baikonur," *Sv. Troitskoe bratstvo*, http://shigri.ru/izgotovlenie_ikonostasov/ikonostas_hrama_svt _nikolaya_v_kazahstane.html#up. On the baptismal font, see Milkus, "'Kosmicheskii' batiushka."

210. "Ikonostas khrama sv. vmch. Georgiia Pobedonostsa."

211. Milkus, "'Kosmicheskii' batiushka."

212. Natalia Burtseva, "V kosmos s blagoslovelniem," *Vesti TV*, 13 December 2008.

213. Milkus, "'Kosmicheskii' batiushka."

214. Indira Shestokova, "Otets Sergii: 'Padali otlo te rakety, kotorye mi ne osveschiali,'" *Metro*, 11 September 2013. On the growing public criticism, see *Kosmos kak poslushanie* (Moscow: Studia ROSKOSMOS, 2010).

215. Indira Shestokova, "ROSKOSMOS prodolzhit osviaschiat' rakety," *Metro*, 11 September 2013.

216. Milkus, "'Kosmicheskii' batiushka."

217. Marina Lev, "Kosmos vo slavu Bozhiiu," *Pravoslavie.ru*, 12 April 2013.

218. Olga Glagoleva, "Zveznyi: Khram," *Pravoslavia.ru*, 30 November 2010.

219. Lev, "Kosmos."

220. Lev, "Kosmos."

221. Marina Gladkova, "Iegumen Yoav dukhovnik otriada kosmonavtov," *Vecherniaia Moskva*, 11 April 2014.

222. Lev, "Kosmos."

223. Milkus, "'Kosmicheskii' batiushka."

224. "Cherez ternii k Bogu," *ROSKOSMOS*, 12 April 2011.

225. Maksim Suraev, *"Dnevnik kosmonavta Maksima Suraeva,"* Roscosmos.ru, 19 November 2009.

226. Virgiliu Pop, "Space and Religion in Russia: Cosmonaut Worship to Orthodox Revival," *Astropolitics*, no. 7 (2009): 158.

227. Lev, "Kosmos."

228. Gladkova, "Iegumen Yoav."

229. *Kosmos kak poslushanie.*

230. It would probably be more precise to say that the reference is to the main bases of the 12th GUMO. It is unlikely that every arsenal of the service had its own church. Also, the reference is not necessarily to the newly constructed temples, but to the existing ones that had functioned next to or within the bases, upon their return to the ROC in the 1990s. These started providing pastoral care and, in some cases, became assigned to the bases. Finally, many of the arsenals are located next to the bases that did have their own churches. In such cases, the GUMO arsenals have been assigned to the churching activities of the nuclear priests and temples of other services.

231. "Doklad predsedatelia OVVSiPU protoierei Dmitriia Smirnova—Arkhiereiskii sobor 2004," *Patriarchia.ru*, 7 June 2008.

232. Vera Nadezhdina, "Khorugvi i iadernui schit," *KZ*, 5 October 2007.

233. Viktor Iuzbashev, "Moleben iadernomu oruzhiiu," *NVO*, 7 September 2007; Dmitrii Andreev, "Garanty iadernogo schita," *KZ*, 3 September 2012. According to the polygon commander, this generation has only heard about nuclear tests but possesses great skill in modern non-nuclear explosive experiments—one of the main directions in the polygon's functioning. Olga Romanova, "Na severnykh rubezhakh Rodiny stroiat khramy," *Arctic Universe*, 11 November 2010.

234. Valentina Muzykina, "Otets Innokentii, monakh poliarnik," *Pravda*, 31 December 2014.

235. "Patriarshaia nagrada vruchena novomu nachal'niku 12-go GUMO," 17 July 2006, *Patriarchia.ru*; "Na Novoi Zemle osviaschen samyi severnyi pravoslavnyi khram Rossii," *Izdatel'stvo Sretenskogo monastyria* (pravoslavie.ru), 20 September 2006.

236. "Arkhipelag Novaia Zemlia: Sviato-Nikolskii khram," *Zolotoshveinaia masterskaia Ubrus*, 5 January 2012.

237. "Na Novoi Zemle osviaschen samyi severnyi pravoslavnyi khram Rossii."

238. "Osviaschenie poligona na Novoi Zemle," *KZ*, 24 November 2006.

239. A reference to two big crosses that were placed at around that time at the maritime entrance to the Belushia Guba—Cape Morozova and Cape Lil'e.

240. "Na Novoi Zemle osviaschen samyi severnyi pravoslavnyi khram Rossii."

241. Igor' Dubonosov, Vsepobezhdaiuschii krest Khristov," *Novozemel'skie vesti*, 25 April 2014. By 2008, the congregation numbered 250 permanent members, out of the settlement's 2,630 residents. Romanova, "Na severnykh rubezhakh Rodiny stroiat khramy."

242. "Valynkin Igor Nikolaevich," *Fond apostola Andreiia Pervozvannogo* (accessed 12 January 2017).

243. "84 mezhvidovyi uchebno-takticheskii tsentr v/ch14258," *Voiskovye chasti Rossii* (accessed 13 January 2017); "Novyi khram v sele Sharapovo," *MEV,* nos. 1–2 (2003).

244. "Istoriia khrama," *Khram Arkhangela Mikhaila derevnia Sharapovo Sergievo-Posadskogo raiona Moskovskoi oblasti* (spasemhram.ru) (accessed 13 January 2017); "Novyi khram v sele Sharapove"; "Istoriia Mikhailo-Arkhangel'skogo khrama, derevnia Sharapovo," *Sergievo-Posadskoe blagochinie* (spblago.ru), 23–24 April 2011; "10 let so dnia osnovaniia garnizonnogo Nikolskogo khrama," *Sergievo-Posadskoe blagochinie,* 19 November 2012.

245. "Istoriia khrama"; "Novyi khram v sele Sharapove"; "Istoriia Mikhailo-Arkhangel'skogo khrama, derevnia Sharapovo"; "10 let so dnia osnovaniia garnizonnogo Nikolskogo khrama." On Sundays the priest conducted within the base catechizational conversations with the compulsory servicemen, analyzed with them documentary movies of spiritual-moral content, and set up a library of religious literature in an officer's house. Since mid-decade, the monk has participated in all the celebrations and official events of the center and contributed to conversations with the conscripts that the administration of Sergiev Posad conducts within the training center twice a year. Annually, the residents of the village and the military and their families conduct a cross procession on the saint's day, moving between both temples. Several times a year commanders of the garrison together with the garrison priest conduct pilgrimage tours to the hallowed sites of the Sergiev Posad region. By the end of the decade, the priest was regularly visiting the military hospital of the 12th GUMO located in Sergiev Posad. He consecrated the administration, surgery, and emergency rooms and has provided pastoral care to the patients, conducting services each time in a different department. In 2007 commanders designated a building for the hospital church. The garrison has been actively involved in restoration work of the main village church, while the servicemen have attended the services in both temples—starting from 2002, between October and April the services regularly take place in the Nikolsky church and the rest of the year in the Mikhailo-Arkhangel'skii temple. See "Istoriia khrama."

246. The ceremony took place on 4 December, following the liturgy of one of the twelve main Orthodox feasts—the Day of the Entry of the Holy Theotokos into the Temple. "Patriarshie bogosluzhenie v den' prazdnika Vvedeniia Presviatoi Bogoroditsy vo khram," *Sedmitza.ru,* 5 December 2003.

247. General-Colonel Igor Valynkin was awarded for "strengthening the spiritual foundation of the military service and realization of the program, developed under his leadership, for construction of the military churches. Today, Orthodox churches are functioning in all garrisons of the 12th GUMO of the RF MoD." "Valynkin Igor Nikolaevich"; "Obiavlenny lauriaty premii 'Za veru i vernost'," *Pravoslavie.ru,* 14 December 2005.

248. "Doklad predsedatelia OVVSiPU."

249. Editorial, "Iz khroniki otdela," *KZ,* 27 October 2004.

250. The career of General Moroz, GUMO's deputy for educational work, is indicative. In 1991 he became deputy of the RVSN commander for educational work, and in 1997 he moved to the 12th GUMO to head its educational work department. Until the Soviet collapse, he served as deputy commander of the RVSN Political Directorate and

headed the agitprop department. Since retiring, he has advised the GUMO commander. "Patriarshie bogosluzhenie v den' prazdnika Vvedeniia"; "General-leitenant: Moroz Nikolai Maksimovich," in G. A. Sukhina and S. B. Maslii, *Voennyi sovet RVSN* (Moscow: TsIPK RVSN, 2007). During his last RVSN position, he was among the architects of cooperation with the ROC and one of the authors of the religious-patriotic curriculum of the FOC in the RVSN Academy. "Nikolai Maksimovich Moroz," *RVSN AAA*.

251. "Patriarshaia nagrada vruchena novomu nachal'niku."

252. The president of Russia designated 4 September as the official annual professional holiday of the service—the Day of the Nuclear Maintenance Specialist—to acknowledge the contribution of the service to the national security of the Russian Federation and to commemorate the same day in 1947 when the service was established in the Soviet Union. "V Vooruzhennykh Silakh otmechaetsia Den' spetsialista po iadernomy obespecheniiu," *RF MoD*, 4 September 2015.

253. "V khrame Khrista Spasitelia nachalis' torzhestva po sluchaiu 60-letiia so dnia osnovaniia iadernogo oruzheinogo kompleksa Rossii," *Patriarchia.ru*, 4 September 2007.

254. "60 let 12 Glavnomy upravleniiu Ministerstva oborony RF," *KZ*, 4 September 2007.

255. "V khrame Khrista Spasitelia nachalis' torzhestva."

256. "I hope that the prayers of St. Seraphim Sarovsky will guide the Fatherland's defenders in all their paths and that the activities in the framework of the agreement will enable further strengthening of our country's security capabilities." "Patriarshee privetstvie uchastnikam prazdnovaniia 60-letiia so dnia osnovaniia 12-go GUMO RF," *Patriarchia.ru*, 4 September 2007.

257. "Serafim Sarovskii—nebesnyi pokrovitel' 12-go GUMO," *VViMD*, 4 September 2007; Iuzbashev, "Moleben iadernomu oruzhiiu."

258. "V khrame Khrista Spasitelia nachalis' torzhestva."

259. "O skite," *Gefsimanskii-Chernigovskii skit* (skit-chernigovsky.ru) (accessed 16 January 2017).

260. Editorial, "Faktu," *KZ*, 11 January 2008.

261. Aleksandr Aleksandrov, "Edinstvo doblesti i very," *KZ*, 19 December 2007.

262. "Osviaschenie pamiatnika svt. Nikolaiu Chudotvortsu i zakladnogo kamnia v osnovanie buduschego khrama TsNII MO RF," *Patriarchia.ru*, 13 December 2007.

263. "Sviatitel' Nikolai, arkhiepiskop Mirlikiiskii, Chudotvorets, 13 dekabria 2007," *Blagotvoritel'nyi fond Sviatitelia Nikolaia Chudotvortsa* (sannicila.ru) (accessed 16 January 2017).

264. Aleksandrov, "Edinstvo doblesti i very."

265. "Sviatitel' Nikolai, arkhiepiskop Mirlikiiskii."

266. Aleksandrov, "Edinstvo doblesti i very."

267. Aleksandrov, "Edinstvo doblesti i very."

268. "Sviateishii Patriarkh Aleksii osviatil pamiatnik Nikolaiu Chudotvortsu v Tsentral'nom nauchnoi-issledovtel'skom institute MO RF," *Patriarchia.ru*, 13 December 2007; "Osviaschenie pamiatnika svt. Nikolaiu Chudotvortsu."

269. The ceremony took place on the fiftieth anniversary of the polygon's establishment. The entire garrison, the residents of the closed city, and the clergy were present. The ceremony followed a similar pattern: consecration, addresses by the Arkhangelsk episcop and the polygon commander, and the garrison marching in parade uniforms, saluting the clergy, the commanders, and the saint. "19 sentiabria 2008, poselok Belushia Guba," *Blagotvoritel'nyi fond Sviatitelia Nikolaia Chudotvortsa* (accessed 16 January 2017); Dmitrii Andreev, "Tainy Novoi Zemli," *KZ*, 8 August 2012.

270. "V glavnom voennom vedomstve iadernogo oruzheinogo kompleksa Rossii osviaschen pamiatnik," *VViMD*, 8 September 2010.

271. "Vesti iz blagochinii: Sergievo-Posadskii okrug," *MEV*, nos. 1–2 (2010); "Nachalo voinskoi ucheby v Sharapovo," *Moskovskaia eparkhiia*, 1 December 2009.

272. "Vesti iz blagochinii: Sergievo-Posadskii okrug," *MEV*, nos. 11–12 (2009).

273. See, e.g., on banners at parades and ceremonies: "Osviaschenie boevogo znameni voinskogo soedineniia Rzhanitskogo garnizona," *Zhukovskoe blagochinie* (zhukovka.prihod.ru), 18 February 2010. On Verkhovtsev: "Medvedev uvolil nachal'nika 'iadernogo glavka,'" *Oruzhie Rossii*, 27 December 2010. On new garrison temples: Editorial, "Novosti," *VPK*, 29 July 2009; "V Voennom poselke postroiat khram," *VViMD*, 12 November 2010.

274. "Poseschenie Sviateishim Patriarkhom Voennoi akademii RVSN," *Patriarchia.ru*, 8 December 2009.

CHAPTER 7

1. Peter Finn, "Saints in Demand in Russia as Church Asserts Tie to State," *Washington Post*, 20 April 2007.

2. Nikolai Grigor'ev, *Vzaimodeistvie Vooruzhennykh sil RF i RPTs v sovremmennykh usloviiakh* (Moscow: RGB OD, 2003), avtoreferat.

3. References to military debacles have been omitted. Nikolai Mitrokhin, "Liubov' bez udovletvoreniia," *Journal of Power Institutions in Post-Soviet Societies*, no. 3 (2005): 6–7.

4. Grigor'ev, *Vzaimodeistvie Vooruzhennykh sil RF i RPTs*, avtoreferat.

5. Vladimir Legoyda, "Not Peace, but a Sword?," *Moscow Defense Brief*, no. 2 (2004): 3–5.

6. Legoyda "Not Peace, but a Sword?," p. 5

7. Mitrokhin, "Liubov' bez udovletvoreniia," pp. 6–7.

8. This would then repeat itself every subsequent anniversary.

9. It first came out with a commercial publisher, but in 2015 the Moscow Patriarchate bought the rights and reissued it in its own publishing house toward the seventieth anniversary of the GPW victory. Andrei Farberov, *Spasi i sokhrani: Svidetel'stva ochevi-dt—* noschi Bozhiei Rossii v Velikuiu Otechestvennuiu voinu (Moscow: *Ine Vse trudnoe legkim sodei': Molitva marshala Chuikova," *KZ*,

ude *Shtrafbat*, *Utomlennie solntsem 2*, and *Pop*. See Sergei Nepod-vershenno sekretno*, 8 December 2014.

11. Sergei Filatov, "RPTs i iubilei Pobedy," *Russkoe reviu*, May 2005.

12. The majority came from the Main Educational Work Directorate.

13. Materialy tserkovno-obschestvennoi konferentsii *"Za drugi svoia": RPT i VOV* (Moscow: Izdatel'skii sovet RPTs, 2005); "Tserkov' v gody voiny," *Tserkovnyi vestnik*, no. 6 (307) (March–April 2005).

14. O. Iu. Vasil'eva, I. I. Kudriavtsev, and L. A. Lykov, *Sbornik dokumentov: RPTs v gody VOV 1941–1945 gg.* (Moscow: Izdatel'stvo Krutitskogo podvoriia, 2009).

15. "Zakliuchitel'noe plenarnoe zasedanie IX VRNS," *VRNS*, 10 March 2005.

16. Sergei Filatov, "RPTs i iubilei Pobedy."

17. Sergei Filatov, "RPTs i iubilei Pobedy."

18. Sergei Filatov, "RPTs i iubilei Pobedy."

19. Sergei Filatov, "RPTs i iubilei Pobedy."

20. Sergei Filatov, "RPTs i iubilei Pobedy."

21. "Protoierei Dmitrii Smirnov: 'Pobeda nad natsizmom stala neizbezhna, kogda Stalin prinial reshenie prekratit' goneniia na Tserkov'," *VViMD*, 23 April 2010.

22. "Rol' tserkvi v Velikoi pobede," *VViMD*, 9 April 2010.

23. See, e.g., Vladislav Maltsev, "Sviaschennaia voina," *Nezavisimoe religioznoe obozrenie*, 19 May 2010.

24. Patriarch Kirill, *Slovo pastyria*, *ORT*, 25 February 2017.

25. B. M. Lukichev, *Patriarkh Kirill i voennoe dukhovenstvo* (Moscow: FIV, 2016), pp. 74–75.

26. "Den' pamiati velikogo kniazia Aleksandra Nevskogo, kontrnastuplenie pod Moskvoi," *VViMD*, 6 December 2010.

27. Mitrokhin, "Liubov' bez udovletvoreniia," p. 7.

28. Brian Whitmore, "Russia's Patriarch Increasingly Becoming Major Force in Politics," *Radio Free Europe*, 6 September 2009.

29. Irina Pavliutkina, "Chasovnia v shtabe DA," *KZ*, 27 August 2002.

30. Virgiliu Pop, "Space and Religion in Russia: Cosmonaut Worship to Orthodox Revival," *Astropolitics*, no. 7 (2009): 157–58.

31. *Kosmos kak poslushanie* (Moscow: Studia ROSKOSMOS, 2010).

32. Pop, "Space and Religion in Russia," pp. 157–58; Marina Lev, "Kosmos vo slavu Bozhiiu," *Pravoslavie.ru*, 12 April 2013; *Kosmos kak poslushanie*.

33. *Kosmos kak poslushanie*.

34. *Kosmos kak poslushanie*.

35. Anti-Religion Community website, "Obraschenie k studii ROSKOSMOS po povodu fil'ma 'Kosmos kak poslushanie,'" 8 December 2010, http://ru-antireligion .livejournal.com/5291179.html (accessed 4 March 2017).

36. "Nebesnye zastupniki," *VViMD*, 31 December 2010; "Sviaschennik Dimitrii Dovbysh: Ikona 'Sobor pokrovitelei voinstva Rossiiskogo,'" *Moskovskie eparkhal'nye novosti*, no. 2 (2016).

37. See Jeffrey Mankoff, *Russian Foreign Policy* (Lanham, MD: Rowman and Littlefield, 2011).

38. Andrei Okara, "Potselui Velikogo inkvizitora," *NG-Religii*, no. 12 (20 July 2

39. Egor Kholmogorov, "Tserkov' osviatila iadernyi schit," *GloboScope*, 11 September 2007.

40. "Serafim Sarovsky predskazal sozdanie 'iadernogo schita' Rossii," *Pravda.ru*, 2 July 2003.

41. V. E. Kostiukov and R. I. Il'kaev, "Lider," *Atomnaia strategiia*, no. 2 (2009): 14.

42. Dmitry Sladkov, "Serafim—znachit plamennyi," *Zavtra*, 8 June 2003.

43. D. V. Sladkov and I. G. Zhidov, "Fiziki bez sviaschennikov—sovremennye papuasy," *FOMA* 16, no. 2 (2003).

44. Feliks Schelkin, *Apostoly atomnogo veka* (Moscow: Deli Print, 2004), pp. 147–48.

45. Fedor Gaiduchkov, "Ot Ioanna do Serafima," *Rossiiskaia gazeta*, 20 July 2006.

46. Following the president's remarks, the ROC issued a statement that "the president assumes that nuclear weapons and Orthodoxy strengthen Russian statehood and national security." "Prezident Putin polagaet, chto rossiiskuiu bezopasnost' ukrepliaiut iadernoe oruzhie i pravoslavie," *Pravoslavie.ru*, 1 February 2007.

47. Aleksandr Kukolevsky, "Kontseptsiia izmenilas'," *Kommersant vlast'*, 10 September 2007.

48. Egor Kholmogorov, "Putin i atomnoe pravoslavie," *Russkaia narodnaia liniia*, 2 February 2007.

49. Kholmogorov, "Putin i atomnoe pravoslavie."

50. Kholmogorov, "Putin i atomnoe pravoslavie"; Egor Kholmogorov, "Atomnoe pravoslavie: Sarovskaia lektsiia," *Russkii obozrevatel'*, 31 August 2008.

51. Kholmogorov, "Atomnoe pravoslavie: Sarovskaia lektsiia."

52. Kholmogorov, "Atomnoe pravoslavie: Sarovskaia lektsiia."

53. Egor Kholmogorov, "Bog kak subject istorii," *Apologia*, no. 5 (5) (July 2005).

54. Kholmogorov, "Tserkov' osviatila iadernyi schit."

55. Kholmogorov, "Tserkov' osviatila iadernyi schit."

56. Jardar Østbø, *The New Third Rome: Readings of a Russian Nationalist Myth* (Stuttgart: Ibidem Press, 2016), p. 236.

57. Kholmogorov, "Tserkov' osviatila iadernyi schit."

58. Kukolevsky, "Kontseptsiia izmenilas'."

59. Kavad Rash, "Iadernaia strazha," *KZ*, 4 September 2007.

60. Rash, "Iadernaia strazha."

61. Rash, "Iadernaia strazha."

62. Viktor Mikhailov, *Ia iastreb* (Moscow: FGUP ISS, 2008), p. 24.

63. Aleksandr Soldatov, "Atomnoe pravoslavie," *Ogonek*, 16 September 2007.

64. Fiona Hill and Clifford Gaddy, *Mr. Putin: Operative in the Kremlin* (Washington, DC: Brookings Institution Press, 2015), p. 252.

65. Dennis Zuev, "A Visual Dimension of Protest: An Analysis of Interactions During the Russian March," *Visual Anthropology*, no. 3 (2010): 221–53; Soldatov, "Atomnoe pravoslavie."

66. Soldatov, "Atomnoe pravoslavie"; "Vsia khronika," *Russkaia doktrina*.

67. For example, the section suggests the establishment of unified special operations and informational operations commands, comprising both the digital-technological and

cognitive-psychological aspects of these operations, augmented by the long-range conventional and nuclear capabilities—indeed the exact military innovations that have occurred since 2014. "Obschie nabroski ustroistva novykh russkikh VS," punkt 7, glava 6, chast' III, in *Russkaia doktrina*. See Dmitry (Dima) Adamsky, *Cross-Domain Coercion: The Current Russian Art of Strategy* (Paris: IFRI, 2015).

68. "Obschie nabroski ustroistva novykh russkikh VS," in *Russkaia doktrina*.

69. "Obraz Rossii buduschego," punkt 5, glava 4, chast' V, in *Russkaia doktrina*.

70. "Vsia khronika," in *Russkaia doktrina*.

71. Soldatov, "Atomnoe pravoslavie."

72. The first edition was published in 2007, and subsequent editions in 2008, 2010, 2014, 2015, and 2016. Andrei Kobiakov, Vitalii Aver'ianov, and Vladimir Kucherenko [Maksim Kalashnikov], *Russkaia doktrina: Russkii shans XXI veka prorvatsia skvoz' globalnuiu smutu*, Maksim Kalashnikov rekomenduet (Moscow: Iauza Press, 2007); V. Aver'ianov, A. Anisimov, I. Brazhnikov, Ia. Butakov, P. Kalinin, A. Kobiakov, V. Kucherenko, E. Kholmogorov, and K. Cheremnykh, *Russkaia doktrina: Gosudarstvennaia ideologiia epokhi Putina* (Moscow: Institute russkoi tsivilizatsii, 2015); Vitalii Aver'ianov, *Strategiia Russkoi doktriny: Cherez diktaturu k gosudarstvu pravdy* (Moscow: Knizhnyi mir, 2016).

73. "Vsia khronika," in *Russkaia doktrina* (rusdoctrina.ru) (accessed 9 September 2016).

74. Soldatov, "Atomnoe pravoslavie." In 2009 the Kremlin, and President Medvedev, exchanged ideas on Russia's modernization and development with Kalashnikov, one of the doctrine's coauthors. Kalashnikov responded in 2009 in an open letter to Medvedev's modernization call "Russia Forward." "Medvedev obratil vnimanie na ratspredlozhenie v Internete," *Vesti programm, TV Channel "Rossiia 24,"* 16 September 2009.

75. Alexei Obukhov, "Nuclear Weapons and Christian Ethics," *Security Index* 13, no. 1 (81) (2007): 88, 103–5.

76. "Historically, it happened that our developments in the nuclear field always went hand in hand with the Orthodox spiritual heritage. The nuclear shield has been forged in Sarov, the place where Seraphim Sarovsky settled his residency. One of the centers of the nuclear R&D, the 12th TsNII, is located on the land of Sergiev Posad. [. . .] Today, we are reviving the connection between military bravery and the spiritual faith, restoring the Orthodox traditions." Aleksandr Aleksandrov, "Edinstvo doblesti i very," *KZ*, 19 December 2007.

77. Kholmogorov, "Atomnoe pravoslavie: Sarovskaia lektsiia."

78. By the second post-Soviet decade, the exhibits at the museum of the RVSN Academy featured a mixture of Soviet attributes, contemporary Russian military symbolism, and icons and religious banners of St. Varvara and Jesus. "Natalia Vladimirovna Kopytova," *RVSN AAA*, 18 October 2010. Similarly, the Sarov museum of nuclear weapons turned into part of the clergy's standard pilgrimage program. It had a special department dedicated to the heritage of St. Seraphim and the religious life of Sarov, as well as a replica of the monastery as it originally stood. Senior and rank-and-file clergy from the local parishes, Moscow, and elsewhere, often personally guided by the VNIIEF se-

niors, became frequent guests. "Istoriia sozdaniia muzeia" and "Fotogalereia," Muzei RFIaTs-VNIIEF (vniief.ru) (accessed 16 February 2017).

79. Sergei Leskov, "My iz Bombograda," *Izvestiia*, 11 November 2009.

80. "Patriarkh: Sozdanie iadernogo oruzhiia—bozhii promysel," *Grani.ru*, 19 September 2009.

81. "Serafim Sarovskii vstanet na zaschitu Otechestva," *Newstube.ru*, 24 July 2009.

82. Dmitrii Andreev, "Mesto sluzhby—Tagil," *KZ*, 4 August 2010.

CHAPTER 8

1. *Religious Belief and National Belonging in Central and Eastern Europe* (Washington, DC: Pew Research Center, 2017); Gregory L. Freeze, "Russian Orthodoxy and Politics in the Putin Era," *Carnegie Task Force White Paper*, 9 February 2017, pp. 2–3.

2. Katarzyna Chawrylo, *The Altar and the Throne Alliance* (Warsaw: Center for Eastern Studies, 2015), p. 5; Freeze, "Russian Orthodoxy and Politics," pp. 2–3; *Religious Belief and National Belonging*.

3. "Otnoshenie k RPTs i patriarkhu Kirillu," *Fond Obschestvennoe mnenie*, 4 March 2012.

4. Freeze, "Russian Orthodoxy and Politics," pp. 2–3.

5. On being Orthodox and belonging, see *Religious Belief and National Belonging*. This situation resonates with that in Israel, where Judaism has become an integral part of the national-cultural identity. Since many pillars of Zionism, the national ideology, and symbols of the modern state of Israel feature essentially religious motifs, secular Israelis identifying themselves as Jewish imply a national, rather than a religious, identity. On cultural-civil self-identification, see Chawrylo, *Altar and the Throne*, p. 5. On the ROC as a trusted institution, see Charles Clover, *Black Wind, White Snow* (New Haven, CT: Yale University Press, 2017), p. 302.

6. "Storonniki i protivniki svetskogo gosudarstva," *Fond Obschestvennoe mnenie*, 2 March 2012. On turning believers into belongers, see Freeze, "Russian Orthodoxy and Politics," pp. 2–3.

7. The number of Orthodox websites, officially affiliated with the ROC as well as independent ones, has grown exponentially and left print media far behind. Freeze, "Russian Orthodoxy and Politics," pp. 4, 6.

8. Patriarch Kirill, while he was a metropolitan, "met with Konstantin Kinchev and Iurii Shevchiuk to discuss the compatibility of contemporary rock music with Orthodoxy." Aleksei Makarin, "The Russian Orthodox Church," *Russian Politics and Law* 49, no. 1 (2011): 20–21.

9. These converted patriotic bikers even moved the opening of the biking season from the Great Lent to Easter. Evgenii Vorob'iev, "Patriarch Kirill blagoslovil 'Nochnykh volkov,'" *Nefakt.Info*, 25 April 2011.

10. "Patriarkh blagoslovil 'Nochnykh volkov' na motoprobeg," *Vesti.ru*, 25 May 2009.

11. These achievements include the introduction of military chaplaincy, restitution of seized properties, and catechization of education and of the public sphere.

12. No tax is levied on the ROC's income from the following: candle making, products of publishing houses and movie companies, icons, religious garments and items of church interiors, any goods sold in the ROC's shops or merchandise produced in its factories, and fees for baptism, wedding, and memorial services. No tax is levied on property, land, and religious tourism businesses, including the ROC's hotel networks.

13. Construction companies affiliated with the ROC conducted state-funded restoration at twelve thousand heritage sites all over Russia that were returned to the ROC by the restitution law. The ROC also benefited from rental income following the restoration. Kseniia Leonova, "Poboisia boga," *OpenSpace.ru*, 15 September 2011; Mikhail Sutnikov, "Moskva otkazivaetsia ot gruza proshlogo," *NG-Religii*, 1 June 2011.

14. Kirill Golovastikov, "Kul't i kul'tura," *Lenta.ru*, 12 January 2011. Public tension around the return of the Isaakievsky Cathedral in St. Petersburg, which had functioned until 2017 as a state museum, was illustrative of this trend. Also see Chawrylo, *Altar and the Throne*, pp. 13–14.

15. Freeze, "Russian Orthodoxy and Politics," pp. 7–8.

16. Aleksei Boiarskii, "Sviataia mera," *Kommersant*, 21 May 2017; Marc Bennetts, "Putin's Holy War," *POLITICO*, 21 February 2017.

17. Chawrylo, *Altar and the Throne*, p. 5.

18. John Anderson, "Religion, State and 'Sovereign Democracy' in Putin's Russia," *Journal of Religious and Political Practice* 2, no. 2 (2016): 249–66.

19. Kirill sees the principles of equality of all confessions postulated by multi-confessionalism as an attempt to impose the American model of state-church relations on Russia. Metropolitan Hilarion (Alfeev) of Volokolamsk, *Patriarkh Kirill: Zhizn' i mirosozertsanie* (Moscow: Izdatel'stvo Moskovskoi Patriarkhii, 2010).

20. Chawrylo, *Altar and the Throne*, pp. 5–6.

21. This relates to the ROC's inability to introduce Orthodox education on a compulsory basis, the slow introduction of the military clergy, the slow process of restitution, and the demand that it follow the Kremlin's line since the beginning of the Ukrainian crisis. Chawrylo, *Altar and the Throne*, pp. 5–6; John Anderson, "Putin and the Russian Orthodox Church: Asymmetric Symphonia?," *Journal of International Affairs* 61, no. 1 (Fall/Winter 2007): 198.

22. "The patriarch and the president don't always see things eye to eye" and "respect their rights to differ." *Tserkovnik* and not *gosudarstvennik*, Patriarch Kirill "formally recognizes the existing state order," but competes with the Kremlin to improve the ROC's positions. Freeze, "Russian Orthodoxy and Politics."

23. The Ukrainian crisis illustrated this well. On one hand, the ROC has been a tool of Moscow's policy in Ukraine, trying to influence hearts and mind. On the other hand, Patriarch Kirill was absent from the "the reunion with Crimea" speech, mindful of potential implications in Ukrainian eparchies.

24. Freeze, "Russian Orthodoxy and Politics," pp. 8–9.

25. Chawrylo, *Altar and the Throne*, p. 5.

26. Marlene Laruelle, "Putin's Regime and the Ideological Market," *Carnegie Task Force White Paper*, 16 March 2017. Also see Yuri Teper, "Official Russian Identity Dis-

course in Light of Annexation of Crimea: National or Imperial," *Post-Soviet Affairs* 32, no. 4 (2016): 378–96.

27. Laruelle, "Putin's Regime."

28. Evan Osnos, David Remnick, and Joshua Yaffa, "Trump, Putin, and the New Cold War," *New Yorker*, 6 March 2016.

29. Fiona Hill and Clifford Gaddy, *Mr. Putin: Operative in the Kremlin* (Washington, DC: Brookings Institution Press, 2015), p. 351.

30. Hill and Gaddy, *Mr. Putin*, p. 273.

31. Ilyin is referred to in Russia mainly as a religious philosopher, but his views about the spiritual and geopolitical renewal of the Russian state appeal to different patriotic-minded constituencies.

32. Anton Barbashin and Hannah Thoburn, "Putin's Philosopher," *Foreign Affairs*, 20 September 2015.

33. Barbashin and Thoburn, "Putin's Philosopher." The authors were less interested in whether Putin personally believed in the ideas that he actively propagated. This book argues that Ilyin's philosophy indeed resonated with Putin, in addition to providing the Kremlin with instrumental tools to communicate with the masses.

34. Osnos, Remnick, and Yaffa, "New Cold War."

35. Such as Vladimir Solov'ev, Ivan Ilyin, Sergei Bulgakov, Nikolai Trubetskoi, Petr Savitskii, and Lev Gumilev. V. V. Afanas'ev, *Pravoslavnaia sotsiologiia* (Moscow: INFRA-M, 2015), pp. 54–73. According to Clover, "Various groups in Putin's orbit—Yakunin's 'Orthodox Chekists,' Malofeev's 'Orthodox Businessmen,' and Father Tikhon's conservative circle within the ROC—all form part of Dugin's contact network within the Russian elite." Clover, *Black Wind, White Snow*, p. 304.

36. Barbashin and Thoburn, "Putin's Philosopher."

37. Clover, *Black Wind, White Snow*, p. 302.

38. "Patriarshee pozdravlenie Predsedateliu Pravitel'stva Rossii V. V. Putinu s dnem rozhdeniia," *Patriarchia.ru*, 7 October 2011.

39. "Patriarkh Kirill: Putin spas Rossiiu ot raspada," *RBK*, 7 October 2011.

40. "Surkov rasskazal o bozhestvennom prednaznachenii Putina," *Letna.ru*, 8 July 2011.

41. "Interviu Predstoiatelia RPTs telekanalu 'Rossiia,'" *Patriarchia.ru*, 9 September 2012. The slogan shouted by the members of Pussy Riot on the altar of the Christ the Savior Cathedral, "Mother of God chase Putin away," illustrates the depth of both the protesters' irritation and the state-church nexus.

42. "I would like to wholeheartedly congratulate you, Vladimir Vladimirovich, with the election, as the majority of our people consciously, reasonably, and freely elected you as the president of the Russian Federation. [. . .] Legitimacy of the president is based on the trust of the people. You possess this trust." "V den' inauguratsii Prezidenta Rossiiskoi Federatsii V. V. Putina Sviateishii Patriarkh Kirill sovershil molebnoe penie v Blagoveschenskom sobore Moskovskogo Kremlia," *Patriarchia.ru*, 7 May 2012.

43. "In order to make your service successful, there is a need to hear people's voices. This is a very difficult art. People's voices can be obscured by well-organized groups, or

by single individuals, who are willing to equate their opinion with that of the people. [. . .] We pray today that your ability to hear people's voices will sharpen every day." "V den' inauguratsii Prezidenta Rossiiskoi Federatsii V. V. Putina Sviateishii Patriarkh Kirill sovershil molebnoe penie v Blagoveschenskom sobore Moskovskogo Kremlia."

44. "Obraschenie prezidenta k Federal'nomu sobraniiu Rossii," *Kremlin.ru*, 12 December 2012.

45. "Propoved' Sv. Patriarkha Kirilla v den' pamiati sviatitelia Iony, mitropolita Moskovskogo," *Patriarchia.ru*, 28 June 2012.

46. Editorial, "Gosudarstvo i tserkov'—pochti sovetskaia model'," *Vedomosti*, 5 February 2013.

47. Since 2010, Putin and Medvedev and his wife, Svetlana, regularly and publicly arrive to congratulate Patriarch Kirill three times a year: on his birthday, his name day, and the anniversary of his installation. For examples, see "D. Medvedev i V. Putin pozdravili patriarkha Kirilla s imeninami," *TV Zvezda*, 24 May 2011; "Godovschina intronizatsii patriarkha Kirilla," *TV Zvezda*, 1 February 2011.

48. "Vystuplenie prezidenta Putina vo vremia prazdnichnogo kontserta po sluchaiu 70-letiia Sv. Patriarkha Kirilla," *Patriarchia.ru*. Also see "Pozdravlenie Prezidenta RF V. V. Putina Sviateishemu Patriarkhu Kirillu s dnem tezoimenintstva," *Patriarchia.ru*, 24 May 2016; "Nachal'nik Voennoi akademii RVSN pozdravil Sviateishego Patriarkha s iubileem," *SOMP VVSiPU*, 5 December 2016.

49. To illustrate the point, he contrasted the female protagonist of the book *Gone with the Wind*, who envisioning hunger as her catastrophe sought material, worldly benefits, with a hypothetical Russian person driven by something much bigger that "stretches beyond the horizon, something spiritual, and connected to God." Consequently, argued Putin, despite being a democracy, the United States had conducted one of the biggest ethnic cleansings of an indigenous population in history; was among the last to abolish slavery, which continued to resonate through the twentieth century (an impression he had from reading Colin Powell's memoirs); and had used nuclear weapons without any operational necessity—something that the Soviet Union or Russia, driven by their values, would never do. "Although Stalin was a dictator and tyrant, I am very doubtful [that] if he had had a bomb in spring 1945, he would have used it against Germany. In 1941 and 1942, when the survival of the state was in question, maybe he would have. But not when the enemy was capitulating and had no chances. But Americans did it against nonnuclear Japan, which was losing the war anyway. This is another difference between [us]." Vladimir Putin, live interview, *RT*, 12 June 2013.

50. Osnos, Remnick, and Yaffa, "New Cold War."

51. Forty-two percent said that government policies should support the spread of religious values and beliefs, and 50 percent approved the state's financial support of the ROC. *Religious Belief and National Belonging*.

52. Official and public figures involved in Russian political life would promote this narrative more directly and implicitly when ideological-political confrontation with the West intensified before and after events in Ukraine. Mikhail Karpov, "Sintez pravoslaviia i sovetskogo proekta," *Lenta.ru*, 11 March 2017.

53. Clover, *Black Wind, White Snow*, p. 302.

54. Arkhimandrit Tikhon (Shevkunov), *Nesviatye sviatye* (Moscow: Izdatel'stvo Sretenskogo monastyria, 2012).

55. Clover, *Black Wind, White Snow*, pp. 302–3.

56. Some even suggested Stalin's canonization.

57. Despite Patriarch Kirill's centralized style, the ROC is not a homogeneous entity and is home to a spectrum of opinions. The three main perspectives include "modernist liberals, pragmatic traditionalists, and nationalist fundamentalists." Freeze, "Russian Orthodoxy and Politics," pp. 4, 8. Although "Orthodox Stalinists" may sound like a contradiction in terms, those who adopted this notion had their logic. Stalinism, as a form of state management, minus traditional Soviet atheism, appealed to them as the desired ideal type of organization—"an authoritarian and self-sufficient state, with the Orthodox ideology instead of the communist one." They were aware of the awful persecution of the ROC during the first Soviet decades, but somehow downplayed them, appealing to the most complicated social-political circumstances of the moment. Their interpretation of Russian history argues: "Jews and Bolsheviks destroyed the great empire, but Stalin destroyed them, and returned to the state the lost imperial chic, although under a different banner." Besides, Stalin restored the ecclesiastical structure with the patriarchate nonexistent for centuries, imposed "traditional ethical values," and gave the ROC his protection, which Nikita Khrushchev later withdrew. Andrei Desnitsky, *Pravoslavnyi stalinism: Pochemu v RPTs poliubili Stalina* (Moscow: Carnegie Moscow Center, 24 December 2015).

58. The ROC's leadership's drift in this direction, even if undesired, resulted from several factors. Rhetorically, at the time when the ROC began emphasizing traditional values and entered the ideological confrontation with the spiritually shallow and decadent West, there was a need to offer a social-political alternative, beyond the pure religious system of views. Revival of the Soviet model, with modifications, was handy. From the historical point of view, it was Stalin who during the war provided the ROC with unprecedented organizational resources. Although this was done for instrumental reasons, a favorable state-church modus operandi emerged back then: the ROC assisted the state in spreading patriotism and a positive image abroad, while the state tolerated certain ROC activities. Finally, the clear resemblances of organizational structure and culture between the authoritarian power verticals of the state and those of the ROC ensured the natural gravitation of both toward each other. Desnitsky, *Pravoslavnyi Stalinism*.

59. "Slovo Sviateishego Patriarkha Kirilla na vstreche s moriakami-podvodnikami Tikhookeanskogo flota RF," *Patriarkchia.ru*, 19 September 2010.

60. During the decade, each of the Kremlin's reception halls acquired special porcelain sets of dishes. The national emblem of St. Georgii decorated the first set, St. Andrei adorned the second one, and the star of St. Alexander Nevsky and his ribbon were on the third one. Since his return in 2012, Putin has preferred traditional Russian cuisine, offering it to the guests and popularizing it during his visits to the regions. The Kremlin's main chef began adapting the menu to the spirit of the times. In 2014, for the first time, all the meals at the Kremlin New Year's reception were made solely from Russian, locally produced products. As the chef put it in 2016, "We rejected fancy desserts and returned to the ancient

[Russian] recipes." This also included serving local Russian wines and locally produced brandy, which Russians call cognac. Elena Filipova, "V Kremle vse bliuda prikhoditsia adaptirovat' pod sovremennyi lad," *Interviewrussia.ru*, 19 January 2015; Eva Merkacheva, "Antikrizisnye sovety kremlevskikh povarov," *MK*, 29 December 2014; Tatiana Melikian, "Politicheskaia kukhnia," *Lenta.ru*, 28 August 2016. Similarly, many popular Moscow restaurants and cafés offer nostalgic menus with Soviet and traditional Russian cuisine. The interiors, music, and atmosphere in these places replicate different Soviet epochs. Many fancy Moscow restaurants offer special wine lists with "Crimea wines" and meals with a more traditional, nostalgic flavor, evident from the course name.

61. Andrei Sebentsov, "Religion in the System of State Power," *Russian Politics and Law* 49, no. 1 (2011): 46–56.

62. The cases of Montenegro and Moldova in 2016 serve as good illustrations. Andrew Higgins, "In Expanding Russian Influence, Faith Combines with Firepower," *New York Times*, 13 September 2016.

63. Patriarch Kirill argues that the current Russian national mentality, self-identity, civil society, and state greatness emerged out of the Time of Troubles and victory over the Polish-Lithuanian invaders in 1612. Under Putin, that date became an official holiday of national unity, an equivalent of sorts to the U.S. Independence Day and a substitute for the Communist-era Revolution Day.

64. Hilarion, *Patriarkh Kirill*, pp. 389–97.

65. Hilarion, *Patriarkh Kirill*, pp. 392–93.

66. Andrei Okara, "Potselui Velikogo inkvizitora," *NG-Religii*, no. 12 (20 July 2011).

67. Marlene Laruelle, "The 'Russian World': Russia's Soft Power and Geopolitical Imagination," *Center on Global Interests*, 21 May 2015. Also see "Former KGB General Kalugin Calls US-Russia Spy Saga a Farce," *Radio Free Europe*, 17 July 2010.

68. Films, music, literature, art, theater, entertainment, Orthodox faith, and patriotism promoted by new and old media and traditional and public diplomacy caused security concerns in several strategic communities in the near and far abroad. Andis Kudors, "Russian World—Russia's Soft Power Approach to Compatriots Policy," *Russian Analytical Digest*, no. 81 (16 June 2010): 2–5; Daniel P. Payne, "Spiritual Security, the Russkiy Mir, and the Russian Orthodox Church," in *Traditional Religion and Political Power*, ed. Adam Hug (London: Foreign Policy Centre, 2015), pp. 65–71.

69. Nikolai Spasskii," Rossiiskii vek," *Indeks bezopasnosti* 16, no. 4 (95) (2010): 41.

70. At around that time, in addition to other activities, the ROC was actively constructing cultural centers worldwide, such as in Paris and Nice. Lidiia Orlova, "Tserkov' boretsia za russkii mir," *Nezavisimaia gazeta*, 2 April 2011.

71. Hill and Gaddy, *Mr. Putin*, p. 352.

72. For analytical pathologies of the intelligence officers, see Uri Bar-Joseph and Rose McDermott, *Intelligence Success and Failure: The Human Factor* (Oxford: Oxford University Press, 2017).

73. In their analysis, oil, nuclear capabilities, and Orthodox spirituality would enable Russia in the observable future to preserve its great power position and to counterbalance the United States.

74. Aleksandr Sytin, "Anatomiia provala: O mekhanisme Priniatiia vneshne-politicheskikh reshenii Kremlia," Bramaby.com (January 2015).

75. Hill and Gaddy, *Mr. Putin*, p. 273.

76. Fay Voshell, "Who Will Save Middle East Christians: Obama or Putin?," *American Thinker*, 6 October 2015.

77. Hill and Gaddy, *Mr. Putin*, p. 368.

78. Jardar Østbø, *The New Third Rome: Readings of a Russian Nationalist Myth* (Stuttgart: Ibidem Press, 2016), pp. 233 34. In November 2014, in Manege Hall, right next to the Kremlin, Patriarch Kirill and Putin opened a multimedia historical exhibition dealing with the history of monarchy and faith in Russia, organized by the ROC and the Ministry of Culture and curated by Archimandrite Tikhon. As part of the exhibition, a conference, titled "Moscow—the Third Rome," was held; it featured Dugin and Reshetnikov, among other participants. The setting of the event, according to Østbø, aimed to present the official version of Russian history and demonstrate that "the myth of the Third Rome has now entered the mainstream." Although Putin and Kirill avoided referring explicitly to this concept in their speeches, "the timing, location, organizers, and participants" of the conference demonstrate that the regime encourages "the mainstream Russian intellectual public" to refer to the Third Rome concept and the Russian World as the framework for interpreting the integration of Crimea. Østbø, *New Third Rome*, pp. 235–37.

79. Dmitri Trenin, "The Mythical Alliance: Russia's Syria Policy" (Moscow: Carnegie Moscow Center, 2013), p. 13.

80. Clare Morris, "Vladimir Putin Vows to Defend Christianity Worldwide," *Christian Post*, 12 February 2012. Middle Eastern religious leaders, such as the patriarch of Jerusalem, also have encouraged Putin in the same direction and praised his personal role in pacifying the region and protecting Orthodox interests and values. "Sostoialas' vstrecha Prezidenta Rossii s Blazhenneishim Patriarkhom Ierusalimskim Feofilom," *Patriarchia.ru*, 28 May 2013.

81. It argued that Washington had demolished the regional order and unleashed chaos, including the refugee problem, but was reluctant to commit boots on the ground to solve the problems it had created. In contrast, Moscow promoted its own image as regional troubleshooter. Dmitry (Dima) Adamsky, "Putin's Damascus Steal," *Foreign Affairs*, 16 September 2015. This stand generated certain support worldwide, especially among those concerned about the eradication of ancient Christian communities. As one commentator put it, "The beleaguered Christians in Syria and elsewhere in the Middle East doubtless see the very recent Russian bombing of ISIS headquarters as a gift from God, and Putin as their potential deliverer from martyrdom." Voshell, "Middle East Christians."

82. For example, the Soviet spread of the Communist ideology clearly was a metamorphosis of the Third Rome motif, which was resurrected when the Kremlin began restoring Russia's greatness.

83. Anna Geifman, "Putin's 'Sacred Mission' in Syria," *BESA Center*, Perspectives Paper no. 335, 27 March 2016.

84. "Russian Church Supports Military Operation in Syria," *Russia Beyond the Headlines*, 7 January 2016.

85. "Patriarch Kirill nazval voinu s terrorizmom sviaschennoi," *Zvezda TV*, 6 May 2016.

86. "Patriarch Kirill Praises Russia's Role in Saving Syria," *Sputnik*, 26 July 2016. By the fifth year of the Syrian civil war, the Russian Imperial Orthodox Palestine Society had an actively functioning special organization for protecting Christians in the Middle East and North Africa. "Khristiane na Blizhnem Vostoke: Est' li shans vizhit'?," *Russkii mir*, 14 March 2016.

87. "Nuzhno pomnit' slova Suvorova: 'Molis' Bogu, ot Nego—pobeda,'" *VVD*, 23 February 2016.

88. See, e.g., "RPTs budet uchastvovat' v vosstanovlenii razrushennykh khramov v Sirii," *RIA novosti*, 7 October 2017; "Bogdanov: Palestinskoe Pravoslavnoe Obschestvo postroit shkolu v Damaske," *RIA novosti*, 17 October 2017.

89. "We attach particular importance to our joint efforts, [. . .] including at the UN, [. . .] aimed at protecting Christians in the Middle East, and drawing attention of the international community to the crimes being perpetrated against them. We intend to continue fruitful cooperation in the interest of strengthening the authority of our country in world affairs, stabilization of the Middle East situation, and promoting inter-civilizational dialogue and the lofty ideals of peace, good, and justice." "Foreign Minister Sergey Lavrov's Greetings to the Participants in the Meeting Devoted to the 135th Anniversary of the Imperial Orthodox Palestinian Society," *MFA* (mid.ru), 2 June 2017.

90. "Russian Church Official Meets Pence," *Radio Free Europe*, 12 May 2017.

91. "RPTs budet uchastvovat' v vosstanovlenii razrushennykh khramov." By 2016, the state of Middle Eastern Christians and normalization in Ukraine became the main themes in all ROC international encounters. Both topics, with a clear pro-Kremlin connotation, loomed large during the patriarch-pope meeting in Cuba in February 2016. The joint communiqué following their encounter called for the eradication of terrorism in the Middle East and pacification of Ukraine—the tone and content favorable to Moscow's agendas.

92. See, e.g., on Medvedev's visits to holy sites: "Palomnichestvo Prezidenta RF Dmitriia Medvedeva v Sviato-Troitskii Serafimo-Diveevskii monastyr'," *Nizhegorodskaia eparkhiia RPTs*, 3 July 2011. On his displayed icon: "Dmitrii Medvedev vstretilsia s direktorom eksportnogo tsentra," *Novosti ORT*, 1 November 2016. On his summer residence: "Usad'ba Milovka," *Fond bor'by c korruptsiei* (fbk.info), 2016.

93. See, e.g., Ivan Krylov, "Sergei Lavrov postavil svechku v Alma-Ate," *Russkii mir*, 14 May 2011.

94. For example, when the first launch from the new Vostochny cosmodrome proved successful in 2016, Vostochny enabled Russia to launch from its own territory and not from the Kazakhstan-owned Baikonur cosmodrome. "Ivanov perekrestilsia pered zapuskom rakety-nositelia," *Zvezda TV*, 28 April 2016.

95. Konstantin Gaaze, "Dvor vmesto Politbiuro," *Carnegie.ru*, 25 August 2017.

96. Previously, it had been called the Jerusalem Gate because Moscow's metropolitan and the tsar passed through it during the processions of the cross at Easter, com-

memorating the biblical entrance of Jesus to Jerusalem. The tradition of passing through the gate without a hat and making the sign of the cross beneath the icon was preserved until the revolution. Romanov rulers en route to their coronation ceremonies, foreign diplomats on official visits, and regiments leaving Moscow for battle or returning passed through the gate. "Ikony na bashniakh Moskovskogo Kremlia," *Patriarchia.ru*, 4 November 2010. In 2007, Putin and Patriarch initiated the restoration of the icon over the entrance. At the opening ceremony in 2010, Medvedev emphasized the importance of this symbol for national identity and for the spiritual protection of Russia. "Vystuplenie na tseremonii otkrytiia nadvratnoi ikony na Spasskoi bashne Kremlia," *Kremlin.ru*, 28 August 2010.

97. The attendees included Deputy Prime Minister Dmitry Rogozin; Minister of Defense Serdiukov; director of ROSATOM, Sergei Kirienko; and the commander of the newly established service of the Russian military, the Airspace Forces. "Putin pribyl v Sarov s rabochim vizitom," *NTA-Privolzh'e*, 24 February 2012.

98. "Vizit v Izrail'," *Kremlin.ru*, 25 June 2012.

99. Interviews with senior Israeli officials, central Israel, summer 2017.

100. "Videomaterial." The patriarch did not address Putin's spouse with the same personal blessing with which he greeted Medvedev's spouse, probably because he was aware of her lesser religiosity and possibly already in the know about Putin's forthcoming divorce (June 2013).

101. "Vzoshel na goru: Komy palomnichestvo Putina pokazalos' intronizatsiei," *Lenta. ru*, 28 May 2016.

102. "Reviving today patriotic values, historical memory, traditional culture, we count on further solidifying our relations. [. . .] Important evidence of the growing ties between Russia and Athos are the relics, which arrive to our country for adoration, among them the Belt of the Mother of God from Vatopedi Monastery [2013] and the right hand of St. George the Victor from the Xenophontos Monastery [2015]. Hundreds of thousands of the Russian Orthodox have had an opportunity to touch them. I would like to thank you wholeheartedly for this." "Vystuplenie na vstreche s chlenami Sviaschennogo kinota," *Kremlin.ru*, 28 May 2016.

103. During the same visit, he opened an exhibition of Russian icons in Greece, featuring works of Andrei Rublev, one of the greatest medieval Russian painters of Orthodox icons. "Vystuplenie na vstreche s chlenami Sviaschennogo kinota."

104. Anastasiia Iakovleva, "Sviaschennik Aleksandr Terpugov: 'Glavnoe, chto my s Gospodom,'" *KZ*, 30 June 2011. For examples of the ROC's media campaign, see "V Minoborony poiavilsia glavnoi po vere," *VViMD*, 28 October 2010; "U voennykh sviaschennikov poiavilsia svetskii rukovoditel'," *VViMD*, 25 October 2010; "U voennogo dukhovenstva osobaia rol'," *VViMD*, 17 March 2010; "Religioznyi faktor—osnova motivatsii," *VViMD*, 1 June 2011; "Prezident Rossii Dmitrii Medvedev vysoko otsenivat vklad RPTs v delo vozrozhdeniia instituta voennogo dukhovenstva v RS," *VViMD*, 26 May 2010.

105. See, e.g., Aleksandr Shirokorad, "Sviaschenniki v voiskakh nauchiat smireniiu," *NVO*, 9 September 2011; A. I. Burkin, "Polkovye sviaschenniki Rossii: Dukhovnaia

priroda voinskogo sluzheniia," *VM*, April 2010, pp. 68–77; Mikhail Ivashko, "Institut voinskikh i flotskikh sviaschennosluzhitelei sovremennoi rossiiskoi armii," *Bezopasnost' Evrazii*, no. 1 (January–July 2013); D. V. Shut'ko, "Pedagogicheskie osnovy primeneniia potentsiala religii v vospitanii voennosluzhaschikh," *Vestnik Voennogo universiteta*, no. 3 (2010): 26–30; V. Iu. Balubashevich and A. I. Gurskii, "Vzaimodeistvie armii i religii: Sostoianie, problemy, perspektivy," *Vestnik Akademii voennykh nauk*, no. 1 (2009); Kh. M. Abdulin, "Chto mozhet bit' priskorbnee takogo bezvykhodnogo polozheniia voennogo sviaschennika," *ViZh*, January 2011, pp. 52–55.

106. See, e.g., Sergei Ivaneev, "Popu vmesto 'komissarov'?," *Ateism.ru*, 28 May 2010; Sergei Ivaneev, "Batiushka komandiru ne pomoshnik," *VPK*, 10 August 2011.

107. "The tradition of the church's participation in the life of the military is deeply rooted in the Motherland's history and is one of the powerful sources of patriotism. [. . .] Let me remind you of recent history—22 June 1941 [. . .]. Metropolitan Sergii appealed to the people to defend the Fatherland [. . .] before Stalin. [. . .] First, Stalin addressed the people as *male and female citizens*; only later, when he assessed the level of the threat, he switched to [a religious appeal] *brothers and sisters*. This was not an accident. [Therefore,] it is important to ensure a proper level of development of the institution of the military clergy." B. M. Lukichev, *Patriarkh Kirill i voennoe dukhovenstvo* (Moscow: FIV, 2016), pp. 84–85.

108. Lukichev, *Patriarkh Kirill*, pp. 60–63; Evgenii Mazurin, "Vvedenii voennogo dukhovenstva—pervyi rubezh vziat," *Tserkovnyi vestnik*, 18 February 2011; "Sostoialos' zasedanie 'voennoi' sektsii Rozhdestvenskikh Chtenii," *VViMD*, 25 January 2011; "Rol' voennykh sviaschennikov v dukhovnom prosviaschenii i nravstvennom vospitanii voennosluzhaschikh," *VVD*, 2 February 2012.

109. "Rezoliutsiia sektsii XIX Rozhdestvenskikh chtenii 'Tserkov' i armiia': Aktual'nye problemy formirovaniia korpusa shtatnykh voennykh sviaschennosluzhitelei," *Patriarchia.ru*, 27 January 2011.

110. For an example of this trend, see Anna Emke, "Otchet o rabote s veruiushimi voennosluzhaschimi na kosmodrome Plesetsk v 2013," *KhSAMM*, 10 January 2014.

111. "Teper' my vse znaem, chem byl zaniat Serdiukov," *Izvestiia*, 25 December 2012; Lukichev, *Patriarkh Kirill*, p. 63; "God na postu: Samye vazhnye resheniia Sergeia Shoigu v NO," *VVD*, 6 November 2013.

112. Lukichev, *Patriarkh Kirill*, pp. 63–65, 86–87.

113. "Sviateishii Patriarkh Kirill posetil Voennuiu akademiiu GS VS RF," *Patriarchia.ru*, 31 May 2011. Upon Shoigu's invitation, in December 2014, Kirill joined the first meeting of the MoD Board at the newly opened National Defense Management Center, where Putin outlined national security goals and priorities for the near- and long-term future. Lukichev, *Patriarkh Kirill*, p. 15.

114. Among 150 staffed positions, there were only two imams and one Buddhist monk; the rest were Orthodox priests. Lukichev, *Patriarkh Kirill*, pp. 101–2.

115. Many within the armed forces strongly disliked Serdiukov, considering him an irrelevant civilian, clueless in military affairs, and driven by the mentality of a furniture manufacturing manager—his actual professional background. Aleksandr Golts, *Military Reform and Militarism in Russia* (Uppsala: Uppsala University Press, 2017)

116. "Sostoialas' vstrecha Sviateishego Patriarkha Kirilla s ministrom oborony."

117. "Sostoialas' vstrecha Sviateishego Patriarkha Kirilla s ministrom oborony." Since his nomination, Shoigu has been intensively investing in military infrastructure, with a strong emphasis on the High North and the Arctic—regions highly prioritized by Putin. "V Minoborony sravnili masshtaby stroitel'stva s poslevoennym vremenem," *Lenta.ru*, 23 January 2017.

118. Since 2015, several shifts of priests, each of several months' duration, have already exchanged.

119. On Easter 2017, Patriarch Kirill blessed several thousand Easter breads and eggs at the Christ the Savior Cathedral, and they were delivered by Russian military-transport aviation to Syria to reach the Easter breakfast tables of the expeditionary forces and military advisers.

120. There, in addition to the pastoral care to the servicemen, they have been interacting with local Christians. For example, the priests joined the mine clearance force in Aleppo, which, among other sites, cleared the mines from the local church. Military priest Ioann Kovalev accompanied them and offered his interpretation of events to the locals and morally supported the unit. "Sapery zavershili v Aleppo razminirovanie drevnogo khristianskogo khrama," *Novosti ORT*, 24 April 2017.

121. The latter reported on the contributory role of the priests, together with officers under his command, to the morale-psychological state of the servicemen. Aleksandr Kolotialo, "Na perednem krae," *KZ*, 15 September 2016; "Na aviabaze Khmeimim v Sirii proshlo osviaschenie dostavlennykh iz Rossii," *mil.ru*, 1 May 2016; Aleksandr Pinchiuk, "K tainstvu Blagovescheniia," *KZ*, 21 April 2016; Vasilii Dandykin, "Frontovaia brigade v Khmeimime," *Voin Rossii*, 5 May 2016; "Boevoe kreschenie na aviabaze Khmeimim," *NG-Religii*, 20 January 2016; "Rossiiskim voennym v Sirii dostavili tri tysiachi kulichei," *Interfax*, 16 April 2017; "Kulichi dlia Sirii," *Khram Voskreseniia Slovuschego na Uspenskom vrazhke* (accessed 20 May 2017); Gennadii Miranovich, "I stal dlia nikh domom Khmeimim," *KZ*, 2 November 2015.

122. "Mitropolit Saratovskii Longin sovershil otpevanie pogibshego v Sirii letchika," *Patriarchia.ru*, 14 July 2016.

123. Olena Iarmoliuk, "Rossiiskie letchiki v Sirii na bombordirovki berut s soboi ikony," *Pressa Ukrainy*, 7 October 2015.

124. Ol'ga Kalshtyk, "Batiushki osobogo naznacheniia," *Suvorovskii natisk*, 7 June 2014.

125. "Na bortu MAK 'Makhachkala' Kaspiiskoi flotilii vpervye proveden prazdnichnyi moleben," *mil.ru*, 8 January 2016.

126. "Na Chernomorskom flote proidut torzhestva posviaschennye Rozhdestvu," *mil.ru*, 6 January 2016.

127. Reporting from an aircraft carrier, a cleric described ideal conditions for pastoral work, asked to be sent more cross pendants, due to high demand for baptism, but complained that sailors had been using coarse and vulgar language—a sin by Orthodox standards. "'Kak v raiu': Sviaschennik na borty 'Admirala Kuznetsov,'" *Newsru.com*, 6 November 2016.

128. "Sostoialas' vstrecha Sviateishego Patriarkha Kirilla s ministrom oborony."

129. Lukichev, *Patriarkh Kirill*, pp. 69–73.

130. "V VDV sviaschenniki podderzhivaiut molodykh desantnikov pered pervym pryzhkom," *Nezavisimaia gazeta*, 6 June 2011.

131. "Minoborony RF priravnialo voennykh sviaschennikov k zampolitam," *RIA novosti*, 5 July 2011.

132. Lukichev, *Patriarkh Kirill*, pp. 83–84. Priests also more frequently organized excursions and sightseeing trips to military-historical sites for the servicemen. "Kolomenskoe blagochestie: Ekskursia dlia voennykh sviazistov," *OVVSiPU*, 25 February 2011; "Kolomenskoe blagochinie: Ekskursia v muzei tekhniki," *OVVSiPU*, 13 March 2011.

133. Lukichev, *Patriarkh Kirill*, p. 85.

134. Nina Doronina, "Sluzhenie voennogo dukhovenstva," *Pravoslavnaia Kamchatka*, 10 February 2016.

135. Valerii Gerasimov, "Mir na graniakh voiny," *VPK*, 15 March 2017.

136. The strategic exercises have included Schit Soiuza-2011, Tsentr-2011, Kavkaz-2012, and Zapad-2013. Evgenii Murzin, "Institut voennogo dukhovenstva v Rossii: Promezhutochnye itogi," *VVD*, 19 September 2013; "Nakanune strategicheskogo ucheniia Tsentr-2011 v 201 voennoi baze proidet moleben i osviaschenie tekhniki," *RF MoD*, 1 August 2011; "Samoe pristal'noe vnimanie na uchenii 'Schit Soiuza-2011' budet udeleno moral'no-psikhologicheskoi podderzhke voennosluzhaschikh," *RF MoD*, 16 September 2011. During Tsentr-2011, three hundred servicemen were baptized. "300 voennosluzhaschikh uchastnikov strategicheskogo ucheniia Tsentr-2011 proshli obriad krescheniia," *RF MoD*, 23 September 2011.

137. "Na Chernomorskom flote osviatili pokhodnyi iconostas," *KZ*, 2 April 2014; Viktor Litovkin, "Batiushka Matros," *NVO*, 2 September 2011.

138. "Pomoshniki komandirov po rabote s veruiuschimi voennosluzhashimi poluchiat voennuiu formu s osoboi simvolikoi," *mil.ru*, 29 October 2014.

139. *Molitvoslov pravoslavnogo voina* (Moscow: Sintagma, 2011); Andrei Pliusnin, *Molitvoslov pravoslavnogo voina* (Moscow: Blagovest, 2011); Elena Eletskaia, *Molitvoslov pravoslavnogo voina* (Moscow: Feniks, 2012); Sviaschennik Aleksandr Shantaev, *Soldatskii molitvoslov* (Moscow: Neugasimaia lampada, 2013).

140. It contained, in addition to the main Orthodox prayers, "Prayers Before the Battle," "Prayers During Emergencies and Enemy Attacks," "Prayers About the Enemy," and an overview of the "Saint Protectors of the Motherland." L. P. Medvedeva, T. A. Levshenko, and E. V. Trostnikova, *Molitvoslov pravoslavnogo voina* (Moscow: Izdatel'stvo MP RPTs, 2015).

CHAPTER 9

1. "Arkhiepiskop Georgii pozdravil sotrudnikov RFIaTs-VNIIEF s 65 letnim iubileem atomnoi promyshlennosti," *Nizhegorodskaia eparkhiia RPTs*, 24 September 2010; "Vladuka Georgii pozdravliaet VNIIEF," *Pravoslavnyi Sarov*, 6 September 2011; "70 let unikal'nykh dostizhenii," *ROSATOM*, 2 August 2016. Annually, Patriarch Kirill has sent official congratulatory notes praising the VNIIEF's work and the faith-atoms nexus. "Svi-

ateishii Patriarkh Kirill pozdravil Rossiiskii federal'nyi iadernyi tsentr s 65 letiem obrazovaniia," *Patriarchia.ru*, 10 June 2011.

2. "Arkhiepiskop Georgii v Sarovskoi pustyne sovershil chin osviascheniia khrama v chest' prepodobnykh Antoniia i Feodosiia Kievo-Pecherskikh," *Nizhegorodskaia eparkhiia RPTs*, 6 September 2011.

3. "Zalozhena kapsula v osnovanii prestola tserkvi Zosimi i Savvatiia," *ProAtom*, 5 July 2010.

4. "Kirienko prinial uchastie v osviascheni khrama v Sarove," *ProAtom*, 28 May 2012.

5. "O festivale atomnykh gorodov 'Serafim Sarovskii,'" *Pravoslavnyi Sarov*, 27 April 2011; "Fotokonkurs 'Pravoslavnye sviatyni atomnykh gorodov,'" *Pravoslavnyi Sarov*, 18 May 2011; "V Dome Uchenykh obsudili proekt 'Serafim Sarovskii i atomnye goroda,'" *Sarovskie novosti* (sarov.net), 25 January 2011; "Dukhovnoe nasledie cherez kino," *Pravoslavnyi Sarov*, 3 November 2011.

6. The 320th anniversary of Sarov, the 302nd anniversary of the Sarov Monastery, and the 65th anniversary of the VNIIEF. "V Rossii vveden v pochtovoe obraschenie convert s izobrazheniem pamiatnika prepodobnomy Serafimu Sarovskomu," *Nizhegorodskaia eparkhiia RPTs*, 2 August 2011.

7. "Kakim budet Dukhovno-nauchnyi tsentr pri Sarovskom monastyre?," *Pravoslavnyi Sarov*, 17 December 2012.

8. "V Sarove obsudili voprosy sozdaniia nauchno-dukhovnogo tsentra," *Patriarchia. ru*, 1 July 2013. The local metropolitan and the scientific head of the VNIIEF have chaired all the center's assemblies.

9. "Deiatel'nost' Dukhovno-nauchnogo tsentra v Sarove dolzhna bit' mnogourovnevoi," *Pravoslavnyi Sarov*, 9 December 2013.

10. "Predsedatel' Sinodal'nogo informatsionnogo otdela prinial uchastie v rabote DNTs pri Sv. Uspenskoi Sarovskoi pustyni," *Patriarchia.ru*, 21 October 2014.

11. "Spiritual Security in the Sphere of Education," with senior academic figures participating, and "Spiritual and Physical Health of the Nation—the Necessary Condition of National Security," with the minister of health care and several deputies from other ministries participating. "Missiia Sarovskogo Dukhovno-nauchnogo tsentra—prorabotka tem obscherossiiskogo masshtab," *Pravoslavnyi Sarov*, 22 December 2014.

12. One of the leading research institutes in the Russian Academy of Sciences on the issues of applied mathematics, informatics, and informational security.

13. As the concluding summary put it, "Although Russia faces external threats, internal problems are more dangerous, because they hinder the state's capacity to adequately address the challenges of the time." "Dukhovnye osnovy otechestvennoi bezopasnosti," *Pravoslavnyi Sarov*, 1 March 2014. Also see "Rossiia—na perelome istorii," *Pravoslavnyi Sarov*, 15 February 2015. To participants who experienced the Soviet collapse, this was not an esoteric, but a historically sound, claim.

14. "Missiia Sarovskogo Dukhovno-nauchnogo tsentra—prorabotka."

15. "Kak nam obustroit' russkii dom?," *Pravoslavnyi Sarov*, 21 March 2015. Another seminar, "Spiritual Aspects of the National Economic Policy," explored the economic dimension of strategic competitions in the modern world. "Ekonomika—sfera manipuliatsii

soznaniem," "Dukhovnye problem ekonomiki," "Ne liudi dlia ekonomiki, a ekonomika dlia liudei," *Pravoslavnyi Sarov*, 29 September 2015.

16. In light of its being designated as a threat by the U.S. 2015 national security strategy.

17. "Mitropolit Georgii: 'Nam nuzhno tselepolaganie,'" *Pravoslavnyi Sarov*, 5 December 2015.

18. "Predstoiatel' Russkoi Tserkvi sovershil liturgiiu v Diveevskom monastyre i vozglavil khirotoniiu arkhimandrita Evgeniia," *Pravoslavie.ru*, 1 August 2016.

19. "Sviateishii Patriarkh Kirill osviatil zakladnoi kamen' v osnovanie Uspenskogo sobora Sarovskoi pustyni," *Patriarchia.ru*, 1 August 2016.

20. The icon with a golden star, incorporating a small piece of Seraphim's remains, depicted the saint in the center, the monastery-VNIIEF buildings in the background, and episodes of contemporary nuclear history: the 1903 canonization in the presence of the tsar, the Cheka shutdown of the monastery and expulsion of the monks, Patriarch Alexey receiving the remains and meeting with scientists at Arzamas-16, and the return of the relics to Diveevo. The hosts put the icon in the exhibition hall of the VNIIEF museum dedicated to the history of the saint's life. "Sviateishii Patriarkh Kirill osviatil zakladnoi kamen'"; "Ikona batiushki Serafima s kleimamy iz noveishei istorii," *Pravoslavnyi Sarov*, 2 August 2016.

21. "V Sarove sostoialas' vstrecha Sviateishego Patriarkha Kirilla s rossiiskimi uchenymi-iaderschikami," *Patriarchia.ru*, 1 August 2016.

22. According to Patriarch Kirill, cultivating the moral-religious component of scientific-technological progress—the ability to differentiate between good and evil—is a natural field for cooperation. "Slovo Sviateishiego Patriarkha Kirilla na vstreche s uchenymi v Sarove," *Patriarchia.ru*, 1 August 2016.

23. "Under the nuclear test ban, we employ new research methods and mathematical models to solve issues related to nuclear weapons' effectiveness and safety. In terms of the hardships, these missions are comparable to the first Soviet nuclear project. During such serious work with formidable weapons, we need high moral standards, and on this matter we much count on the ROC's support." The rector of Moscow State University continued this theme, arguing that religion and science complement each other and are necessary in a person's development and praising the opening of churches at his and other universities. "V Sarove sostoialas' vstrecha Sviateishego Patriarkha Kirilla."

24. "Sovremennoe gosudarstvo: Dukhovno-nravstvennye osnovy i pravo," *Pravoslavnyi Sarov*, 19 December 2016; "Sarovskii dukhovno-nauchnyi tsentr beretsia razrabotat' kontseptsiiu razvitiia Rossii na sto let," *Pravoslavnyi Sarov*, 5 February 2017.

25. Vladimir Moiseev, "Sviaschenno-iadernyi soiuz," *Russkii Reporter*, 18 October 2012.

26. "O khrame," and "Povsednevanaia rabota khrama," *Khram pri NIIaU MIFI*. In the same year, blessed by Patriarch Kirill and ROSATOM senior officials, MIFI signed a cooperation agreement with the Synodal Department of Social Service, according to which the university would provide preparatory courses and reserve quotas for gifted children from low-income families, who are taken care of by the ROC eparchies all over

Russia. "Podpisanno soglashenie o sotrudnichistve mezhdy Sinodal'nym otdelom po sotsial'nomu sluzheniiu i Natsional'nym issledovatel'skim iadernym universitetom MIFI," *Patriarchia.ru*, 2 May 2012.

27. Elena Komleva, "Ot pravoslaviia k fenomenu iadernoi energii," *Pravo i bezopasnost'*, nos. 1–2 (44) (2013): 48–53.

28. For the faculty's critical debates, see "Kafedra teologii," *Entsiklopedia MIFI* (accessed 18 February 2017). For the scientific conferences, seminars, and roundtables of the faculty, see "Nauchnaia deiatel'nost'," *Kafedra teologii NIIaU MIFI* (theology.mephi.ru) (accessed 18 February 2017). The initial attitude of students and faculty was mixed. However, as it became obvious that the initiative belonged to the rector, those with a negative attitude gradually gravitated toward a neutral-indifferent position. Some thought this reflected a genuine quest on the part of the devout rector, while others saw it as a purely instrumental move, ensuring the support of an influential political actor, against the backdrop of the overall religiosity of the Kremlin and the pro-religious position of the ROSATOM minister. Moiseev, "Sviaschenno-iadernyi soiuz"; "Krest vozle glavnogo korpusa," *Entsiklopedia MIFI*.

29. Dmitry Anokhin, "Fizika, lirika, i bogoslovie," *ZhMP*, 5 November 2013. The fact that the priest of the university's house church had graduated from MIFI with a doctorate in physics enabled him to skillfully navigate the catechization efforts. He positioned faculty activities as liberal arts studies that aimed to provide appropriate education to the future Russian nuclear elite, and he compared it to technological universities worldwide hosting schools of theology. The courses indeed covered subjects beyond Orthodox culture, and visiting professors lectured on history of religion and science. The core faculty has promoted and conducted research on the religious history of Soviet nuclear scientists. Dmitry Anokhin, "Zachem fiziku teologia," *ZhMP*, 19 October 2016.

30. "Troinoi prazdnik strategicheskikh pastyrei," *VVD*, 29 April 2013.

31. For example, in 2017, on the Baptism of Jesus feast day, at the Vlasikha base, several hundred servicemen participated in the procession of the cross and then dove inside Iordan—the icy baptismal font named after the Jordan River, where St. John had baptized Jesus. "V Moskovskoi oblasti raketchiki RVSN sovershili Krestnyi khod i omovenie v ledianoi vode," *RF MoD*, 19 January 2017.

32. See, e.g., "Paskhal'noe torzhestvo v v/ch no.83320 gorodskogo okruga Domodedovo," *OVVSiPU*, 17 June 2011.

33. "Troinoi prazdnik strategicheskikh pastyrei."

34. For example, the newly opened Kapustin Ian garrison church was located within the patriotic club building, which was consecrated and decorated with religious paraphernalia and had a cross placed on its dome. It was turned into a church but preserved its function as the patriotic club. Its entrance features portraits of Marshal Georgy Zhukov, Red Square, and the Kremlin. Referring to the church, the local clergy and military commentators call it the "spiritual-patriotic center" of the base. "Den' rozhdeniia RVSN," *SOMP VVSiPO*, 20 January 2016.

35. In 2007 the MoD decided to exchange the old Soviet unit banners for the new ones. The process started in the RVSN around 2010 and lasted for about six years. Priests

providing pastoral care to the RVSN consecrated the banners during official ceremonies. "Sostoialos' osviaschenie boevogo znameni chasti RVSN," *VViMD*, 13 December 2010. Dmitrii Andreev, "Boevye znamena—raketchikam," *KZ*, 13 September 2011; "Raketnoi divizii RVSN vrucheno boevoe znamia novogo obraztsa," *RF MoD*, 12 September 2011; "Iasenskomu raketnomu soedineniiu RVSN vruchili boevoe znamia," *RF MoD*, 9 September 2011. Since then, during parades within the garrisons, three types of banners are often carried in front of the marching RVSN columns: the Russian Federation flag, the RVSN unit flag, and a religious banner. "Den' rozhdeniia RVSN."

36. "Predsedatel' Synodal'nogo otdela po vzaimodeistviiu s VS pozdravil vypusknikov Voennoi akademii RVSN," *Patriarchia.ru*, 27 June 2016.

37. "Nuzhno pomnit' slova Suvorova: 'Molis' Bogu, ot Nego—pobeda,'" *VVD*, 23 February 2016.

38. "Sotrudnichestvo RVSN and RPTs prodolzhaet razvivatsia," *RF MoD*, 17 February 2011; "V dvukh raketnykh soedineniiakh RVSN na dolzhnosti pomoshnikov komandirov po rabote s veruiuschimi naznacheny voennye professionaly," *RF MoD*, 15 November 2011; "V Voinskikh chastiakh RVSN rabotaiut predstavitel voennogo synodal'nogo otdela RPTs," *RF MoD*, 20 July 2011.

39. "V dvukh raketnykh soedineniiakh RVSN."

40. One of them for about a decade has been a confessor of the Tagil missile division, where his son was serving at the rank of captain. "V dvukh raketnykh soedineniiakh RVSN."

41. "V Novosibirskom raketnom soedinenii naznachen pomoshnik komandira po rabote s veruiuschimi," *RF MoD*, 12 April 2012.

42. B. M. Lukichev, *Patriarkh Kirill i voennoe dukhovenstvo* (Moscow: FIV, 2016), p. 66. The FOC students have been regular participants in the annual Christmas readings and other catechization events organized by the ROC and, as such, were well trained to conduct similar activities within the troops. "Fakul'tet pravoslavnoi kul'tury Voennoi akademii RVSN otmechaet svoe 15-letie," *RF MoD*, 3 October 2011.

43. "Pomosch' batiushki neobkhodima," *VVD*, 31 July 2012.

44. For one of the earliest examples of the trend, see "Ekaterinburgskii Arkhipastyr' sobiraetsia v gosti k voinam RVSN," *Novyi den'* (urfo.orf), 20 May 2002. In a more recent example, in 2014 an RVSN priest went to conduct a regular pastoral conversation with officers and cadets of the Serpukhov RVSN Academy and, for the first time, consecrated an operational training version of the Topol ICBM; he was even allowed "to drive this formidable missile." "V Serpukhovskom filiale Voennoi akademii RVSN osviatili uchebnye puskovye ustanovki 'Topol','" *RF MoD*, 19 February 2014.

45. For example, in December 2012, following an address to the combat crew and consecration of the RS-20 Voevoda ICBM, the cleric joined the servicemen in the command post and "blessed the exercise, asking for God's help." The warhead hit the designated targets in Kamchatka, at the Kura ballistic missiles testing range, where the garrison church in the Kliuchi base had been functioning. "Pravoslavnyi sviaschennik prinial uchastie v puske mezhkontinetal'noi ballisticheskoi rakety," *SOMP VVSiPO* (pobeda.ru) 26 December 2006; "Osviaschenie rakety voennymi sviaschennikami," *Orenburgskaia i*

Buzulukskaia eparkhii, 17 August 2011. By then, priests were permanently present at the main RVSN testing ranges—Plesetsk and Kapustin Iar. Anastasiia Iakovleva, "Dukhovno-iadernnye sily Rossii," *VViMD*, 17 December 2010. Putin personally allocated funds for the garrison church construction within the latter's polygon. The local governor matched the contribution with another half million rubles. Lukichev, *Patriarkh Kirill*, p. 199.

46. "Voennyi sviaschennik Dal'nekonstantinovskogo garnizona osviatil kazarmu," *VViMD*, 6 May 2010.

47. It also funded Orthodox literature departments in the garrison libraries. "Rukovoditel' eparkhial'nogo otdela po vzaimodeisitviiu s VS prot. Viktor Poliakov posetil Dal'nekonstantinovskii garnizon RVSN," *Nizhegorodskaia mitropoliia*, 16 March 2012.

48. "V RVSN poiavitsia pervyi mobilnyi khram," *RF MoD*, 18 June 2012.

49. "Voiny ot Boga," *VViMD*, 20 September 2011. A field church, mobile or air-dropped, includes a tent and a life-sustaining module decorated with icons and a dome with the cross on the roof. It is parachuted from the same platform that carries the VDV armored vehicles and heavy equipment. "Wind and a Prayer: Army's 'Flying Priests' to Win War Souls," *RT*, 8 March 2012.

50. "Polevye ucheniia Irkutskoi divizii RVSN," *Irkutskaia eparkhiia*, 14 October 2016.

51. "Upravlenie vospitatel'noi raboty RVSN," in *Slovari, MoD*, http://encyclopedia.mil.ru/encyclopedia/dictionary/details_rvsn.htm?id=14036@morfDictionary (accessed 7 July 2016).

52. "Voennyi sovet: Andrei Filatov," *Ekho Moskvy*, 11 May 2013.

53. "Upravlenie vospitatel'noi raboty RVSN."

54. "Upravlenie vospitatel'noi raboty RVSN." The directorate is also responsible for "monitoring of the social atmosphere among the troops and in military-social work." This includes preserving the social rights of the servicemen and members of their families, as well as maintaining the servicemen's aesthetic education, and arranging cultural and entertainment activities, vacations, health care, and welfare.

55. "Upravlenie vospitatel'noi raboty RVSN." The three departments: Moral-Psychological Maintenance, Education, and Culture; Military Discipline and Military-Social Work; and Informational Maintenance. In 2009 an organizational reform of the directorate significantly downsized its orbit and led to the hiring of civilian psychologists and sociologists. "Voennyi sovet: Andrei Filatov."

56. "Voennyi sovet: Andrei Filatov."

57. One of the previous directorate commanders, Lieutenant General Moroz, was one of the leading forces in integrating the ROC into the RVSN and then into the 12th GUMO.

58. "Pomosch' batiushki neobkhodima"; "V RVSN poiavitsia pervyi mobilnyi khram."

59. "Sbor rukovodiaschego sostava Vladimirskogo raketnogo obedineniia," *VVD*, 21 January 2013.

60. Standard topics covered included "legal order maintenance, strengthening military discipline, prevention of suicidal events in the troops, social adaptation of demobilized

servicemen and members of their families." "V RVSN nachalsia sbor rukovodiaschego sostava organov po rabote s lichnim sostavom," *RF MoD*, 19 September 2011.

61. "V RVSN nachalsia sbor rukovodiaschego sostava organov po rabote s lichnim sostavom"; "Sotrudnichestvo RVSN and RPTs prodolzhaet razvivatsia."

62. The priest of the RVSN garrison in Vlasikha and the head of the Synodal Department's RVSN section conducted a workshop for the participants on "cooperation of the commanders' assistants for work with the faithful and division commanders for the sake of the spiritual-morale education of servicemen and their families." "V RVSN prokhodit uchebno-metodicheskii sbor s rukovodiaschim sostavom organov po rabote s lichnym sostavom," *RF MoD*, 11 September 2013; "Sbory ofitserov po rabote s lichnym sostavom i sviaschennosluzhitelei RVSN proshla v Altaiskom krae," *VViMD*, 17 September 2013.

63. "Sovmestnye sbory ofitserov po rabote s lichnym sostavom i sviaschennosluzhitelei RVSN," *Irkutskaia eparkhiia*, 23 September 2013.

64. On the final day of the gathering, the supplication service and liturgy took place at the main church of the RVSN in Vlasikha. "V RVSN prokhodit uchebno-metodicheskii sbor s rukovodiaschim sostavom organov po rabote s lichnym sostavom," *RF MoD*, 20 October 2015; "Sbor rukovodiaschego sostava RVSN i voennykh sviaschennikov," *Sobor RVSN*, November 2015.

65. "V RVSN nazvany luchshie spetsialisty psikhologicheskoi raboty," *RF MoD*, 24 March 2016.

66. "V Irkutskoi oblasti proshli sbory DA," *VViMD*, 29 May 2011.

67. "Voennoe dukhovenstvo DA," *VViMD*, 16 December 2011.

68. Anastasiia Iakovleva, "Novye gorizonty DA," *KZ*, 3 June 2011.

69. "Pervyi iubilei: Voennye sviaschenniki o sluzhbe i sluzhenii," *VVD*, 21 July 2014.

70. See, e.g., on liturgies: Vladimir Malyschev, "Sorabotnichestvo vo imia zhizni," *KZ*, 25 February 2005; on icons in cockpits: Marina Vasil'eva, "Ot Soltsov do Tambova," *KZ*, 27 April 2007; on the increase of both in garrisons: Iakovleva, "Novye gorizonty DA."

71. Ol'ga Kalshtyk, "Batiushki osobogo naznacheniia," *Suvorovskii natisk*, 7 June 2014.

72. "V Riazane osviaschennye strategicheskie samolety," *VVD*, 24 February 2014.

73. "Sovershenno osviaschenie voinskogo znameni Engel'sskoi aviabazy," *VVD*, 15 January 2012.

74. "Pervyi iubilei: Voennye sviaschenniki o sluzhbe."

75. In 2015 Engels Air Base was at the center of the controversy over the icon of Stalin. Aleksandr Prokhanov, an ultraconservative writer and public figure, brought the icon to the base during the visit of the Izborsky Club delegation. In parallel, the local garrison priest arrived to bless the crew before a regular operational mission. Both events coincided. Eventually, against the backdrop of a Tu-95MS that was about to take off for a combat mission, the priest sprinkled holy water on the crew and Stalin's icon. Following a wave of public opposition, the ROC officially criticized the cleric who used the noncanonic icon for such an important mission. "PRTs obvinila predsedatelia Izborskogo kluba Aleksandra Prokhanova v provokatsii," *Pskovskaia lenta novostei*, 17 June 2015.

76. Anastasiia Iakovleva, "Protoierei Konstantin Tatarintsev: 'Vo vsekh garnizonakh DA provoditsia reguliarnaia rabota voennykh sviaschennosluzhitelei,'" *RPTs—Moskovskii patriarkhat*, 28 June 2016.

77. Iakovleva, "Novye gorizonty DA"; Marina Vasil'eva, "Granitsa pod dukhovnoi zaschitoi," *KZ*, 3 July 2010; Editorial, "Krepnuschee sodruzhestvo," *KZ*, 29 December 2009; "Okhraniaia rubezhu otechestva," *VViMD*, 7 July 2010.

78. "Voennoe dukhovenstvo DA."

79. "Pervyi iubilei: Voennye sviaschenniki o sluzhbe."

80. During Easter week of 2011, the commander of the LRA presented to Tikhon an icon with the relics of St. Iliia Muromets, the LRA patron saint. "Obraz s moschami nebesnogo pokrovitelia DA peredali Sretenskomu monastyriu," *VViMD*, 3 May 2011.

81. For the admirals' participation in the services, see "V Sevastopole proshol moleben v pamiat sviatogo pravednogo voina Fedora Ushakova," *RF MoD*, 5 August 2011; "Chernomortsy pomniat svoego admirala," *KZ*, 26 August 2011. The Navy commander in chief at the time, Admiral Vladimir Vysotsky, kept a big icon of St. Fedor Ushakov on the wall of his office. "Glavkoma VMF uvolili iz-za otkaza perevesti shtab v Peterburg," *Lenta.ru*, 12 May 2012.

82. Patriarch Kirill presented the church with an icon of Ioann Kronshtadtsky and an altar Bible decorated with jewels. "Piatnadtsataia godovschina osviascheniia garnizonnogo khrama," *Pravoslavnaia Kamchatka*, 15 December 2013; "Predstoiatel' Russkoi Tserkvi vstretilsia s moriakami-podvodnikami Tikhookeanskogo flota," *Pravoslavie.ru*, 19 September 2010; "Pervosviatitel'skii vizit na Dal'nii Vostok: Poseschenie voennoi bazy 16-i eskadry podvodnykh lodok Tikhookeanskogo flota VMF Rossii," *Patriarchia.ru*, 19 September 2010.

83. "Predstoiatel' Russkoi Tserkvi vstretilsia s moriakami-podvodnikami." Upon completion of the ceremony, about three hundred nuclear submariners marched with their flags in several formations and saluted Patriarch Kirill and the commanders as they passed the tribune. "Pervosviatitel'skii vizit na Dal'nii Vostok."

84. "Slovo Sviateishego Patriarkha Kirilla na vstreche s moriakami-podvodnikami Tikhookeanskogo flota RF," *Patriarkchia.ru*, 19 September 2010.

85. "Slovo Sviateishego Patriarkha Kirilla na vstreche s moriakami-podvodnikami."

86. The churches are open to the shipyards' workers and to the submarines' crews. "Atomnyi podvodnyi kreiser 'Vladimir Monomakh' osviatili v Severodvinske," *Arkhangel'skaia eparkhiia*, 3 January 2013; "Domovyi khram vo imia sviatogo kniazia Vladimira otkrylsia v soedinenii moriakov-podvodnikov," *VViMD*, 27 August 2015; "K-550 'Aleksandr Nevsky': Istoricheskaia spravka," *Russkii podplav* (accessed 9 January 2017); "Na severodvinskom sudoremontnom zavode 'Zvezdochka' budet postroen khram sviatogo Feodora Ushakova," *VViMD*, 7 May 2011; "Khram-chasovnia Fedora Ushakova," *Biblioteka Krugozor* (iagry.ru) (accessed 4 January 2017).

87. "Na Kamchatke planiruetsia vozvesti pravoslavnyi khram dlia moriakov-podvodnikov," *RF MoD*, 11 September 2012; "Chem sil'nee ispytaniia, tem krepche druzhba," *Pravoslavnaia Kamchatka*, 21 November 2011.

88. "Kto v more ne khodil, tot Bogu ne molilsia," *Pravoslavnaia Kamchatka*, 21 June 2011.

89. Iulia Liatskaia, "Khram postroim—tochki vozvrata ne suschestvuet," *Pravoslavnaia Kamchatka*, 18 April 2012. "Piatnadtsataia godovschina osviascheniia."

90. For example, in 2011 monks from the Vatopedi Monastery on Mount Athos brought their most important relic to Russia—the Belt of the Virgin Mary. During a monthlong stay in Russia, it was taken to fourteen cities across the country and everywhere attracted lines of people several kilometers long seeking to venerate it. All over Russia about 3.1 million pilgrims came to venerate the relic, about 1 million in Moscow alone. "Okolo milliona chelovek poklonilos' Poiasu Presviatoi Bogoroditsy v Moskve," *Edinnaia Rossiia* (er.ru), 28 November 2011. Also see Sergei Kulichkin, "My—glavnyi argument Rossii," *Pravoslavnaia Kamchatka*, 9 January 2011.

91. "Podvodniki proshli krestnym khodom po Severodvinsku," *VViMD*, 23 October 2012.

92. On the first day, hundreds of closed city residents venerated the relic located within the garrison church and consecrated their home icons with it. The garrison priest drove with the icon around residential areas and military installations. Reciting prayers, he stopped to bless each district of the city, the barracks, the staffs, the warehouses of armaments and spare parts, and the piers with the anchored submarines. Eventually, he put this icon, which was several meters high, on the upper deck of an icebreaker and took it around Krasheninnikov base. Passing along the piers, he blessed the submarines and the crews. "Chudotvornaia v Rybachem: Den' pervyi," and "Chudotvornaia v Rybachem: Den' vtoroi," *Pod Andreevskim flagom*, 22–23 January 2010.

93. The FSB helicopter with the icon and priests aboard conducted an aerial procession of the cross, flying over the peninsula's bases, blessing the submarines, the crews, and members of their families. Then the icon arrived at the nuclear submarine base. The squadron commander and the entire garrison, in parade uniform, but with hats off, welcomed the icon in front of the Main Staff. Following the service, the metropolitan and the squadron commander explained the significance of the icon for the Russian warriors and for the submariners' service, and then the entire squadron marched, saluting the icon, while the metropolitan sprinkled holy water on them. Then a long line of nuclear submariners began venerating to the icon and received from the metropolitan a blessed miniature replica of it. To enable the crews on duty to be blessed by the icon, a small military ship took it around the bay so that all the crews could see it as they stood on the upper decks of their vessels. "Moriaki-podvodniki vstrechaiut ikonu prepodobnogo Sergiia Radonezhskogo," *Pravoslavnaia Kamchatka*, 11 September 2014.

94. To bless the submarines deployed at the base, the priests conducted a naval procession of the cross in the bay, blessing all the squadron submarines moored along the piers. "Tikhookeanskii flot: Po bukhte Krasheninnikova sovershen krestnyi khod," *Pravoslavie.ru*, 18 June 2015.

95. The squadron commander said:

St. Prince Vladimir baptized Holy Rus in 988 and united all the Slavic peoples under one faith. During his reign statehood was strengthened, state-building was actively pursued, the spiritual foundations of the state were created and the whole state in which we live and which we serve. Special attention Prince Vladimir paid to his warriors, to strengthen their prowess and combat abilities, and he highly respected them. [. . . .] Let me thank again the representatives of our eparchy for the opportunity given to us—to venerate the relics of the saint. [. . .] On behalf of the nuclear submarine forces' command and all the submariners, let me express deep gratitude that despite your busy schedule the representatives of the ROC have paid such attention to the underwater forces.

The metropolitan responded:

Dear sailors and submariners, God-loving warriors of the Christ! [. . .] The first place the relics are arriving at in Kamchatka, for prayer and blessings, is of course Viliuchinsk [the nuclear submarine base]—a forward post of eastern Russia and the power of our state. But we should remember that the power of our state was not always only in the sharp sword and in the modern weapons, but also in the power of the spirit. Celebrating the great Prince St. Vladimir, equal of the apostles, we are celebrating the whole history of Russia. Specifically, Prince Vladimir not only laid the foundation of the state, not only established the great military force, but also gave the historical vector of development of Russian statehood, choosing Orthodoxy as the state religion and backbone for many centuries. [. . .] Today each of you will touch the relics of the saint, [. . .] then you will become undefeatable, and through you Russia will be undefeatable.

"Sviatye moschi sv. Ravnoap.kn. Vladimira na Kamchatskoi zemle," *Pravoslavnaia Kamchatka*, 26 September 2015.

96. "Voennosluzhaschie podvodnykh sil TOF poklonilis' moschiam sv. prav. voina Feodora Ushakova," *Pravoslavnaia Kamchatka*, 6 August 2016.

97. For example, in 2010, during his visit to the Viliuchinsk nuclear submarine base, Patriarch Kirill presented the crews with small icons of St. Andrei the First Called. Explaining the icon's meaning, Patriarch Kirill said: "Behind the face of Andrei the Apostle we see the cross on which he was crucified. Not accidently the Andreevsky cross became the symbol of the Russian Navy. It symbolizes sacrifice and readiness to defend the Fatherland until death. Under this cross our fleet conducted great and glorious deeds. Let this icon refer each of you to the Andreevsky banner and to the notion that it promotes." "Predstoiatel' Russkoi Tserkvi vstretilsia s moriakami-podvodnikami."

98. "Episkop Arkhangel'skii i Kholmogorskii Tikhon sovershil oschiaschenie atomnoi podvodnoi lodki 'Severodvinsk,'" *VVIMD*, 25 June 2010; "Spusk na vody APL 'Severodvinsk,'" *Smotr program, NTV*.

99. "V Severodvinske osviatili raketonosets Ekaterinburg," *Patriarchia.ru*, 20 December 2014.

100. "Mitropolit Daniil blagoslovil zakladku APL Arkhangel'sk," *Arkhangel'skaia eparkhiia*, 20 March 2015.

101. For the new nominees, see "Dolzhnost' pomoshnika komandira po rabote s veruiuschimi poiavilas' v TOF," *RIA novosti*, 7 July 2011. For the former submariners, see "Chem sil'nee ispytaniia, tem krepche druzhba."

102. "Den' moriaka-podvodnika," *Pravoslavnaia Kamchatka*, 24 March 2015.

103. Liudmila Selivanova, "V more za Slovom Bozhiim," *VViMD*, 20 September 2013; Mikhail Bokov, "MIFI, komandovanie podlodkoi, kreschenie na glubine sta metrov," *Pravmir.ru*, 19 March 2014.

104. Born in the closed city of Chelyabinsk-70 and trained initially as a nuclear physicist, he left his studies for a military career and retired as 1st rank captain after serving for two decades on nuclear submarines of the NF. He became religious while still serving, and in parallel with his service at the Navy Main Staff in Moscow, he attended classes at St. Tikhon Orthodox University. In 1998 he retired, worked for a while in the naval sector of the Synodal Department, and then became a monk in the Sanaksarsk Monastery, which hosts the tomb of the admiral and patron saint of the Navy, St. Fedor Ushakov. Upon introduction of the institution of military clergy, a counter-admiral from the NF and a former colleague, during a pilgrimage to the monastery, asked Father Veniamin to consider continuing as a monk in service at the nuclear submarine base as an assistant to the commander of the repair and construction brigade. Bokov, "MIFI, komandovanie podlodkoi, kreschenie"; Selivanova, "V more za Slovom Bozhiim"; "U voennykh moriakov budet dykhovnyi nastavnik," *VViMD*, 11 May 2012.

105. For this reason, most of the tsarist chaplains on Navy ships were monks. Bokov, "MIFI, komandovanie podlodkoi, kreschenie."

106. "Episkop Iakov sovershil pervyi monasheskii postrig," *Arkhangel'skaia eparkhiia*, 19 July 2012.

107. Nina Doronina, "Vozrozhdenie voennogo dukhovenstva," *Pravoslavnaia Kamchatka*, 7 March 2012.

108. Nina Doronina, "Sluzhenie voennogo dukhovenstva," *Pravoslavnaia Kamchatka*, 10 February 2016.

109. In 2015 Artemy became the metropolitan of Argentina and South America.

110. "Den' moriaka-podvodnika" (2015).

111. "Sviaschenniko pozdravili kollektiv morskogo poligona s iubileem," *VViMD*, 8 November 2014. In 2013 the nuclear submarine *St. Alexander Nevsky*, armed with torpedoes, cruise missiles, and sixteen Bulava-type ICBMs, entered the state tests—the final check under operational conditions. During the entire testing period, Father Veniamin was among the crew and conducted supplication services daily. To him, spiritual support of the servicemen is especially important under real operational conditions when the submarine tests "all regimes of its functioning, including under extreme conditions: at maximum power and full speed." "Ieromonakh Veniamin (Kovtun): 'Vykhod v more— eto extrem,'" *VViMD*, 17 September 2013.

112. Bokov, "MIFI, komandovanie podlodkoi, kreschenie"; "Na Kamchatke atomnoi podlodke podarili sobstvennyu khram," *Pravoslavie.ru*, 10 January 2012.

113. Following the submarine commander's salute and brief oral report on the combat mission's accomplishment to the commander of the squadron, clerics have blessed the crew with icons and holy water. "Na Kamchatke atomnoi podlodke podarili sobstvennyu khram"; "Torzhestvennaia vstrecha," *Pravoslavnaia Kamchatka*, 24 December 2012; "Glavnoe, chto boevaia zadachia vypolnena," *Pravoslavnaia Kamchatka*, 29 December 2011.

114. Bokov, "MIFI, komandovanie podlodkoi, kreschenie."

115. Selivanova, "V more za Slovom Bozhiim." By 2014, according to the surveys that the monk Veniamin conducted among his submarine flock, the percentage of practicing Orthodox was below 10 percent. "About 87% position themselves as Orthodox and have been baptized. However, the role of the church in their regular life ashore is not high," and "their churching is insufficient." "Thus, not only pastoral care, but missionary work and catechization are the primary tasks of the military priesthood." Bokov, "MIFI, komandovanie podlodkoi, kreschenie."

116. During nuclear submarine raids, he also usually takes aboard with him icons of Jesus and of the Mother of God; always an icon of St. Feodor Ushakov from the Sanaksarsk Monastery, where the remains of the admiral are kept; and relics of St. Zosima and Savvatii Solovetsky. Bokov, "MIFI, komandovanie podlodkoi, kreschenie."

117. Bokov, "MIFI, komandovanie podlodkoi, kreschenie."

118. "Fond OMORF peredal pokhodnyi khram dlia atomnogo kreisera 'Petr Velikii,'" *Pravoslavie.ru*, 27 April 2006.

119. "Flagman Baltiiskogo flota esminetz 'Nastoichevyi' obrel pravoslavnyi khram," *Russkaia narodnaia liniia*, 20 February 2015.

120. Sergei Gurov, "Vitse Admiral Brazhnik peredal pokhodnyi khram ekipazhu APL 'Kazan',"' *Iantarnyi ostrov*, 5 April 2017; "V Severodvinske osviatili pokhodnui khram dlia podvodnogo kresiera 'Vladimir Monomakh,'" *Tserkovnyi vestnik*, 26 November 2013; "Na Kamchatke atomnoi podlodke podarili sobstvennyu khram"; "Pokhodnyi khram poiavilsia na podvodnoi lodke 'Cheliabinsk,'" *Pravoslavnaia Kamchatka*, 10 January 2012.

121. "Na podlodke 'Aleksandr Nevsky' poiavitsia pravoslavnyi khram," *Sedmitza.ru*, 8 December 2011; "Pokhodnyi khram osviatili dlia podvodnoi lodki 'Vladimir Monomakh,'" *Arkhangel'skaia eparkhiia*, 26 November 2013; "Na Kamchatke planiruetsia vozvesti pravoslavnyi khram."

122. An extract from the address to the crew of the nuclear submarine *Vladimir Monomakh* in 2014 is indicative. "Establishing a temple aboard the cruiser, we testify that a submariner's service is linked to the readiness to sacrifice life for your brothers, and has the highest moral dimension. In the military system of values, faith in God has always occupied a central space. Although the sailors today are only starting to learn the faith of the fathers, this crew already has an opportunity to enjoy God's grace, which strengthens spiritual unity, so necessary for successful accomplishment of the combat tasks." "Atomnyi podvodnyi kreiser 'Vladimir Monomakh.'"

123. "Pokhodnyi khram poiavilsia na borty atomokhoda 'Georgii Pobedonosets,'" *Rossiiskoe atomnoe soobschestvo*, 16 June 2011; "U podvodnikov poiavilsia pokhodnyi khram," *VViMD*, 16 June 2011; "Fotoreportazh: 'Omofor' privez podarki," *Pravoslavnaia Kamchatka*, 15 June 2011; "Atomnyi podvodnyi kreiser 'Vladimir Monomakh'"; "V Severodvinske osviatili pokhodnui khram."

124. "Predstoiatel' Russkoi Tserkvi vstretilsia s moriakami-podvodnikami"; "Slovo Sviateishego Patriarkha Kirilla na vstreche s moriakami-podvodnikami."

125. Selivanova, "V more za Slovom Bozhiim."

126. "V Severodvinske osviatili raketonosets Ekaterinburg."

127. "Den' moriaka-podvodnika," *Pravoslavnaia Kamchatka*, 19 March 2014.

128. "Den' moriaka-podvodnika" (2015).

129. "Den' moriaka-podvodnika" (2015).

130. The addresses of the local metropolitan to the nuclear submariners in 2015 and 2016 exemplify this role: "I think that in the nuclear triad our submarine forces occupy the leading place. As long as these forces will be in combat state, and on combat duty, and there are people who command them, Russia will make such political decisions and build such internal life, which we have been preserving for centuries." "Den' moriaka-podvodnika" (2015); "Your service, in terms of its responsibility, difficulty, and danger is not less, and [is] even higher[,] than in any other corps. On an autonomous raid deep in the ocean, there is a bigger demand to lean on professionalism, [on] loyalty to the oath of allegiance, on the crew's coherence, and of course on the fortitude of spirit." "Den' moriaka-podvodnika," *Pravoslavnaia Kamchatka*, 20 March 2016.

131. "V Tveri podveli itogi vzaimodeistviia Tserkvi i armii," *Pobeda.ru*, 7 October 2011.

132. Although 80 percent of the conscripts identified themselves as Orthodox and had been baptized, according to the SF priests they did not know much about religion, services, and rituals and had only a vague understanding of how and why they became Christians. "Vzaimodeistvie s vooruzhennymi silami i pravookhranitel'nymi organami," *Arkhangel'skaia eparkhiia*, 19 September 2011.

133. See, e.g., "Schelkovskoe blagochinie: Vstrecha v Kosmicheskikh voiskakh," *OV-VSiPU*, 8 April 2011.

134. For celebrations of holidays, religious and secular, see, e.g., "Prazdnovanie Rozhdestva Khristova v Pushkinskom blagochinii," *Moskovskaia eparkhiia RPTs*, 13 January 2010; "Pozdravlenie zaschitnikov Otechestva v Sofrino," *Moskovskaia eparkhiia RPTs*, 23 February 2011; "Prazdnik v Sofrinskoi shkole," *Moskovskaia eparkhiia RPTs*, 28 February 2011; "Paskha v Pushkinskom blagochinii," *Moskovskaia eparkhiia RPTs*, 9 April 2010; "Moleben v divizii PRO Sofrino 1," *Moskovskaia eparkhiia RPTs*, 6 May 2012. For baptisms, see, e.g., "Kreschenie soldat v garnizone KV Sofrino 1," *Moskovskaia eparkhiia RPTs*, 6 October 2011.

135. "Ofitserskoe popolnenie v garnizone Sofrino 1," *Moskovskaia eparkhiia RPTs*, 5 October 2013; "Moleben pered nachalom ucheniia: 5 brigadi sil VKO," *OVVPU*, *Moskovskaia eparkhiia RPTs*, 2 September 2011.

136. See, e.g., "Voinskoi chasti soedineniia protivoraketnoi oborony vrucheno novoe boevoe znamia," *RF MoD*, 18 July 2011; "Osviaschenie boevogo znameni voiskovoi chasti 71615," *Novomoskovskoe blagochinie Tul'skoi eparkhii*, 6 May 2011; "Voinskoi chasti Glavnogo tsentra preduprezhdeniia o raketnom napadenii vruchili novoe boevoe znamia," *RF MoD*, 15 July 2011; "Vesti iz blagochinii: Chekhovskii okrug," *Moskovskie eparkhial'nye novosti*, nos. 1–2 (2010). Svetlana Pimenova, "Protoierei Artemy Emke osviatil novoe boevo znamia v/ch 14276," *KhSAMM*, 14 June 2011.

137. "V Orenburgskoi oblasti osviatili nachalo stroitel'stva protivoraketnoi radiolokatsionnoi sistemy," *Pravmir.ru*, 15 August 2013.

138. "Iubilei voisk voenno-kosmicheskoi oborony v Sofrinskom garnizone," *Moskovskaia eparkhiia RPTs*, 21 January 2012; "Ustanovka kupola i kresta na kolokol'niu v garnizone Sofrino-1," *Obschina khrama Spasa Nerukotvornogo v Muranovo*, 23 May 2014; "Vstrecha s voennosluzhaschimi KV," *Moskovskaia eparkhiia RPTs*, 31 January 2011; "Pervoe bogosluzhenie v khrame-chasovne garnizona Kosmicheskikh voisk," *VViMD*, 29 March 2011. In 2015 construction of the new and bigger Dmitry Donskoy church started in the garrison. "Moleben pered nachalom stroitel'stva novogo khrama," *Moskovskaia eparkhiia RPTs*, 20 April 2015.

139. Svetlana Pimenova, "Raketa-nositel 'Soiuz 2.1b' s navigatsionnym sputnikom 'Glonass,'" *KhSAMM*, 29 November 2011; "Osviaschennaia raketa 'Soiuz' vyvela na orbitu voennyi sputnik," *VViMD*, 27 June 2011.

140. The blessing rite was exactly the same as the one practiced in Russia. "Nastoiatel' Spaso-Preobrazhneskogo sobora sovershil osviaschenie rakety 'Zenit,'" *Russkaia Pravoslavnaia Tserkov' zagranitsei*, 2 August 2012.

141. "Operatsii i eksperimenty na MKS," *ROSKOSMOS*, 7 January 2014.

142. "'Soiuz TMA-21' dostavit na MKS Kazanskuiu ikonu B. Materi," *ROSKOSMOS*, 5 April 2011; "Kosmonavty dostaviat na orbitu ikony B. Materi," *VViMD*, 15 March 2011.

143. "Kosmicheskii korabl' 'Gagarin' s novym ekipazhem pristykovalsia k MKS," *RIA novosti*, 7 April 2011.

144. "Pochtovyi iaschik kosmonavtov MKS," *ROSKOSMOS*, 25 April 2011.

145. Svetlana Pimenova, "Bilo zhal' rasstavat'sia," *KhSAMM*, 25 March 2012.

146. "Krestnyi avtoprobeg s ionoi prp. Sergiia Radonezhskogo po poselkam Kamchatkogo kraia," *Pravoslavnaia Kamchatka*, 15 September 2014; "V ramkakh arkhipastyrskogo vizita v Ust'-Kamchatkii arkhiepiskop Artemii proinspektiroval," 13 October 2014.

147. Olga Glagoleva, "Zveznyi: Khram," *Pravoslavia.ru*, 30 November 2010.

148. Glagoleva, "Zveznyi"; "Sviateishii Patriarkh osviatil khram," *ROSKOSMOS*, 28 November 2010. Following the official part, Patriarch Kirill was taken on a tour of the Preparation Center, where he was shown cosmonauts' gear and the replica of the space station that was for training purposes. "Sviateishii Patriarkh osviatil khram." During tea with the ROSCOSMOS head and with the cosmonauts who were about to go into orbit, Kirill expressed his desire to go into space on one of the expeditions. The ROSCOSMOS head saw it as possible in principle, given the patriarch's earlier training with the Russian AF (nineteen flights on a MiG jet). "Patriarkh Kirill reshil otpravit'sia v kosmos," *Lenta.ru*, 1 December 2010.

149. For the garrison in Sergiev Posad, see, e.g., "Vstrecha s predstaviteliami silovykh struktur v Sergievom Posade," *Moskovskaia eparkhiia RPTs*, 18 February 2011; "Sergievo-Posadskoe blagochinie: Soveschanie s voennym dykhovenstvom," *Moskovskaia eparkhiia, OVVSiPU*, 2 August 2011. For the garrison in Novaia Zemlia, see, e.g., "Novogodnii moleben," *Arkticheskoe blagochinie* (arctic.prihod.ru), 1 January 2014; "Voennaia prisiaga na Tsentralnom iadernom poligone Rossii," *Arkticheskoe blagochinie*, 30 June 2014 and 21 January 2014; Igor' Dubonosov, Vsepobezhdaiuschii krest Khristov," *Novozeml'skie vesti*, 25 April 2014.

150. "Klirik Brianskoi eparkhii stal shtatnym voennym sviaschennikom," *Brianskaia eparkhiia*, 12 October 2013; "Tserkov' i silovye struktury: Khronika vzaimodeistviia," *VVD*, 11 August 2016.

151. "Sergievo-Posadskoe blagochinie: Soveschanie s voennym dykhovenstvom," *Moskovskaia eparkhiia, OVVSiPU*, 2 August 2011.

152. The ceremony in the nuclear arsenal at the closed city of Briansk-18 aptly illustrates this. Garrison commanders, nuclear industry officials, and the Briansk regional governor were standing on both sides of the priest, who performed the consecration rite over the new military banner. Junior officers stood next in line and held the silver cup with the holy water and the brush for sprinkling it. "Osviaschenie boevogo znameni voinskogo soedineniia Rzhanitskogo garnizona," *Zhukovskoe blagochinie* (zhukovka.prihod. ru), 18 February 2010.

153. "Brianskuiu oblast' obleteli s ikonami na voennom samolete," *Pravosalvie.ru*, 23 August 2014.

154. See, e.g., "O dne zachitnika Otechestva," *Sergievo-Posadskoe blagochinie*, 22 February 2011; "Prazdnovanie Paskhi 2011," *Sergievo-Posadskoe blagochinie*, 23–24 April 2011; "Voinskii prazdnik v Sergievo-Posadskom blagochinii," *Moskovskaia eparkhiia RPTs, OVVSiPU*, 22 February 2011; "10 let so dnia osnovaniia garnizonnogo Nikol'skogo khrama," *Sergievo-Posadskoe blagochinie*, 10 November 2012.

155. "Tsentral'nyi poligon Rossii nagrazhden ordenom Suvorova," *RF MoD*, 17 September 2014; "Ocherednoi pamiatnik v Belushei," *Vse ob arkhipelage Novaia Zemlia* (belushka.ru), 16 October 2014. In subsequent years, the garrison priest together with the city mayor addressed the audience during the celebrations. "Prazdnovanie dnia Tsentral'nogo poligona Rossiiskoi Federatsii," *Gorodskoi okrug Novaia Zemlia* (novzemlya.ru), 18 September 2015.

156. "Iubilei mezhvidovogo tsentra po perepodgotovke i povysheniiu kvalifikatsii spetsialistov VS Rossii," *Moskovskaia eparkhiia*, 9 October 2015; "10 let so dnia osnovaniia garnizonnogo Nikol'skogo khrama"; "Sviaschennik Brianskoi eparkhii naznachen pomoshnikom komandira po rabote s veruiuschimi," *VVD*, 15 October 2013.

157. Dubonosov, "Vsepobezhdaiuschii krest Khristov"; "Klirik Brianskoi eparkhii stal shtatnym voennym sviaschennikom"; "Sviaschennik Brianskoi eparkhii naznachen pomoshnikom komandira."

158. "Klirik Brianskoi eparkhii stal shtatnym voennym sviaschennikom."

159. Dmitrii Andreev, "Garanty iadernogo schita," *KZ*, 3 September 2012.

160. "Khranitelei iadernogo oruzhiia proveriat na narkotiki i prestupnii umisel," *Izvestiia*, 9 September 2016. A staunch supporter of the newly introduced institution of the military clergy, he was especially eager to dispatch clerics to the faraway garrisons and small closed cities "where opportunities to satisfy religious needs are limited." Evgenii Murzin, "Institut voennogo dukhovenstva v Rossii: Promezhutochnye itogi," *VVD*, 19 September 2013.

161. "Sbory voennykh sviaschennikov i ofitserov po vospitatel'noi rabote proshli v Murmanske," *VViMD*, 25 March 2014; "V Minoborony Rossii proshel uchebno-

metodicheskii sbor s rukovodiaschim sostavom organov po rabote s lichnym sostavom," *RF MoD*, 28 March 2014.

162. For example, in 2016 the pupils of the MoD secondary school in the closed city Briansk-16, the children of the 12th GUMO servicemen of the local nuclear arsenal garrison, joined the Yunarmiia and named their platoon Peresvet, after the famous Orthodox monk-warrior, a hero of the battle of Kulikovo. The oath of allegiance ceremony took place within the GUMO base, in the presence of the deputy commander for educational work, the base commander, the garrison priest, the head of the regional administration, and the servicemen. According to the movement's regional head, the Yunarmiia will teach the schoolchildren military-applicable skills and provide them with patriotic education. The military-applicable skills will be taught at the facilities of the GUMO base, while the spiritual education of the youngsters will be the responsibility of the local protoierei, assistant to the commander for work with the faithful servicemen. Viktor Khudoleev, "V 'Iunarmiiu' vstupaet 'Peresvet,'" *KZ*, 14 July 2016. In the same year, the commander of the service addressing another Yunarmiia platoon within the school of the 12th GUMO closed city in the Murmansk region said, among others things, that the youth of the closed cities, thanks to the firsthand examples of their fathers and mothers, know the meaning of serving the Fatherland and respect its heroic past. "Vserossiiskoe voenno-patrioticheskoe obschestvennoe dvizhenie Iunarmii popolnilas' novym otriadom," *RF MoD*, 16 December 2016.

163. Roman Biriulin and Aleksandr Tikhonov, "Reserv vysokoi kvalifikatsii," *KZ*, 10 July 2016.

164. Aleksandr Khvastov, "Iz auditoria—na polygon," *KZ*, 14 April 2015.

165. "Protoierei Sergei Privalov prinial uchastie v otpravke prizyvnikov v nauchnye roty MO Rossii," *Pobeda.ru*, 9 July 2015.

166. "Prisiaga v nauchnoi rote," *VNIIEF*, 27 January 2016.

167. Aleksandr Pinchiuk, "Ot znaniia k zvaniiu," *KZ*, 20 December 2016; "Operatoram pervogo prizyva nauchnoi roty 12-go GUMO prisvoeny ofitserskie zvaniia," *RF MoD*, 13 December 2016; "V Sergievom Posade nachalos' formirovanie novoi nauchnoi roty v interesakh 12-go GUMO," *RF MoD*, 27 October 2015.

168. "V ramkakh osennego prizyva na voennuiu sluzhbu napravleno okolo 85% novobrantsev," *RF MoD*, 12 December 2016; "Okolo 400 novobrantsev vesennego prizyva otobrany dlia sluzhby v nauchnykh rotakh," *RF MoD*, 7 July 2016.

CHAPTER 10

1. Metropolitan Iliia of the Lebanon Mountains never passed the authority of the Mother of God to the Soviet government to conduct processions of the cross over Moscow, Leningrad, Stalingrad, Kursk, Königsberg, or elsewhere; these processions never happened, and Stalin never met him. Sergei Bolotov, "Stalin i Tserkov': Piat' faktov," *FOMA*, 5 March 2013.

2. Sergei Bolotov, *RPTs i mezhdunarodnaia politika SSSR v 1930–1950 gody* (Moscow: Izdanie Krutitskogo podvor'ia, 2011); also see Sergei Nepodkosov, "Bog voiny," *Sovershenno sekretno*, 8 December 2014.

3. For the divine assistance narrative, see Nikolai Blokhin, *Rubezh: Khristianskaia povest' o sobytiiakh Velikoi Otechestvennoi voiny* (Moscow: Izdatel'skie resheniia, 2014). Nepodkosov, for example, refuted the story of Marshal Golovanov having flown over Moscow with an icon and three priests aboard and direct radio transmission of the prayer to the Kremlin, and, among other things, he mentioned the following discrepancies: the Kazanskaia Mother of God icon was not in Moscow at that time; the specific type of airplane could not have carried that number of people; and radio transmission was technically impossible. The author also demonstrated that the successful counterattack of the battle of Moscow in 1941 was due to reserve divisions that had been redeployed from the Soviet Far East and not due to St. Matrona Moskovskaia. See Nepodkosov, "Bog voiny."

4. "Pravoslavnaia Tserkov' v gody Velikoi Otechestvennoi voiny," *VViMD*, 28 April 2010.

5. The Synodal Commission for Saints Canonization established an expert group to formulate a canonical version of Matrona's life in preparation for her official canonization as a saint in 2004. Many of the facts were sanitized, including the story of Stalin's blessing. Andrei Zaitsev, "Kanonizatsia snizu: Dva zhitiia Matrony Moskovskoi," *Neskuchnii sad*, 2 May 2012; Bolotov, "Stalin i Tserkov'."

6. See, e.g., Svetlana Volkova, *Pokrov Bozhii nad Rossiei* (Moscow: Sibirskaia Blagozvonnitsa, 2012); A. I. Farberov, *Spasi i sokhrani: Svidetel'stva o pomoschi Bozhiei v Velikuiu Otechestvennuiu voinu* (Moscow: Izdatel'stvo Moskovskoi Patriarkhii, 2015); Vladimir Zobern, *Na altar' Pobedy: Voevali, verili, pobedili* (Moscow: Eksmo, 2016); Sergei Galitskii, *Iz smerti v zhizn': Zapiski voennogo sviaschennika* (Moscow: Grad Dukhovnyi, 2014); *Iz smerti v zhizn': Chast' 1. Svidetel'stva voinov o pomoschi Bozhei na voine* (Moscow: Grad Dukhovnyi, 2015); *Iz smerti v zhizn': Chast' 2. Svidetel'stva voinov o pomoschi Bozhei na voine* (Moscow: Grad dukhovnyi, 2013); Dmitry Linchevsky, *Rasskazy o chechenskoi voine* (Moscow: Alta Print, 2014).

7. See, e.g., Nataliia Skorobogat'ko, *Chudesa Bozhii na frontakh Otechestvennoi Voiny: Svidetel'stva ochevidtsev* (Moscow: Belyi gorod, 2012); Aleksandr Ananichev, *Sviatye voiny prepodobnogo Sergiia Radonezhskogo* (Moscow: Izdatel'stvo Moskovskoi Patriarkhii, 2013).

8. Nepodkosov, "Bog voiny."

9. Anastasia Iakovleva, "Protoierei Mikhail Vasiliev: 'Mi trudimsia ne radi deneg, a za Rodinu,'" *KZ*, 26 August 2011.

10. Aleksandr Cherkasov, "Dukhovnaia osnova voinskoi kul'tury," *KZ*, 29 January 2011. According to the article, originally the ROC introduced the military slogan "For the Holy Rus! For the Orthodox Faith!" Then, reflecting the rising role of the absolute monarchy, since Peter the Great, the slogan turned into "For Faith, Tsar and Fatherland." The Soviet slogan "For the Motherland! For Stalin!" popularized during the GPW, was essentially an extension of the same idea. The subtext equated Stalin with tsar, the national leader. Exchanging *Fatherland* with *Motherland* evoked a religious association—Motherland, referring to Russia, meant Holy Rus. The iconic and most famous wartime Soviet poster "Motherland—Mother Calling" underscored this subtext

through the resonance of the poster image with the Mother of God in Russian icons. Moreover, in the first weeks of the war, Stalin introduced its official name—the Great Patriotic War, which reads literally in Russian as "Fatherland's War." By doing so, he covered all three pillars of the traditional slogan. In parallel, to strengthen the resonance, Stalin ordered Soviet composers to produce an anthem for the war. The crash program resulted in the most famous Soviet war song, *Holy War*, saturated with patriotic-religious motifs. As Patriarch Kirill said on the matter of the slogan to an audience of the GS Academy, even if "we change the words, we still think about the same things." "Vystuplenie Sviateishego Patriarkha Kirilla v Voennoi akademii GS VS RF," *Patriarchia.ru*, 31 May 2011.

11. B. M. Lukichev, *Patriarkh Kirill i voennoe dukhovenstvo* (Moscow: FIV, 2016), pp. 80–81; "Vystuplenie Sviateishego Patriarkha Kirilla v Voennoi akademii."

12. "Sviateishii Patriarkh Kirill: 'Nuzhny pravil'nye slova, nuzhna sil'naia molitva,'" *KZ*, 30 June 2011.

13. Lukichev, *Patriarkh Kirill*, pp. 82–83.

14. For example, in 2014 Kirill referred to the divine predestination of the war: "The GPW put an end to the terrible and bloody period of the church's persecution and the destruction of its sanctuaries. We know what a terrible price our people paid for stepping out of faith. [. . .] God punished our people but not to death because some portion of the faith was preserved. In the severe years of the war faith grew stronger among the people and turned into their main cementing factor and spiritual staple." Lukichev, *Patriarkh Kirill*, p. 97.

15. Lukichev, *Patriarkh Kirill*, p. 82.

16. Consider the 2017 ceremony of the Fatherland's Defender Day in the Kremlin. President Putin, DM Shoigu, foreign minister Lavrov, FSB head Patrushev, other senior officials of the strategic community, governors, and Metropolitan Iuvenalii, a close associate of Patriarch Kirill and the oldest of the serving metropolitans, stood in the first row and several hundred top military brass were in the audience. Putin addressed them with the Soviet term *comrades*. His speech, which praised historical and current military achievements and outlined future priorities, was followed by a concert. The first song was titled "Bless Us for the Acts of Bravery and Glory." The solo singer, standing in front of the military chorus, wore white clothing and a white head covering—a silhouette strongly resonating with the image of the Mother of God. The song included the phrases "save us by your prayer" and "bless the Holy warriors of Russia." The word *bless* was the chorus. During the song, two huge red stars decorated the background. The climactic finale was a big red star rising over the stage, with Orthodox cathedral bells ringing in the background. When the song ended, the master of ceremonies opened the concert, saying that faith and truth had made Russian soldiers undefeatable throughout history. The repertoire of military and popular songs and videos during the concert clearly praised the continuity of the Soviet military tradition and linked it to the heroism of the Russian military in Syria. "Prazdnichnyi kontsert k Dniu zaschitnika Otechestva," *ORT TV Channel*, 23 February 2017.

17. Mikk Marran, *International Security and Estonia* (Tallinn: Teabeamet, 2016), p. 19.

18. Lukichev, *Patriarkh Kirill*, p. 77.

19. The linkage between the two Vladimirs is similar to the linkage that Stalin popularized between himself and Ivan the Formidable (Ivan IV) and his positive role in Russian history.

20. Lukichev, *Patriarkh Kirill*, pp. 95–96.

21. Lukichev, *Patriarkh Kirill*, p. 96.

22. Lukichev, *Patriarkh Kirill*, pp. 97–98.

23. For example, the Baikonur cosmodrome priest argued that relatives of the first cosmonauts clandestinely met clergy for prayer and to receive blessings. Natalia Burtseva, "V kosmos s blagoslovelniem," *Vesti TV*, 13 December 2008. He also referred to documented evidence demonstrating that Korolev, the father of the Soviet space program, was faithful and donated to churches and monasteries. Aleksandr Milkus, "'Kosmicheskii' batiushka otets Sergii," *Komsomol'skaia pravda*, 10 April 2015. Protoierei Chaplin, the then head of the ROC's department of relations with society, argued that "spiritual feelings were not strange to the first cosmonauts." "Sviaschennosluzhiteli o kosmonavtike," *VViMD*, 12 April 2011.

24. Milkus, "'Kosmicheskii' batiushka."

25. At the bottom of the Ivan the Formidable bell tower in the Kremlin's Uspensky Cathedral, there is the church of St. Ioann Listvichnik, which functions as a museum. Protoierei Smirnov saw this as God's will. To illustrate the parallels, he placed a picture of Gagarin next to the image of the monk and a picture of the space rocket next to the picture of the Uspensky Cathedral's bell tower. The protoierei tried to convince the authorities to conduct the service on Cosmonautics Day there, and toward the fiftieth anniversary, he redoubled his efforts to regain the church, but in vain. Interestingly, Elena Gagarina, daughter of the first Soviet cosmonaut and head of the Kremlin museum authority, repeatedly declined his request. "Obraschenie k Elene Iur'evne, docheri nashego natsional'nogo geroia Iuriia Alekseevicha Gagarina," *Mil'timediinyi blog protoiereia Dimitriia Smirnova*, 4 April 2011.

26. Consider the following supporting evidence that the speaker brought: "[aviation pioneer] Sikorsky in his leisure time was occupied with theology and authored several theological texts. Another inventor, Polikarpov, dubbed the king of fighter aviation, was a priest's son and a deeply faithful person, who each time, before the test of a new airplane, energetically prayed." "50 let v kosmose: Vchera, segodnia, zavtra," *VVD*, 3 May 2011.

27. "50 let v kosmose."

28. Every Soviet pupil knew the mantra about cosmonauts who went into space but saw no God.

29. According to Yoav, since 2005–6, he commemorates and mentions Gagarin during every service and liturgy he conducts. Marina Lev, "Kosmos vo slavu Bozhiiu," *Pravoslavie.ru*, 12 April 2013.

30. "Prazdnik v kosmicheskom garnizone v Pushkinskom blagochinii," *Moskovskaia eparkhia RPTs, OVVSiPU*, 30 May 2011. Also, during the consecration ceremony of a new military banner within one of the SF units, the priest offered the following blessing: "Dear comrades! The fact that today the clergy is invited to the ceremony of receiving the banner of the unit, and that we decided to consecrate it, means we desire that the

weapons that you are entrusted would be not only for defense of lives, but also that this would be God's sword, given to you by God, to punish the evil and to defend the good." "Vruchenie boevogo znameni v v/ch 73570," *Informatsionnyi portal Krasnogorsk*, 10 February 2011. Also, decorations of places of worship in the SF also merged images from several epochs. For example, during the mission descents, SF priests put altars and iconostases in the soldiers' club right under a huge mural featuring portraits of Korolev, Gagarin, space launches, ICBMs, and military satellites. On another occasion, a priest heard soldiers' confessions beneath a portrait of Suvorov, a legendary and pious Russian military commander of the eighteenth century. Svetlana Pimenova, "Den' zaschitnika Otechestva na kosmodrome," *KhSAMM*, 23 February 2012.

31. "Ot RVSN zavisiat suverenitet Rossii i mir na vsei planete," *VVD*, 17 April 2012.

32. Andrei Mel'nikov, "Atomnoe pravoslavie poluchit tselevuiu auditoriiu," *NG-Religii*, 17 February 2016.

33. "People should be brought here and told about everything, so that even those distanced from the church, God, and faith will see that God is present in everything." "Slovo Sviateishego Patriarkha Kirilla posle zakladki Uspenskogo sobora v Sarovskoi pustyne," *Patriarchia.ru*, 1 August 2016.

CHAPTER 11

1. In militaries influenced by an organized religion, if, in addition to other considerations, commanders have the freedom to decide when, where, and how to fight, "they can align these choices with advantageous religious conditions." Ron Hassner, *Religion on the Battlefield* (Ithaca, NY: Cornell University Press, 2017), p. 15.

2. These "commemorate triumphal martyrdom or celebrate religious victories, as well as holy places that honor martial deities." Hassner, *Religion on the Battlefield*, p. 17. "Believers perceive these times as possessing unique value and power," since "the gods have designated certain periods as being more 'important,' 'lucky,' 'strong,' or pure than others." Hassner, *Religion on the Battlefield*, p. 31.

3. Hassner, *Religion on the Battlefield*, p. 33.

4. Hassner, *Religion on the Battlefield*, p. 32.

5. It seems that relative to the Russian case, U.S. and U.K. commanders have been ambivalent about blessing weapons systems. Hassner, *Religion on the Battlefield*, p. 116.

6. In addition, of course, to the desire to enable service members to practice their faith.

7. Hassner, *Religion on the Battlefield*.

8. Hassner, *Religion on the Battlefield*, p. 93.

9. Oleg Falichev interviewing Andrei Kartapolov, "Pravo pervim podniatsia v ataku," *VPK*, 11 September 2018.

10. Hassner, *Religion on the Battlefield* , p. 96.

11. Fiona Hill and Clifford Gaddy, *Mr. Putin: Operative in the Kremlin* (Washington, DC: Brookings Institution Press, 2015), p. 253.

12. Developments around the *Matilda* movie might be seen as one of the first indications.

13. For example, in spring 2017, DM Shoigu outlined his vision of nuclear triad modernization and maintaining parity with the West in light of its military innovations. Within expansion and upgrade of all three legs of the triad, greater emphasis on naval and air nuclear components was a novelty. According to Russian commentators, the growing potential a U.S. prompt global strike makes ICBMs, the traditional backbone of the Russian nuclear triad, most vulnerable and thus demands a better diversification of the arsenal, in terms of numbers and sophistication. "Ministr oborony vystupil na zasedanii Soveta Federatsii," *Mil.ru*, 24 May 2017; Pavel Felgenhauer, "NATO and US: Enemies of Choice for Russia's Military," *Eurasia Daily Monitor* (Jamestown Foundation) 14, no. 72 (25 May 2017).

14. Felgenhauer, "NATO and US."

15. On several occasions mentioned in the book, nuclear priests emphasized their specific sectarian nuclear flock as being the most important leg of the triad. The possible subtext of such a statement is for a preference in funds allocation. Also, there have been several examples of bureaucratic wars when Patriarch Kirill intervened on behalf of a specific corps and appealed to the senior military-political leadership. His efforts in 2009–11 and then eventual success to preserving the Air Defense Academy illustrated this trend. B. M. Lukichev, *Patriarkh Kirill i voennoe dukhovenstvo* (Moscow: FIV, 2016), p. 29.

16. During the Cold War, the majority of the RVSN crews had been composed "entirely of communist officers or party candidates," and over 90 percent of the SSBN's officers and 80 percent of the Air Force crews had been party members. About 40 percent of the Soviet military, and three quarters of its officers, were Communist Party members. Stephen M. Meyer, "Soviet Nuclear Operations," in *Managing Nuclear Operations*, ed. Ashton Carter, John Steinbruner, and Charles Zraket (Washington, DC: Brookings Institution Press, 1987), p. 493. Also see Susan Curran and Dmitry Ponomareff, *Managing the Ethnic Factor in the Russian and Soviet Armed Forces* (Santa Monica, CA: RAND, 1982).

17. Hassner, *Religion on the Battlefield*, p. 16.

18. Hassner *Religion on the Battlefield*, p. 7.

19. Hassner, *Religion on the Battlefield*, pp. 88, 98–99.

20. For example, anecdotal evidence from Israel suggests that during the previous decade, on at least one occasion, an observant senior political decision maker speculated along these lines when engaged in dealing with a major national security challenge. His decision-making style was shaped by the belief that if one is driven by the right cause, divine predestination will eventually lead to victory, even if in objective military terms the correlation of forces is not in one's favor. "There is God's guiding hand that knows better, while man is unable to understand God's will." Moreover, a strategic debacle or the loss of a battle, to such a believer, is not a terrible thing, but part of God's plan, the price that God exacts upon the faithful for eventual victory. Interviews with senior Israeli practitioners, central Israel, 2017.

21. Hassner, *Religion on the Battlefield*, p. 10.

22. Hassner, *Religion on the Battlefield*, p. 41; Shmuel Bar, "God, Nation, and Deterrence: The Impact of Religion on Deterrence," *Comparative Strategy* 30, no. 5 (2011):

428–52. Moreover, in the militaries that emphasize morale over material factors as sources of military effectiveness, the observant may believe that there is a causal link between fulfillment of religious commandments and correlation of forces on the battlefield.

23. For example, Morielle Lotan argues that tailoring a deterrence program to the strategic level of command is as important as influencing the cost-benefit calculus of nuclear operators, who, given their responsibilities, in certain situations become not merely executors but also decision makers. Morielle Lotan, "Strategic Dilemmas of WMD Operators," *Comparative Strategy* 34, no. 4 (2015): 345–66.

24. Lawrence Freedman, *Deterrence* (London: Polity, 2004). See also T.V. Paul, Patrick Morgan, and James Wirtz, eds., *Complex Deterrence: Strategy in the Global Age* (Chicago: University of Chicago Press, 2009).

CHAPTER 12

1. Ron Hassner, *Religion on the Battlefield* (Ithaca, NY: Cornell University Press, 2017), p. 113.

2. See, e.g., Stuart Cohen, "Israel," pp. 114–43; Mahsa Rouhi, "Iran," pp. 143–59; and Aysegul Komsuoglu and Gul Kurtoglu Eskisar, "Turkey," pp. 208–27, in *Religion in the Military Worldwide*, ed. Ron Hassner (New York: Cambridge University Press, 2014); Yagil Levi, *Mefaked ha-alion* (Tel Aviv: Am Oved, 2015); Gilad Wenig, "Egypt's Army of God: The Largest Arab Military Is Not as Secular as It Seems," *Foreign Affairs*, 31 October 2014.

3. According to some interpretations, in Eastern Orthodox tradition, in contrast to the Roman Catholic, war is seen as a minor moral good, rather than a necessary moral evil. See Alexander Webster and Darrell Cole, *The Virtue of War* (Salisbury, MA: Regina Orthodox Press, 2007); Yuri Stoyanov, "Norms of War in Eastern Orthodox Christianity," in *World Religions and Norms of War*, ed. Vesselin Popovski, Gregory Reichberg, and Nicholas Turner (Tokyo: United Nations University Press, 2009), pp. 205–11. The ROC's 2000 Sobor document outlined church and state interaction; the chapter "War and Peace" includes several references to the *jus ad bellum* and asserts that resorting to war is desirable in certain circumstances, such as national self-defense, defense of neighbors, and restoration of trampled justice. "Osnovy Sottsyal'noi Kontseptsii RPTs," *Arkhiereiskii Sobor RPTs 2000*, Moscow Patriarchy.

4. Hassner, *Religion on the Battlefield*, p. 95.

5. Hassner, *Religion on the Battlefield*, p. 122.

6. Hassner, *Religion on the Battlefield*, p. 134.

7. Similarly, Hassner argues that faith and religious practices have been influencing battlefield decision-making and may act as a force multiplier enabling military operations and as a force divider constraining them. Hassner, *Religion on the Battlefield*, p. 1.

8. To illustrate his concern with the subjective hesitations of the operators, Dougherty referred to a genuine Cold War incident with one of his subordinates, Major Harold Hering, who during the human reliability program questioned the sanity of the authenticator. "Yes, he would turn keys upon receipt of an authentic order from the proper authority: if he thought the order was legal; if he thought the circumstances necessitated

an ICBM launch; if he was convinced that it was a rational, moral necessity and so on." Russell Dougherty, "The Psychological Climate of Nuclear Command," in *Managing Nuclear Operations*, ed. Ashton Carter, John Steinbruner, and Charles Zraket (Washington, DC: Brookings Institution Press, 1987), pp. 413–14. Also see Ron Rosenbaum, *How the End Begins* (New York: Simon and Schuster, 2011), pp. 31–44.

9. "The ever-present human factors involved require constant care and surveillance at all levels of command—and they get it. This is a 'first call' on the time and attention of all commanders with nuclear responsibilities." Dougherty, "Psychological Climate of Nuclear Command," pp. 414–15.

10. Dougherty, "Psychological Climate of Nuclear Command," pp. 417–18.

11. "No one could predict how the duty officer would react in such an extraordinary moment, at the edge of the abyss." David Hoffman, *The Dead Hand* (New York: Anchor Books, 2010), p. 153.

12. Hassner, *Religion on the Battlefield*, pp. 1, 17.

13. In the cyber era, religious soldiers might be seen as more reliable in keeping secrets and less likely to leak them.

14. Hassner, *Religion on the Battlefield*, p. 127.

15. Hassner, *Religion on the Battlefield*, pp. 93–94.

16. Similarly, anecdotal but growing evidence from the Israel Defense Forces' (IDF) operations of the past decade support this assertion. Religious soldiers, when opening fire and when under fire, report themselves, and are reported by their commanders, to be more motivated and less hesitant to take life and risk death, which they see as a noble mission and even potential martyrdom, and are more trigger-happy and indiscriminate than their secular peers, since many of them see the battlefield through the prism of "fighting against the Amalek." They feel more self-confident, less hesitant to encounter grave danger, and ready to go to extremes. Interviews with senior and mid-level IDF commanders, central Israel, 2015–17.

17. Stephen M. Meyer, "Soviet Nuclear Operations," in Carter, Steinbruner, and Zraket, *Managing Nuclear Operations*, p. 492.

18. This included even a case of justifying civilian carpet bombings. Hassner, *Religion on the Battlefield*, pp. 99–100.

19. A sub-scenario of this might be when the "main executive authority" is decapitated or unreachable by communication.

20. For example, see Russian officers discussing the dilemma of executing a morally inappropriate order from the political leadership. Natalia Gugueva, *Krym: Nebo Rodiny*, documentary, *ORT*, 2017.

21. Fiona Hill and Clifford Gaddy, *Mr. Putin: Operative in the Kremlin* (Washington, DC: Brookings Institution Press, 2015), pp. 271–72.

22. Andrei Kolesnikov, "The Burden of Predictability: Russia's 2018 Presidential Election" (Moscow: Carnegie Moscow Center, 18 May 2017).

23. During the war with the Amalekites, the prophet Samuel accused King Saul, whom he previously had anointed as the first king of Israel, of being in violation of the Lord's commandment of total destruction of the Amalekites. Saul indeed spared the

enemy's king and the livestock. For his wartime disobedience, the prophet Samuel announced that God, who had made Saul king, could also unmake him, and anointed David as king instead. "Now go and strike Amalek, and utterly destroy all that they have, and spare them not; but slay both man and woman, child and infant, ox and sheep, camel and donkey." 1 Samuel 15:3.

24. See, e.g., "Sviatitel' Filipp, mitropolit Moskovskii," and "Sviaschennomuchenik Arsenii, mitropolit Rostovskii," *Pravoslavie.ru* (accessed 13 June 2017); Dmitry Pavliuchenkov, "Konflikt patriarkha Nikona i tsaria Alekseia Mikhailovicha," *Pavluchenkov. ru* (accessed 13 June 2017).

25. This event seemed to be not an isolated extremist episode, but a possible symptom of a broad political phenomenon, both on the elite and grassroots levels, potentially undermining the Kremlin's authority, as this conservative opposition, both secular and religious, is loyal not so much to the Kremlin as to the national ideology that it promotes. See, e.g., Alexander Baunov, "Is Putin Losing Control of Russia's Conservative Nationalists?," *Foreign Affairs*, 10 October 2017.

CPSIA information can be obtained
at www.ICGtesting.com
Printed in the USA
JSHW021222170123
36374JS00002B/225

9 781503 608641